Marketing and Financial Management

New Economy – New Interfaces

David Walters
Michael Halliday

First published 2005 by
PALGRAVE MACMILLAN
Houndmills, Basingstoke, Hampshire RG21 6XS and
175 Fifth Avenue, New York, N.Y. 10010
Companies and representatives throughout the world

PALGRAVE MACMILLAN is the global academic imprint of the Palgrave
Macmillan division of St. Martin's Press, LLC and of Palgrave Macmillan Ltd.
Macmillan® is a registered trademark in the United States, United Kingdom
and other countries. Palgrave is a registered trademark in the European
Union and other countries.

ISBN 1–4039–4097–5

This book is printed on paper suitable for recycling and made from fully
managed and sustained forest sources.

A catalogue record for this book is available from the British Library.

Library of Congress Cataloging-in-Publication Data

Walters, David, 1936–
    Marketing and financial management : new economy—new interfaces / David
Walters, Michael Halliday.
        p. cm.
    Includes bibliographical references and index.
    ISBN 1–4039–4097–5 (pbk.)
    1. Marketing—Management. 2. Strategic planning. 3. Corporations—Finance.
    I. Halliday, Michael, 1947– II. Title.

    HF5415.13.W254 2004
    658.8′02—dc22   2004052488

10   9   8   7   6   5   4   3   2   1
14   13   12   11   10   09   08   07   06   05

Printed and bound in China

In memory of
George Wright
1930–2004

Contents

List of Figures

List of Tables

Introduction

Business operates everywhere in an environment that is increasingly dynamic and challenging. In the emerging 'New Economy' markets have globalized, technology has become all-embracing, and relationships with suppliers, customers and competitors are undergoing constant change. *New business models* are emerging, ones in which competitive advantage is based upon *managing processes* that facilitate rapid and flexible responses to 'market' change, and ones in which new *capabilities* are based upon developing unique relationships with partners (suppliers, customers, employees, shareholders, government and, often, with competitors). The business model has often taken second place to strategy in management thinking and focus. Normann (2001) discusses 'a new strategic logic'. He suggests that: 'managers need to be good at *mobilizing, managing,* and *using* resources rather than at formally *acquiring* and necessarily *owning* resources. The ability to reconfigure, to use resources inside and particularly outside the boundaries of the traditional corporation more effectively becomes a mandatory skill for managements.'

Drucker (2001) has identified some of the changes that have occurred already within the largest US corporations suggesting these have changed many fundamental philosophies, views and practices. A similar shift, some years ago, sponsored the development of vertical integration on a large scale – and did so for many years. Drucker cites Standard Oil and Ford as examples of this earlier phenomenon. It is noticeable that large corporations are leading the changes in strategic posture. General Motors for example, have created a business that will buy for the ultimate car consumer – they will make available whatever 'make' of car and model most closely fits the consumer's preferences. As Drucker notes, the changes go beyond this, into design and development, and production. Products and services now have multiple applications and business organizations are redefining their core capabilities and processes. In other words 'value chains' are competing with 'value chains'. The value chains are organization structures, or confederations, that are developing from traditional corporations.

Another example of the approach to the 'new economy is provided by *Millennium Pharmaceuticals*. This company was founded in 1993 and is specializing in performing basic research on genes and proteins using automated R&D technologies. In an interview with the CEO (Champion 2001) described the reasons why the company was repositioning itself in the value chain. The reasons given by Mark Levin (the CEO) were that the value in the industry has changed. Value has migrated:

> Value has started to migrate downstream, toward the more mechanical tasks of identifying, testing, and manufacturing molecules that will affect the proteins produced by the genes, and which become the pills and serums we sell. At Millennium, we've anticipated this shift by expanding into downstream activities across several major product categories. Our ultimate goal is to develop capabilities and a strong presence in every stage of the industry's value chain-from gene to patient.

Levin argues that the value chain for other high-tech products has, after all, tended to break down into a few separate, largely independent industries (each specializing in specific value positioning characteristics). The computer industry is used as an example with chip manufacturing, computer assembly and delivery and software. Where once IBM was dominant, Intel, Dell and Microsoft now coexist as a value chain. Millennium sees problems with the current structure of the industry; the profitable areas of the value chain are not in the R&D process alone. Levin suggests the future of the industry lies in personalized medicine: 'One day, everyone will have their own genomes mapped out and stored in memory chips, and doctors will look at the information in those chips and prescribe accordingly.'

The implications for management are immense. One is very clear. Unless managers operate on a basis of cross-functional decision making most organizations will not survive. This text introduces this notion by considering the interrelationships that exist between marketing and financial decision making. This is considered to be a prime requirement of managers aiming to make their mark in 'new economy' organizations.

This book is aimed at undergraduate students who have an understanding of marketing and finance, postgraduate students and experienced managers seeking a better understanding of the interrelationships that exist between marketing and financial management decisions. It assumes a familiarity with the basic concepts of both disciplines. It also assumes a shared view that any manager has a responsibility to work towards the overall objective of increasing the value of the shareholders' investment within the company.

The purpose of this text is to explore marketing decisions that have implications for financial management. This approach is taken on the basis that successful business decisions are those based upon achieving customer satisfaction and are, therefore, initially marketing-led. The authors have found from experience that many marketing managers often pursue opportunities without considering the wider implications of their decisions for the company, particularly for the financial management of the business.

Some examples based upon our own experiences may help to explain the basis of our concern. In one instance, a consumer durable goods manufacturer shifted its distribution emphasis away from its traditional distributors towards an emerging discounter network. The rate of growth demonstrated by the new channel of distribution was impressive and promising. As soon as the company's intentions became apparent to its existing distributors (electrical multiple retailers, department stores, large independent retailers and electrical wholesalers), they either delisted the company or made it a number two or three brand and reduced their stock cover and service facilities. As a result, it faced a major reduction in sales volume which created large inventory surpluses. The discounter network failed to sustain its initial rate of growth and, furthermore, the key companies refused to hold stock, demanded large discounts to maintain their price competitiveness and were very slow to pay for product purchased.

The financial implications were serious. The build-up of inventories required additional working capital funds. In addition, the physical storage space requirements became such that external facilities were rented at excessive rates. The reduction in sales volume exacerbated the financial problems. Reduced sales and contribution (and therefore margins) had serious implications as the company was a high fixed-cost operation. As a consequence the implications for capacity utilization and labour utilization soon required dramatic action. The decision to change its distributor network had resulted in a very large increase in working capital requirements, an under-recovery of overhead costs and serious under-utilization of fixed and human assets. In addition, the decision had put the company in an impossible situation with the established distribution channels.

Clearly, closer liaison with financial management may have identified many of these problems, could have considered their implications and may well have resulted in a different decision being taken.

In another situation an industrial equipment manufacturer sought to increase the manufactured content of its product range. At the point in time at which the decision was made it manufactured some 60 per cent of the finished product. It considered that by increasing this amount to 85 per cent it could increase its profit margin and be in a stronger position to meet increasing price competition. It underestimated the plant and equipment costs required for manufacturing the additional product components as well as the human resources costs (which included considerable training costs). The company's problem was fundamental in that it overlooked the fact that the components it had decided to manufacture required specialist equipment and highly trained and skilled operators. The technology required to manufacture the new components was very different from that used for the more simple manufacturing and assembly activities already performed. As a result, not only did the investment costs exceed expectations, requiring additional funding, but the process was slow to come on stream and there were numerous quality control problems resulting in customer dissatisfaction and, subsequently, loss of major customers.

Once again, a joint review of the proposal (with marketing and finance together and, in this instance, with operations management as well) would have probably rejected the proposal.

These two examples are typical of the many decisions and outcomes that are made in industry. By developing a better understanding of the financial managers' role, and of the aspects of their job which are influenced by marketing decisions, the marketing manager can play a more effective role in increasing the value of the business.

This book has been developed around a number of marketing and financial management topics. The overall direction of the text is to consider the financial implications of strategic and operational marketing decisions. The text first considers the role of management in its responsibility to the shareholder. Recent views on the implications of shareholder value management on corporate decision making and performance are introduced. From these we develop a set of criteria, *shareholder value drivers*: profitability, productivity, cash flow and growth. Growth is essential for all businesses and during our discussions throughout the text it will be considered as an implicit influence on shareholder value. Typically, managers are confronted with choices between high rates of return, that is, for profitability, productivity and cash flow – in other words choices concerning projects with various rates of growth but having various levels of accompanying risk.

Chapter 1 introduces and explores the implications of shareholder value management for marketing decision makers. Shareholder value drivers are identified and discussed within the context of margin management, asset base management, and financial and investment management activities. Each is introduced in the chapter and they are then considered within the context of strategic marketing options such as: consolidation and productivity, market penetration, product and market development, and diversification.

The Du Pont approach to planning and control is introduced and is worked into the discussion. The subsequent development of the Du Pont model into the strategic profit model is also reviewed and examples are worked through to demonstrate the basic concepts of the model. Margin and asset base management are explored to identify examples of importance to the marketing/finance interface by introducing corporate activities (such as R&D, procurement and materials management, and manufacturing and logistics operations) and identifying issues of importance to marketing and finance and their interface.

Chapter 2 introduces a number of topics that are important in the business environment of the 'new economy'; the growth of customer centricity, customization and mass customization, the notion of 'value' and its application to both customers and 'organizations', the importance of planning and monitoring cash flow performance rather than just profitability, the decline of the vertically integrated organization and the growing importance of virtual structures, the preference for asset 'leverage' rather than ownership, the growth of the importance of intangible assets and the decline of tangible assets, the emergence of the notion that processes and capabilities are resources and a move away from functional 'silo' thinking, and introduction to the concept of value migration.

Chapter 3 considers the impact of the 'new economy' on current and new management thinking. It starts by revisiting Ansoff and discusses enterprise growth in the context of his model. Value-based management is reviewed with an emphasis on a stakeholder approach. The essentials of establishing and maintaining sustainable competitive advantage within the context of the 'new economy' explores new options and considers the implications for financial management. Identifying, generic business processes and their characteristics and the implications of new organizational structure options are considered. Finally, the processes and components of business model development are discussed.

The capacity size decision influences production investment and operating costs. Clearly these are all influenced by marketing strategy decisions. Chapter 4 identifies the need for a joint approach by marketing and finance. The chapter initially establishes a process by which the market volume available to the firm may be determined. Given a realistic forecast of volume potential the company should then consider the implications this presents for structuring production and specifically the implications for cost structures. The discussion considers economies of scale and the shape of long run cost curves in the determination of cost behaviour. This leads us into a discussion of strategic revenues and their implications for cost structures at a strategic level.

Operational implications are considered in Chapter 5. Topics addressed include the consideration of risk and the cost structure of the business. (Business and financial risk characteristics are discussed.) The chapter then looks at the influence of the nature of the manufacturing process on cost structure, and in particular decisions influenced by fixed and variable cost structure alternatives. We discuss the complexity of manufacturing processes and marketing influences, which includes a review of break-even analysis and its responses to price and volume changes together with consideration of capacity expansion. The experience effect is discussed and this concept links the earlier discussion of cost structures, technology and economies of scale. Chapter 5 includes a discussion on value systems and introduces the notion that cost structures, which are an influence on product market price, can be considered as inter-company decisions as well as intra-company decisions. The principle espoused is simply that more effective decisions may be made by analysing the value chains of all members of a value-generating system (or supply chain) – that is, manufacturers, distributors and the end-users. This approach identifies the benefits that may accrue to the entire system and which, through effective distribution policies, may be both increased and delivered more equitably. Product profitability and its components are introduced in Chapter 5. The discussion considers the implications of product management decisions such as product range rationalization, value analysis, and the role of direct product profitability in pricing decisions.

Chapters 6–11 are concerned with the implications of marketing decisions for the more common financial management areas of: working capital management (Chapter 7); managing fixed assets (Chapter 8); managing cash flows (Chapter 9); capital structure decisions (Chapter 10); and investment appraisal (Chapter 11). The chapters are introduced by a discussion of financial structure and performance characteristics (Part III). Part III reviews some of the fundamental issues of the marketing/finance interface including the funds flow cycle, working capital cycles, managing fixed assets, managing cash flow and funds flows, financial structure, and investment decisions. Both marketing and finance decisions require performance measurement criteria. These are introduced in Part III, together with a simple model that considers the marketing/finance decision-making complex. The matrix used relates the decision-making process to the shareholder value drivers introduced in Chapter 1.

Chapter 6 considers the marketing influence in the creation of shareholder value. The discussion introduces and reviews recent approaches to measuring shareholder value and compares these with earlier marketing-led approaches to strategic marketing and financial performance analysis proposed by the Boston Consulting Group (BCG). The chapter concludes by using these earlier shareholder value management models to develop a marketing based model.

Working capital management is discussed in Chapter 7. A comprehensive discussion considers the implications of marketing decisions on the components of working capital. The chapter commences with a review of the company's operating cycle, identifying important marketing/finance interface issues. This is followed by a review of working capital funding requirements for the primary components of current assets and examples are given. The topics discussed include inventory, accounts receivable and cash management. A similar treatment of current liabilities follows and here the discussion includes accounts payable (and the use of credit), bank overdrafts and other forms of short-term financing. The management of working capital and management performance criteria conclude the chapter. Examples are used to illustrate the impact that rigorous working capital management (influenced by marketing decisions) can have on the shareholder value drivers.

Managing the fixed asset base is discussed in Chapter 8. The chapter commences with a review of asset base components of particular interest to marketing decision makers. These concern the role of fixed assets in the production and delivery of an appropriate market offer. Fixed asset considerations include intangible factors such as R&D and branding. The performance of fixed assets is a concern for both marketing and financial managers. The criteria typically used are introduced and common influences are also introduced and discussed. Financing options are introduced and considered with a view to their influence on corporate performance, and debt and equity considerations. Off-balance sheet financing and leasing are all funding alternatives available to the firm which, depending upon varying circumstances, may have advantages or disadvantages.

Cash flow management is a vital activity for any organization and Chapter 9 considers the issues important to the marketing/finance interface. Cash flow and profits are distinguished, and the sources and applications report is reviewed to identify both marketing and financial points of interest. Examples are used. A marketing perspective of cash flow is taken and the Boston Consulting Group's growth/share matrix is discussed in this context. In order that marketing managers may gain a better perspective on cash flow issues (and management), the text develops a model that considers both the strategic and operational management aspects. We take the view that cash flow management requires a time perspective over which cash flow requirements and sources may be planned and controlled, with both internal and external aspects considered.

Chapter 10 considers the interface implications presented by capital structure decisions. The chapter discusses the role of gearing in the capital structure and managerial attitudes towards financial risk. The examples explore the major issues of concern to both marketing and financial management. The cost of capital is discussed and we consider both the qualitative costs (the influence on corporate control) and the quantitative costs (the interest return required by shareholders and investors). The means by which capital is obtained are also discussed and worked examples are given. As with other chapters the marketing/finance interface issues are explored and a comprehensive model is developed which identifies issues that both marketing and finance managers should consider when deciding upon an appropriate financial structure.

In Chapter 11 we consider investment decision issues. Alternative investment appraisal methods are reviewed and their relevant advantages and disadvantages discussed. The link between net present value (NPV)/discounted cash flows (DCF) and shareholder value is discussed. The role of the capital asset pricing model (CAPM) within the context of marketing/financial investment decision making is explored in some detail, with its implications for both return and risk as a major consideration. The spread of returns generated by a project or product investment and the risk acceptable to management is seen as an important issue in the marketing/finance interface with much of the chapter spent on exploring the factors that should be considered when appraising returns available from alternative strategies.

Chapter 12 considers the marketing and financial aspects of portfolio management. The work of the Boston Consulting Group during the 1960s and 1970s is well documented and widely known and used. Our approach to the topic is first to review the product life cycle theory and its implications for cash flow management. The discussion moves on to consider a portfolio effect of products or strategic business units at different stages of their development and the implications this has for funding growth activities. We discuss the BCG growth/gain model in some detail, using it to explore its linkages with shareholder value management through margin, asset base, and financial and investment management decisions. The relationship between growth and internal and external funding options is also discussed using this BCG model and frontier curve analysis. We also consider the financial management approach to portfolio design and management to demonstrate an alternative method of considering return and risk. The chapter concludes with a proposed marketing/finance model for portfolio planning. This model considers business growth rate, risk and shareholders' expectations for returns and identifies the trade-off potential among these criteria.

Chapter 13 considers planning and control issues. Planning and control is discussed in some depth and the influence of organizational structure is introduced. The concept of responsibility centres is explored within the context of organizational issues. The chapter is very much concerned with performance measures and the use of budgets in planning and control performance monitoring is a major topic. The use of PPBS (programme–planning–budgeting–systems) or output budgeting is discussed within the context of the marketing/finance interface. We also consider how value chain analysis may be used as a planning and control mechanism. Performance is a relative measure and the company should therefore monitor its own success against that of its competitors. If it performs better than its competitors it enjoys real success. A company/competitor performance evaluation is developed for this purpose.

Marketing and Financial Management aims at promoting a better understanding between these two important management disciplines. We hope that as a result of reading this book greater cooperation will be achieved and improved performance realized.

REFERENCES

Champion, D. (2001) 'Mastering the Value Chain', *Harvard Business Review*, June.

Drucker, P. (2001) 'Will the corporation survive?', *The Economist*, 1 November.

Normann, R. (2001) *Reframing Business*, Wiley, Chichester.

PART

I

Marketing and Finance Interface Issues for Marketing Strategy, Analysis and Decisions

Implementing the strategy decisions

The purpose of any business is to identify market-based opportunities and to apply its resources to them such that value is created for both the customer and the shareholder. While it is the responsibility of marketing to identify opportunities, it is a responsibility of financial management together with marketing to ensure that resources are used cost-effectively. The relationship is one which should aim to optimize customer and corporate value creation. It should be managed as a cooperative, rather than an adversarial, relationship.

An understanding of how marketing decisions can influence key areas of performance is often expressed in terms of their impact on the primary financial reporting instruments. The implications of marketing strategy decisions on margin performance, asset base productivity and the return on shareholder and investors' funds should be understood and considered by marketing management.

In this opening section we consider how best use may be made of analytical tools which may be used to bridge the marketing/finance interface.

We also consider the marketing strategy decision and implementation processes. A review of recent, relevant contributions to the marketing strategy literature is conducted. Implementing marketing strategies considers how resources may be allocated to meet the marketing objectives which result from a review of the opportunities offered by the environment in which the firm operates. Essentially, implementation is an operational activity, in which decisions are typically short term and often require changes to make responses to unexpected shifts in the organization's business environment. We have used *productmarket scope* and *operational resource allocation* as terms to describe the implementation process. The section offers a foundation on which to begin to explore the marketing/finance interface.

Current Perspectives of the Marketing/ Finance Interface

The purpose of any business is to convert its resources profitably into a product which creates value for another business or an end-user. In this context the accounting and financial manager views customer satisfaction and the profitable deployment of resources as components in the overall task of generating wealth for the owners of the business, the shareholders.

In recent years there has been an emphasis on creating shareholder value. Variously defined, this suggests that growth of the share price, dividend payments and positive economic cash flow are the primary concerns of the shareholder. Creating shareholder value requires both the marketing and the finance management to understand the implications their decisions have for each other.

In this chapter we shall explore this relationship by tracing the responsibilities of both marketing and finance in the creation of shareholder wealth.

During the 1980s many large companies directed their management activities towards 'value-based management' (VBM). The thesis behind VBM was (and remains) the notion that corporate objectives and strategies should be directed towards maximizing the return to shareholders – towards creating shareholder value. Creating shareholder value (although variously defined) essentially suggests that growth of the share price, dividend payments and positive economic cash flow are the primary concerns of the shareholder as an investor.

In some ways VBM was a response to the events of the 1970s and early 1980s which saw a large number of acquisitions, many of which were prompted by low share prices. Typical targets were businesses whose management had not performed very well, allowing their share price to fall such that an aggressive predator could make an attractive offer for the business. The exponents of value-based management argue that if shareholders' wealth is maximized, then share price and dividend yields will be high enough to discourage any bids from wouldbe predators. A healthy share price will discourage potential acquisitors.

The second area of interest in creating shareholder value, dividend payments, should clearly compensate the shareholders' investment at a level which recognizes both comparable market returns and the risk involved in the investment. Economic cash flow, the third concern, is important from two points of view. One is that the informed investor will want to take into consideration the present value of future income streams – the cash flow (this will have been discounted to reflect the risk that it is perceived the company is undertaking). We shall return to this topic in detail in later chapters. The second and more immediate view is that cash flow within a business is important for three practical reasons. The first is to enable the firm to meet its transactions commitments, such as payments to materials suppliers, employees and other suppliers of factors; dividend payments are also made from cash flow. The second reason is to provide for unexpected contingencies. The third is a speculative reason: to allow the business to be able to make an acquisition quickly and at a relatively low cost or, in a more routine situation, take advantage of low supply prices. Typically companies generate excess cash to cover contracted debts but also to ensure flexibility.

1.1   Creating shareholder value

Figure 1.1 traces the structure of the marketing/finance interface, from the recognized desired result of shareholder return, through the layers of actual operation, back to the decisions of each management area. If we look at the level of shareholder value, we can see the three criteria we have already identified. In practice, the overall return to shareholders is a combination of the performance of these three criteria. It is generally not possible to maximize all three concurrently. The task of management is to identify *optimal combinations* of share price, dividend and cash flow growth. It may be that retaining a higher than average proportion of the company's profits in the business (increasing retained earnings but *reducing* the dividend payment) will ultimately result in higher levels of profitability, thereby resulting in an increase in both share price and cash flow.

The marketing interface refers to an area of decision making within which there are implications for each function. For example, a decision by marketing management to expand market share will have implications for operating expenditures (i.e., promotional costs etc. requiring cash and increases in inventory holding to provide customer service). Before implementing such a decision the implications for the company's financial management should be

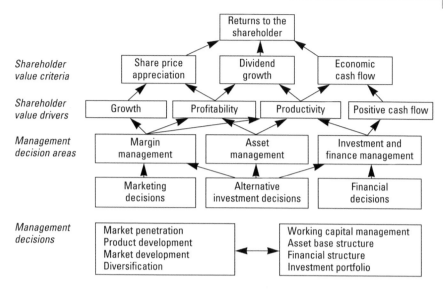

Figure 1.1   Structure of marketing/finance interace

discussed by senior marketing and financial managers. This ensures that objectives that have been set for profitability, productivity and cash flow will continue to be met or perhaps will show improved performance.

Of more interest for the marketing/finance interface are the *shareholder value drivers*, also shown in Figure 1.1. Management literature has started to make considerable use of the concept of a driver (or critical success factor). Drivers are those characteristics or features which, if managed appropriately, will lead to high performance. The drivers listed in Figure 1.1 are profitability, productivity, positive cash flow and growth.

Profitability is a function of the relationship between sales revenue and the costs of generating revenues. The ratio between profit and sales is a function of margin management. We shall expand upon this in the latter part of this chapter.

Productivity of the resources consumed by the business is another expectation of shareholders. The business is expected to use resources effectively. If inadequate resources are used it is likely that product quality will be inferior but overuse of a resource will result in excessive costs, low margins or high prices, and subsequently a loss of sales.

The importance of *cash flow* has been discussed earlier. The concept of cash flow has two components. Operational cash flow includes receipts from sales activities, in other words cash generated from the primary activity of the business. It also includes cash disbursements, payments to suppliers of primary goods (raw materials and components), labour, depreciation, service functions and activities and the payment of taxes. Negative cash flows place the business in a difficult situation because it becomes unable to meet trans-action commitments without assistance (typically from banks), and this imposes an additional cost (and outflow of cash) in the form of interest payments.

Strategic cash flow, the second component, covers cash flows (into the business and from it) derived from the sale and acquisition of fixed assets and from changes in the status of funding (the sale of shares or their repurchase, the increase in long-term loans and the receipt of capital allowances). Corporate cash flow is the sum of the two operational and strategic flows. We shall return to this topic in Chapter 9.

Growth is essential for all businesses and is assumed to be a primary value driver. Throughout this book we shall make this assumption and consider growth to be a necessary component without which profitability, productiv-ity and cash flow performances are unlikely to achieve acceptable levels. Clearly the expectations for shareholder value performance will be influenced by the growth rate planned (and actually achieved) for the business. This requires management to consider risk as well as the growth of performance characteristics. It is important that growth occurs at a planned rate. If the firm does not plan for growth then imbalance may develop. The firm should avoid two undesirable situations: having too large an asset base (excess capacity); or too little capacity, which may result in lost sales through poor deliveries. Planned growth facilitates the planning and acquisition of resources. Both marketing and finance have influence and interest here.

If profitability, productivity, positive economic cash flow and growth – the shareholder value drivers – are to match shareholder expectations margin and asset base management, investment and financial management are required. *Margin management* ensures that planned profitability is achieved. The primary objective of a business is for revenues to cover the costs of producing a specified level of output. Traditionally margin management was based upon the notional mark up on production costs; market-based pricing was not seen as being particularly important. Over time customer response and competitor activities have introduced other components into the equation. Margin management, for the competitive business, requires an understanding of the relationship between market share volumes, competitive pricing (which may involve a range of customer-based techniques), production capacity profiles, materials acquisition prices, labour rates and even the cost of funds to finance operations.

Asset base management is also volume and market-position based. Clearly an achievable, realistic forecast of market share is essential. A forecast of likely volume throughput provides an indication of the size of manufacturing facilities required to meet sales forecasts and customer expectations of product availability. The positioning strategy indicates the company response to researched customer expectations for exclusivity, quality and variety (among other attributes). This is important because the flexibility capability of the manufacturing facility is influenced by positioning decisions. Specific capacity and flexibility required for the company to allocate the appropriate level of resources to the market opportunity should emerge. Once the resource requirements are known, decisions may be made on how to organize them. This may not be a simple task, and it is influenced by the pattern of demand. For example, erratic market demand may lead management to plan a base level of capacity and add to production requirements by using overtime or outsourcing as and when needed. Clearly a wide range of issues needs to be considered.

Investment and financial management must ensure that the capital required by the firm is available and at optimum cost. The issue is one of balance and is linked to margin and asset base management. Given a potential market share and a profile for direct and indirect costs, financial managers must ensure that their business can fund the required asset base at a cost of capital (and using a method of funding) that is realistic to the cost structure of the firm. For example, it would be unrealistic for a small manufacturing business to undertake a market opportunity which, in a short space of time, would increase its size some tenfold. The problems of financing the activity would be large and would introduce risk into the equation. Investors would view the proposal with considerable scepticism and seek high levels of interest to offset risk. Thus much of what the marketing group may see as opportunity might require consideration in the context of the investment and financial management reality.

We shall return to each of the managerial activities in detail in subsequent chapters.

The process of creating shareholder value is one in which marketing decisions (such as consolidation and productivity, market penetration, product and market development, and diversification) are considered within the context of their investment requirements and their implications for funding requirements (working capital, asset base structure, financial structure and the impact on the portfolio balance of company strategies, product groups, divisions and other strategic business unit definitions).

Market penetration is a strategy by which the company seeks to expand its market share. This may be achieved in one of two ways. Existing customers may be encouraged to increase their use of a product, either by increasing the frequency of use or by using more of the product each time. Another possibility is to expand the customer base. This strategy may create a new group of customers or attract competitors' customers. Variations of these will exist. What are the implications for finance of a decision on market penetration?

Clearly the precise nature of the financial response depends upon what the decision is, but, for example, we can see that a decision to increase volume will require additional product inventories if orders are to be met promptly. This in turn may require additional capacity for production and raise the level of customer credit allowed. The additional stocks and accounts receivable increase the working capital requirements and may introduce some unknowns. For example, new customers' purchasing patterns may not be similar to those of existing customers; they may buy a limited range of products. Furthermore they might expect deliveries more frequently and take longer to pay outstanding accounts. In this scenario it is clear that the costs of the company will increase. Marketing and finance need to agree whether or not the incremental increase in working capital funding is offset by the increase in the business generated. In reaching a decision they will need to consider the overall impact on the business.

Diversification decisions should be evaluated in much the same way. Here the issues are more expansive. Typically, diversification is undertaken to provide opportunity for additional growth. Often existing markets have plateaued and more attractive growth opportunities exist elsewhere. Pursuing such an opportunity requires an increase in investment by the business. This may take the form of an acquisition of another firm currently competing in the market under review, or it may be preferable to develop a new business in the marketplace and pursue organic growth. The decision process is complicated and both marketing and finance will need to address such essential issues as the amount of capital required, the cost of capital and its availability, together with an estimate of volume potential and growth rate, profit margins likely to be generated, cash flow generation and a host of market characteristics such as customer and competitor profiles.

1.2 Management decisions and performance

We have so far explored qualitative issues and relationships, establishing a link between marketing and finance decisions in the process. We can now explore the quantitative links.

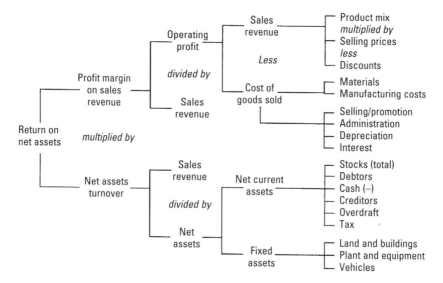

Figure 1.2   Du Pont system of financial analysis

Some years ago the Du Pont Company developed an approach to planning and control which was designed to monitor divisional performance. This system of financial analysis has subsequently been used by numerous companies. Its attraction is that it brings together the *activity ratios,* which measure how effectively a firm or its strategic business units (SBUs) employs the resources it controls with the profit margins on sales; it also shows how these ratios interact and determine the profitability of the assets. Figure 1.2 outlines the nature of the ratio system. The lower half of Figure 1.2 develops a net asset turnover ratio, or asset productivity measure. The upper part of the figure develops operating profit (or the margin percentage) on sales. When the net asset turnover ratio is multiplied by the operating margin the result is a return on net assets (RONA).

The Du Pont model has been modified to suit a number of purposes. One such model, the strategic profit model (SPM), has been varied by many authors and is shown in Figure 1.3. This model allows us to relate management activity components quantitatively. It helps with managerial decisions in four ways:

• It identifies the principal objective of the business: to maximize the return to the shareholders.
• It identifies the growth and profit paths available to a business (improve the margins earned, increase asset productivity, increase gearing).

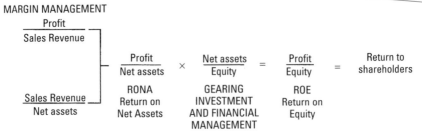

Figure 1.3   Strategic profit model

- It highlights the principal areas of decision making: asset management, margin management and financial management.
- It provides a useful model for appraising the marketing and financial aspects of strategy options.

A review of the decision-making areas helps us to understand the marketing/financial decision interface.

Asset base management (sales revenues/net assets) measures the effectiveness of the management's employment of capital. It reveals the judgements that were made in applying capital to pursue opportunities. As a ratio, it is particularly useful because it indicates the level of commitment required to pursue opportunities. This allows the business to examine the alternative means of acquiring the necessary assets, for example purchasing against leasing.

Margin management ('profit'/sales revenues) measures management's ability to recover the cost of materials and manufacturing, distribution (channel margins and physical distribution), depreciation, interest payments, overheads, and to provide a contribution towards shareholder compensation. 'Profit' in quotation marks implies that profit has a number of measures or levels, for example, gross, operating, EBIT or net, hence ' ' suggests that any are relevant at this point. The marketing influence here is concerned with the positioning of the business. Typically, the margins generated reflect the positioning of the business, its market position, and the expenses managers consider necessary to make a significant impact in the market. The relationship between margins generated and the asset base productivity infer its positioning. For example, low margins and high asset base productivity suggest a price led (or discount led) business. The reverse is typical of companies offering some exclusivity in their product and/or service offer. High gross margins suggest exclusive distribution into niche markets accompanied by high levels of service. Low gross margins, by contrast, usually imply mass distribution using high volume, low cost distribution with a level of promotional expenditure sufficient to effect projected sales.

Return on assets managed ('profit'/net assets). Neither of the above measures (sales revenue/net assets and 'profit'/sales revenues), taken on its own, is an adequate performance measure. The relationship between the two measures suggests that an increase in one, for example the profit margin, will increase the overall efficiency of the business:

$$\frac{\text{'Profit'}}{\text{Sales}} \times \frac{\text{Sales}}{\text{Net assets}} = \text{ROAM (return on assets)}$$

The strategic profit model may be used to evaluate alternative strategies. For example, an increase in price may increase total sales revenue and the profit margin. Alternatively, a reduction in stockholding (following a range reduction decision) would result in a reduction in net assets and this would be reflected as an increase in asset circulation. A plant or warehouse closure would have a similar effect, but this would influence fixed asset efficiency whereas the previous example would affect working capital. Both could have an adverse effect on revenue and profit.

Gearing (net assets/equity) reflects the business's dependency on borrowed funds for both short- and long-term needs. Low ratios suggest the business is conservative in its attitudes towards risk, preferring to rely upon shareholders' funds for financing activities. Such businesses are more likely to expand along product- or market-related vectors rather than to opt for diversification strategies. The reverse does not necessarily follow. Clearly the highly geared firm is less risk-averse but it must be remembered that the use of debt capital means the firm has to meet fixed interest payments regardless of its success (or lack of success). Thus, while a business may appear cavalier in its sourcing of funds, it may not necessarily reflect this attitude in its marketing strategy.

Return to shareholders ('profit'/shareholders' equity). The purpose of a business is to maximize the return on shareholders' investment in it and this ratio measures the success of its activities towards that end. The return on equity (ROE) is a measure of the return generated on the shareholders' investment (the equity or net worth) in the business. Reasons for high (or low) performance will vary and may reflect ineffective management decisions (such as a failure of the marketing strategy) or an inappropriate financial structure for the marketing opportunities the company attempted. Inadequate control of

Table 1.1   Wombat Holding results

WOMBAT HOLDING PTY LTD Profit and Loss Account 1995/1995 ($000)		
Sales		30,000
Less cost of goods sold		17,500
Gross profit		12,500
Less operating expenses		
Materials	1,500	
Manufacturing	3,000	
Selling and promotion	350	
Administration	550	
Depreciation	1,000	
	6,400	
Operating profit		6,100
Less other expenses		
Interest	700	
Profit before tax		5,400
Corporation tax (40%)	2,160	
Net profit after tax available to shareholders		3,400

production or distribution operations, leading to high costs and low margins, may be another cause of poor performance, as may the impact of recession or some other external influence over which the firm has no control.

We can explore the relationships the strategic profit model suggests using the results of Wombat Holding Pty Ltd (a fictitious company) (see Table 1.1).

Wombat Holding's net profit for 1995/1996 is $3.4 million and sales are $30 million. The net assets are $17 million and the shareholders' equity is $10 million. Using the strategic profit model we have:

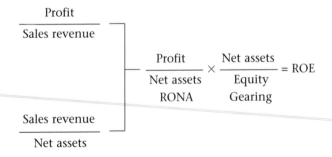

which gives us:

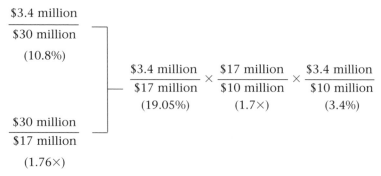

$$\frac{\$3.4 \text{ million}}{\$30 \text{ million}}$$
(10.8%)

$$\frac{\$3.4 \text{ million}}{\$17 \text{ million}} \times \frac{\$17 \text{ million}}{\$10 \text{ million}} \times \frac{\$3.4 \text{ million}}{\$10 \text{ million}}$$
(19.05%)   (1.7×)   (3.4%)

$$\frac{\$30 \text{ million}}{\$17 \text{ million}}$$
(1.76×)

We can now ask a few 'what if' questions to explore our model. For example, what if the profit margin could be improved and the profit was $4 million instead of $3.4 million, and the return on sales increased to 13.3 per cent? The return on net assets would then be 23.4 per cent and the return to the shareholders almost 40 per cent (39.89 per cent). This suggests that if costs could be controlled more effectively, perhaps by reducing the range of product choice or by eliminating product features, then profit and return to the shareholder could be improved significantly.

Another 'what if' question concerns asset base management. What if the assets could be made more productive? What if, by reducing stocks, or perhaps by selling land, buildings or equipment that are surplus to requirements, we reduced the net asset figure of Wombat Holding from $17 million to $15 million? This would give an asset turnover of $30 million/$15 million; or two times. At the original level of profit margins on sales, 10.8 per cent, the increased asset turnover would improve the return on net assets to 21.6 per cent. Gearing would be changed because the $2 million received from the sale of the assets would be used elsewhere in the business and would generate additional revenue and earnings. The company would ideally prefer to improve its margins as well as the productivity of the asset base. Thus if the profitability of the business could be improved beyond the $3.24 million to say $3.75 million and the asset turnover to 2, then we would have:

$$\frac{\$3.75 \text{ million}}{\$30 \text{ million}}$$
(12.5%)

$$\frac{\$3.75 \text{ million}}{\$15 \text{ million}} \times \frac{\$15 \text{ million}}{\$10 \text{ million}} \times \frac{\$3.75 \text{ million}}{\$10 \text{ million}}$$
(25%)   (1.5)   (37.5%)

$$\frac{\$30 \text{ million}}{\$15 \text{ million}}$$
(2 ×)

In most instances we try to increase the sales generated from the assets. Returning to our original situation and assuming a 15 per cent increase in sales (together with a similar increase in profit) but with no change in the assets we would expect to see:

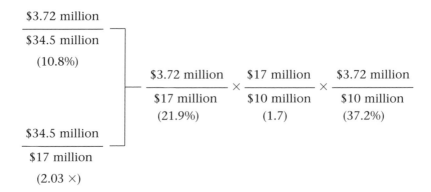

$$\frac{\$3.72 \text{ million}}{\$34.5 \text{ million}}$$
(10.8%)

$$\frac{\$3.72 \text{ million}}{\$17 \text{ million}} \times \frac{\$17 \text{ million}}{\$10 \text{ million}} \times \frac{\$3.72 \text{ million}}{\$10 \text{ million}}$$
(21.9%)   (1.7)   (37.2%)

$$\frac{\$34.5 \text{ million}}{\$17 \text{ million}}$$
(2.03 ×)

Clearly an increase in sales makes a significant improvement to the performance of the business.

1.3   Margins, productivity and the use of assets

From the proposition made by the strategic profit model, the interface between marketing and financial performance can have significant implications for the overall performance of the business. Figure 1.4 expands the strategic profit model (Figure 1.3). It identifies decision options to increase the overall return on assets deployed within the business. From Figure 1.3 we have a basic proposition:

$$\frac{\text{Sales revenue}}{\text{Assets}} \times \frac{\text{Profit}}{(\text{Sales revenue} - \text{Costs})}{\text{Sales revenue}} \times \frac{\text{Profit}}{\text{Assets}}$$

Figure 1.4 therefore identifies some of the components of Figure 1.3. Sales revenue decisions require associated decisions concerning research and development investment, capital requirements, market development, differentiation, etc. Asset decisions include production capacity and methods and process and product technology, etc. These suggestions are by no means all the decisions that are involved.

The financial interest in *sales revenue* generation may influence the entire product-market strategy. Research and development investment is required

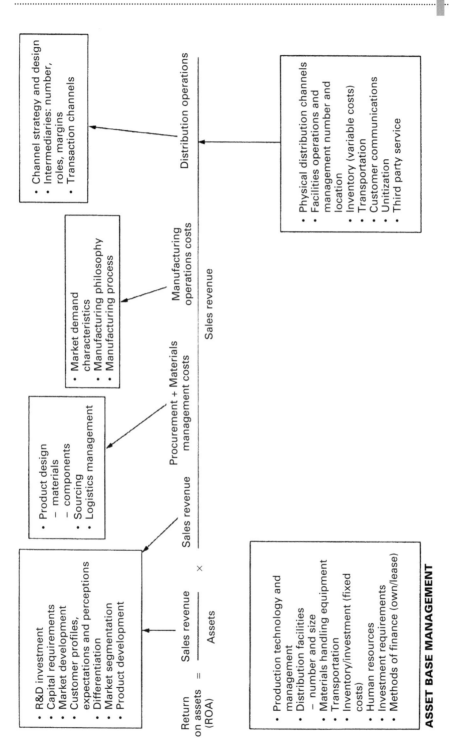

Figure 1.4 Margin and asset base management in detail

for both product and market development. Capital requirements and the attitude towards risk will influence the company's response to the opportunities
of the marketplace. Other important considerations are those of product
differentiation and market segmentation. These are important because they
influence volume and margins and therefore profitability, and return on capital employed and to the shareholders.

Procurement and materials management brings together finance, marketing and
logistics issues. Finance/marketing considerations are linked in product
design. Marketing activities can enhance overall margins by establishing
detailed performance specifications across a product range. In this way the
potential for using common components and materials and the effect on
costs can be explored. Consumer durables manufacturers make considerable
use of this principle at the design stage by making replacement peripheral
items and internal microswitches, timers and so on as common to as many
models as possible, without detracting from performance or differentiation
specifications. As a result, purchasing may be rationalized (within the context
of securing continuity of supplies) and buying margins enhanced by greater
purchasing volumes. This clearly has an impact on logistics management by
improving warehousing and transport utilization.

Manufacturing operations have both marketing and financial interests. The
size of a market, product characteristics, customer purchasing frequencies (and
processes) will determine the manufacturing philosophy and process adopted.
This will be accompanied by financial management issues concerning plant size,
infrastructure and other factors. These issues will also be influenced by the
nature of the demand profiles of customers. For example, both industrial and
consumer durables manufacturing are strongly influenced by just-in-time (JIT)
philosophies and processes and customers in these markets require quite different supply service arrangements from customers who operate on a production
inventory system. The implications for both marketing and finance of these two
operations are different. Marketing concern is for high levels of customer service.
Finance, while contented with improved cash flow and in particular the low
levels of stockholding which accompanies JIT, will seek to maintain high levels
of production efficiency which may require more frequent plant replacement.
This in turn may require accelerated plant depreciation and write off procedures.

Distribution operations have two major areas of joint concern: the transaction
channels and physical distribution channels. Marketing decisions aim to
develop sales and maintain high levels of customer service. To that end
managers identify the tasks to be performed in the process of achieving
customer satisfaction (ensuring product quality, service support etc. at
competitive prices). The issue for the marketing manager here is to identify
where value is added during this process and then to identify the most cost

effective means by which this may be achieved. Often this is resolved by using intermediaries (to whom a payment is made which dilutes the overall margins generated) or by conducting the transactions directly with customers which creates costs.

Similarly, physical distribution channel decisions are about identifying end-user expectations and designing a system to deliver the level of service required by the customer (or perhaps customers if a sequence of intermediaries is involved). As Figure 1.4 implies, there are a number of cost entities to be considered.

Essentially the marketing decision is one of 'make or buy'. As we shall see in subsequent chapters, it is here that the marketing/finance interface can operate effectively. 'Make or buy' may be interpreted extensively to include the comparison of direct versus indirect selling in transaction channels as well as considering the use of third party distribution services in physical distribution channels.

The *asset base* decision should also be considered as a joint concern. Financial managers typically prefer to restrict ownership to those assets which are likely to increase in value or those which are readily disposable. The marketing preference is for an asset base structure that offers customers 100 per cent of their expectations. This preference risks excess capacity in production and distribution facilities, product ranges with extreme Pareto profiles, generic rather than selective customer service offers and a range of other similar excesses, all of which erode profit margins. The asset base decision should be one which optimizes the level of investment and achieves customer satisfaction levels resulting in revenue, profit and cash flow performances that meet the financial and marketing objectives.

1.4   Elements of shareholder value

To conclude this first chapter we will consider the primary activities that are included in the marketing/finance interface by looking at the relationships among the four areas discussed in this chapter: margin management, asset management, investment and financial management and cash flow management. Figure 1.5 illustrates how the profit and loss account may be viewed from a *margin management* perspective by identifying the components of gross margin, operating margin and net profit. Each of the component expenses is influenced by marketing decisions at the gross and operating profit levels.

Asset management comprises fixed assets and working capital issues. Again there are both marketing and financial considerations to decisions about these.

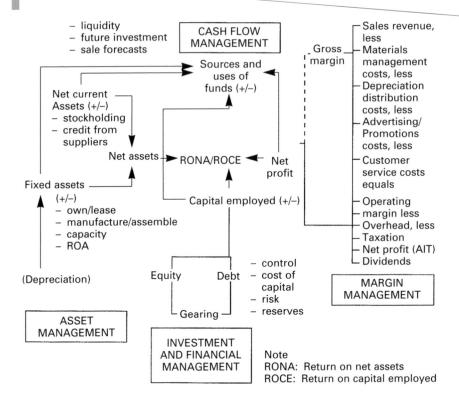

Figure 1.5 Overall model of the firm

Fixed assets decisions are based upon the manufacturing and distribution response to market expectations. The marketing view will seek to maintain high levels of product availability, customer service(s) and competitive price levels. The finance manager is concerned with ensuring that the level of return generated from the marketing activity will provide satisfactory profit and cash flow streams to ensure profitable continuity. In this respect the financial appraisal of a marketing opportunity will not only consider the return on assets but also how best this may be achieved by viewing a range of fixed asset and working capital combinations. Issues such as the owning versus leasing of facilities, the manufacturing process and its impact on costs will be of major concern.

Working capital decisions (net current assets) will consider the costs and ways of achieving marketing objectives. They will require evaluation to ensure that given the estimates of stock and service levels, together with the proposed customer credit policy, the most cost-effective means of financing the requirements is found. A financial management concern is the extent to which items that are essentially working capital items (such as inventory held for safety stock) may become a permanent feature and as such require long-term funding.

Financial management issues have some interface concerns of their own. The balance of funding (i.e., proportions of equity and debt) depend upon the business's view on control. Often there is reluctance to expand the funds of the business and finance growth by issuing more shares, the preference being either to use reserves or to expand using long term debt. A number of issues are involved here. While control is contained, debt finance does bring with it the commitment to pay interest charges regardless of how well the project actually succeeds. If there is doubt concerning the level and continuity of the return from a project funded in this way the riskaverse firm would probably not proceed.

The cost of capital is also a factor. The decision to take on long-term debt clearly is influenced by the interest rate. Interest rates can vary from lender to lender but they can also vary because of the lenders' views concerning the level of debt currently in the firm. If they consider it to be too high then interest rates will be adjusted to compensate for what amounts to a perception of high risk.

Again there are further issues here. Clearly marketing must ensure that it investigates the proposed opportunity in detail, ensuring that the characteristics of it that introduce risk to the firm (for example, volumes to be achieved, margins or initial investment) are thoroughly evaluated.

Cash flow management also has marketing/finance interests. Any business is concerned about liquidity – the ability to meet operating expenses from the revenues generated. It follows that reliable and accurate sales forecasts are required and that the financial management group will use market forecasts to reach decisions on future investment requirements. Again it becomes clear that marketing has a major responsibility to ensure that it identifies the relevant data if financial managers are to be able to plan for efficient funds flow and availability when they are required at a cost which will ensure that the planned opportunity will make a satisfactory return on investment.

1.5   The strategic profit model

Another view of the marketing/finance interface may be seen in Figure 1.6, which expands upon the margin and asset components of Figure 1.3. Here

Figure 1.6 Expansion of the stratgic profit model

we see Gross profit influenced by product range and mix decisions, together with market segmentation. As we saw earlier, decisions about market characteristics and the supply chain (inbound) will influence manufacturing costs.

Product-market strategy decisions will determine features of the (outbound) supply chain. In particular here are distribution and promotional costs. Clearly the available channel strategy alternatives will be influenced by the necessary expenditure levels, and these will include distributor margins and promotional costs.

Working capital components (inventory, accounts receivable) will also be influenced by supplier/distributor relationships. Other aspects of net current assets will be influenced by decisions concerning relationships with suppliers, notably the levels of accounts payable and the time period allowed by suppliers for payment.

Fixed assets are influenced by decisions requiring investment in production and distribution facilities. The intangible assets of human resources and brand names are also influenced by productmarket development strategy and relate to the longer-term characteristics of market positioning.

Margin and asset management identify the areas in which the marketing and finance managers work closely together. The SPM extends the earlier discussion by adding the financial structure to the picture. The major benefit of the SPM is the facility it offers to explore alternatives. For example, given specific requirements for the return on equity and perhaps a constraint on the gearing relationship, it is possible to probe alternative strategic positions to identify the most suitable strategy for the company to pursue.

We shall return to the SPM in subsequent chapters in order to use its flexible approach to planning and control.

1.6 Summary

This first chapter has served to introduce a number of concepts which bring together the marketing and financial decision processes. We identified shareholder satisfaction as an overall objective for any business and identified the drivers and management decisions involved in achieving shareholder value. In order that we might consider these components in more detail we introduced the strategic profit model which has been derived from earlier work pioneered by Du Pont for divisional planning and control purposes.

Finally, the point should be made that there are clearly quite different views between marketing and finance concerning performance achievements

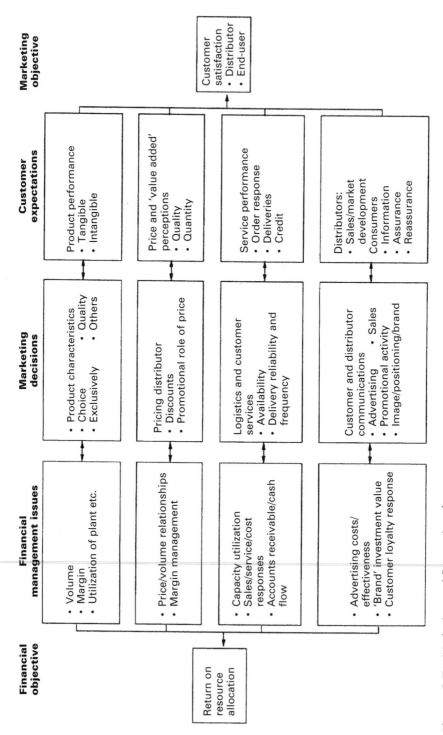

Figure 1.7 Marketing and finance interfaces

(see Figure 1.7). The objective from a corporate point of view is to achieve the level of customer satisfaction determined by customer research, at a level of profitability that satisfies return on investment expectations, and to meet the shareholders' value expectations by maintaining a healthy share price, acceptable dividend payments and strong cash flows.

2 Marketing and Finance in the 'New Economy': New Roles – New Relationships

2.1 Introduction

Changes in the business environment have resulted in changed roles for business disciplines and changes in the ways in which they relate to each other. Among the many changes that have occurred (and are ongoing) the following are important in that they identify the increasing need for marketing and financial management to be increasingly aware of the impact and implications that each have upon each other:

- The growth of customer centricity, customization and mass customization.
- The notion of 'value' and its application to both customers and 'organizations'.
- An emphasis on cash flow performance rather than just profitability.
- The decline of the vertically integrated organization and the growing importance of virtual structures.
- Asset 'leverage' rather than ownership.
- The growth of the importance of intangible assets and the decline of tangible assets.
- Processes and capabilities as resources and a move away from functional 'silo' thinking.
- Value migration.

The changes in the requirements for competitive leadership are suggested in Figure 2.1, which identifies the changing nature of competition over recent years. It also suggests the changing response of business organizations. The traditional marketing approach has evolved: 'customer centricity' has developed

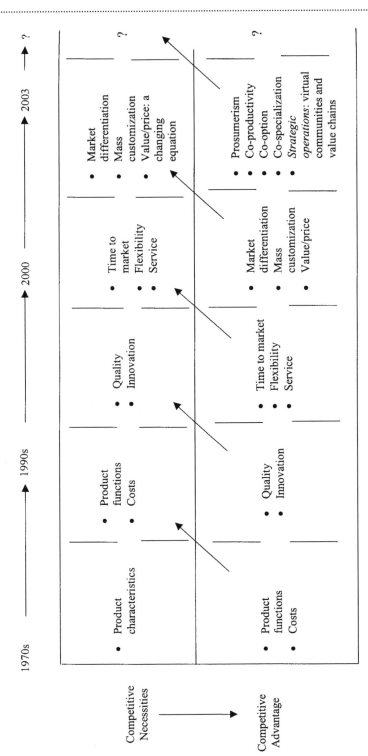

Figure 2.1   The transitional stages of competitiveness: new economy – new competitiveness

from a product-led marketing philosophy. Among the interesting issues to emerge one clearly concerns the need for marketing managers to understand the accounting and financial implications of the decisions they make currently and in the future. The 'real' costs of differentiation and the fixed and variable costs of alternative organizational structures are becoming increasingly important and as such need to be identified and understood.

2.2   The growth of customer centricity, customization and mass customization

'Customer-centric' thinking

Slywotzky and Morrison (1997) suggest the customer becomes the first link and everything else follows: '. . . everything else is driven by the customer'. Managers should think of:

(1)   their customers' needs and priorities;
(2)   what channels can satisfy those needs and priorities;
(3)   the service and products best suited to flow through those channels;
(4)   the inputs and raw materials required to create the products and services;
(5)   the assets and core competencies essential to the inputs and raw materials.

Additionally they are becoming required to consider:

(6)   relationships between revenues and costs that occurs when customer expectations are focused on
(7)   alternatives available to an organization to create and deliver customer value

And they add an important perspective:

> The value of any product or service is the result of its ability to meet a customer's priorities. Customer priorities are simply the things that are so important to customers that they will pay a premium for them or, when they can't get them, they will switch suppliers.

Slywotzky and Morrison are suggesting that value opportunities are distinguished by understanding customers' priorities and monitoring priorities for change. They give examples: Nicolas Hayek (Swatch) understood that a growing segment of consumers would buy watches based upon taste, emotion and fashion rather than on prestige; and Jack Welch (General Electric) identified customers who saw less value in the product and more in services and financing.

This suggests a broad perspective of value, well beyond direct benefits and one that encompasses the nuances of basic criteria. Basic value criteria are broad characteristics like security, performance, aesthetics, convenience, economy and reliability. However, at the next level these may be seen to be wide-ranging criteria.

The approach suggested by these authors would change the traditional customer-driven perspective. Slywotzky and Morrison go further:

> In the old economic order, the focus was on the immediate customer. Today, business no longer has the luxury of thinking about just the immediate customer. To find and keep customers, our perspective has to be radically expanded. In a value migration world, our vision must include two, three, or even four customers along the value chain. So, for example, a component supplier must understand the economic motivations of the manufacturer who buys the components, the distributor who takes the manufacturer's products to sell, and the end use-consumer.

Clearly the ability to be 'customer specific' is only possible in a limited number of markets and this was not the authors' message. What Slywotzky and Morrison are suggesting is that an analysis of product-service delivery alternatives may result in identifying an option that maximizes customer satisfaction at an acceptable level of cost. The issue becomes one of understanding not only the cost issues but also the full range of alternatives.

Customization and mass customization

Customer centricity was not meant to imply customer specifity. Indeed there are very few product-service offers that are required to meet such a stringent specification. Typically the customers' focus is on product-service aspects that may be 'mass produced'. Pine has identified some interesting and related issues. Mass production has a goal shared by both business and consumers and raises an interesting interface between technology management and relationship management. Consumers accepted standard products, which facilitated market expansion and reduction of prices through economies of scale. The restricted capabilities of manufacturers to produce differentiated products at similar prices to those of mass produced goods further encouraged the emphasis on demand from homogeneous markets. This relationship interface became institutionalized in a stable market environment. Pine points towards an inherent logic. He argues that generating cash flow and profit are essential if companies are to remain in business. Both are a function of volume and margin – margins are increased if costs are kept as low as possible. Homogeneous markets are volume markets, hence an increase in volume decreases cost still further and, typically, as they are elastic, price reductions can (at least for some time) increase volume and revenues. Further cost reductions can result in price levels at which niche market customers will succumb. Those niche markets that remain were left to fringe manufacturers. The homogeneous product manufacturers apply technology (automated processes) that increase fixed costs but lower unit costs; pricing is used to expand volume still further. Product life cycles are long, and maintained that way, so as to ensure that costs can be amortized over the large volumes produced and sold. Internally the organization operates a tightly controlled production system that uses incentives to achieve volume targets. Externally distributors accept (prefer) few product changes and customer satisfaction is realized through a combination of acceptable levels of quality and service at low prices.

However, technology has enabled large manufacturers to compete. Mass customization was a response to changing customer circumstances and expectations. Consumer disposable incomes increased, thereby increasing their spectrum of choice; these included variety and an immediacy in demand satisfaction. Through the application of 'new technology' (computer-based design and manufacturing) together with new approaches to management, industry created an alternative paradigm. Here the objective is to 'deliver' affordable products and services with sufficient variety and customization such that; '. . . nearly everyone finds exactly what they want'. This differs markedly from the proposition offered by mass production in which 'nearly every one can afford them'. Pine offers a logic for mass customization. Unstable demand for specific products results in market fragmentation; product variety becomes an essential feature of customer satisfaction. Homogeneous markets become heterogeneous. Niches become important. Manufacturers undertake specific niches with a view to meeting specified and feasible customer requirements, typically through post-production methods. This is not profitable and production systems change. Initially, the requirements were for shorter production runs accompanied by expensive loss of production time and 'set-ups'. However, niche customers accept premium prices that compensate manufacturers. Experience eventually enables production costs to be reduced and product variety is achieved at the same, or even lower, costs. Varying consumer demand requires a rapid time-to-market response with shorter product development cycles, which in turn result in shorter product life cycles. Demand fragments but individual producers find stability in their operations with selected niche segments.

The concept of 'product platforms' has also had an impact. The concept of product platforms is well known and the application of the concept first introduced by Black and Decker has expanded across a number of industries. A skillful approach of the concept can reap benefits of economies of scale, economies of differentiation and economies of integration. Meyer and Lehnerd (1997) describe the role and the importance of product platforms in the strategic planning of an organization:

> They know they must generate a *continuous stream* of value-rich products that target growth markets. Such products form the product family, individual products that share common technology and address related market applications. It is those families that account for the long-term success of corporations.

> Product families do not have to emerge one product at a time. In fact, they are planned so that a number of derivative products can be efficiently created from the foundation of common core technology. We call this foundation of core technology the 'product platform,' which *is a set of subsystems and interfaces that form a common structure from which a stream of derivative products can be efficiently developed and produced.*

The authors argue that the approach dramatically reduces costs in procurement and manufacturing, because so many costs are amortized across the product range. Furthermore, the 'building blocks' of product platforms can be integrated with *new* components to address new market opportunities rapidly. Hence, *time-to-market*, an important value driver and competitive advantage feature, can also be developed. Product platforms must be managed. Failure to monitor the development of customer expectations *and* to use developments in related technology implies that such derivatives that do emerge will fail 'customers in terms of function and value'.

2.3 The notion of 'value' and its application to both customers and 'organizations'

Value is a term frequently used but infrequently understood and for which numerous interpretations exists. In a business context, value implies stakeholder satisfaction, which is a broader consideration than simply customer satisfaction. Stakeholder satisfaction ensures that not only are customers' expectations met, but also those of employees, suppliers, shareholders, the investment market influencers, the community and government. It follows that stakeholder satisfaction presents the business with a broader range of decisions and typically, a larger number of ways in which satisfaction can be delivered.

Value is an interesting concept. The underlying motivation for changes in customer expectations is a shift in the consumer perspective of value which has moved away from a combination of benefits dominated by price, towards a range of benefits in which price for some customer segments, has very little impact. Value is assumed to be the benefits received from a product choice less their costs of acquisition. Porter (1996) offers a view of the role of 'value' in a strategic context:

> A company can outperform rivals only if it can establish a difference that it can preserve. It must deliver greater value to customers or create comparable value at lower cost or do both. The arithmetic of superior profitability then follows: delivering greater value allows a company to charge higher average unit prices; greater efficiency results in lower average costs.

Value is not a new concept. It will be recalled that Adam Smith introduced the notion of 'value in use' in 1776. He argued two aspects of value. He was of the view that value was determined by labour costs (subsequently modified to 'production costs'). Smith also argued that 'value in use' from a user's point of view is important. It is only when it is used that the full costs and benefits of a product-service may be identified. A number of companies use the 'value in use' concept to arrive at pricing decisions. The notion that an end-user should consider all aspects of a product-service purchase, not simply the price to be paid, enables both vendors and purchasers to identify all of the elements of the procurement–installation–operation–maintenance–replacement continuum. The process encourages both parties to look for trade-off situations such as high acquisition costs with low operating and maintenance costs, together with relevant supplier services packages. This approach introduces the possibility of integrated activities in which the supplier–customer relationship expands from a one-to-one relationship into a fragmented, but economically viable, value delivery system.

This situation is currently more the exception than the rule. Creating customer value (for that is what stakeholder value actually is about) has a history of development. Band (1991) traces the history of value creation, comparing North American interpretations with those of Japanese management philosophies which, ultimately, defines what it is the customer is offered and how this is accomplished, by whom, how, when and, of course why (which is usually the reference to corporate/stakeholder objectives). Band suggests that during a whole range of changes occurring in the 1980s: 'Executives who got the quality and service "religion" . . . failed to remember that quality and service are the means, but *value for the customer* is the end'.

Band interprets this simply and succinctly: 'The idea of creating value may, indeed, be reduced to a concept as simple as striving to become ever more "useful" to customers'.

And:

> But of course good intentions must be transformed into practical reality. The businesses that will succeed in the decades ahead are not those with advantages defined in terms of internal functions, but those that can become truly market focussed – that is, able to profitably deliver sustainable superior value to their customers'.

This means being able to do the following:

- Choose the target customer and combination of benefits and price that to the customer would constitute superior value; and
- Manage all functions rigorously to reflect this choice of benefits and prices so that the business actually provides and communicates this chosen value, and does so at a cost allowing adequate returns.

Looking more closely at the question of user value, the following characteristics are found:

- Quality – expressed in terms of features of products or services that are consistently valued by customers.
- Cost – the 'sacrifice' required of the user (in terms of money, time, risk or self-esteem).
- Schedule – the delivery of user-valued features in the correct quantity, time and place.

It follows that it is management's responsibility to identify what the end-user and indeed other 'customer groups' value and to create, monitor and modify organizational systems that add value to the product-service. Thus, for Band, the assertion is that creating and delivering value is much more than 'a passing business fad'. Rather it is an approach to strategic management that can be used to ensure that organizations respond to customer expectations, doing so with organizational structures that are flexible. Value creation, he suggests is *strategic* (because it entails both organizational and behavioural change), and it is *continuous* (because the challenge of delivering customer satisfaction in a dynamic market place requires unrelenting attention to achieving higher and higher levels of performance).

Differentiation has been an acknowledged component of competitive advantage for some time. While many companies focus on products or services, MacMillan and McGrath (1997) argue that the customer life cycle, or the consumption chain, is a means by which; 'they can uncover opportunities to position their offerings in ways that they, and their competitors, would never have thought possible'. Using a process they have labelled 'Mapping the Consumption Chain', they capture the customer's total experience with a product or service. Such a process identifies numerous ways in which value can be added to a product or service. The mapping process to identify the consumption chain comprises a series of questions aimed at establishing aspects of behaviour that occur:

- How do people become aware of their need for a product or service?
- How do consumers find a specific offering?
- How do consumers make final selections?
- How do customers order and purchase a product or service?
- How is the selected product or service delivered?
- What happens when the product or service is delivered?
- How is the product installed?
- What is the customer really using the product for?
- How is the product or service paid for?
- How is the product stored?
- How is the product moved around?
- What do customers need help with when they select a product?
- What about returns or exchanges?
- How is the product serviced?

An omission is a question concerning disposal or recycling of the product, which is becoming an important consideration. Essentially the authors are applying Kipling's 'six loyal serving men' to an audit of customer product selection and use behaviour. Their argument is reinforced with numerous examples. The mapping process is an ideal method for identifying 'value adding' opportunities, but another benefit, not identified as such, is the opportunity it offers to review the value creation processes and consider alternative delivery methods. Clearly these may not be 'in-house' and the analysis therefore encourages the use of external suppliers who may add even greater value to the product-service, either through extended differentiation or by cost reductions. This is the very essence of value chain strategy and management.

Anderson and Narus (1998) adopt a similar approach. They argue that very few suppliers in business markets are able to answer questions concerning what value actually is, how it may be measured and what the suppliers' products (or services) are actually worth to customers. They comment:

Customers – especially those whose costs are driven by what they purchase – increasingly look to purchasing as a way to increase profits and therefore pressure suppliers to reduce prices. To persuade customers to focus on total costs rather than simply on acquisition price, a supplier must have an accurate understanding of what it is customers value, and would value.

The authors suggest that the successful suppliers in business markets are successful because they have developed *customer value models,* which are data-driven representations of the worth, in monetary terms, of what the supplier is doing, or could do, for its customers. Customer value models are based on assessments of the costs and benefits of a given market offering in a particular customer application.

Value is defined by Anderson and Narus as follows: 'Value in business markets is the worth in monetary terms of the technical, economic, service, and social benefits a customer company receives in exchange for the price it pays for a market offering.' Value is expressed in monetary terms. Benefits are net benefits; any costs incurred by the customer in obtaining the desired benefits, except for the purchase price are included. Value is what the customer gets in exchange for the price it pays. Anderson and Narus add an important perspective concerning a market offer. A market offer has two 'elemental characteristics: its value and its price. Thus raising or lowering the price of a market offering does not change the value such an offering provides to a customer.' And, finally, value takes place within a competitive environment; even if no competitive alternative exists the customer always has the option of 'making' the product rather than 'buying' it. The difference between value and price equals the customer's incentive to purchase. In other words, the equation conveying the customer's incentive to purchase a supplier's offer must exceed its incentive to pursue the next best alternative.

Anderson and Narus are offering a structured approach to 'value in use' pricing, or life cycle costing. They consider the activities involved in generating a comprehensive list of value elements which are: 'anything that affects the costs and benefits of the offering in the customer's business. These elements may be technical, economic, service or social in nature and will vary in their tangibility.' The authors consider both tangible and intangible aspects of value, commenting on the difficulties that exist in ascertaining the value impact of benefits such as design services. They also discuss the problems associated with establishing monetary values to many of the elements, such as social factors like 'peace of mind'. Depending upon the nature of 'peace of mind' it is possible to consider the monetary outcome if it does not exist. For example, peace of mind may be available from an alternative because it eliminates pollution or some other problem. Not to choose that particular alternative may result in prosecution for pollution offences – the legal costs and potential fine does have monetary values!

Anderson and Narus are aware of the need to match value delivered with costs. They identify what they label as *value drains* – services that cost the supplier more to provide than they are worth to the customers receiving them and that offer no competitive advantage. They also identify two important advantages of the approach. Given the understanding of their customers' businesses, customer value models enable an organization to be specific concerning its value proposition and from this position of advantage another follows: customer relationships are strengthened. Possibly the most important benefit comes from the fact that understanding value in business markets and translating this into delivered value, gives suppliers the means to receive an equitable return on their efforts and resources.

2.4 An emphasis on cash flow performance rather than just profitability

There have been a number of global accounting-based crises which suggest that the often-cited quotation 'profit is opinion, cash flow is fact' is a major consideration for corporate governance regardless of size and structure.

It should be pointed out that even the conventional (accounting-based) approach to cash flow management is limited, being developed for statutory reporting purposes. An alternative model is offered as Figure 2.2. This model

Revenues Less Discounts less Wages and Salaries less Materials, components and services Less Capital servicing and maintenance costs less Overhead expenses **= Operating Cash Flow**

Operating Cash flow +/- Short-term Working Capital Requirements +/- Capital structure (restructuring) costs = **Cash Flow from Assets**

Cash flow from Assets +/- Fixed Assets (Tangible & Intangible) +/- Long-term Working Capital Requirements+/- 'Entry and Exit' Costs = **Strategic Cash Flow**

Strategic Cash flow +/- Changes in Equity & Debt funding = **Free Cash Flow**

NB: Tax payments have been omitted. These may occur at operating, asset management and strategic cash flow management levels depending upon tax regulations. Other charges may also be relevant

Figure 2.2   The determinants of free cash flow: a primary objective

identifies the operational and strategic decision areas that impact on cash flow planning and management and breaks these down into three broad categories the sum of which gives the firms *free cash flow*.

The first category is quite familiar – *operating cash flow*. Cash flow analysis at this level in the context of a 'new economy' business structure allows the identification of options based around delivering both customer and corporate value either by enhancing product features or by reducing costs. These options may be internal to the organization or may be external. Basic options such as outsourcing production to lower component costs or to obtain a more reliable component can be evaluated, as can the impact on both customer service (and cash flow) that may result from a shift in the companies policy towards intermediaries.

At the second level the model enables the impact on assets of alternative production and distribution strategies to be evaluated. *Cash flow from assets* describes the cash flow profiles that may result from alternative decisions. The options available each have significant implications for inventory, receivables and payables together with cash flow impacts from changes in the 'structure and ownership' of production and logistics in the organization.

Strategic cash flow decisions include investment in long-term fixed tangible and intangible assts. They also concern working capital to the extent these are essentially long term. Considering not simply work in progress and finished goods inventories, but strategic sourcing issues that are involved with the design of products to benefit from the advantages of product platforms and buying exchanges, established on an industry wide basis. In addition, we are also concerned with the difficult, but nonetheless important, entry and exit costs that are associated with strategic cost decisions.

The eventual success of the business is the *free cash flow* that is generated. To calculate this we need to consider the additional funding required by the business if it is to achieve its objectives. These will be equity and/or debt combinations. This introduces not only the cost considerations but also the perceptions of risk that the 'market' may assume and issues of corporate control. The 'value of the business' then becomes the discounted value of the free cash flow at a discount rate that is judged to be appropriate reflecting this risk.

The characteristics of the target market have a strong impact on cash flow management decisions. For example, highly competitive markets in which margins are 'difficult' due to market structure (in which concentration has resulted in a few influential companies with large market shares, seasonal and fashion driven products, or 'luxury' products that are prone to mark downs) may require equally competitive pricing strategies if positive cash flow are to be maintained.

2.5 The decline of the vertically integrated organization and the growing importance of virtual structures

There can be little doubt that the changes that have occurred in the business environment have brought about fundamental shifts in the response of businesses. Both philosophy and structure are undergoing significant changes. Increasingly alliances and partnerships are extended. The importance of 'distributed operations' (and therefore assets), the notion that core processes may be inter-organizational rather than intra-organizational, and the increasing frequency of the inclusion of customers in the design, development and production of products, suggests the need to expand the concept and the role of operations management into a planning and coordinating role. The issue that needs to be addressed is not where and how large should a manufacturing or logistics facility be; but rather do we need to own the facility(ies) at all!

Clearly some lessons have been available (if not learnt) and issues for consideration have been identified. Boulton *et al.* (2000) make a useful contribution. They contend:

> The encompassing challenge that companies face in this new environment is how to identify and leverage all sources of value, not just the assets that appear on the traditional balance sheet. These important assets including customers, brands, suppliers, employees, patents, and ideas – are at the core of creating a successful business now and in the future . . . But what assets are most important in the New Economy? How do we leverage these assets to create value for our own organizations in a changing business environment? What new strategies are required for us to create value?

The authors continue by making the point that the new business models comprise asset portfolios whose success is influenced by the interaction of the assets. Furthermore, in the new economy business model, asset portfolios are far more diversified than those of traditional organizations and include intangible assets such as relationships, intellectual property and leadership. They suggest that new business models are becoming commonplace in 'every industry' in the new economy.

> In these emerging models intangible assets such as relationships, knowledge, people, brands and systems are taking center stage. The companies that successfully combine and leverage these intangible assets in the creation of their business models are the same companies that are creating the most value for their stakeholders. (Boulton *et al.* 2000)

In an attempt to establish a 'model' to identify assets that create value the authors propose five core categories of assets: physical, financial, employee and supplier, customer and organization. Examples are given of companies that have focussed on a specific asset group to create above average value.

For Boulton *et al.* it is clear that: 'the ultimate success of each of these companies depends not on its ability to make the most of just one or two assets, but on its skill in optimizing all assets that make up the business model'. They broaden the definition of an asset by the following comments:

- Assets are tangible and intangible and extend beyond the balance sheet. They should be located where they will be strategically effective.
- Assets are, therefore, both owned and leased, controlled and uncontrolled. They offer sources of value that are within an organization's control and outwith it.
- Assets are sources of both financial and non-financial benefits. Intangible assets such as customers provide information as well as cash from sales revenues. Employees provide skills and ideas and, over a period of time, knowledge and learning. Organizations provide processes and systems.
- Assets have distinct life cycles.
- Assets include internal and external sources of value. The asset base of the virtual organization includes numerous external relationships.

In describing the development of virtual organization structures in the oil industry, Pebler (2000) offers a prescription for the future virtual organization:

> The virtual enterprise of the future will be much more dynamic and sensitive to the need for tuning operational parameters of the enterprise as a whole, including capital spending for both producers and service companies, optimizing the whole chain of value creation. The future world will be characterized by knowledge management and collaborative decision-making by way of virtual teams. Virtual enterprises will be empowered by a willingness to do business in more productive ways and by information technologies that eliminate barriers between stakeholders and radically improve work processes.

It is arguable that the changes that have occurred are all due to the 'new economy.' However there can be little doubt that the changes have brought with them a response from corporate thinkers. Whittington *et al.* (2000) comment:

> Increasingly competition, new information technologies, the rise of the knowledge economy, and extended global scope are all forcing many large

companies to experiment with new forms of organizing themselves. The concepts vary – they are seeking to become networked, virtual, horizontal or project based. But all these concepts express a need at the dawn of a new century to develop flatter, more flexible and intelligent forms of organising.

2.6   Asset 'leverage' rather than asset ownership

Drucker (2001) notes that while the traditional response to market pressures was vertical integration on a large scale – he cites Standard Oil and Ford as leading examples – today even the large corporations are leading the changes in strategic posture. For example, General Motors are creating a business for the ultimate car consumer – they aim to make available what car and model most closely fits that consumer's preferences. As Drucker notes, the changes to facilitate this are not just sales and marketing driven, but encompass design and development, and production. Products and services now have multiple applications and business organizations are redefining their core capabilities and processes.

Normann (2001) considers the new economy to be an opportunity to create more value and wealth. He adopts economic productivity as a measure of value, arguing that increases in productivity and wealth creation are positively correlated. He also argues that traditional 'value-creating' institutions have been replaced by new structures that use technology and new practices, such as outsourcing, to create value. This, he contends, resulted in a temporary focus on shareholder value, but argues that in the long term, shareholder value is generated by the creation of customer value. While this view might be contested, Normann's 'new strategic logic' is relevant. He suggests that:

> managers need to be good at *mobilizing, managing,* and *using* resources rather than at formally *acquiring* and necessarily *owning* resources. The ability to reconfigure, to use resources inside and particularly outside the boundaries of the traditional corporation more effectively becomes a mandatory skill for managements.

The result is a 'low capital intensity (investment/sales ratio)' that facilitates achieving maximized targeted cash flow and rate of return objectives. Furthermore, by adopting this strategy there is an implication that less funds have to be re-invested by each partner, making more funds available for discretionary purposes (i.e., reinforcing their distinctive competences, or distribution to shareholders).

A low level of capital intensity provides flexibility for marketing strategy options. It widens the price point options available by making lower price segments attractive and feasible. High-growth markets may be funded from internal funding (with cash still available for discretionary purposes). It is difficult, usually impossible, for capital-intensive businesses to fund high growth rate from internal sources without the 'benefit' of monopolistic price advantages or perhaps some other characteristic that affords sustainable competitive advantage. Furthermore the low capital intensity model also offers operational flexibility. By maintaining an optimal balance between fixed and variable costs production volumes can be made more responsive to market volumes thereby avoiding break-even crises. At the same time market response times are not inhibited. The application of flexible manufacturing systems (FMS) and just-in-time (JIT) philosophies and techniques compensate for the loss of control that a shift from vertical integration to virtual integration *may* imply.

2.7 The growth of the importance of intangible assets and the decline of tangible assets

The 'new economy' has been developing over the past decade. Customization, flexible response, models based upon inter-organizational interdependencies and the virtual oganization were concepts of the late 1980s. Business historians point to craft and merchant structures of the Middle Ages as the forerunners of the virtual model. The more recent changes in the structure of demand and supply have been accompanied by changes in inter-organizational relationship management and the investment and ownership of assets. Companies such as Dell Computer refer to 'asset leverage' (commented on above) as possibly the only option for effective competitive organization. Indeed evidence exists to show the decline in tangible assets and the growth of 'capability, based' intangible assets.

The increasing significance of intangible assets is emphasized by findings from the Brookings Institution. Brookings has been monitoring the changes in the financial structures of large US mining and manufacturing companies. Since 1982 fixed tangible assets as a proportion of total assets has declined steadily. In 1982 fixed tangible assets, as a proportion of total assets, were some 67 per cent. By 1992 this was 38 per cent and by 2000 the figure was reported to be less than 30 per cent.

Of interest here is the implications this places on both marketing and financial managers. Marketing managers need to be aware of the 'asset value' of brands, R&D, exclusive processes and, increasingly, customer relationships and customer databases. Financial managers are responsible for making marketing managers (and other managers with senior responsibilities) aware of the value of intangible assets and offer advice when strategies are discussed that may either enhance or damage their value.

2.8 Processes and capabilities: a move away from functional 'silo' thinking

More recent views of the value chain model point to the importance of taking a *process*-based perspective of the organization and extend this with the view that processes are not simply *intra-organizational* but have become *inter-organizational* and often *intercontinental*! Value chain analysis identifies the core capabilities and core processes involved in meeting the essential corporate and customer value drivers.

'A core business process "creates" value by the capabilities it gives the company for competitiveness': (Johansson *et al.*, (1993). Core business processes are the processes identified by the organization as being central to its strategy for competitive advantage. Normann (2001) suggests that the core business process of a company in the long term is to form new 'dominating' ideas. There is a similarity here with Porter's argument for long-term success. Over the long term the company requires a strategy for value delivery that not only offers competitive advantage through differentiation but one built around a core process to renew (or perhaps form new) 'dominating' ideas – the drivers of long-term competitive advantage. Normann contends:

> No other process in any organization is more fundamental in the long-term than this renewal of the dominating ideas, this reappreciation of an organization's identity and the way of manifesting it, in the face of environmental change.

Hammer (2001) argues that as businesses become accustomed to the *customer economy* 'process thinking' becomes essential: 'In order to achieve the performance levels that customers now demand, businesses must organize and manage themselves around the axis of process; moreover, they must apply the discipline of process even to the most creative and heretofore most chaotic aspects of their operations.' And: '. . . processes are what create the results that a company delivers to its customers'. Hammer continues by providing a *customer economy* definition of a process. He offers: 'an organized group of related activities that together create a result of value to customers'.

Hammer's discussion of this definition suggests increasing opportunities for the virtual organization. He establishes a process as a *group* of related activities that work *together*, pointing to the fact that value is created by the entire process. It is the result of 'value production and coordination'. Activities are *related* and *organized* with no irrelevant activities and performed sequentially giving some structure to the process and requiring process management. Effective process management is *result* oriented.

A strategic perspective is adopted by Armistead *et al.* (1999). The authors identify themes 'associated' with business process management. Strategic choice and direction suggests that because an organization cannot pursue every opportunity it makes choices, or trade-offs and these determine the resource patterns of organizations and, eventually, the development of core competencies. These, in turn, lead to competencies that influence subsequent strategy. Strategic business process management forces companies to 'examine their form and structure' having an influence on boundaries, structure and power within organizational design. An important component of the authors' model is the market value chain that 'links the stages which add value along a supply chain'. They suggest that *within* an organization the market value chain is taken to be the conceptualization of the core processes and activities which represent the organization in process terms: 'They capture the activities which start and end in the organization and link with other organizations in the chain.' They further suggest that the market value chain reinforces the resource-based view of the organization because it forces the identification of core processes from which core competencies and competitive advantage emerge. Performance management is another perspective of strategic business process management that 'relies on the management of resources and on a series of measurement systems', without which progress towards goals and any necessary corrective action is not possible. Organizational coordination occurs internally and externally (i.e., with suppliers and customers). This is particularly pertinent 'as the boundaries of internal processes become more ill-defined'; it could be argued that it is even more important for the boundaries between value chain organizations (such as the prosumer relationship between customer and supplier). This perspective adds emphasis to the importance of relationship management. The authors also identify knowledge management as a component of their model. Business process management enhances organizational learning and knowledge management. It 'provides a framework for organizational learning and can incorporate the management of knowledge'. In particular, it identifies the essential need for marketing and finance management to obtain greater understanding of each other's roles.

2.9   Value migration

Normann and Ramirez (1994) suggested that value is created, not in sequential chains, but in constellations: 'the role of business is to involve customers in creating value, taking advantage of the expertise, skills and knowledge possessed by each member of the value creation system'. As value-creating systems become complex and varied so do the component transaction relationships needed to produce and deliver the value offer. A company's principal task becomes the reconfiguration of its relationships and business systems. However, it should not overlook the production, logistics and service activities in value production. For example, automobiles and consumer durable products are a complex of each of these.

Normann and Ramirez were predicting the growth of the virtual organization in which the 'company's principal task becomes the configuration of its relationships and business systems'. However, for this to be managed effectively both upstream and downstream relationships are involved, and the task becomes one of identifying specific partners for specific processes; the coproductivity concept becomes multi-directional. In such circumstances Slywotzky and Morrison's (1997) comment concerning the importance of considering value migration assumes even greater significance. There are important issues such as conformity, consistency and continuity of the value offer to be managed. Not only do these have to meet the customers' expectations but they become part of the 'brand'. Thus the company should be mindful of the fact that for the end-user customer the product is an entity and the 'brand owner' is responsible for coordinating conformity, consistency and continuity of all aspects of product performance and support service.

It has been suggested that many arguments about creating value are only about customer satisfaction and assume profit may be taken for granted. However, companies need to think about their comparative advantages in their business model even before they start thinking about how to reconfigure it for their customers. If they do not, they are not making strategy; they are simply engaging in business process re-engineering.

Value migration occurs as both economic and shareholder value flows away from obsolescent (and obsolete) business models. Slywotzky (1996) argues that new models offer the same benefits to customers, but at lower cost, by changing the model structure. This change often results in a restructuring of profit sharing throughout the business model. Uren (2001) quotes Schremp (CEO, Daimler Chrysler) who expresses the view: 'within 10 years the price of a car will represent only a quarter of the total value provided to a customer with the balance consumed in maintenance, finance and other services'.

Uren also identifies differences between Qantas and Ansett, suggesting that Qantas, with its international networks and travel agency links, together with an investment in services is building a strong advantage. Similarly in the B_2B sector Amcor and Visy (both in packaging) are using IT-based e-commerce systems to increase customer service. In each of these examples, four basic issues emerge. First the 'value' of the brand is enhanced by service extensions or additions to the basic product. Second is the increased importance of intangible assets and the shift in investment patterns. Third is the importance of partnerships/alliances in the containment of fixed asset investment and, therefore, increased utilization albeit the assets are shared. And fourth is the acknowledgement that business organization or 'models' have changed. Virtual enterprises have expanded and the principle of outsourcing has expanded such that the maxim of 'Why own it when you can rent it?' has resulted in many businesses opting for a new model.

The basis for adopting the alternative (or new model) is based upon a simple thesis. Some competencies or capabilities are 'distinctive' and as such offer possibilities of sustainable competitive advantage, others – the 'reproducible' capabilities – offer no such benefits and in fact are readily available in supply markets (Kay 2000). Uren's observations suggest that typically distinctive competencies/capabilities are 'intangibles' and substantiates the inference to be drawn from findings from the Brookings Institution concerning the changes in asset structure in US large manufacturing and mining companies.

Value migration, it will be recalled, is the shift of business designs away from outmoded designs toward others that are better designed to maximize utility (value) for customers and profit for the company. Slywotzky contends that business designs (similar to products) also have cycles and reach a point of economic obsolescence. Customer expectations have a tendency to change over time but business model designs tend to stay fixed. By combining both, alternative added value structures may be evaluated.

Slywotzky measures the value migration process by using market value relative to the size of the company; size is measured as revenue. Thus we have:

$$\text{Power of business design} = \frac{\text{Market value}}{\text{Revenue}}$$

Where market value is defined as the capitalization of a company (shares outstanding multiplied by current share price plus long-term debt).

Gadiesh and Gilbert (1998) argued that: 'Successful companies understand that profit share is more important than market share', suggesting that by identifying the profit pools within the value creation system the company would understand the 'actors and processes' involved. Their argument continued by suggesting that profit pools differ within segments and by value chain and that profit pools shift as structural changes occur within both segments and/or value chains. They also argued that many companies: 'chart strategy without, a full understanding of the sources and distribution of profits in their industry'. Plotting the revenue profits, cost and productivity profiles of alternative business models enables the options to be identified in the knowledge of critical financial *and* structural criteria.

2.10   Summary

Day (1999) identifies five 'transitions' that are having (or will have) disruptive effects. These include *more supply and less differentiation* (or excess capacity for commodity-type products) that results in product-service imitation. Day cites the athletic shoe market as an example for which imitation reaches well beyond products and into delivery methods. The 'net'-based shopping offers of the major food retailers are another example. Globalization, *more global and less local* trends are another important transition. Globalization is being fuelled by the convergence, or homogenization, of customer needs, trade liberalization and the opportunities offered by international trends in deregulation. Day refers to the move from a 'marketplace' to a 'marketspace' perspective (a concept introduced by Rayport and Sviokla). Day suggests that this is a new emphasis not only on marketing communications, but also on product-service characteristics and transaction payment systems. The marketspace removes the need for dominant location; 'customers can shop across the globe or country, dramatically cutting the advantage of local presence that is the mainstay of many retailers'. *More competition and more collaboration* imply a shift away from self-damaging behaviour (such as that inflicted by price competition) towards a more collaborative approach to customer satisfaction. Day identifies an arrangement between Sony and Philips who are working together to develop common optical media standards and supplying components for one another. Collaboration in the European automotive industry has resulted in shared diesel engine developments. As Day comments: 'There are many markets in which a firm can be a customer, supplier and rival at the same time.'

The preference among most organizations for long-term customer relationships rather than expanding the 'new customer base' is identified by Day as *more relating and less transacting*, reflecting the move towards customer retention and points to the organizational changes occurring in many companies whereby they organize around customers rather than products or sales districts. The adoption of customer profitability and retention are becoming important as performance measures. Day's final 'transition' concerns response to customer requirements. Again this considers both strategic and operational aspects. *More sense-and-respond and less make-and-sell* suggests an increasing application of computer-aided design and manufacturing systems and a departure from traditional make-to-forecast manufacturing and response-based logistics systems based upon economies of scale and vertical control structures. *Economies of integration*, the coordination of capacities and capabilities on an inter-organizational basis are rapidly replacing economies of scale in manufacturing strategy.

Clearly a number of changes have occurred to the business environment within which marketing and finance operate. It is suggested that the changes and trends identified are sufficient motivation for a closer working relationship between marketing and finance.

REFERENCES

Anderson, J. C. and J. A. Narus (1998) 'Business marketing: understanding what customers value', *Harvard Business Review*, November/December.

Armistead C., J.-P. Pritchard and S. Machin (1999) 'Strategic business process management for organizational effectiveness', *Long Range Planning*, vol. 32, No. 1.

Band, W. (1991) *Creating Value for Customers: Designing and Implementing a Total Corporate Strategy*, Wiley and Sons, Toronto.

Boulton, R. E. S., B. D. Libert and S. M. Samek (2000) 'A business model for the new economy', *The Journal of Business Strategy*, July/August.

Brookings Institution (2001).

Day, G. (1999) *The Market Driven Organization*, The Free Press, New York.

Gadiesh, O. and Gilbert, J. L. (1998) 'How to map your industry's profit pool', *Harvard Business Review*, May/June.

Hammer, M. (2001) *The Agenda*, Crown Publishing Group, New York.

Johansson, H. J., P. McHugh, A. J. Pendlebury and W. Wheeler III (1993) *Business Process Reengineering*, Wiley, Chichester.

Kay, J. (2000) 'Strategy and the delusion of grand designs', *Mastering Strategy*, Financial Times/Prentice Hall, London.

MacMillan, I. C. and R. G. McGrath (1997) 'Discovering new points of differentiation', *Harvard Business Review*, July/August.

Meyer, M. H. and A. P. Lehnerd (1997) *The Power of Product Platforms*, The Free Press, New York.

Normann, R. (2001) *Reframing Business*, Wiley, Chichester.

Normann, R. and R. Ramirez (1994) Designing Interactive Strategy: *From Value Chain to Value Constellation*, Wiley, New York.

Pebler, R. P., (2000) 'The virtual oil company: capstone of integration', *Oil & Gas Journal*, March 6.

Pine III, B. J. (1993) *Mass Customisation: The New Frontier in Business Competition*, Harvard Business School Press, Boston.

Porter, M. E. (1996) 'What is strategy?' *Harvard Business Review*, November/December.

▶

Slywotzky, A. J. (1996) *Value Migration*, Free Press, New York.

Slywotsky, A. J., D. J. Morrison with Bob Andelman (1997) *The Profit Zone*, Wiley, Chichester.

Uren, D. (2001) 'To winners go more spoils in rivalry tango', *The Australian*, 10 March.

Whittington, R., A. Pettigrew and W. Ruigrok (2000) 'New notions of organizational "fit" ', *Mastering Strategy*, Financial Times/Prentice Hall, London.

Business Planning in the 'New Economy' – an Integrated Approach

3.1   Introduction

It is interesting to note that very few approaches to business planning include consideration of both marketing *and* financial issues let alone operations concerns. Chapter 2 identified a number of changes occurring in the 'new' business environment. As a reminder these are:

- The growth of customer centricity, customization and mass customization.
- The notion of 'value' and its application to both customers and 'organizations'.
- An emphasis on cash flow performance rather than just profitability.
- The decline of the vertically integrated organization and the growing importance of virtual structures.
- Asset 'leverage' rather than ownership.
- The growth of the importance of intangible assets and the decline of tangible assets.
- Processes and capabilities as resources and a move away from functional 'silo' thinking.
- Value migration.

It is very obvious that a business plan that only has a marketing approach or a financial approach or indeed that is simply concerned with operations issues is unlikely to be successful. Best (2004) is concerned that strategic marketing planning does consider financial performance characteristics but he does not raise the operations issues and the increasing need to consider alternative structures. Given the recent emphases of the new and successful

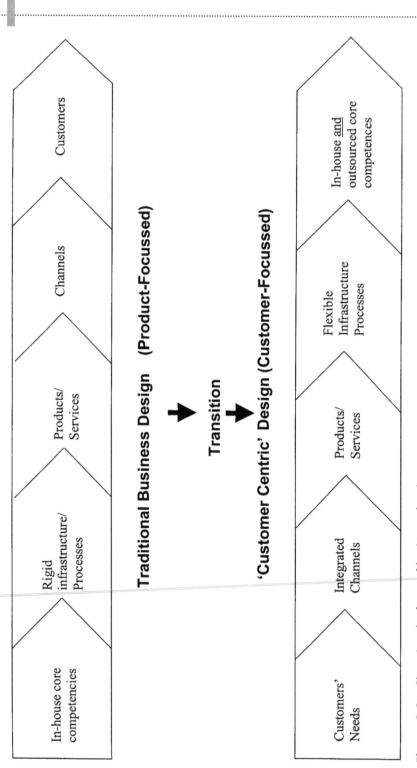

Figure 3.1 Changing the focus of business planning

Source: Based on paper given by A. Lai, HP Greater China Marketing Director: Global, 23/4 June 2000.

organizations (such as Dell and Nike) and an increasing involvement in part-nership and collaboration by a number of other large organizations (Ford, General Motors, etc.) we suggest any approach to marketing planning would be incomplete without consideration of these important functions. It is also important to remember that the move towards customer centricity has resulted in a *process management focus* to business operations and therefore individual functional planning is being abandoned in favour of an overall business approach.

The market–customer focus adopted by Best (2004), Day (1999), Slowotzky *et al.* (1997) has clear advantages and these have been seen and adopted by both large and medium-sized organizations globally. In Southeast Asia Hewlett Packard restructured their organization around a customer require-ments approach based upon Figure 3.1. Best's approach proposes a: 'a careful assessment of current *business performance, market attractiveness,* and, *competi-tive advantage* for each product-market a business wishes to consider over a three-to-five year strategic planning horizon'. Business performance includes: share position, sales growth and profitability. Market attractiveness comprises market forces, competitive intensity and market access. Differentiation, cost and marketing are the factors considered under the heading of competitive advantage. Best's approach offers a useful point of departure from which to build a more comprehensive planning model that can include some of the pressing issues of the 'new economy'.

3.2   Ansoff and enterprise growth

Ansoff's pioneering work in strategy forms the basis of many, if not most of the subsequent approaches to marketing, market and business planning. It is interesting to note that nowadays it rarely receives the credit to which it is clearly entitled. The philosophy of incremental performance growth based upon core capabilities and the avoidance of unnecessary risk is inherent in many of the current models.

A current application of Ansoff's approach would be to consider the need for strategies that focus on customer retention, customer attraction, opera-tional efficiency improvements and product-market development. Each would be explored with a view to evaluating its contribution to developing *sustainable competitive advantage.* The argument for this is made by Kay (2000) who suggests that sustainable competitive advantage is a measure of the strategic (*effective*) and operational (*efficient*) use of resources. Kay argues for the concept of added value as 'the key measure of corporate success' and he defines it thus:

Added value is the difference between the (comprehensively accounted) value of a firm's output and the (comprehensively accounted) cost of the firm's inputs. In this specific sense, adding value is both proper motivation of corporate activity and the measure of its achievement.

Kay calculates added value by subtracting from the market value of an organization's output the cost of its inputs:

Revenues
Less (wages and salaries, materials, capital costs)
Equals
Added Value

He suggests that added value is a measure of the loss that would result to national income and to the international economy if the organization ceased to exist:

Adding value, in this sense, is the central purpose of business activity. A commercial organization which adds no value – whose output is worth no more than the value of its inputs in alternative uses – has no long-term rationale for its existence.

Added value in this context includes the depreciation of capital assets and also provides for a 'reasonable' return on invested capital. Calculated this way added value is *less than* operating profit, the difference between the value of the output and the value of materials and labour inputs and capital costs. It also differs from the net output of the firm: the difference between the value of its sales and material costs (not labour or capital costs). Kay's measure of *competitive advantage* is the ratio of added value to the organization's gross or net output:

$$\text{Competitive Advantage} = \frac{\text{Revenues} - (\text{Wages} + \text{Salaries} + \text{Materials} + \text{Capital Costs})}{\text{Wages} + \text{Salaries} + \text{Materials} + \text{Capital Costs}}$$

There is a similarity here with the Stern Stewart's EVA measure (economic added value). Both approaches use a 'comprehensive' cost of capital that includes not just depreciation but interest and dividend payments, management and employee development, and investment in intangible assets.

We will return to Kay's model later in this chapter.

3.3   Value-based management: a stakeholder approach

Essentially Kay offers a 'simple' means by which competitive advantage may be calculated and compared across organizations. However, it too does not address some of the current issues that are common across 'new economy' enterprises. We suggest that these shifts do require a further step in the planning process. In Figure 3.2 we identify a number of considerations that have accompanied the 'new economy' and are essential features of current planning models. As the diagram suggests, a *value-based management* approach is taken. This expands the 1990s view of value-based management that was primarily focused on generating shareholder returns (shareholder value) in the form of share price and dividend growth. The emerging perspectives of shareholder value are based upon the admission that the early approaches failed because they omitted customer and other stakeholder interests from the calculation. Typically there was resentment among these groups and often the 'means-to-the-end' required extensive and expensive activities in developing the required information.

The current view of value-based management includes corporate, stakeholder and customer interests as well as enterprise value. The argument made here is that there is interdependency across the model. For example, the fact that collaborative partnership is an increasing feature of current business

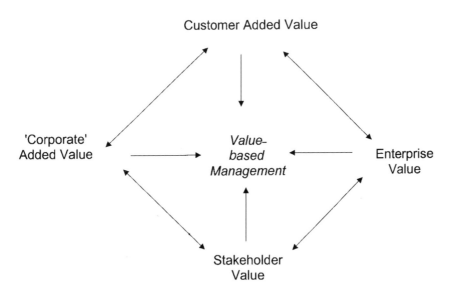

Figure 3.2   Value-based management: a stakeholder approach

process development implies that any planning requires agreement among the partners on both direction and returns to the partners, without such a 'win–win' understanding the partnership would struggle to survive and is more than likely to fail. The inclusion of enterprise value ensures that all relevant and realistic options to maximize free cash flow (the primary measure of success) are evaluated. This would appear to suggest that only quantitative objectives are worthy of consideration. Clearly this is not so. Qualitative concerns would include such aspects as the continued development of partner core capabilities such as brand reputation, RD&D (research, design and development) processes, knowledge bases and customer relationships.

3.4   The essentials of sustainable competitive advantage

However, creating sustainable competitive advantage becomes an important and primary activity. Figure 3.3 identifies the generic components, although clearly the emphasis placed on each will vary from one business organization to another and these will depend upon the product-market characteristics in each of them.

Customer delivered value has a number of aspects. 'Value' has numerous definitions. The one favoured here is based upon the concept of 'value-in-use'. Value-in-use considers all aspects of vendor–customer transactional features, being based upon the notion that while customers look for, and receive benefits from transactions, the process is not cost free; in fact the 'value' received is the sum of the benefits received *less* the costs incurred in obtaining them. This is proposed in the diagram suggesting that benefits comprise time and performance benefits while the acquisition costs include specification and evaluation, and operating and maintenance costs.

Product-market differentiation is another obvious characteristic. As suggested in Chapter 2, consumer/customer expectations are based around differentiation, choice and speed of response. These features are often at odds with each other, creating complex problems for an organization. For example, delivering value containing any of these features can become expensive to the point at which it becomes difficult, if not impossible to compete effectively. Some of the important developments in operations management have been targeted at these problems such that many of the theoretical arguments made concerning the restrictive nature of differentiation are no longer valid because CAD/CAM (computer aided design/computer aided manufacturing) and FMS (flexible manufacturing systems) have reduced set-up costs and

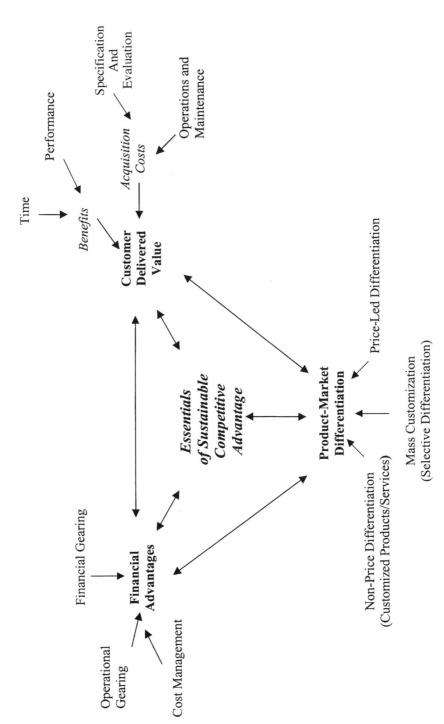

Figure 3.3 The essentials of sustainable competitive advantage

times and lead-times in manufacturing. The principles of JIT (just-in-time) have been applied throughout operations processes and as a result time required and process costs have been dramatically reduced. Chapter 4 continues this discussion by introducing and exploring the benefits delivered by 'mass customization' and the application of 'product platforms'.

Financial advantages are essential. Best (2004) acknowledges the importance of this characteristic by identifying *cost advantage* as a key feature of competitive advantage. Best proposes lower variable costs, a marketing cost advantage and operating cost advantage as important. Unit cost advantages (variable costs) are associated with high volume throughput and Best includes economies of scale and scope in his argument together with the learning benefits from experience effects. A 'new economy' approach includes the impact of collaboration in a value chain (see Chapter 2) with other 'value creators' and the impact this has on operational gearing (the relationship between fixed and variable costs), the financial structure of the organization – its financial gearing (the combination of equity funding and debt) and the ability to achieve low operating expenses/sales ratios and, at the same time, to remain competitive with the value proposition that is made to the customer. These topics will be explored in more detail later in this chapter.

3.5   Financial management considerations

Financial management considerations are considered to be an important feature of business planning. Figure 3.4 identifies some important relationships in this respect. Chapter 1 discussed the strategic profit model at length, giving some examples. At this point we should consider the model in more detail and explore the relationships from a 'new economy' perspective. It will be recalled that profitability management, productivity management and financial management were 'arithmetically linked' to identify decision options resulting in alternative performance outcomes. It is worthwhile to consider other useful features of this model.

For example, alternative partnership structures may improve *return on investment (ROI)*. ROI can be influenced by considering each structure which may offer the opportunity to improve ROI performance. *Co-productivity* is the concept by which the production process is distributed within the value chain and is conducted by members with specific skills (such as initial component manufacture) followed by assembly later in the process chain because of cost advantages that can be realized. IKEA is an example of co-productivity. IKEA designs products and works with a selected number of suppliers who manufacture part or all of an individual product. The product is 'purchased'

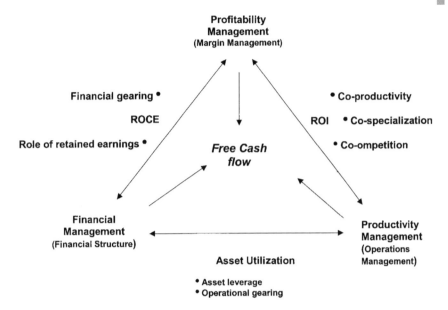

Figure 3.4   Financial management considerations

by the customer in a flat-pack format who then complete the distribution and production processes.

Co-specialization is the synergistic value creation that results from combining separate resources, positions, skills and knowledge sources. 'Partners' contribute unique and differentiated resources – tangible and intangible – to the success of an alliance. They became substantially more valuable when bundled together. Co-specialization becomes increasingly important and a central feature of a partnership as companies refocus on a narrower range of capabilities (core skills and activities) as opportunities become systems and solutions rather than discrete products. Individual companies become less likely to own all the necessary resources.

Co-ompetition turns potential competitors into allies and suppliers. Both competitors and 'complimenters' need to be co-opted into coalitions. Possibly the most extensive example of co-ompetition is occurring in the automotive industry. Prominent manufacturers are sharing design expertise across a range of engine, transmission and body components. This occurs both internally and externally. Within the Ford product range the company 'shares' these components across a range of competing products such as Volvo, Land Rover, Jaguar, Aston Martin and the Ford LtD. This is achieved through the concept of product platforms and is discussed in Chapter 4. The external application occurs when one competitor collaborates with another to share what they would see as non-competitive components, such as floor pan/chassis components, in an effort to boost the productivity and profitability of both organizations that share the benefits from increased production volumes.

Asset utilization is a concept that has had (and continues to have) a strong influence on 'new economy' business decisions. The concept of *asset leverage* is simple: why build and operate a manufacturing (or distribution) facility when there is available capacity within an industry? Michael Dell, who has built a very successful value delivery system around the concept, brought the notion of asset leverage into focus. Dell uses a BTO (build-to-order) model to meet customer orders. Components are purchased from a range of selected suppliers and assembled to meet specific customer requirements (their order) and shipped within a very short order cycle period. The benefits for both Dell and his suppliers are very obvious. Dell avoids the capital investment in production facilities while suppliers benefit from increased capital (plant) utilization. By implementing JIT systems linked by EDI communications other cost savings become available. Inventory holding costs are lower, the space required for storage is lowered (thereby decreasing fixed costs of facilities) and product obsolescence costs are also reduced. *Operational gearing* is linked to asset leverage. Operational gearing measures the relationship between fixed and variable costs. It is high if the proportion of fixed costs exceeds that of variable costs in the total cost amount. The implications of the operational gearing decision are that if it is high then profit margins are also high, but an organization becomes vulnerable to demand/volume fluctuations because in order to achieve the full benefits of high operational gearing it must achieve high production volumes. Clearly this is reversed with a low value. If components are purchased rather than manufactured the fixed content of total costs is lowered and while the suppliers earn margin from the transactions with the assembler organization, they also share the risk if a market downturn occurs. This topic is discussed at length in Chapter 5.

ROCE (*return on capital employed*) is an important planning and control metric linking financial structure and profitability management. *Financial gearing* describes the relationship between equity funds (provided by shareholders) and debt funding (funds borrowed from banks and other lenders carrying a fixed term of interest over a fixed period of time). While the implications for tax and profitability are discussed in Chapter 10 the implications for profitability and cash generation will be considered here. With a high level of debt funding an organization has an obligation to meet the required interest payments before distributing profit to shareholders (dividends) or recycling the profit into expanding the business. Clearly this has implications for operational cash flow as a high-interest payment obligation reduces this. It follows that under these circumstances, to sustain a healthy level of cash flow, an organization requires a stable and high level of revenues. If revenues decline the company is in a high-risk situation as failure to meet the interest payments can result in insolvency and, ultimately, bankruptcy. A decision to expand the business through the use of debt funding can be accompanied by a high level of risk in some industries. The 'bio-techs' will identify with this, as did the 'dot.coms'. Both require large amounts of capital for R&D development activities. However, without a revenue stream to provide this cash they have little choice but to resort to external funding. Typically this comes with conditions. Venture capitalists will insist on very tight performance measures (often overseen by their implanted CEO), together with an agreement that, as and when, the organization is 'floated' on the stock market it will also profit from its agreed shareholding. Conventional bank lending is difficult to obtain because of the perceived high level of risk that is unattractive to them. Ongoing, successful, organizations do have some options. Depending upon the level of success so the perceptions of risk will vary and the funding options will widen. Furthermore they will have generated profit and cash flow and as a result of this will have the options of paying dividends or *retaining the earnings* and using these as a source of funds. Clearly there is no interest commitment, but there is an implied commitment to the shareholders in that the use of *retained earnings* to expand the business will increase the financial value of the organization and this will be reflected in the growth of the share price, thereby providing a capital gain on their initial investment.

Marketing managers should be aware of these issues and relationships. Having this knowledge will help in the product and market evaluation and selection processes. Clearly in a start-up situation the attraction of the product to a market should be considered in terms of the financial risk it imposes. Similarly seasonal, fashion and fad markets need to be approached with caution, often requiring a collaborative approach with partners willing to share financial success and risk in both the short and the long term. The message that the failure of many of the 'dot.coms' in the period 2000/2001 delivers is still very strong – there is a period of time beyond which the financiers expect results! Thus 'time-to-market' is an important planning criterion. The role of marketing as a conduit with the marketplace is expanding to identify how competitive organizations manage the value creation, production and delivery process and to offer a considered view on alternative approaches. Unless the implications of the alternatives on the financial health of the organization are understood, marketing managers cannot be expected to fulfil this role.

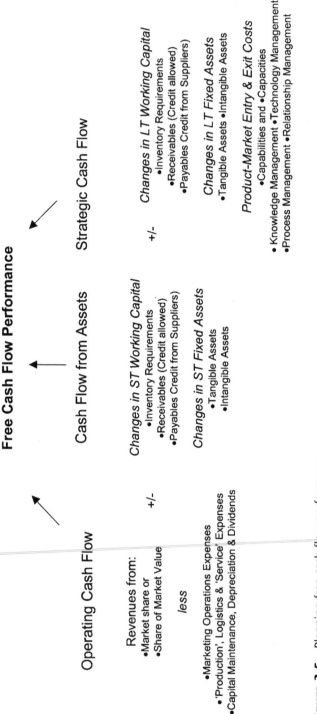

Figure 3.5 Planning free cash flow performance

Figure 3.5 identifies these issues in generic terms. Clearly the importance of each is influenced by the context of the sector an organization works within.

3.6 Maintaining sustainable competitive advantage

We have discussed the necessity of developing a competitive advantage and considered the need for linkages and their implications to be identified and evaluated. For any competitive advantage position to be sustainable a number of its aspects should be monitored and reinforced as and when necessary. Four important features are identified in Figure 3.6.

'Value' and 'ownership' of the asset base is important. We have argued above that asset leverage is an attractive strategic planning alternative; however, the potential negative considerations should also be discussed. One concern is *control*. An asset upon which an organization becomes dependent, but that is in the control of a partner organization, can create difficulties if it poses supply continuity problems. Clearly to this situation there are solutions. Acquisition is one alternative, but this contradicts the ethos of asset leverage

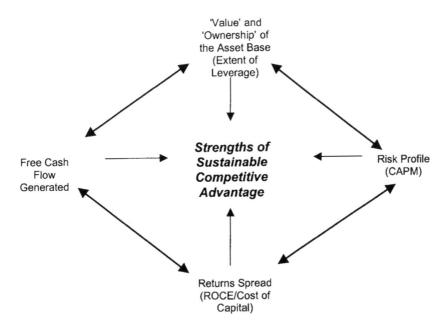

Figure 3.6 Maintaining competitive advantage

and optimal capital utilization. However, if the resource input is of such importance and the strength of the organization's competitive advantage is highly sensitive to the resource, an acquisition may be the optimal decision. The criteria involved are based upon sensitivity and cost, and the 'added value' that can be expected to be realized. The issue is one that concerns both tangible and intangible assets. For example, the acquisition of a manufacturing facility should be approached with caution to ensure that its capacity can be utilized at beyond break-even levels, thereby avoiding the risk of losses. A 'low cost' option is to identify alternative suppliers or to operate a multi-supply strategy. This also has its problems because despite rigorous attempts to ensure that performance and quality specifications are established and monitored, problems can occur with continuity and compatibility in assembly operations.

Return spread (ROCE/cost of capital) is linked to the previous topic. The return spread is simply the margin difference between the return on capital employed generated by an organization and the cost of the capital used to produce the result. Thus it follows that asset leverage can increase this measure. By working closely with partner organizations, without problems of supply continuity and performance and quality conformance, the 'burden' and cost of owning the assets are minimized and the return spread performance increased.

Risk profiles can be identified and evaluated. This is a topic that will receive detailed discussion in Chapter 11. The CAPM (*capital asset pricing model*) is helpful in this respect. The CAPM is based upon the assumption that investors are risk-averse and the greater the risk of a variable return on an investment, the greater will be the actual return expected by investors. It follows that there is a trade-off between market risk and expected return that must be reflected in the required rates of return from the investment alternatives. The capital asset pricing model was developed to evaluate securities in the investment market. It considers risk to have two components: market risk that affects all securities to much the same degree, and unique risk that is specific to a specific investment and may be reduced by diversifying the investments or product-market activities. The underlying principle of the CAPM is that the *expected return* on an investment comprises two components – a *risk-free return* and a *risk premium*:

$$\text{Expected return} = \text{risk-free return} + \text{risk premium}$$
$$ER = Rf + \beta(Emr - Rf)$$

where

ER = expected return

Rf = the current short term risk-free interest rate (e.g., government bond rates)

ß = the coefficient that measures the market risk of the individual share, investment or product market project.

Emr = the expected market return from an investment in *all shares* available in the market – it is a market return.

The beta factor (ß) is determined by calculating the relationship between the returns on a specific asset (investment or product-market project) and those of the market. For our purposes we can consider it to reflect the relationship between alternative organizational structures, such as a partnership or a structured collaboration, and an identified market opportunity.

CAPM is of interest here because it provides a forward-looking 'project'-based variable interest rate evaluation model, in which the required rate of return (and therefore the rate of interest used for discounting) can be related to risk as suggested by the beta value. If we use the beta concept in the context of organizational options and the risk of each alternative the notion of the beta value as an indication of risk does not change: in effect, the beta should reflect the risk involved from the adoption of any of the options identified. Clearly the purpose of considering a partnership structure is based on the assumption that the better the 'fit' the more relevant the structure between the market opportunity becomes. As will be demonstrated later the investment market view of new (and unrelated) product-market expansion by an organization with little or no experience would be met with some doubt concerning its potential success. Typically this is expressed by adjusting their expectations through the beta value used to reach the 'expected market return'. Consider the situation in which a manufacturer of commercial refrigeration identifies an opportunity to enter a segment of the consumer market. Not only would it prove difficult and expensive without a partner(s) who can provide the additional expertise the response from lending institutions would be based upon their view of the risk involved. To diversify without access to necessary skills and resources would attract high levels of risk and the institutions' response would be to apply an adjusted beta vale. Using the beta concept facilitates the process by which the structure that *optimizes* both the expected and the risk of the structure is derived. Chapter 11 will provide more expansive coverage of this topic.

Free cash flow generated has been demonstrated as a primary performance requirement. Given the assumption that the primary objective of the organization is to generate (and maximize) free cash flow (albeit within legal, social and corporate imposed constraints) the ultimate, comparative, performance model will be the net present value (NPV) of the free cash flow generated. A strong positive NPV of the free cash value indicates the business or combination of businesses is increasing its (their) value. A negative value implies that the value will decline if the strategy or structure option selected is pursued. . Using a partnership/ collaborative approach the objective then is to consider and evaluate the alternatives available to optimize the free cash flow objective.

3.7　Identifying generic business processes and their characteristics

As Magretta (2002) points out, the business model is the 'system, how the pieces of a business fit together', while a firm's strategy is the choices made about how to deploy that model in the marketplace. Using the example of American Express and the invention of the traveller's cheque in the nineteenth century, that: 'a successful business model represents a better way than the existing alternatives. It may offer more value to a discrete group of customers. Or it may completely replace the old way of doing things and become the standard for the next generation of entrepreneurs to beat.' In particular:

> all new business models are variations on the generic value chain underlying all businesses. Broadly speaking, this chain has two parts. Part one includes all the activities associated with making something: designing it, purchasing raw materials, manufacturing and so on. Part two includes all the activities associated with selling something: finding and reaching customers, transacting a sale, distributing the product or delivering the service. A new business model's plot may turn on designing a new product for an unmet need . . . Or it may turn on a process innovation, a better way of making or selling or distributing an already proven product or service.

However, this is often much easier said than done. Many businesses are too structured, needing to review these structures against the changing business environment. Hagel and Singer (1999) argue that the traditional organization comprises three basic types of business: a customer relationship business, a product innovation business and an infrastructure business. They suggest each of these differ concerning the economic, competitive and cultural dimensions. They argue that as the exchange of information and 'digestion' increases through electronic networks, the traditional organization structures will become 'unbundled' as the need for flexible structures becomes an imperative and 'specialists' offer cost-effective strategy options in each of these basic businesses (see Figure 3.7).

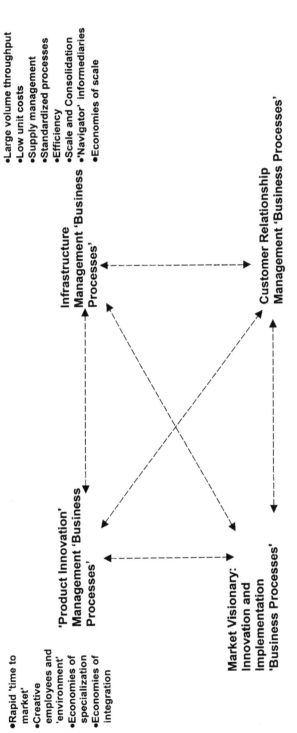

- Large volume throughput
- Low unit costs
- Supply management
- Standardized processes
- Efficiency
- Scale and Consolidation
- 'Navigator' informediaries
- Economies of scale

Infrastructure
Management 'Business
Processes'

Customer Relationship
Management 'Business Processes'

- High order/visit frequencies
- High aggregate 'spends'
- Develop strong customer loyalty
- Economies of scope

- Rapid 'time to market'
- Creative employees and 'environment'
- Economies of specialization
- Economies of integration

'Product Innovation'
Management 'Business
Processes'

Market Visionary:
Innovation and
Implementation
'Business Processes'

- Identifying 'market opportunities' and 'alternative responses'
- Identifying, locating and coordinating the core capabilities and capacities required for successful value delivery
- Creating and coordinating multi-enterprise value creation systems/networks
- Economies of differentiation
- Economies of integration

Figure 3.7 Identifying generic business processes and their characteristics

They also suggest that this is leading to car manufacturers, for example, adopting outsourcing models for manufacturing operations (as is beginning to occur) and to enter the after-market through partial acquisitions or partnerships or even fully acquiring downstream companies.

The argument underlying Hagel and Singer's model concerns a conflict of production economics. They argue that customer relationship businesses are essentially driven by the need to achieve economies of scope and do so by seeking to offer customers a wide range of products and services. By contrast, product innovation is driven by speed: by minimizing its time-to-market the company increases the likelihood of capturing a premium price and a strong market share. Infrastructure businesses are dominated by economies of scale. They are typically characterized by capital-intensive facilities that entail high fixed costs. Given the relationship between throughput and fixed cost it follows that large volumes of product throughput is essential.

> these three businesses . . . rarely map neatly to the organizational structure of a corporation . . . Rather than representing discrete organizational units, the three businesses correspond to what are popularly called 'core processes' – the cross functional work flows that stretch from suppliers to customers and, in combination, define a company's identity.

The solution for Hagel and Singer is to 'unbundle the organization' and to restructure based upon maximizing the effect of the economic characteristics of each of the individual businesses.

Hagel and Singer conclude that: 'The secret to success in fractured industries is not to unbundle, but to unbundle and rebundle, creating a new organization with the capabilities and size required to win.' This requires identifying and understanding fully the economics of scale, scope, specialization and integration. Figure 3.7 explores this proposition. In addition to the three 'business processes' suggested by the authors a fourth, 'market visionary: innovation and implementation' has been included. *This addition is justified by the increasingly important role that is now played by the 'virtual organization'.*

Business processes have a clear impact on business performance and structure options. It follows that in a dynamic business environment organizational flexibility is required. Hagel and Singer suggest frequent reviews of organizational capabilities and as and when necessary making relevant changes to ensure market relevance and optimal performance.

3.8   Organizational structure options

In an argument that concludes with the view that organizations are changing rapidly and dramatically, Drucker (2001) comments on recent events and trends in organizational development. He suggests these have changed many fundamental philosophies, views and practices. Such a view sponsored the development of vertical integration on a large scale – and did so for many years. Drucker cites Standard Oil and Ford as examples.

It is noticeable that large corporations are leading the changes in strategic posture. General Motors, for example, have created a business that will cater for the ultimate car consumer – they will make available what car and model most closely fits the consumer's preferences. As Drucker notes, the changes go beyond this, into design and development, and production. Products and services now have multiple applications and business organizations are redefining their core capabilities and processes. In other words 'value-creating systems' are competing with 'value-creating systems'. Each component of the systems are organization structures, or confederations, that are developing from traditional corporations.

Campbell (1996) offers a typology of virtual organizational forms that helps identify the various alternative structures available:

- *Internal virtual organizations:* autonomous business units are formed within a large organization: '. . . to provide operational synergies and tailor responses to specific customer demands'.
- *Stable virtual organizations:* these are conventionally structured organizations that outsource non-core activities to a small network of suppliers whose processes and activities become integrated with the initiator.
- *Dynamic virtual organizations:* organizations that focus on core capabilities and introduce external partners in cooperative ventures.
- *Agile virtual organizations:* temporary networks that are rapidly formed: '. . . to exploit new market opportunities through the mutual exchange of skills and resources'.

It is interesting to note three points. First, the typology identifies a progressive move towards a structure built around 'intangibles' and, second, the typology reflects the growing confidence of these organizations in the continuous developments in process, knowledge, technology and relationship management applications. The third point concerns the ability to match structure with risk. For example, *internal virtual organizations* can manage low-risk situations such as brand leverage accompanying an extension of a product range. However, *product differentiation* required to meet the expectations of a small segment of a large market may be best resolved by working with an established partner – a *stable virtual organization*. For unrelated product-market developments, developments requiring additional expertise to that available within the organization, *dynamic virtual organizations* offer a suitable structure. Short life-cycle opportunities, such as those often found in the 'fashion' segments of apparel markets, an *agile virtual organization* may prove to be more appropriate.

The issue here is for the 'business organization' to be responsive and flexible such that it can optimize financial and market success at an acceptable level of risk.

3.9 Developing a business model

It is suggested that in the modern global marketplace, traditional hierarchical models based on the deployment of ever-increasing amounts of capital to achieve market dominance through large-scale virtual or horizontal market integration are unlikely to be flexible or adaptable enough to succeed. While size still matters and it is not suggested that the large 'corporates' are yet heading the way of the dinosaur, traditional models require re-examination.

In particular, it is suggested that the 'new economy firm' should focus on five key attributes in developing and designing their business models, all of which are discussed in detail below. These attributes are:

- The firm should be *cash flow driven.*
- It should focus on *return on investment.*
- It should function with *'distributed assets' (low capital intensity).*
- It should develop a more single-minded *focus on core assets (R&D, brands) and distinctive capabilities only.*
- A principal element of its competitive advantage should come from successfully and appropriately *positioning itself in its industry value chain.*

These components are interdependent and are illustrated in Figure 3.8.

Cash flow driven

The first of these structural imperatives is a focus on cash flow as opposed to traditional notions of profitability. There have been a number of global accounting-based crises that suggest the often-cited quotation 'profit is opinion, cash flow is fact' is a major consideration for corporate governance regardless of size and structure.

It should be pointed out that even the conventional (accounting-based)

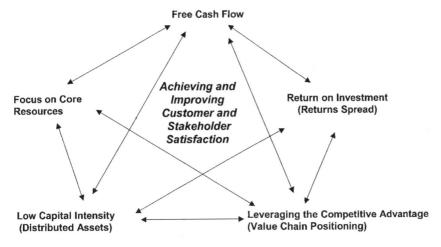

Free Cash Flow

Achieving and
Improving
Customer and
Stakeholder
Satisfaction

Focus on Core
Resources

Return on Investment
(Returns Spread)

Low Capital Intensity
(Distributed Assets)

Leveraging the Competitive Advantage
(Value Chain Positioning)

Figure 3.8   The business model component

approach to cash flow management is limited, only being developed for statutory reporting purposes. An alternative model is offered as Figure 3.9. This
model identifies the operational and strategic decision areas that impact on
cash flow planning and management and breaks these down into three broad
categories the sum of which gives the firms *Free Cash Flow*.

The first category is quite familiar – *Operating Cash Flow*. Cash flow analysis at this level in the context of a 'new economy' business structure allows

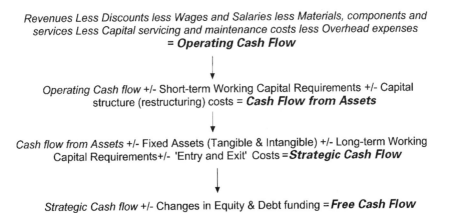

*Revenues Less Discounts less Wages and Salaries less Materials, components and
services Less Capital servicing and maintenance costs less Overhead expenses*
= ***Operating Cash Flow***

*Operating Cash flow +/- Short-term Working Capital Requirements +/- Capital
structure (restructuring) costs = **Cash Flow from Assets***

*Cash flow from Assets +/- Fixed Assets (Tangible & Intangible) +/- Long-term Working
Capital Requirements+/- 'Entry and Exit' Costs =**Strategic Cash Flow***

*Strategic Cash flow +/- Changes in Equity & Debt funding =**Free Cash Flow***

*NB: Tax payments have been omitted. These may occur at operating, asset
management and strategic cash flow management levels depending upon tax
regulations. Other charges may also be relevant*

Figure 3.9   The determinants of free cash flow: a primary objective

the identification of options based around delivering both customer and corporate value either by enhancing product features or by reducing costs. These options may be internal to the organization or may be external. Basic options such outsourcing production to lower component costs or to obtain a more reliable component can be evaluated, as can the impact on both customer service (and cash flow) that may result from a shift in the companies policy towards intermediaries.

At the second level the model enables the impact on assets of alternative production and distribution strategies to be evaluated. *Cash Flow From Assets* describes the cash flow profiles that may result from alternative decisions. The options available each have significant implications for inventory, receivables and payables together with cash flow impacts from changes in the 'structure and ownership' of production and logistics in the organization.

Strategic cash flow decisions include investment in long-term fixed tangible and intangible assets. They also concern working capital to the extent these are essentially long term, considering not simply work in progress and finished goods inventories but also strategic sourcing issues that are involved with the design of products to benefit from the advantages of product platforms and buying exchanges established on an industry-wide basis. In addition we are also concerned with the difficult, but nonetheless important, entry and exit costs that are associated with strategic cost decisions.

The eventual success of the business is the *free cash flow* that is generated. To calculate this we need to consider the additional funding required by the business if it is to achieve its objectives. These will be equity and/or debt combinations. This introduces not only the cost considerations but also the perceptions of risk that the 'market' may assume and issues of corporate control. The 'value of the business' then becomes the discounted value of the free cash flow at a discount rate that is judged to be appropriate reflecting this risk.

The characteristics of the target market have a strong impact on cash flow management decisions. For example, highly competitive markets in which margins are 'difficult' due to market structure (in which concentration has resulted in a few influential companies with large market shares, seasonal and fashion-driven products, or 'luxury' products that are prone to mark downs) may require equally competitive pricing strategies if positive cash flow is to be maintained.

A focus on return on investment

While we maintain that free cash flow should be the primary measure of success there are a number of reasons for including ROI within a 'portfolio' of performance measures. Using an ROI measure facilitates comparisons not only between businesses but also between components *within* a business. This is particularly important when considering the potential returns from alternative investments within an organization. The efficiency of capital within specific functions, such as physical distribution and manufacturing within a virtual organization, differ widely, and it is for these reasons that decisions to seek partner organizations occur.

Rappaport (1983) offers the *value return on investment (VROI)*. VROI uses discounted cash flows to compare strategic alternatives. Rappaport's approach is to measure the value created per discounted dollar of investment. Thus, it offers management the means to evaluate which alternative offers the largest benefit. Rappaport's model is simply stated by:

$$VROI = \frac{Post\text{-}strategy\ Value - Pre\text{-}strategy\ Value}{Present\ Value\ of\ Projected\ Investments}$$

The existing strategy value is derived by discounting the past year's cash flow. The post-strategy value is similarly arrived at by using a DCF technique, but being careful to consider planning horizons and by using a risk-adjusted discount rate such as that used by the capital asset pricing model. One further element is required – the present value of projected investments, which comprises the present value of the stream of incremental investments in fixed and working capital.

The VROI model offers a useful means by which the likely results of alternative business models may be evaluated. Income streams (and their capital and operating costs) can be compared using a *beta-adjusted* discount rate to reflect the alternative perspectives of risk that each of the structures would involve. As an example, consider the partnership between an f.m.c.g. producer and a consumer durable manufacturer moving into industrial catering systems. Clearly, they both lack specific experience in the industry sector and this inexperience should be reflected objectively by considering its impact on the venture. Investors' views of risk would be reflected in the borrowing rates offered. In contrast, in a scenario in which two or more organizations can bring a 'synergy' into the organization structure, and in doing so *lower* the risk rather than raise it, then the discount rate used for the NPV calculation is likely to be lower.

Clearly VROI must be greater than zero if it is to create value for the shareholder. It can also be assumed that a negative value would indicate that not only is it not creating shareholder value, but it is also unlikely that customer value expectations are being met, or if they are it suggests something is wrong with the project costings and that future activities are unsustainable. There are other considerations. An organization's target ROI and its financial structure are closely related. In turn both are influenced by market characteristics. It follows that operational gearing is closely linked to the expected ROI of the business. If fixed costs are a relatively large proportion of total costs then pricing and gross margin ratios must be made to reflect the financial structure if a required ROI (and cash flow) are to be met. Sensitivity analysis on cause and effect relationships within alternative markets and market segments will add insight into the impact on ROI (and cash flow) on making changes in not only the financial variables but also the structure of alliances and partnerships within the virtual organization.

'Distributed assets'/low capital intensity

The benefits accruing to this aspect of the model have been well developed by firms such as Dell and Nike. Low capital intensity (investment/sales ratio) facilitates achieving maximized targeted cash flow and rate of return objectives. Furthermore, by adopting this strategy there is an implication that less funds have to be re-invested by each partner, making more funds available for discretionary purposes (i.e., reinforcing their distinctive competences, or distribution to shareholders).

A low level of capital intensity provides flexibility for marketing strategy options. It widens the price point options available by making lower price segments attractive and feasible. High growth markets may be funded from internal funding (with cash still available for discretionary purposes). It is difficult, usually impossible, for capital-intensive businesses to fund high growth rates from internal sources without the 'benefit' of monopolistic price advantages or perhaps some other characteristic that affords sustainable competitive advantage. Furthermore, the low capital-intensity model also offers operational flexibility. By maintaining an optimal balance between fixed and variable costs, production volumes can be made more responsive to market volumes thereby avoiding break-even crises. At the same time market response times are not inhibited. The application of FMS and JIT philosophies and techniques compensate for the loss of control that a shift from vertical integration to virtual integration *may* imply.

A focus on core resources/assets

It follows that the emergent 'new economy' focus on virtual structure encourages partners in an alliance to develop their core resources and assets. Indeed it is the reason that each component in an alliance has attraction for the other members. Kay (2000) identifies two categories. The first category are *distinctive capabilities* such as institutional sanctioned items – patents, copyrights, statutory monopolies and so on, but which also feature 'powerful idiosyncratic characteristics . . . built by companies in competitive markets'. These include strong brands, patterns of supplier and/or customer relationships, specialist skills, knowledge and processes.

In contrast, *reproducible capabilities* can be created, purchased or leased by any company with reasonable management skills, skills of observation, and the financial resources. Both process and product technology are reproducible capabilities; the automotive industry is but one example.

Quinn (1992) emphasizes the need to cultivate a core competence (capability) and suggests that manufacturing companies are becoming more and more dependent within the value chain on links consisting of services or intellectual activities. Olve *et al.* (1997) suggest that the underlying driver of long-term strategic performance is intellectual capital and used Stewart's (1997) definition to give the term meaning, that is 'packaged useful knowledge'. They suggest it is this approach that is the reason why a company may be valued at more than the sum of its 'hard' assets. Other approaches suggest the term 'intangible assets'. This has the advantage of including or detailing specifics seen as brand values, R&D and management development.

This is an interesting concept for strategic organizational structures. Given the proposal that the dynamics of the business environment will lead to a situation where knowledge and core capabilities will be viewed as having specific shelf lives, the onus is on the company to identify the core capabilities necessary for its future. Olve *et al.* (1997) extend their argument by describing a capability *balance sheet*. They argue that a traditional way of evaluating a company is to analyse its balance sheet and use the notion of gearing to explore the value of the business. A feature of the balance sheet is the ratio of shareholder equity to total assets, that is the financial gearing of the company. They cite the usual arguments concerning the extent, and influence of gearing, suggesting that if the company is overly self-financed (i.e. it relies too heavily on its own capabilities), it will need to earn profits in excess of 'normal' levels to ensure shareholder satisfaction. Therefore, they suggest, few companies are totally self-financing.

The analogy of planning capability requirements uses the principles of financing for growth. The 'assets' required for success are identified as capabilities and the 'liabilities' indicate how the capabilities are to be financed – that is, who is to provide them. The authors continue with the notion that capabilities have limited life expectancies and therefore suggest that the liabilities reflect a degree of 'capability leverage'. The capabilities are largely 'financed' by value chain partners. The contribution made by partners is large and is complemented by externally sourced temporary capabilities, required to meet specialist needs.

Hamel and Prahalad (1994) commented that:

Preemptive investment in a core capability is not a leap into the dark . . . it is the simple desire to build world leadership in the provision of a key customer benefit, and the imagination to envision the many ways in which that benefit can be delivered to customers, that drives the capability-building process.

They continue by suggesting that capabilities that are most valuable are those representing a gateway to a wide range of potential product markets – a core capability leader possesses the option to be a major participant in a range of end-product markets. This is a particularly important issue for strategic operations management because the options become much wider when a value chains approach is considered. Hamel and Prahalad consider this with their capability matrix. Implicit in Hamel and Prahalad's original model is the requirement that some forward thinking be undertaken to determine the direction of 'potential product markets' prior to investing in core capability leadership. Indeed the virtual organization/value chain approach offers an option to spread risk reflected by an even greater proportion of externally sourced temporary capabilities.

The link here with the cash flow and 'distributed assets'/low capital intensity' features of the model becomes quite clear. Organizations in virtual structures are able to focus investment on distinctive capabilities thereby reinforcing their differentiation and that of the alliance. There is a minimum of investment made into what Kay describes as 'reproducible capabilities'. More importantly, each member is not investing in 'duplication' of essential distinctive capabilities because these already exist.

Leveraging competitive advantage: a 'positioning' decision

Potential competitive advantage in the marketplace and its potential for delivering superior shareholder value (as opposed to market positioning that attempts to deliver superior customer value) is very much based on adopting the low capital-intensity model, but also identifying *where within the virtual network the capabilities of individual organizations can best be deployed.* Recognition of the fact that not all of the necessary capabilities and/or capacities are internally available leads the progressive business towards identifying where in the value chain its resources are most effectively applied. Value chain positioning and competitive advantage strategy is therefore a critical activity

In a qualitative context successful 'leveraged competitive advantage' is assumed to be the successful management of one or more 'market-based' characteristics that offer the organization a competitive edge. These may be located in either the demand chain or the supply chain, but for them to be significant they should be exclusive to the organization. It could be argued that effective strategic management identifies what these are and creates an appropriate virtual structure.

Normann and Ramirez (1994) suggested:

> strategy is primarily the art of positioning a company in the right place on the value chain – the right business, the right segments, the right products and market segments, the right value-adding activities. [And] The focus of strategic analysis is not the company or even the industry, but the value creating system (the value chain) itself, within which different economic actors – suppliers, business partners, allies, customers – work together to co-produce value. Their key strategic task is the reconfiguration of roles and relationships among this constellation of actors in order to mobilize the creation of value in new forms and by new players . . . their underlying strategic goal is to create an ever improving fit between competencies and customers.

Of more interest to shareholders and partners is a quantitative measure of 'value' delivered by this set of 'competitive advantages' Kay (2000) offered such an approach. It will be recalled from earlier in this chapter that he suggested that the added value generated by an organization could be measured simply and effectively by deducting operating expenses and a 'cost of capital' from revenues. If the result is positive the organization is 'adding value', if not then it is 'destroying value'. However, Kay extends his argument by using it to provide a quantitative measure of competitive advantage. Kay's measure of competitive advantage is relatively simple; it is the added value divided by the operating costs and capital charges. Kay argues that added value and competitive advantage may be calculated from published accounting information. However, it may take some searching of the 'notes to the accounts' to identify some of the cost items.

Figure 3.10 suggests how, using Kay's model, competitive advantage may be further 'leveraged' by exploring the opportunities offered by the virtual organization model. In particular:

Revenues may be enhanced by partnerships that result in more effective responses to key customer value drivers (such as time-to-market, QR (logistics responses), flexibility, and customized service packages). Revenues may also be improved by such initiatives as cooperative R&D and product-market development with complementary and competitive organizations.

Labour cost profiles are influenced by outsourcing to obtain specialist skills or preferential labour rates. 'Capitalizing' production processes is also a well-used

Enhance revenues by cooperative:

- RD&D
- Product development
- Market development
- 'Brand' leverage; and
- Responses to key customer value drivers

Labour, materials and services cost profiles influenced by:

- Outsourcing
- 'Capitalizing' the manufacturing and distribution processes
- Purchasing and assembly of components and 'modules' rather than 'materials conversion'
- Membership of web-based interaction and transactions structures
- Utilizing partner specialization and differentiation capabilities
- Outsourcing non-core/reproducible service process and activities

$$\text{Competitive Advantage} = \frac{\text{Revenues} - (\text{Labour costs} + \text{Materials Costs} + \text{Services Costs} + \text{Capital Costs*})}{\text{Labour costs} + \text{Materials Costs} + \text{Services Costs} + \text{Capital Costs*}}$$

* Capital costs may be optimized or reduced by:

- Partnerships to leverage 'tangible assets' facilities
- Partnerships with owners of 'intangible assets'

Figure 3.10 Influencing competitive advantage in the virtual organization

alternative. Becoming more important is the use of design (for example, by designing around 'platforms') to reduce intra- and inter-organizational costs and in some circumstances eliminating duplications of process, activities and, therefore, costs.

Materials and services are also influenced by inter-organizational cooperation. The automotive, pharmaceutical and chemicals industries have pioneered web-based supply chain partnerships. 'Elemica' is a global electronic network comprising 22 of the largest international chemical corporations. By forming a negotiations/transactions hub interactions and transactions costs are significantly reduced and asset productivity throughout the 'organization' was improved by the elimination of unnecessary inventories, automated transaction systems, reduced transportation costs (not to mention a vast improvement in 'mode' utilization) and storage costs.

Capital costs are optimized or reduced by improving the productivity of tangible assets such as manufacturing facilities and distribution systems. Partnerships in product-market development or with the application of product innovations (e.g., the biotech industry) increase overall productivity and decreases unnecessary investment. Working capital productivity may be improved by optimizing inventory allocation and location supported by applying electronic systems to intra- and inter-organizational interactions.

An effective value chain strategy, therefore, takes an organization beyond its own boundaries. It involves identifying the core capabilities necessary to compete and to produce and deliver customer value expectations and to *coordinate* the value production process. The well-known examples, such as Dell and Nike, have established models that are being implemented by a number of industries through a value chain approach. But less well-known examples of value chain positioning also exist.

An example: the Australian wine industry

Developments in the Australian wine industry are typical of a model based upon distinctive capabilities (discussed below) with little or no fixed investment and the minimization of working capital. The objective is to achieve a low investment to sales ratio. This takes into account assumptions concerning inventory levels that service target markets, realistic receivables and payables and a targeted pricing policy that generates target gross margins. The compelling philosophical attractiveness of the model can be demonstrated by the following two simple examples that compare a virtual wine business with a typical traditional wine business (which grows, makes and stores around 70 per cent of its sales volumes).

In a low capital-intensity (virtual winery) model the investment/sales ratio is typically lower than that of traditional models by a significant amount – 30 per cent compared with as much as 120 per cent. Assuming similar costs and product quality the *required* EBIT/funds employed ratio becomes a much lower figure. For example, with a capital intensity ratio of say 40/50 per cent compared to the traditional level of between 100 and 200 per cent the required EBIT/funds employed figure can be as low as 10 per cent, considerably lower than the 30 per cent required for viability by the traditional model. It follows that target revenues are also lower, often by some 30 per cent – in retail terms this may be as much as 25 per cent less per bottle for the same quality wine! As a result the EBIT/funds employed ratio can show an impressive 75 per cent for the 'virtual' model compared to approximately 5 per cent for the traditional winery model.

Cash flow improvements are equally significant. It can be calculated that, based on the assumptions of same revenues, EBIT/funds employed and debt, the cash generated can be shown to improve by a factor of between three and four times.

Clearly, the low capital-intensity model begs the question as to whether a secure long-term supply of input product and supplementary services are available from third parties. In the context of the Australian wine industry historically, a significant proportion of the wine industry's production volume has been traded between industry members as bulk 'commodity product' and specialist bulk businesses have been established whose sole purpose is to supply bulk inputs (to other businesses). Huge volumes enabled these businesses to supply input product at very attractive prices on flexible payment terms. Rosemount is one such example. Until the early 1990s Rosemount was a traditional wine business. It effectively adopted the low capital-intensity model in the mid-1990s in order to fund its growth. This was achieved during a period of relative under supply and rising grape prices. The strategy is particularly attractive if it is perceived that over supply and falling prices have at least 3–4 years yet to run.

Under such circumstances a *virtual winery* would adjust the proportion of requirements supplied between 'spot' purchases (under short-term contracts), and longer-term contracts. Supplementary services are typically available from third party sources for operational tasks such as facilities where it can 'fine-tune' and store 'product' prior to final processing and contract storage of finished goods.

Other evidence of the success of the approach is suggested by the following recent commentary:

> In the rapidly evolving wine industry, Foster's will have to be careful it remains competitive with the emerging virtual winemakers operating without heavy investment in vineyards.

Relying instead on purchased grapes and some bulk wine, they invest in capable management and brand building.

The cost advantage can be significant, with one industry source saying the virtual winery might invest only 50c for each $1 of sales compared to $2 or even $2.50 of capital for the more traditional winemaker.

To be fair to Foster's the virtual winemaking concept was one of the key attractions of Beringer, where the zinfandel product is completely outsourced.

Chief financial officer Trevor O'Hoy likes to call it 'chateau cash flow'.

Wine traditionalists might blanch, but the reality is the myth and magic surrounding the wine industry is fast being replaced by a focus on shareholder value. (Richard Gluyas (2001) 'Foster's winery is no small beer', *The Australian*, 29 October)

And:

The 'big 4' Orlando Wyndham, Southcorp, BRL Hardy and Beringer Blass realize the equity within their brands and they have managed to turn what otherwise would be ordinary wines into sought after brands. 'Simply put a strong brand should defy economic logic by selling more wine of equal quality at a price higher than its competitors'. Undoubtedly brands increase the financial position of a company and make them attractive to takeovers and acquisitions, which have managed to build these four companies into the leaders they are today. (Jean-Michel (1998))

The Australian wine industry has clearly undergone some significant changes that have resulted in the repositioning of a number of organizations within the industry value chain (for example, 'brand managers', producers, distributors, etc.). Given the importance of economies of scale, differentiation and integration, and the fact that lifestyle is an important consideration in wine marketing, the larger companies have been taking steps to acquire and manage major brand names. Companies in other sectors of the industry have driven much of the acquisition activity. Their knowledge and experience, together with a cost-efficient infrastructure, has enabled them to invest in brand marketing and to manage the economies of scale and of integration by outsourcing wine production. The result then has been a major repositioning of organizations within the industry. The industry is moving towards brand management as being a major element in its value chain positioning and competitive advantage strategy. Wine production remains important, but appears not to be as important as brand marketing when cash flow generation and contribution to earnings is considered.

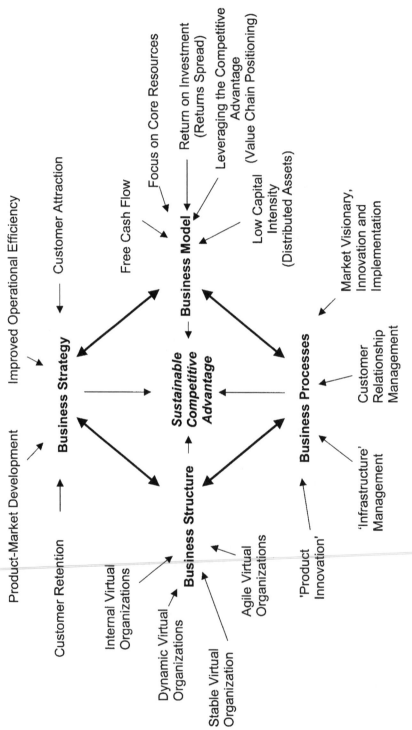

Figure 3.11 An integrated business planning model

3.10 Summary

This chapter has reviewed current business planning issues against the background of a constantly changing business environment. This process has resulted in the development of a model that comprises each of the major topics discussed: business strategy, business processes, business structure and the current views on business models. These are combined into an integrated business planning approach and this is offered as Figure 3.11. The model's objective is to offer a basis for identifying and evaluating the optimal approach for any organization to develop sustainable competitive advantage in a selected product-market. The thesis adopted is one that proposes that the current and developing business environment demands a number of basic requirements. Organizations are expected to be:

- Customer/market focussed.
- Process-rather than function-led.
- Capable of working across inter-organizational boundaries.
- Aware of the changing nature of market-based opportunities offered as value migrates and capable of supplying the organizational responses required to maximize their share of market value rather than simply attempting to maximize market share.

REFERENCES

Best, R. (2004) *Market Based Management*, Prentice Hall, New Jersey.

Campbell, A. (1996) 'Creating the virtual organization and managing the distributed workforce', in P. Jackson and J. Van der Weilen (eds), *New Perspectives on Telework – From Telecommuting to the Virtual Organization*, Report on workshop held at Brunel University.

Coase, H. R. (1991) *The Nature of the Firm: Origins and Evolution*, Oxford, Oxford University Press.

Day, G. (1999) *The Market Driven Organization*, The Free Press, New York.

Drucker, P. (2001) 'Will the corporation survive?', *The Economist*, 1 November.

Hagel, J. III and M. Singer (1999) 'Unbundling the Corporation', *Harvard Business Review*, March/April.

Hamel, G. and C. K. Prahalad (1994) *The Core Competences of the Corporation*, Harvard Business School Press, Boston.

Jean-Michel, G. (1998) *The Value of a Wine Brand*, Hambrecht and Quist, New York.

Kay, J. (2000) 'Strategy and the delusion of Grand Designs', *Mastering Strategy*, Financial Times/Prentice Hall, London.

▶

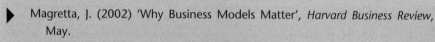 Magretta, J. (2002) 'Why Business Models Matter', *Harvard Business Review*, May.

Normann, R. and R. Ramirez (1994) Designing Interactive Strategy: *From Value Chain to Value Constellation*, Wiley, New York.

Olve, N.-G., J. Roy and M. Wetter (1997) *Performance Drivers*, Wiley, Chichester.

Quinn, J. B. (1992) *Intelligent Enterprise*, Free Press, New York.

Rappaport, A. (1983) 'Corporate Performance Standards and Shareholder Value', *The Journal of Business Strategy*, Spring.

Slywotzky, A. J. and D. J. Morrison (1997) *The Profit Zone*, Wiley, New York.

Stewart, G. B. (1997) *Intellectual Capital: The New Wealth of Nations*, Currency Doubleday, New York.

II Cost Implications and Cost Characteristics Affecting Marketing Strategy Decisions

The previous chapters have reviewed the process by which marketing strategy decisions may be determined and implemented. Before we begin to further explore the financial issues and implications of these decisions for financial management we should first understand some of the cost implications and cost characteristics.

To do this requires a recap of the categories of costs that occur in business, specifically in marketing. This will be used to develop, through cost–volume–profit analysis, an understanding of how marketing decisions impact upon cost structures and the implications for profitability, productivity and cash flow in both the operational and strategic contexts of the business.

First we review cost definitions and their responses to changes in the levels of business activity. We consider the implications for these across a range of marketing activities and decisions.

A review of costs relevant to marketing decision making

In this section we discuss the various views of cost classification. From a marketing point of view it is necessary to understand the relationships that exist because decisions are continually made concerning the profitability of markets, market segments, products and entire product ranges and customers. Clearly, it is important to be certain about the performance of costs as volumes change.

Much of the terminology of cost classification was established for cost accounting purposes:

The classification of costs as direct or indirect, fixed or variable, period or product, and so on was useful for cost accounting, but became particularly important with the development of management accounting. The recognition that different cost concepts are needed for different purposes gave a new emphasis to cost classifications (Scapens 1991).

Scapens continued by suggesting that the current focus of management accounting texts gives particular attention to the classifications of costs as fixed or variable. This reflects the short run decision making orientation of much current management accounting thought. He added: 'Long-run incremental cost concepts are sometimes included in discussions of relevant costs for decisions, but generally the decision situations involve fixed capacity. In such cases, the distinction between fixed and variable costs is important.' This is emphasized in product mix and customer profitability decisions. The cost–volume–profit analysis model will describe this relationship and the implications for marketing decisions, in Chapter 5.

Tomkins (1991) made a similar observation. He suggested that: 'Another broad area in which management accounting practices may influence resource allocation is in the analysis of cost behaviour and product costing: accounting practices here may substantially affect the perception of a project's incremental cash flows.' An understanding of the definitions of cost categories and their application is vital to the marketing decision making process together with a knowledge of their behaviour characteristics.

Another view of costs and their implications for strategic management was offered by Hosking (1993). Hosking's approach was based on a view that suggests that cost analysis should be seen as a means of selecting an investment 'in addition to redefining cost in a way that makes proactive management possible it is important to make a distinction between efficiency and effectiveness. Efficiency involves doing things quickly and well, while effectiveness involves doing things that optimize the results of an organization's overall activities.'

Hosking reinforced this view with the suggestion that while most companies focus 90 per cent of their cost structure improvement efforts on increasing *efficiency*, often with limited impact, 90 per cent of an organization's added value is created by activities that increase *effectiveness*. Thus we have, in many companies, a situation in which 'a reactive approach emphasizes efficiency while a proactive approach focuses on creating a more effective organization'. The inference is, therefore, that proactive companies are those more likely to be organizations that improve the overall value of the business in the context of shareholder value – that is, growth, profitability, productivity and cash flow.

Hosking argued that the concept of cost and time (i.e., fixed costs and variable costs) inhibits strategic decision making. He argued that a fixed/variable cost focus may lead to management decisions where the concern is more with volume and achieving a break-even objective, from which follows corporate strategic priorities: profit is maximized by maximizing revenue, which is achieved by higher sales volumes or by higher prices. Thus the secret of success is to balance price and volume in a way that optimizes the organization's profitability. This is not necessarily increasing the value of the business. Hosking would see the assumption that a fixed cost is 'fixed' over the entire length of a planning cycle or horizon (and therefore has to be 'managed' rather than changed) as philosophically wrong. Moving on from his thesis it follows that the response of management to volume and profit reductions should not be to reduce operating (essentially variable) costs, but to restructure the total costs of the business by reconfiguring the way business is done, rather than attempting to lower the level of the existing cost structure. In other words, 'All cost is variable – over sufficient time. Strategic cost managers do not accept the limitations of fixed cost. They empower themselves by being proactive about cost, seeing it as something they shape consciously, as a selective investment in revenue, not an unchangeable and permanent burden.'

Hosking was offering a philosophical approach to strategic management as well as to strategic cost management. Indeed, it could be argued that his approach would benefit the strategic and operational planning processes because it broadens the available options and may make the implementation task a little less difficult. We shall return to this view in Chapter 5. Here we shall continue with a consideration of other cost categories.

Cost categories

It will be remembered that it is important that time is introduced into the discussion at an early stage. 'The nature of most costs changes depending upon the time-scale involved, with more costs becoming variable as the time-scale increases. This means that all costs have to be classified by reference to the appropriate time-scale for the particular decision being considered' (Ward 1992). For the purposes of operational decision making, such as the decisions to be made when implementing strategy, we can assume a finite time horizon and this will influence the nature of the costs to be discussed.

The simplest and most useful cost classification is that distinguishing fixed costs and variable costs. *Fixed costs* are costs that are unaffected by variations in levels of activity in a given period. They are expected to remain constant throughout a period of time and are independent of the level of output produced or the inputs used. *Variable costs* are affected by the level of activity. Thus if we are considering the marketing planning activities for, say, the coming year, we can assume that certain costs will remain constant because of commitments made, for example, contractual arrangements concerning occupancy, costs such as rent, and other planned costs for salaries, administration, promotion etc. These are fixed cost items.

Variable costs (influenced by levels of activity) include sales persons' commission payments; distribution (delivery) costs; after-sales servicing costs; customer credit financing; order processing, assembly and invoicing. These are activities that vary with servicing customer transactions. Clearly, if we make no sales there are no activities involved in servicing customer orders, nor their after-sales needs.

There are some situations for which costs are described as *semifixed costs*, for example, supervisory activities, equipment rental, and additional sales staff for peak selling times. They are fixed with regard to ranges of activity but may be influenced by expansions or contractions of the activity level. An obvious example is the addition of an extra shift in the manufacturing activity in response to increased demand.

Kaplan (1982) identified two other fixed cost variations. *Committed fixed costs* are the costs of plant, equipment and key personnel (for example, depreciation, rent, insurance, salaries of dedicated management). These costs are budgeted for the long term, the life of the project, and are unlikely to be affected by changes in the level of activity.

Discretionary fixed costs arise from decisions to incur cost in areas in which the relationship between outputs and inputs is not obvious and have little or no relationship to short term variations in activity levels of the firm. Such costs include expenditure on; research and development, management development, and advertizing and sponsorship activities.

Variable costs are directly influenced by variations in the levels of activity. The assumption is that variable costs bear a linear relationship with changes in the level of activity. However, other relationships do occur as in the case when additional shifts are required and premium hourly rates are paid to production staff. Another exception is that of the 'experience effect', or learning curve, whereby cost decreases as throughput (activity) is expanded. We shall return to these characteristics later.

Variable costs may be viewed as direct or indirect variable costs. *Direct variable costs* occur because of the direct relationship between input and output. Each unit of output has specific input requirements. As output expands (or contracts) so too does the level or amount of input resource. If production was ceased direct variable costs would become zero.

Indirect or overhead costs vary with output, but the relationship may not be close. Kaplan suggests they may have a fixed cost component suggesting a stand-by capacity cost. Cost categories include indirect materials (maintenance supplies), indirect labour (handling, storage etc.) and utilities (power for equipment, lighting etc.). One other category of variable costs is that of *discretionary variable costs*, which are usually fixed costs but may be linked to an activity level. One example is the linking of advertizing and promotion to sales. Clearly, such a policy may be damaging. By linking advertizing to sales volume (fixed as a percentage) the impact is somewhat negative; if sales decline so too does advertizing expenditure, at a time when expenditure should be increased rather than decreased. Kaplan also identifies three other cost categories of importance to the marketing/finance interface.

Incremental costs are related to changes in total costs caused by a change in the level of activity. These can be important when an increase in the level of activity is contemplated. For example, a market penetration strategy may be accompanied by an increase in both variable and semifixed costs. The decision should consider the impact on variable costs of production and the costs of selling and promotion necessary if the strategy is to be successful. There may also be an impact on investment: additional capacity may be required which will result in an increase in fixed costs. This aspect of incremental costs raises the issue of reductions in activity levels. A reduction in the level of activity may result in *escapable or avoidable costs*. However, if the market penetration strategy (suggested above) proves unsuccessful the result is more significant because resources will have been wasted. This situation raises the issue: what else could have been achieved if the resources had been committed to an alternative project?

Opportunity costs consider this issue. The opportunity cost of a response is its value when it is used in its next-best alternative. In the market penetration example the incremental investment in additional capacity should be investigated within the context of the return it could have made if deployed on some other project. However, it is not quite that simple. We need to consider risk. As we saw in Chapters 2 and 3, risk varies with the nature of the activity undertaken. The alternative may have been to pursue a product-market development option, which may have had a higher risk profile! Kaplan referred to 'downtime' aspects of opportunity cost. For example, under-utilized warehouse capacity has an opportunity cost. It may be used for stocking alternative products, which may increase the customer service offer in another product group or, it may be rented by another company. Thus assets do not have zero costs.

Sunk costs are elements of cost not influenced by the choice available among current alternatives. The costs of equipment purchased for a specific project (or research and development costs) are not relevant, once spent it becomes a sunk cost. Another aspect of sunk costs concerns the marketing decisions related to a product manufactured on existing plant and equipment. The cost of the equipment should have no influence on pricing decisions as the relevant cost is its current market value, that is, the cost recoverable if the product is sold.

Joint costs occur when one or more products share a common resource. The problem that arises is the allocation of the resources used when essentially the products are inextricably linked, with neither product capable of being produced without the production of the other occurring. The management accounting literature deals with this problem by calculating a 'net realizable value' for each of the products at what is called the 'split-off point' – the point at which production for each separates. If the product can be sold at that point its net realizable value is the selling price less any selling costs at that point. If it has no market value at that point, its net realizable value at the split-off point is the selling price after further processing, less the further processing costs and any subsequent selling costs. Clearly, this may have significant implications for marketing decisions. The pricing of jointly produced costs may not, due to market forces, enable the costs of some products to be covered and the implications for the entire product range must then be considered.

The importance of time on the planning horizon is a critical issue in terms of decision making. In the long run in the strategy decision-making process, there are no fixed costs but once the decision to implement a strategic option is made planning horizons become finite and time perspectives are established. We continue with this approach in Chapter 4 (strategy decisions and cost implications when there are no fixed costs). Chapter 5 considers operational/implementation cost issues (when fixed costs exist and are important in the decision making process).

REFERENCES

Hosking, G. (1993) 'Strategic Management of Costs', *Planning Review*, Sept/Oct.
Kaplan, R. S. (1982) *Advanced Management Accounting*, Prentice Hall.
Scapens, R. (1991) *Management Accounting*, Macmillan, London.
Tomkins, C. (1991) *Corporate Resource Allocation*, Blackwell.
Ward, K. (1992) *Strategic Management Accounting*, Butterworth Heinemann Ltd.

The Financial Implications of Strategic Marketing Decisions

4

4.1   Ascertaining available market volume

Strategic marketing decisions are initially concerned with market size and volume potential. It is important to have a realistic estimate of both the market and the part of it (the market share) that is available to the company. The reason is quite obvious: given an expected volume of production a decision on plant size and the likely structure of costs can be reached.

Kotler (1994) suggested a way in which market potential could be evaluated. The basis of Kotler's approach is to measure *market demand*. Demand is measured by identifying the relevant *product levels*, the potential 'territories' or *space levels*, and the planning horizon or *time level*. This will result in a number of sector forecasts. For example, Kotler identified six product levels, five space levels, and three different time levels.

The product levels suggested by Kotler are product item, product form, product line, company sales, monetary sales and total sales. Space levels include customers' territory/region, country, and global volume. Time levels reflect the specific planning horizons relevant to the business. For example, a forestry products company would have a long-term horizon of some 20 to 30 years, compared with a long-term horizon of less than one year for a ladieswear manufacturer in the high fashion sector. Thus time levels are key to business decisions; the longer the overall planning horizon the more levels there are likely to be.

Within this framework we need to identify a specific market to measure. Figure 4.1 outlines the procedure from the establishment of potential market to the specific portion available to target. It also identifies some problem areas needing clarification. Kotler reminds us that there are several levels of a market. The *potential market* comprises buyers who have the three important

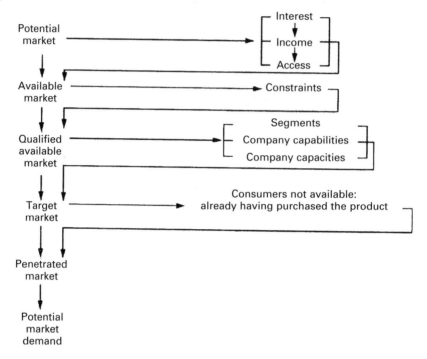

Figure 4.1   Ascertaining the market volume available to a firm

characteristics of interest, income and access. Clearly many consumers have *interest* in a product, but not all have the *income* (and therefore disposable income) to afford a purchase. *Access*, or the availability of the product in distribution terms, is an obvious criterion. If the product is not available locally and conveniently neither high levels of interest nor purchasing power will be sufficient for a sale. Thus all three issues should be considered and qualified because they have an impact on the *available market*.

Often constraints are imposed on the available market. Governments may prohibit the sale of a product or may impose quotas. Alternatively, producers may be unable to supply a market or, as part of their marketing strategy, not make the product available at the time of the research.

The *target market* is the result of the adjustments that have been made to the available market. However, this too may require modification. For existing products there is always a proportion of the market that is not available because consumers have already made recent purchases. The significance of this sector varies. For frequently purchased products, typical f.m.c.g. items, the problem is not as great as it may be for consumer durable products, for which purchasing cycles are infrequent and first-time purchases may represent only a small part of the volume demanded, replacement purchases accounting for the rest. This represents the *penetrated market*. The volume remaining is the *potential market*. From the potential market we can then estimate *potential market demand*.

Kotler's view of market demand for a product is that it is the *total volume* that would be purchased by a *defined* customer group in a *defined* geographical area in a *defined* time period in a *defined* marketing environment within a *defined* marketing programme. This suggests that marketing management, if it is to provide operations and financial managers with useful planning data, should be diligent in its market evaluation and volume forecasting. A major concern for any business is the size of the plant to be built, which will have an impact on cost structures and therefore the competitiveness of the firm in the marketplace. This is not to suggest that costs determine pricing policy, but it is important to consider issues such as margins and the impact of competition on their structure over a range of throughput. Figure 4.2 extends the analysis of the market, beyond the point at which we have estimated potential market demand.

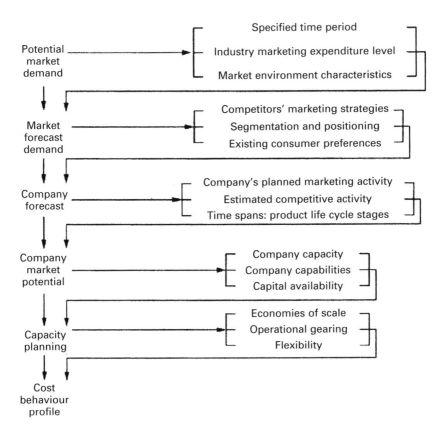

Figure 4.2 Relating market volume to capacity decisions

Potential market demand will be influenced by a number of factors. Three are common to all firms. The first is the time perspective we are considering and this is influenced by the nature of the market. If the market is stable with relatively slow changes in the production process technology, (and of the technology of the product) then a longer-term view might be taken than would be the case with a much more dynamic production process/product combination. Similarly, the level of marketing expenditure and the extent of active competition will influence the perceptions of the marketplace partici- pants, as will (thirdly) the forecast market environment characteristics. For example, decisions taken during (or in the approach to) a recession will differ markedly from those taken after the recession. All of these issues will influ- ence the *market forecast demand*.

Other competitive influences should also be considered. One is clearly related to the strategies adopted by the major competitors within the company's productmar- ket scope. Typically there will be an acknowledged market leader, which usually acts as a focal point for competitors to challenge, imitate or to avoid. The strategy currently pursued by the market leader will be influenced by its view of the growth potential of the market. If the market is expanding, the leader's view will be more relaxed towards competitors than it would be if the market is contracting; in this case the market leader's actions will be more defensive, seeking to protect market share.

A market challenger may choose to attack the position of the leader; or alternatively may seek growth by attacking firms that are either its own size – but have obvious marketing or financial deficiencies – or smaller companies (either regionally based or perhaps with a limited product-service offer), which likewise will lack the financial resources necessary to survive under competitive pressure. Kotler (1994) has a thorough treatment of these topics.

Time span is important once more. In this context we are interested in the stage of the product life of the product (or the product group) because this has a number of implications for the marketing activities of all companies within the market. We shall return to this topic later.

The outcome of considering these influences will be a quantified view of the company's market potential. Nevertheless there is (or may be) a limit on the capacity available with which to pursue a market opportunity; there is also a limit to the level of expertise (company capabilities) available within the firm. If either (or both) of these are less than adequate we must then consider the availability (and cost) of capital within reach of the firm. Each of these items will influence the decision on the size of the reply by the firm to the market opportunity.

Capacity planning then becomes a process by which decisions are made on the optimum size of plant to build and the level of costs this will imply. It is also necessary to make decisions concerning the relationship between fixed costs and variable costs (i.e., the operational gearing of the firm) and, closely related to this, management must decide upon the level of flexibility (i.e., the range of volumes that can be produced at specified levels of cost and the range of products to be produced from the facilities). This will give a *cost behaviour profile.*

4.2 Cost behaviour profile of strategic decisions: identifying economies of scale

The behaviour of costs is largely determined by the extent to which economies of scale may be obtained. Managerial economics offers some interesting insights into the theoretical analysis of business cost structures. It suggests that the costs of production and distribution, together with those of managing and controlling the business, should be considered when comparing options in which varying levels of business activity are involved. These affect both manufacturing and distribution equally and are based upon the debate surrounding the characteristics of the long-run cost curve.

There are a number of sources of economies of scale that are both internal and external to a firm. Here we consider those arising from production/capacity: procurement, promotional activities, technological, financial, and property development activities, replication, stochastic, specialization, and managerial activities, and economies of scale due to indivisibilities and economies of scope.

Production/capacity economies

The basis for the mathematics of the economies of scale is as follows: In an industrial process relating the surface area of a container to the volume of its contents, the material required to manufacture the container increases much less rapidly than does the volume of the capacity as the size of the 'container or activity' is expanded. In other words, the productive capacity of capital equipment increases at a greater rate than does its purchase price: a warehouse capable of twice the throughput of one half the size will typically be built and commissioned for less than twice the cost of the smaller unit. Evidence on maintenance and repair costs suggest a similar relationship.

This relationship explains the move towards the centralization of both manufacturing and distribution operations. Clearly the impact on operating margins will be significant if the investment/cost per unit relationship can be managed to ensure that high levels of throughput will be achieved. It follows that provided the cost of the activity which responds in this way represents a significant proportion of total costs, then expansion of the business to take advantage of the available economies of scale (all other things being equal) makes good business sense. Global business operations are evidence of the efficacy of such an approach. The vehicle manufacturers provide examples of how the benefits may be obtained. By locating the manufacturing of specific vehicles in a minimum number of locations (often only one location) they are able to produce vehicles at optimum cost levels and to benefit from economies of scale in distribution when vehicles are allocated to markets.

Procurement economies

By aggregating purchasing requirements, firms can use the high volume of purchases to obtain preferential terms. BOC Ltd, the industrial gases company, has an international purchasing activity for this very reason. Clearly the less fragmented the product range the more the benefits will be. In addition to the preferential buying terms there is an impact upon organizational costs. The increase in variable costs necessary to service large increases in purchase volumes serviced by the same cost infrastructure is relatively lower, and therefore creates an opportunity to be more competitive due to the impact on overall costs. This is particularly noticeable in large-scale multiple retailing where the merchandise assortment comprises a significant proportion of 'commodity'-type products for which consumers express little or no brand loyalty. As the business expands so too do the volumes purchased, but with a centralized procurement function fixed costs remain constant – or if they increase at all they do so at a much lower rate. Consequently in the long term, operating and net margins become greater.

Promotional economies

Promotional economies occur in two ways. First is the benefit from large purchases of media space and time, for which discounts and preferential times or journal space locations are given, thereby lowering the overall cost of promotion and possibly increasing its effectiveness.

Secondly, there is the benefit that is obtained by large multiple distributors from national campaigns because the campaigns benefit all of the company's outlets. By contrast, regional and local operators find primetime television prohibitively expensive. Concentrated promotions typically generate high sales volumes and these benefit distributors through a buying margin and operations/distribution cost advantage. Often these benefits can be significant, particularly when a range of products is promoted in a high population density area, where the volumes realized can be high.

Technological economies

Again there are benefits of economies of scale for large companies which are able to invest in technological applications. Size is a benefit because it enables a business to make extensive use of technology in manufacturing and distribution. Often this becomes a competitive advantage because the small or medium business has neither the financial capabilities nor often the scope of applications.

Large manufacturing companies have taken advantage of CAD/CAM and FMS manufacturing systems, while their distribution counterparts have used their financial strengths to install EPOS/EFTPOS systems which have enabled them to develop cost-effective operations. Combined manufacturer–distributor use of technology in applications such as EDI has resulted in economies of scale shared jointly.

Financial economies

It has been suggested (in the financial management literature) that there are benefits from corporate size when funds are required. It is suggested that sources of funds are wider and costs of funds are lower. Clearly the lender's view of the risk is based upon the size of a borrower together with a record of successful operations. Furthermore, the large 'listed' company has more options. Funds can be raised by expanding the equity base as well as by short- and long-term borrowing. Moreover the large company has access to overseas sources of funds. This is not without its own problems, and it has been suggested that large companies are able to obtain funds too easily. Many of the leveraged acquisitions of the late 1980s were eventually seen as high-risk investments because the companies involved struggled to service the interest payments from declining revenues during the subsequent recession.

Property development economies

This is also a size-based topic. Both large manufacturing and distribution companies benefit from the establishment of property development and management functions within the firm to handle their property requirements. Size of a business is of particular importance when dealing with property developers and agents, and even more so when negotiating with government at federal and local levels. A specialist activity enables a company to make fuller use of expertise across its property-related activities.

Economies of replication

Economies of replication occur when a business expands by reproducing its format. This is particularly noticeable in distribution. Multiple retailers which expand by increasing the number of outlets of similar design and operating method benefit from economies of replication.

Clearly, they also benefit from other scale effects discussed above as the overall size of the business is increased. The benefits may be large because the increase in business is likely only to carry variable costs, as recovery of most of the fixed costs will have already largely been achieved and the fixed cost element of the business does not require further expansion.

Stochastic economies

This scale effect is associated with inventory levels held to provide 'assurance' to customers against a distribution failure. Typically safety stocks are increased as the size of the business increases, when expressed as an amount per outlet or as an overall percentage of overall stockholding. Calculation of safety stock levels is based upon a simple formula:

$$\text{Safety stock} = \text{safety stock } \sqrt{n}$$

where n is the number of stockholding points. Thus while the stocks do increase, they do so at a decreasing rate.

It follows that by operating centrally based distribution activities (and reducing the value of n) the level of safety stock required can be considerably reduced. This assumes that distribution failures do not occur at the same rate at which the business expands.

Specialization

Economies of scale due to the specialization of labour and equipment are not confined to the manufacturing process. It is well known in both manufacturing and distribution that focussing upon core activities offers benefits in the form of lower operating costs. The result has been a growth of specialist service companies (for example, distribution companies such as, TNT or DHL) which develop businesses based upon economies of scale, which are then passed on to client companies in the form of lower service prices.

Managerial economies

With developments in information technology have come facilities for increasing the effectiveness of managerial control and decision making. A major benefit of information technology is that it enables management to increase its span of control. Timely, accurate information enables management to review the performance of longer-term activities more effectively.

Diseconomies of scale

Davies (1991) has suggested that while it is not difficult to argue that economies of scale are present to one degree or another in large-scale manufacturing, it is difficult to determine whether or not firms face diseconomies of scale beyond a certain size. He argued that 'If attention is restricted to technological factors there is little reason to suppose that diseconomies of scale exist'. He continued by suggesting that there may be a point at which further economies are not available and the long-run cost curve becomes flat, but that it is unlikely that the forces which operate to generate the scale economies are likely to work in reverse.

However, it is possible for diseconomies to occur due to managerial factors. Here Davies argued that as output is expanded managerial control becomes increasingly difficult to exercise due to 'span of control' issues – managers' ability to coordinate the activities of an increasing number of staff reporting to them. This may occur because an increased hierarchy causes delays and 'noise' in information flows. In such situations it is possible that *managèrial diseconomies of scale* become larger so output is decreased. At some point the managerial diseconomies of scale eventually outweigh the technological economies.

4.3   The economics of value creation and production in the 'new economy'

Management accepts the economies of production discussed so far, but their relevance will differ according to industry sector. The increasing tendency towards partnership and alliance structures introduces a different (and for some organizations a new) perspective. The economies of 'added value', or perhaps adding value, offer an opportunity to review strategies and structures. There are four components:

- The economics of transformation.
- The economics of interaction and transaction.
- The economics of competition.
- The economics of organizational architecture.

See Figure 4.3.

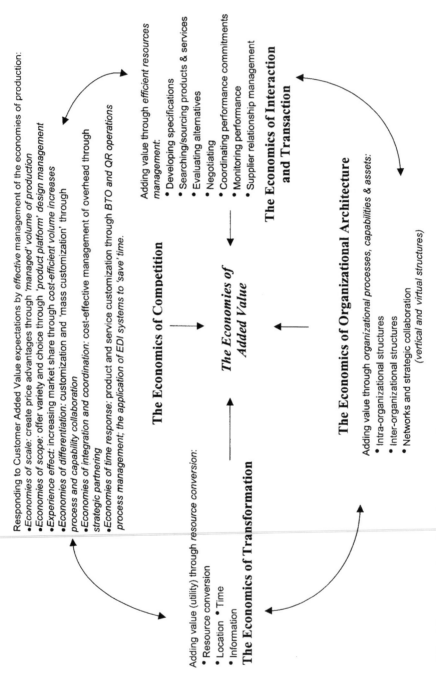

Responding to Customer Added Value expectations by *effective management of the economies of production:*

- *Economies of scale:* create price advantages through *'managed' volume of production*
- *Economies of scope:* offer variety and choice through *'product platform' design management*
- *Experience effect:* increasing market share through *cost-efficient volume increases*
- *Economies of differentiation:* customization and *'mass customization'* through process and capability collaboration
- *Economies of integration and coordination:* cost-effective management of overhead through strategic partnering
- *Economies of time response:* product and service customization through *BTO and QR operations* process management; the application of EDI systems to *'save' time.*

Adding value through *efficient resources management:*

- Developing specifications
- Searching/sourcing products & services
- Evaluating alternatives
- Negotiating
- Coordinating performance commitments
- Monitoring performance
- Supplier relationship management

The Economics of Interaction and Transaction

The Economics of Competition

The Economics of Added Value

The Economics of Organizational Architecture

Adding value through *organizational processes, capabilities & assets:*

- Intra-organizational structures
- Inter-organizational structures
- Networks and strategic collaboration *(vertical and virtual structures)*

Adding value (utility) through *resource conversion:*

- Resource conversion
- Location • Time
- Information

The Economics of Transformation

Figure 4.3 The economics of the 'new economy'

The economics of transformation

The economics of transformation extend the concept of form utility. Adding value (utility) through resource conversion considers the value added by converting resources into useable products. The economist's view of the concept has largely been concerned with the conversion of physical resources. However, by broadening the view to consider 'transformation' in a context of adding features to a 'product' that are valuable to a customer the concept considers the processes that either save time or cost or add features that are otherwise unavailable to the purchaser. The conversion of raw materials into more useable physical products (such as happens in the manufacture of components in the automotive industry) is an obvious example of the economies of transformation, but possibly more significant is the use of inventory and the rapid assembly, interpretation and dissemination of information. For example, the customer service programmes of large fmcg (fast moving consumer goods) companies often include vendor-managed inventory facilities whereby the manufacturer is responsible for the ownership and management of merchandise 'sold' to retailer customers. Payment to the manufacturers is made as and when the product is sold to the end-user. Similarly extended credit arrangements add value to the purchaser because it enables the purchaser to use the cash for other purposes virtually at no cost.

The case of McKesson HBOC is an example of how an organization can make use of the economics of transformation when under competitive pressures. In 1988 its revenues were US$6.7 billion and it was considered successful. It also enjoyed a reputation for innovative applications of it to improve customer service. To this point in time, it was wholesale distributor with its future tied to the success of the independent drug stores it sought to service.

McKesson became threatened by fierce competition from large, integrated drug store chains, which were eliminating the independents. McKesson converted this threat into an opportunity, by introducing a 'rudimentary order-entry system' for their customers. The system reduced order processing costs by expediting inventory checking, order transmission and recording and the packing and shipping to customers. Order assembly to meet customer display formats made in store merchandizing more cost-efficient.

More innovation followed. Software was developed to help retailers set prices, design store layout and plan profitable operating activities and financial reporting. In addition, McKesson recognized the value of its aggregated information to suppliers. The information was sold to suppliers who used the information to increase their own distribution efficiencies. Computer-computer order enabled McKesson to make significant labour savings. The company also used its systems to help process insurance claim applications for reimbursements. This strengthened links among insurance companies, customers and drug stores by decreasing payment times and administrative problems. Through its visionary approach, McKesson restructured the 'economics of transformation' by adding value to customer transactions data and thereby providing value that they otherwise would not have had, or at best would have absorbed a large amount of their own resources to provide.

The economics of interaction and transaction

Butler *et al.* (1997) note what they call 'Interaction Costs' namely 'the money and time that are expended whenever people and companies exchange goods, services and ideas . . . In a very real sense, interaction costs are the friction in the economy.' This same notion can be applied at the level of the firm. The process of transactions between vendors and purchasers is not a smooth synchronous link – it has its own friction and its own interaction costs. It is suggested that much of this friction arises as core demand and supply processes interact and fuse. A firm will create value when what the customer demands can be brought into synchronization with what the firm can supply, minimizing friction and internal interaction costs and maximizing the dynamic forces of the interaction. Where they are not synchronized, value will either not be realized or will actually be destroyed. This may sound simple, but is the reality of the economics of interaction and transactions between complex organizations and is such that this *process fusion* represents the key tactical task for management on a day-to-day basis.

There are numerous examples of how the interaction and transaction costs may be better managed. The use of electronic data interchange (EDI) for routine purchasing and payments is an example of a technology-based solution. Close liaison between customer design staff and vendor engineers is another example of how a well-designed customer relationship management may reduce customer R&D costs and, at the same time, increase vendor revenues. On a more simplistic basis the provision of in-store merchandising services and inventory management by f.m.c.g. companies is a long-standing example of the economics of interaction and transformation.

The economics of competition

Responding to customer added value expectations by *effective* management of the economies of production in order to provide a stronger competitive position for both the purchaser and the vendor is the ideal outcome of a programme designed to increase the economics of competition. Typically, the traditional application of economies of scale and scope and the cost benefits of the experience effect were used to provide customers with lower costs (to be used either as price incentives or to increase profitability and cash flow for expansion or dividend payment purposes). More recently, the notion of outsourcing and of virtual structures such as value nets and value chains has expanded the opportunities to increase the benefits of the economics of competition. The economies of differentiation operate through a process of managed specialization in which the costs of customization and 'mass customization' can be better managed by using production methods designed for differentiated low-volume product-markets through process and capability collaboration. Examples are provided in a subsequent section of this chapter. The economies of integration and coordination result in cost-effective management of overhead through strategic partnering across a range of processes and activities. The well-documented collaboration between Wal-Mart and Procter & Gamble is an example of success. The programme includes shared information on sales and involves both in a cost-efficient inventory management programme that results in improved availability at the point-of-sale and lower customer prices. The economies of time response have a number of applications. One example of this is the product and service customization through BTO and QR operations as discussed later in this chapter in an example of mass-customization in the automotive industry. The application of EDI systems to 'save' time can be seen as a 'facilitating' factor in the economics of competition. The electronic transfer of product-service expectations, the details of an order or a request for order progress information add 'the cost-efficient management' of time to a competitive advantage portfolio.

The economics of organizational architecture

Adding value through *organizational processes, capabilities and assets* was addressed by Kay (1993). He considers capabilities as comprising architecture, reputation, innovation and strategic assets. While they all have significance *architecture (the network of relational contracts within, or around, the firm)* is particularly interesting. He suggests:

> the value of architecture rests in the capacity of organizations which establish it to create organizational knowledge and routines, to respond flexibly to changing circumstances, and to achieve easy and open exchanges of information. Each of these is capable of creating an asset for the firm – organizational knowledge which is more valuable than the sum of individual knowledge, flexibility, and responsiveness which extends to the institution as well as to its members.

This is particularly relevant to the virtual structure to which Drucker referred in 1995 and which are now becoming significant as organizational structures.

Kay describes three *types of architecture*; *internal*, between the firm and its employees and among employees; *external* architecture structures between the firm and its suppliers and customers; and *networks* which comprise groups of collaborating firms. These have similarities with Campbell (1996) whose typology of virtual organization alternatives bring out some important differences that impact on performance outcomes. These were discussed in the previous chapter and comprised: *internal virtual organizations* (relatively autonomous SBUs are formed within a large conventional business to provide operational synergies and 'customised' customer responses); *stable virtual organizations* (conventional business organizations outsource non-core activities to a small network of key suppliers whose activities become integrated and interdependency with the large organization); *dynamic virtual organizations* (organizations concentrating on core capabilities but that introduce external partners in cooperative ventures); and *agile virtual organizations* (temporary networks rapidly formed 'to exploit new market opportunities through the mutual exchange of skills and resources'). Each structure has as its purpose the notion of adding value through *organizational processes, capabilities and assets* by changing (temporarily or permanently) the structure of the organization by introducing intra-organizational structures and inter-organizational structures, together with variations of networks and strategic collaboration.

It is suggested that increasingly it is the 'economics of adding value' that are becoming important in the attempt to develop sustainable advantage. Clearly this suggests new criteria are required for effective planning and control purposes. This topic will be considered in Chapter 13, the final chapter of the volume.

4.4   The shape of strategic long-run cost curves

Within the framework of decision making for both the managerial economist and the strategic planner there are no fixed costs. This implies that capacity planning decisions may be made without the constraints of the existing cost structure. The size of a manufacturing facility, and indeed its format, may be decided upon within the situation prescribed by the marketplace and within the structure of the objectives of the firm and taking into account its attitude towards risk. Typically the decisions facing the business relate to market volume and capacity (as described in Figures 4.1 and 4.2) but eventually the firm must decide upon the size of plant (i.e., its capacity). It is also useful for the company to identify the shape of alternative cost forecasts in order to make a decision that it will possibly need to live with over the long term.

There are a number of factors which influence the plant size decision. One of these is the shape of the long-run cost curve (or cost curves, because invariably a number of options are available). Eventually decisions concerning the fixed and variable cost characteristics will be required. One other issue concerns the structure of the market: the size of major competitors and their market shares and, therefore, the extent of their influence. The shape of the demand function in the proposed market is also a major consideration. More helpful than a demand curve as such is a view of the product life cycle likely to confront the firm, because this introduces time effects.

Before discussing the relationship of the product life cycle with long-run costs we should first consider the shape of the cost curves. Figure 4.4 identifies the different shapes of long-run curves. The curve depicted in Figure 4.4(a) suggests that after the output level at V has been reached diseconomies of scale occur, due possibly to the effect discussed above (i.e., the benefits of technological economies of scale being outweighed by managerial diseconomies of scale). The curve in Figure 4.4(b) shows a situation where there are continuous economies of scale to be obtained while 4.4(c) represents a situation where, beyond a certain level of throughput, no further economies of scale are likely. This point, the minimum efficient scale (MES), is the point beyond which no further scale economies are available from this specific plant format.

The MES value, and particularly the relationship between MES and the size of the market, or particular market share, are of interest to both marketing and financial managers. Clearly the issue that concerns both is whether the market share value which will give the firm a dominant position is close to the MES value. If it is, it suggests that once the MES level is reached the firm is operating at a point of lowest costs and is in a position to begin to exert competitive pressure on those companies that have not yet reached this level of output. Thus, a strategic decision might be taken to build a facility which enables the firm to reach this optimum MES/market share volume quickly (in production volume terms as well as time). If this is achieved the firm moves into a very strong competitive position with considerable advantage.

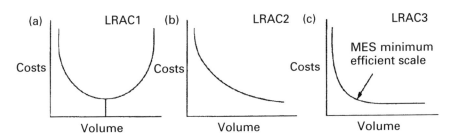

Figure 4.4 Shape of the long-run average cost curves

The cost curves depicted in Figure 4.4 are long-run average curves. For strategic marketing planning purposes it is more useful to consider the relationships between the revenues and costs in order that changes in profit margins (if any) may be identified. Figure 4.5 shows this; the total revenue curves are adjusted on the realistic assumption of declining prices, as individual output (and aggregate market output) is expanded and a market matures. Figure 4.5(a) represents the situation in which there are ultimately diseconomies, and eventually it becomes unprofitable to continue production beyond the point at which TR = TC. However, a range of profitable volume is available between M1 and M2 with maximum profits reached at M3.

In Figure 4.5(b) continuous economies of scale are depicted. Given the same revenue relationship (as at 4.5(a)) the cost function offers a wider range of volume across which to operate. Clearly the margin will depend upon individual revenue and cost relationships. In Figure 4.5(c) the situation of constant returns to scale is illustrated. It also shows the volume at which MES occurs, and the range of market volume available is shown between M1 and M2. Because of the shape of the cost curve, once the MES is realized the range of market volume available is determined by the intensity of the price competition. In a relatively noncompetitive market, margins may be held across a wider range of market volume. TR1 illustrates a competitive situation while TR2 implies little or no price competition. Figure 4.6 illustrates the relationships between economies of scale, revenue, profit and plant capacity.

Davies (1991) acknowledged that:

> [because] theory has failed to discriminate between these alternative forms of the longrun, cost function it is natural to turn to the empirical evidence in an attempt to resolve the issue. Unfortunately, the difficulties of estimating the extent of scale economies in a satisfactory way are so great that it is not possible to reach an 'unambiguous conclusion'.

Davies did suggest three options to attempt to derive the curve: by using statistical estimation, an engineering approach, or the 'survivor' technique.

Statistical estimation is a method by which we can make observations of the costs of producing a 'product' in firms operating at different levels of output and then use statistical analysis to fit equations to the data. However, there are problems with this method. The first concerns the availability of data: the 'ideal' data are rarely available, being confidential to the firm, and those data that are available often do not reflect relevant cost data; activity costs and opportunity costs are two examples. Two other problems concern the product mix, which may have a large influence on

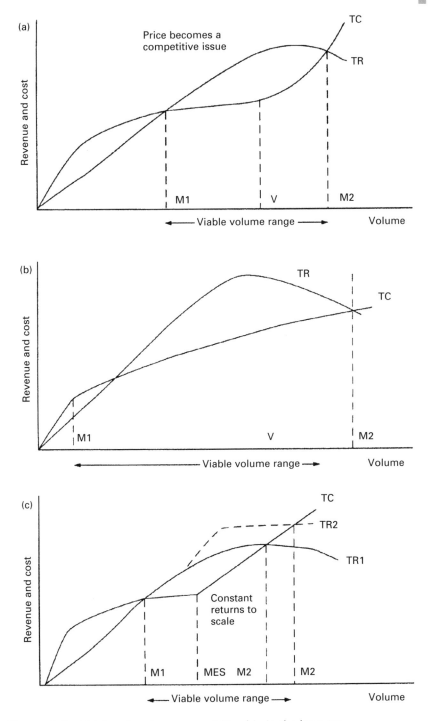

Figure 4.5   Total cost and revenue relationship in the long run

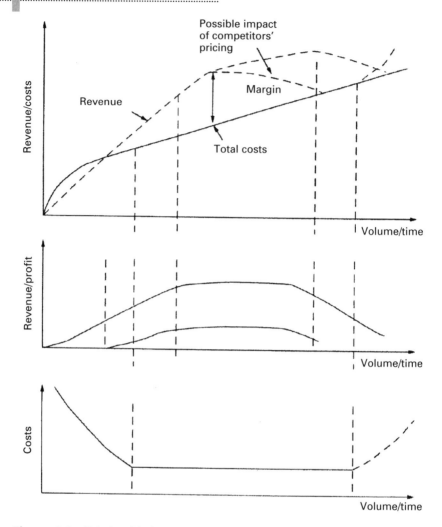

Figure 4.6   Relationship between economies of scale, the product life cycle and plant capacity

costs, and the technology, which may differ markedly between companies (depending upon investment capabilities, volumes and specific product characteristics).

The *engineering approach* attempts to avoid these problems by using the expertise of production engineers to design alternative 'sets' of plant appropriate to the production of different levels of output. Conceptually this approach has appeal but in practice there are usually problems reconciling the accounting and economics concepts of costs. Another problem concerns the apportioning of total cost amongst different products – an issue we shall address in

Chapter 5. Davies suggests that while the engineering and production costs are relatively easy to handle, distribution, administration and management are much more difficult. Experience suggests that it is time-consuming and expensive to calculate costs of a wide range of options, and therefore efforts are typically directed towards identifying all known technical scale economies (thereby developing a LAC curve, depicted in Figure 4.4(c)). Two points are estimated: the MES and a point corresponding to 50 per cent of MES, thereby identifying cost penalties should the 'production' volume be below the optimal scale.

The 'survivor technique' developed by Stigler (1958) assumes that market forces work efficiently, so that firms in the most efficient size category take an increasing share of the market, while firms in less efficient size categories must accept smaller shares (see Figure 4.7). The assumptions made by Stigler are very restrictive: all firms are pursuing the same objectives; are operating in a similar business environment; are faced with similar factor prices; technology remains constant over the period of observation; and market forces work effectively without 'arrangements' or barriers to entry. It is possible that these assumptions may be valid in times of prolonged recession during which the survivor technique offers management a basis for deriving strategic options.

Another issue is the influence of global activities. The scope of international operations is such that the global firm can change the environment in which it operates and with this factor price options and technology options.

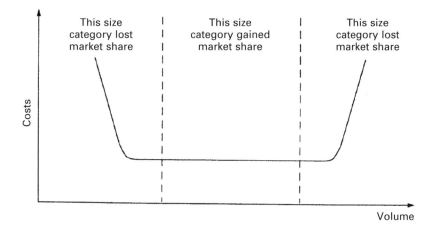

Figure 4.7 Stigler's survivor approach

4.5   Developing a perspective on strategic revenues

The product life cycle is a useful vehicle for a discussion on strategic revenues and their growth.

Product life cycle

Kotler (1994) suggested the value of the product life cycle is 'that it provides insights into a product's competitive dynamics. At the same time the concept can prove misleading if not carefully used'. He suggested further:

> The product life cycle portrays *distinct stages* in the *sales history* of a product. Corresponding to these stages are distinct opportunities and problems with respect to marketing strategy and profit potential. By identifying the stage that a product is in, or may be headed toward, companies can formulate better marketing plans.

Kotler's words of caution were reinforced by comments concerning the level of aggregation used to apply the life cycle theory. He used an illustration based on the work of Page (unpublished) which suggested three levels of analysis. Page produced evidence to suggest that we should consider product category, product form and brand, and used alcohol beverage as an example. Page's case example suggested that over time, depending on which level the analysis is conducted, the 'stage' of the product life cycle might differ from the life cycle stages at other levels. Furthermore, as Kotler ably demonstrated, there are many shapes that product life cycles may adopt. This raises an issue concerning the reliability of the PLC for planning purposes.

Doyle (1994) had similar, if not stronger views, and added, 'despite the popularity of the product life cycle, there is unfortunately no evidence that most products follow such a four stage cycle! Nor is there evidence that the turning points of the different stages are in any way predictable. On the contrary, the shape of the sales curves appears to be completely idiosyncratic.' And finally, 'To summarise, the product life cycle is not much use for marketing decision making'. Doyle then offered six reasons: it is an undefined concept; has no common shape; has no predictable turning points; has unclear implications for decision making; is not exogenous to the firm (i.e., can be and often is influenced by management decisions); and finally it is product oriented (meaning that by becoming product-oriented management loses sight of facts that shape the ability to satisfy customer needs).

Market dynamics: implications for growth

It would appear that the product life cycle is not as reliable a model as we might have hoped, particularly if large-scale investment is required. An alternative approach offered here is one based on proposals by both Doyle (1994) and Aaker (1995).

Doyle proposed that if there is no predictable life cycle and similarly no standard pattern of market evolution, alternatives are required. He suggested there are common processes that shape markets and consequently that, by analysing these, managers can anticipate new markets and how competition will develop, and in so doing determine the likely shape of market volumes. This 'can develop strategies both to capitalise on these changes and to influence those forces of change'. The forces – or common processes – he identified are customers, competition, new entrants, substitute products and technologies, and supply relationships.

Aaker (1995) suggested a process of market analysis within which there are seven dimensions: actual and potential market size; market growth; market profitability; cost structure; distribution systems; trends and developments; and key success factors. Aaker's argument is similar to that of Doyle: it is an understanding of consumer response and competition that shapes the pattern of market development.

To emphasize his new focus Doyle replaced the notion of the product life cycle with one of an 'evolutionary market'. This has four phases: the emerging market; the high growth phase; the mature phase; and the decline.

The major difference between Doyle's approach and that of the product life cycle is that it does not assume that cycles will occur and that strategy should be predicated on them; rather Doyle's approach assumes that the forces of technology and competitive activity will operate and that any product will have a finite existence.

Strategic business areas: a guide to future revenue plans

The scope of a business, defined as being a combination of customer needs, functions, customer groups/segments and technologies, is a viable market cell within which the business can focus its capabilities and capacities to service customer needs and segments within the current technology base. We can consider the market cell as a strategic business area (SBA) and utilize this idea for strategic market planning decisions.

Figure 4.8(a) illustrates how the strategic business area idea may be applied within the overall market demand life cycle. The *demand technology cycle* provides the *market cell* or *strategic business area* within which the firm is to apply its capabilities and capacities. *Product applications* describes the product

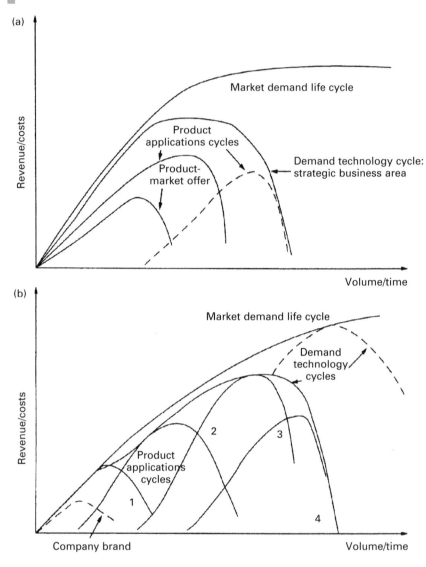

Figure 4.8 The strategic business area as a focal point for strategic market planning

variants possible within the available technology. The approach is essentially customer/market led and linked with R&D activities which identify emerging customer needs and technological feasibility, and a number of companies take this approach. Sony, however, considers that it is unlikely that customers are able to relate latent need with emerging technology. However, if the order is changed and a corporate view taken concerning technological development and its capabilities, and this is compared with emerging consumer use, the process has more direction and is more cost effective. In Figure 4.8(b) a time perspective adds a further demand technology cycle. This illustrates the choice confronting a company. Assume that the firm is working within the product application cycle 2. It then has to make the decision whether to invest further within this demand technology cycle (strategic business area) or have R&D work towards the successor. From a risk consideration it may be less risky to compete in application cycles 3 or 4 (this would be a product-development strategy) and the investment requirement would be lower. However, in terms of opportunity cost, the firm is likely only to be able to commit funds to one opportunity. Its low-risk choice is whether to stay with the revenues from its offer in product application cycle 2 or become a low-risk innovator and potentially make higher profits from an innovatory product by investing in either applications 3 or 4. The higher-risk alternative is to attempt to become the market innovator/leader in the emerging strategic business area. Clearly the decision will be influenced by the rate of change of technology within the overall market demand life cycle and competitive activities.

The possible cost implications are illustrated in Figure 4.9. Figure 4.9(a) depicts the revenue flows that may be expected from participation within a specific product application cycle. Choice often concerns size of plant (and therefore investment) and timing. If the company can confidently forecast that it will develop a strong response (option 2) it should opt for a larger plant as shown by Figure 4.9(b). The cost behaviour will follow the shapes depicted by LRAC1 and LRAC2 (long run average cost). Market effectiveness may possibly be made sooner with the smaller plant but economies of scale are less advantageous than the situation depicted by LRAC2 in Figure 4.9(c).

Figure 4.10 suggests a different, but not unusual, situation. Figure 4.10(a) identifies an opportunity which often occurs and concerns capacity decisions, for example, a new product for which demand expands rapidly once it becomes established. In Figure 4.10(b) the cost options are illustrated. Clearly this hypothetical organization would benefit from the opportunity offered by revenue 2 opportunity, but as Figure 4.10(c) suggests there are investment cost implications. The situation offered by revenue 1 opportunity is likely to cost appreciably less and may be operational earlier; however, the profit potential of revenue 2 opportunity would appear to be more attractive. Clearly we need more information before a decision of this nature can be made. Here our concern has been to demonstrate the cost implications and issues accompanying strategic marketing decision making.

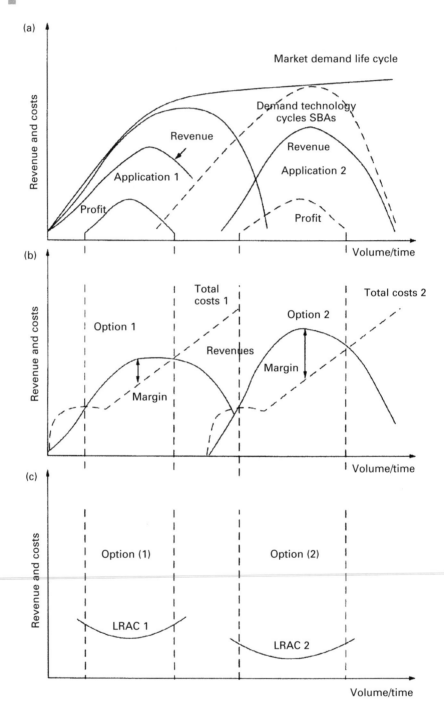

Figure 4.9 Cost implications of alternative investments

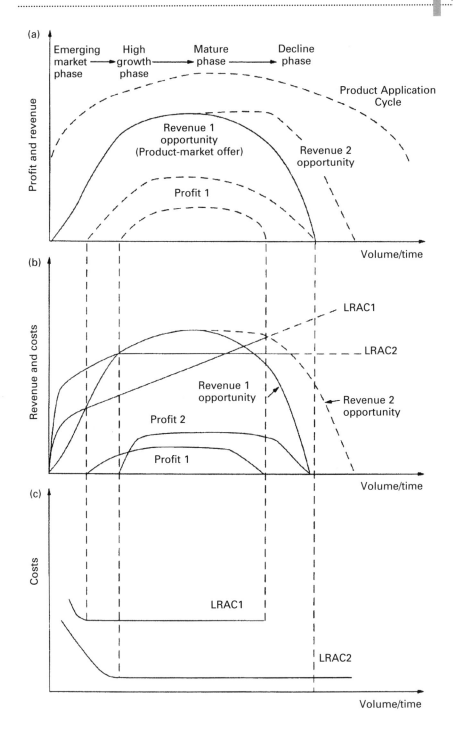

Figure 4.10 Selecting capacity levels to match market volumes

4.6 Managing the costs of differentiation and mass customization through product platforms

Porter's (1996) argument to differentiate between strategy and what he labels *operational effectiveness* requires either the support of partner organizations or the recognition that within a vertically integrated organization some internal disaggregation be pursued:

> A company can outperform rivals only if it can establish a difference that it can preserve. It must deliver greater value to customers or create comparable value at lower cost or do both. The arithmetic of superior profitability then follows: delivering greater value allows a company to charge higher average unit prices; greater efficiency results in lower average costs.

But this suggests that operational effectiveness alone is insufficient for long-term competitive success: '(competitive strategy) is about being different . . . the essence of strategy is in the activities – choosing to perform activities differently or to perform different activities to rivals.' In essence, Porter is suggesting that strategic effectiveness is about doing the right things; operational effectiveness is doing the right things right!! Perhaps his concept is better labelled *operational efficiency*. Thus the dilemma for many organizations is that to remain competitive they need some feature(s), either product or service characteristics, that maintain a position of *sustainable competitive advantage*. Often these are only available outside the organization.

This approach has tended to shift the focus of organizations. While economies of scale and scope continue to have important contributions to make, it is *the economics of differentiation* and of *integration* that are becoming important. Figure 4.11 illustrates how the economics of differentiation influence an organization's strategy. Following Porter's argument that differentiation can be non-price value based, it follows that quite different market expectations will exist. Furthermore, these may require quite different 'value creation, production, delivery and service structures', often necessitating additional investment or perhaps collaborative arrangements. Figure 4.11 suggests that for different differentiation strategies the *operational effectiveness profiles* will differ substantially.

Figure 4.12 extends the argument. Given a highly segmented market an organization will find constraints on its ability to compete effectively. It will experience constraints on its ability to offer either non-price value differentiation or price-led differentiation. For companies operating in simpler market structures the opportunities to expand their operational effectiveness are clearly greater.

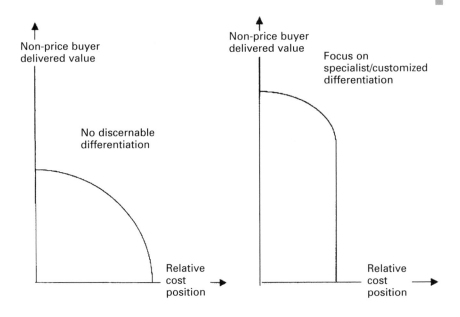

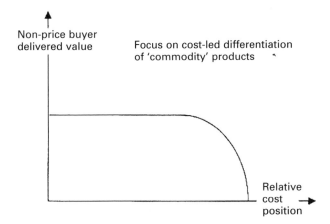

Figure 4.11   Strategic differentiation or operational efficiency? The choices

Product platforms

The concept of product platforms is well known and the application of the concept first introduced by Black and Decker has expanded across a number of industries. A skillful application of the concept can reap benefits of economies of scale, economies of differentiation and economies of integration. Meyer

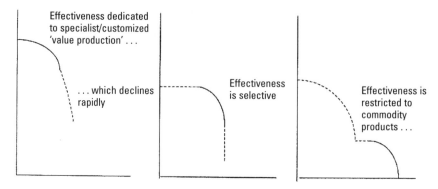

To be competitive requires some difficult decisions

Attempting to create dominant 'operational efficiency' may restrict a successful response to market opportunities. Understanding the characteristics of the market becomes essential

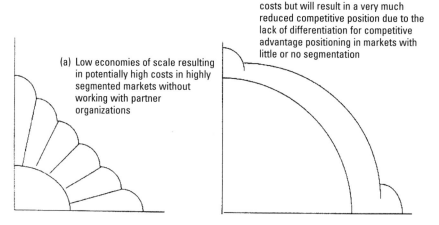

Figure 4.12 The 'economies of integration and differentiation' enable the design of a combination of product-service offers

and Lehnerd (1997) describe the role and the importance of product platforms in the strategic planning of an organization:

> They know they must generate a *continuous stream* of value-rich products that target growth markets. Such products form the product family, individual products that share common technology and address related market applications. It is those families that account for the long-term success of corporations.

Product families do not have to emerge one product at a time. In fact, they are planned so that a number of derivative products can be efficiently created from the foundation of common core technology. We call this foundation of core technology the 'product platform', which *is a set of subsystems and interfaces that form a common structure from which a stream of derivative products can be efficiently developed and produced.*

The authors argue that the approach dramatically reduces costs in procurement and manufacturing, because so many of costs are amortized across the product range. Furthermore, the 'building blocks' of product platforms can be integrated with *new* components to address new market opportunities rapidly. Hence, *time-to-market*, an important value driver and competitive advantage feature, can also be developed. Product platforms must be managed. Failure to monitor the development of customer expectations *and* to use developments in related technology implies that such derivatives that do emerge will fail 'customers in terms of function and value'.

Meyer and Lehnerd (1997) offer a conceptual model that with modification reflects the process of platform development and application. Figure 4.13 depicts the principles of the benefits of taking an integrated and long-term perspective of product-market development.

Market applications identify the range of market segments and price points that define the scope of market opportunity. The notion of the product platform concept is that while it may not be economically feasible to pursue each cell in the market segment matrix at the same time, by using an incremental and integrative approach it may become possible. *Product platforms*, as already established, are the set of subsystems and interfaces that form a common structure for the cost-effective development of a stream of derivative products. For Meyer and Lehnerd, the *common building blocks* comprise consumer insights, product technologies, manufacturing processes and organizational capabilities. The rate of change in the business environment (discussed earlier) suggests a need to rethink these topics. A broader view, one less focused on the existing business sector, would be to consider the relevant developments in knowledge, technology, relationship and process management. The growth of partnership and alliance agreements (as well as technology) is making collaboration between the most unlikely partners an everyday occurrence. An additional feature has been included that of the *value proposition*. It is very clear (from the preceding section) that the customer is playing an important role in product specification and development (Toffler's *prosumer* in Future Shock); accordingly it is suggested that customer involvement in the overall process is becoming a norm, rather than an exception. Furthermore, not only does the value proposition reflect the nature of the overall response to the customer, but it also serves the purpose of communicating the roles and tasks agreed by the 'organization'.

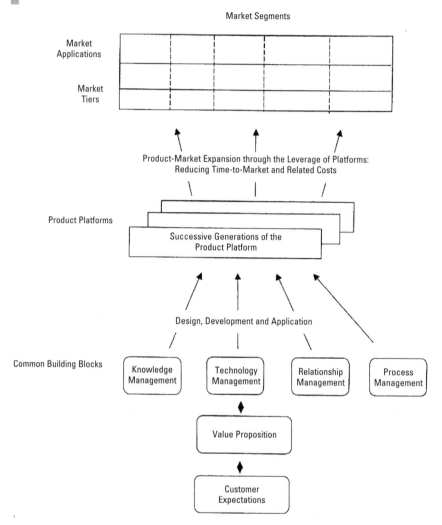

Figure 4.13 The product platform model of product and process innovation and management

The mission statement, popular in the 1980s and 1990s, attempted to package a number of corporate messages. As well as identifying its values and its objectives, the mission statement attempted to identify its response to the customer. Very occasionally it included the internal issues that needed to be resolved and identified the roles and tasks of its internal and external partners that were required for success. The events of the recent past have caused a number of organizations to rethink their mission statements. Many have become so brief that they are meaningless; others focus more on conformance, conservation and the organization's responsibilities to the community. The customer and partner response is now made explicit by its *value proposition*.

To be effective, a value proposition should identify for the customer just how customer expectations are to be met. But given the increasingly important role that partnerships and alliances are now playing it should also identify how they are expected to contribute.

A value-based approach to product-service platforms

If the customer centricity approach suggested by Slywotzky and Morrison (Chapter 1) is adopted then a product-service platform approach becomes essential. Examples of how a product-service platform approach can enhance the flexibility and focus of customer responses are given as Figures 4.14 and 4.15. Figure 4.14 considers the ranges of response available to each aspect of customer expectations. Figure 4.15 identifies ways and means by organizations can (and do) convert customers' costs into value benefits by either reducing the cost items, offering a service that creates greater benefits, or, possibly, offering a benefit that is both less expensive and delivers increased value.

The argument in favour of intangible, (or value-based) platforms is that they facilitate cost-efficient responses in what was described earlier as an increasingly turbulent market environment. Capital commitments can be reduced and, with this, there will be a significant reduction in risk.

In the model described by Figure 4.16 detailed changes to the Meyer and Lehnerd model are proposed. The value proposition assumes a more dominant role, one prescribed by ongoing customer research and joint development projects. By considering customer value drivers and expectations the value creation, production, delivery and servicing processes become more aligned with the underlying characteristics that are responsible for customer behaviour.

It is essential that the organization first understands the generic nature of the market in which it operates and the necessary capabilities and processes that are required for success. Figure 4.17 explores some of these issues. For markets demonstrating a range of segment options, it is unlikely that it can be successful in all of them unless some collaboration with partner organizations is possible. Understanding the value expectations of customers and aggregating these into relevant 'packages' makes matching these against the capabilities required to compete much easier, as well as providing an in-depth understanding of a customer's business. The fact that they are intangible reduces the risk of inappropriate investment. For partner organizations the argument is the same. While they are offering a specialist solution to the primary supplier, they are, in fact, operating with standard, albeit narrower,

	Value Expectations	Value Platform Alternatives	Examples
• Security	• Warranty • A/S service delivery/continuity • Insurance • Product liability (recall/recovery) package	• Strong brand/franchise a well known brand • Customer service/service organization • R and D – product design (product platforms) • Establish an emergency product recall network	• Mercedes/BMW/Caterpillar have developed strong brands and strong service organizations to reinforce their product reputation with end users. Resellers and service organizations are linked to the supplier organizations by IT communications
• Performance	• Quality • Consistency • Continuity • Variety/suitability } 'Solutions' relative to existing market offers that are currently available (product and service)	• TQM throughout operations (manufacturing and logistics/use inputs/components with strong identify • Partnership arrangements with high VA resellers • Use partner's information systems to customize value proposition	• Computer manufacturers use 'Intel' in hardware manufacturing and 'Microsoft' software as partner organizations • Reseller reputations (Harrods, Nieman Marcus, etc) endorse' recommend and support products)
• Aesthetics	• Styling/design • Image/appearance'	• Develop prestige brands/franchise prestige brands • Partnership arrangements with prestige resellers and service organizations • Leverage the reputation of well known customers	• Motor vehicle manufactures (and other industrial product producers) use design services for 'exterior', design performance
• Convenience	• 'Product formulation' flexibility • Time availability • Location availability • Information availability	• 'Multi media' distribution } 'supported by 'easy • High 'access' distribution } access' information } facilities • Increase physical availability through increased field presence using service organizations with specialist service attributes	• Manufacturers and distributors are using telecommunications networks for order processing and progressing and service distribution companies to provide location availability (Telstra, Australia)
• Economy	• Competitive pricing of original equipment • Competitive pricing: service parts • Competitive pricing: service activities • Ownership alternatives	• Product design (product platforms, value engineering), coproductivity with suppliers and customers • Develop industry standards for common or similar replacement parts • Reduce, reformulate ownership/transaction costs using finance specialists	• Consumer durables manufacturers design 'standardization' into products, resulting in cost-efficient and time-efficient servicing
• Reliability	• Availability (time) • Availability (product and services formulation) • Availability (location) • Conformance • Continuity	• Leverage suppliers and resellers fixed assets and working capital • Integrate operating technology • Product development and design 'committees' which incorporate suppliers, resellers and end-users	• Computer manufacturers coordinate manufacturing and supply chain activities to offer customized products within advertised delivery lead times and contain costs (Dell)

Figure 4.14 Examples of a range of customer expectations

Customer Acquisition Costs	Value Expectations	Value Platform Alternatives	Examples
• Specification	• Information and technical advice on product-service suitability (relevance of input) • Assistance in developing input performance criteria for NPD	• Communicating through multi-media networks eg, net based systems, direct technical representation or VA intermediary (distributor or 'consultant' operation) • R&D based upstream and downstream working with suppliers, resellers, relevant intermediaries and end users to develop longitudinal perspective of all needs.	• Fiat product development using internet on Punto • Electronics manufacturers working on problems with customers in partnership R&D ventures • Industrial designers are used to advise on 'packaging' • 'Turkey' consultants offer IT specification services
• Search	• Supplier competence profiles: capabilities, capacities, location	• Maintain web based information of products, services and NPD • Close liaison with key and development customers	• Computer components manufacturers using websites to communicate problem solving abilities, manufacturing capabilities and capacities
• Transactions	• Ownership requirements	• Customize ownership packages (owned, leased, financed options) • Use partner organizations to develop finance/ownership packages	• Sale and lease back facilities permit customers use of capital in core company activities. Examples are extensive in airlines
• Installation/delivery	• Minimum time to full operations	• Skilled installation personnel • Ongoing training programs for staff	• Consumer durables manufactures and retailers use specialist companies for this essentially labour-intensive activity
• Operations	• Standardize inputs • Minimal operating costs • Simplify operations	• 'On-line' technical support • Ongoing training programs for staff	• Computer and photocopier companies offer integrated services which manage installation, operations, maintenance and copy paper replenishment. Elements of these processes are outsourced. IT services are also commonplace.
• Maintenance	• Minimize service intervals/parts costs • Maximum productivity	• Maximum service coverage • Service parts availability • Planned maintenance	• Military operations and maintenance (RAF) are increasingly managed by specialist service companies
• Disposal	• Maximum terminal value (ROI) • Repurchase options/price • Removal and resale	• Remove and dispose of replaced equipment • Develop resale markets • Planned replacement/finance packages	• Commercial aircraft are recycled using 'reseller' specialists

Figure 4.15 Examples of a range of customer acquisition costs

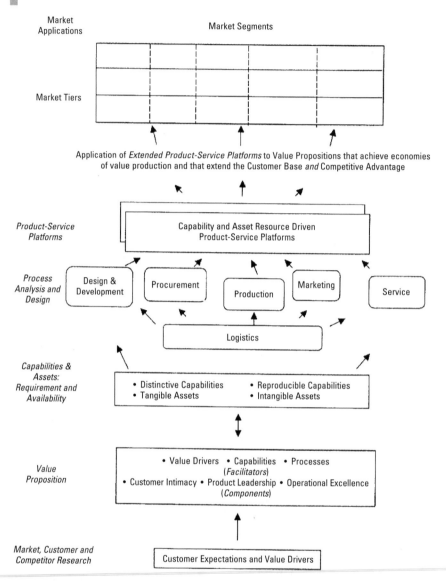

Figure 4.16 An approach to developing product-service platforms

value platforms. Figure 4.18 suggests how vehicle manufacturers are approaching product planning using value platforms. Essentially product-service platforms are used up to the point at which customer differentiation expectations become a major marketing consideration. Thus, the use of common floor pans, engines, transmission and braking components is typical. However, depending upon the expectations of the target market

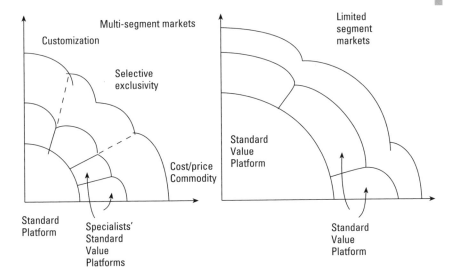

Ideally an organization will prefer to pursue a limited number of product-service platforms. In this way cost economies will be maximized. But if they are pursued beyond a point at which any further exploitation is likely to meet with customer resistance because of the lack of customer expected differentiation the organization must adopt an alternative strategy. The solution is to identify the limit to which a 'standard' production platform may be used and then seek partners with specialist expertise. The automotive industry is an example. Ford Motor Company has a number of major brands Jaguar, Land Rover, Volvo, Aston Martin as well as the existing Ford groups. It operates a platform strategy up to a point where customers begin to perceive value similarities. At this point they are no longer able to extend the application of the platforms and seek to add partners to add the differentiation important to customers

With markets that demonstrate few segment variations the opportunity to expand the application of a standard product-service platform is possible. The use of specific partners who can contribute expertise adds the necessary differentiation *but* the costs are contained at competitive levels due to the effects of the economies achieved with the initial design of the business model. This structure is typical of 'generic' product-markets, such as food and drink, in which segment volumes vary. The difficulty is to maintain productivity in the filling processes. Often the solution is resolved by using specialist partner. In this instance the platforms are process based, having cost (and therefore price & competitiveness) implications

Figure 4.17 Strategic market differeniation and product-service platforms – developing the economics of integration and differentiation

constraints may appear sooner in some segments than in others. Here it is Porter's notion of value differentiation that becomes important. Clearly, more price-sensitive segments are willing to trade-off aspects of differentiation for price concessions. By contrast, the non-price sensitive segments will be less inclined to do so. Successful companies identify theses tolerances before extending platform features too extensively.

To be effective, mass customization strategies should be based upon a

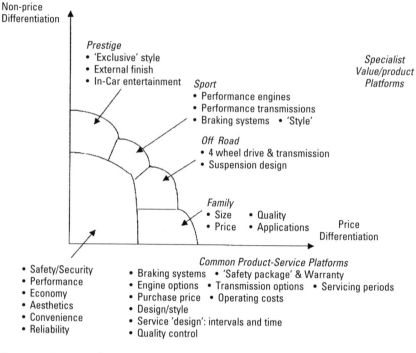

Figure 4.18   Automative Industry 'Product-Service Platforms'

very simple concept: that while a large range of product-service variation may be offered, typically the selection is made from a limited range. The success therefore depends upon managing the cost structures that surround these offers. Figure 4.19 represents the effect on cost structures that an effective 'platform strategy' can have on costs. Overhead costs incurred in the management of design and development, procurement etcetera are amortized across a large volume of activity and the use of a standard components in manufacturing (see earlier in this chapter). The impact of platforms can be increased through design and development partnerships between companies. This can occur through acquisitions (or mergers) such as VW/Skoda and Renault/Nissan or it may simply be a working arrangement such as that between Ford and Mazda to use common components.

Agrawal *et al.* (2001) identify many of the problems involved in mass customization. They suggested 'daunting challenges'

But making mass customization in the auto industry real, particularly in North America, would require carmakers to deal with enormous changes in design, sourcing, manufacturing, marketing and distribution.

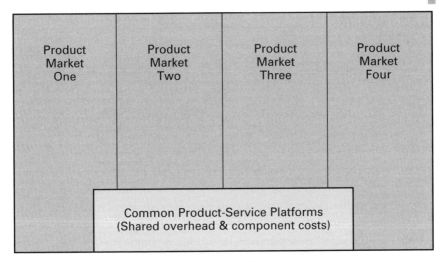

Figure 4.19(a) Limited application of product platform components

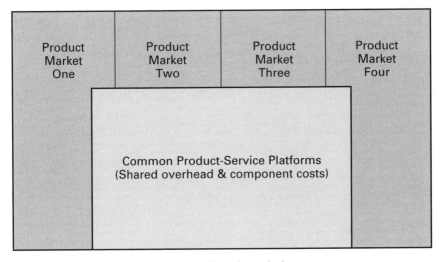

Figure 4.19(b) Wide application of product platform components

Figure 4.19 Extending the cost-effectiveness of product-service platforms

And:

Achieving the strategic manufacturing flexibility required for mass customization would require many operational changes. Customers may like to choose the color of their cars, for instance, but paint shops at car plants run in batch mode to cut costs and to minimize the emissions and waste that are generated every time paint guns receiving new colors are flushed.

Other strategies are to change the design of the product *and the manufacturing process* – modularization is one option gaining favour. The vehicle is designed such that it is initially manufactured in modules that are delivered to a final assembly plant. This reduces the number of suppliers from 'thousands to mere dozens'. However, there are additional costs:

> because car makers might have to carry a range of modules (some of which may vary slightly in color, choice of fabric, or even an individual part) modules could involve greater inventory redundancy and waste within the supply chain than do non modular components, which can be configured exactly according to demand. In addition, modules take up more floor space than do loose parts and are costlier to ship.

The authors have identified basic differences between the traditional 'push' model and the emerging 'pull' approach, as shown in the table opposite.

Clearly, there are a number of marketing and finance issues here as well as operations management decisions. A number of alternatives exist. *Forbes Global* (2003) report a proposed facility in Austria that will be manufacturing 'Saab convertibles and Mercedes-Benz station wagons'. The plant is owned by Magna International, a Canadian-based auto-parts manufacturer, which has converted its European subsidiary into a fully outsourced engineering and production facility. The vehicle manufacturer provides Magna with the styling for a new model and a chassis to build it off, and Magna conducts the engineering, builds an assembly line and produces the vehicles. The practice offers vehicle manufacturers a number of advantages:

- Time-to-market is reduced.
- Labour costs may be reduced by up to 30 per cent.
- Start-up costs can reduced considerably – BMW suggest that for one vehicle these will be $100 million rather than the $400 million required to expand its existing capacity.
- The ability to focus on the manufacturing of its core (volume) product ranges.

The larger US manufacturers (most of whom have capacity problems and therefore are not seeking to close plants) are not participating in this venture at present. However, the high relative wage rates are beginning to take their toll and Magna anticipates that this factor alone will encourage the shift.

	'Push' Model	'Pull' Model
Design	• Wide range of vehicles with mass appeal. • Limited customer input.	• Collaboration between suppliers and OEMs on design & development. • Higher level of customer input.
Sourcing	• Adversarial relationships with suppliers. • Component sourcing. • High levels of inventory.	• More collaborative relationships with suppliers; more suppliers located at plant. • Module sourcing. • JIT processes lower inventory levels.
Manufacturing	• Goal: volume through maximum production. • Manufacturing as core capability. • Downtime unacceptable.	• Goal: increased profit through reduced inventories and overhead costs. • Manufacturing scheduled by customer orders using BTO schedules. • Downtime acceptable when orders are slow.
Marketing	• Pricing based on budget target volumes. • High incentives to generate volume sales through customer incentives.	• Market-driven pricing strategy on order-by-order basis. • Fewer vehicle incentives and discounts – increased profits
Distribution	• Orders based on allocation and capacity constraints. • 60-day order to delivery time. • Price discounting.	• Customer-originated orders. • 20- to 30-day order period. • Low inventory levels, higher revenue for dealers as a result of less discounting.

• (OEMs: Original equipment manufacturers.   • (BTO: Built-to-order
Source: Based on Agrawal *et al.* (2001).

4.7 'New economy' perspectives of market dynamics: directions and options for growth

The popular myth that cost cutting enhances shareholder value is being increasing discredited (Kilroy, *Australian Financial Review*, 17 April 2002). The notion that rationalization can deliver long-term shareholder value is dangerous from two points of view. As Kilroy has demonstrated, not only is it a short-term, almost reflex response that restricts future strategic choice, but it also conditions managerial creativity.

Well-known 'management gurus' (such as Drucker, Hammer and Normann) are suggesting that the necessary management skills are moving away from acquiring and owning resources to coordinating the skills and resources that they and their partners possess. Successful businesses such as Dell and Nike have replaced (and embraced) the concepts of *virtual integration* rather than vertical integration and the *economies of integration* have replaced the economies of scale in importance. This is 'new economy' creativity or innovation: innovation is also about structures and processes, not simply about 'better mousetraps'.

There are a number of models that explore the coordination and cooperation approach. Virtual organizations, value nets and value chains share a common approach. Processes are inter-organizational and have replaced the 'functional silo' mentality. Knowledge management is essential. Technology management is not simply about products and processes, but is now much more concerned with integration and coordination on a (often-global) partnership basis. Relationship management is the nerve system that communicates, consults and builds trust throughout the 'organization'.

Furthermore, this is not a new phenomenon. The Brookings Institution has been monitoring the changes occurring in the asset structures of large manufacturing and mining organizations in the US. Their findings are a significant indication that a number of organizations have been addressing these issues for some time. Fixed tangible assets in these companies fell as a proportion of total assets from 67 per cent in 1982 to 38 per cent by 1992. By 2000 the firgure was reported to be less than 30 per cent. Clearly the concept that you do not necessarily need to 'own-to-control' has been prevalent within some large American organizations for a number of years.

Identifying and evaluating alternatives is not difficult; different, yes, but not difficult. It requires an innovative approach to structure. Given that shareholders are investing in the belief of future wealth from economic cash flow, management's task is to maximize the return at minimal risk. *Enterprise value* (an approach discussed by Knight and Pretty, *The Financial Times* 2000) is maximized, and risk optimized, by managing a mix of tangible and intangible assets (that may or may not be owned) together with improvements in the existing asset infrastructure see Chapter 2).

Knight and Prettyargue that tangible value has been downgraded as the market valuation of internet based companies: 'with a little or no book value but promises of great wealth outshone their traditional competitors'. The events since June 2000 suggest that this is not the case, but it is interesting to note that the emphasis on intangible assets persists and is a major contribution to the growth of virtual enterprises.

The *enterprise value model* described by the authors has a simple structure:

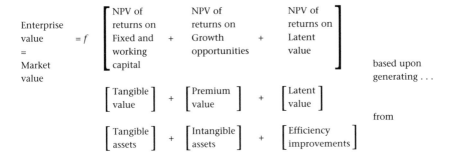

... where *market value* is derived by multiplying share price by the number of shares outstanding and subtracting long-term debt but could be replaced by aggregate economic cash flow.

As soon as the ownership myth is relaxed, the range of alternatives expands rapidly. What follows is routine for a few successful organizations and bewilderment for most. The *traditionalist's approach* – reducing existing operations, and therefore costs (and very often vital customer service – may have a short-term positive impact on investors, but it inevitably overlooks the long-term customer response. The recent NAB action has cast serious doubts upon the efficacy of such a strategy in both the short term and the long term (see Figure 4.20).

The virtual community adopts a quite different approach. The creative manager audits the organization's capabilities-set against those capabilities required for success in the market environment. *Distinctive capabilities* are developed or acquired through partnership alliances and the *reproducible capabilities* are purchased as services as and when required. The result is an 'investment' in a *value chain* comprising a mix of tangible, intangible and existing assets, all having distributed ownership (see Figure 4.21).

Uren (2001) identifies trends in the role of intangible assets as capabilities (notably brands and services) in the competition between airlines and in automotive markets. He noted the differences between Qantas and Ansett, suggesting that Qantas, with its international networks ('One World' and the links with travel agents) together with an investment in service, is building both capabilities and competitive advantage based upon intangible service-based assets. The recent events appear to give credence to this view. In another example, Uren uses the packaging rivals, Amcor and Visy, who seek to differentiate a basic commodity product; both are using IT-based e-commerce systems to increase customer service. In each of these examples a basic issue is emerging.

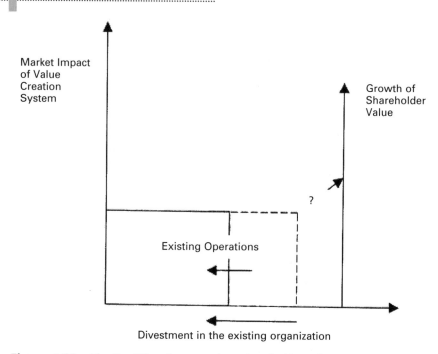

Market Impact
of Value
Creation
System

Growth of
Shareholder
Value

?

Existing Operations

Divestment in the existing organization

Figure 4.20 The 'traditional' approach to shareholder value

Service extensions or augmentation of the basic product enhances the value of the 'brand'. These intangible service items are the result of investment in intangible assets and/or the result of partnership arrangements with specialist providers.

Clearly some lessons have been available (if not learnt) and issues for consideration have been identified. Boulton *et al.* (2000) make a useful contribution. They contend:

> The encompassing challenge that companies face in this new environment is how to identify and leverage all sources of value, not just the assets that appear on the traditional balance sheet. These important assets including customers, brands, suppliers, employees, patents, and ideas are at the core of creating a successful business now and in the future. . . . But what assets are most important in the New Economy? How do we leverage these assets to create value for our own organizations in a changing business environment? What new strategies are required for us to create value?

The new economy business model asset portfolio is far more diversified than that of the traditional organization and includes intangible assets such as relationships, intellectual property and leadership. They suggest that new

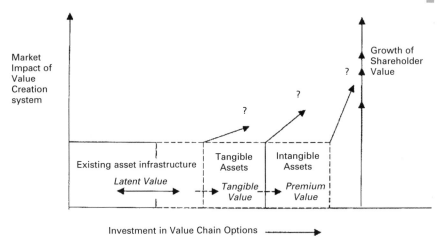

Figure 4.21 The 'new economy' approach to shareholder value

business models are becoming commonplace in 'every industry' in the 'new economy':

> In these emerging models intangible assets such as relationships, knowledge, people, brands and systems are taking center stage. The companies that successfully combine and leverage these intangible assets in the creation of their business models are the same companies that are creating the most value for their stakeholders.

Shareholder value can be (and increasingly is) created by a disciplined and innovative approach to value chain management. There are five basic principles:

- Identify the value chain.
- Evaluate the opportunities it addresses.
- Identify where customer value is created and who is creating that value.
- Question whether additional value can be created – and how.
- Identify a role for the individual organization, one in which its capabilities and assets can best be deployed.

4.8 Summary

This chapter has brought together many of the marketing and finance issues concerned with strategic market decision making. It has dealt with the need for and the process of identifying the market characteristics and influences which eventually qualify and quantify the target market for the firm. This was shown to be a necessary input into planning the capacity requirements of the firm.

Following this discussion we introduced the issues to be considered when making capacity decisions. We suggested that an understanding of the cost behaviour profile of strategic decisions is necessary for marketing managers. A particular influence on strategic costs is the effect of economies of scale and these were identified and discussed.

The shape of long-run cost curves was considered in detail, including problems in estimating their shape and methods for overcoming these.

Strategic market decisions (within a context of strategic business areas) and their cost implications (and options) concluded the chapter. It was emphasized that the analysis was hypothetical in that any company facing such decisions must first identify all the options, the costs and the strategic implications of choices. The vehicle used for the analysis was an adaptation of the work of both Aaker and Doyle.

REFERENCES

Aaker, D. (1995) *Strategic Market Management*, 4th edn, Wiley, New York.

Agrawal, M., T. V. Kumaresh and G. A. Mercer (2001) 'The false promise of mass customization', *The McKinsey Quarterly*.

Ansoff, H. I. (1984) *Implanting Strategic Management*, Prentice Hall, New York.

Butler, P., T. W. Hall, A. M. Hanna, L. Mendoca, B. Auguste, J. Manyika and A. Sahay (2001) A Revolution in Interaction, *The McKinsey Quarterly*, Number 1.

Campbell, A. (1996) 'Creating the virtual organisation and managing the distributed workforce', in P. Jackson and J. Van der Weilen (eds), *New Perspectives on Telework: From Telecommuting to the Virtual Organisation*, Report on Workshop held at Brunel University.

*Davies, H. (1991) *Management Economics*, 2nd edn, Pitman, London.

Doyle, P. (1994) *Marketing Management and Strategy*, Prentice Hall, London.

Forbes Global (2003) September 1.

Kay, J. (1993) *Foundation of Corporate Success*, Oxford University Press, Oxford.

Kotler, P. (1994) *Marketing Management*, 8th edn, Prentice Hall, New York.

Meyer, M. H. and Lehnerd, A. P. (1997), *The Power of Product Platforms*, The Free Press, New York.

Porter, M. E. (1996) 'What is strategy?', *Harvard Business Review*, November/December

▶

▶

Stigler, G. J. (1958)* 'The economies of scale', *Journal of Law and Economics*.

Toffler, A. (1980) *The Third Wave*, Morrow, New York.

Uren, D. (2001) 'To winners go more spoils in rivalry tango', *The Australian*, 10 March.

*See Davies for a detailed discussion on Stigler's work and its implications.

5 The Financial Implications of Operational Decisions

Chapter 4 discussed cost issues and structures which need to be considered in strategic decision making. Once the size of plant capacity and the characteristics of the technology process have been decided, the management task is to achieve volume and cost objectives. In this chapter then we turn to the implementation process which is concerned with a specified planning horizon in which fixed costs appear.

The chapter commences by considering the implications of capacity/technology decisions on the company's operational gearing. This discussion identifies important factors which will influence the company response to the identified market opportunity. Risk, flexibility and added value for the customer (to develop competitive advantage) are discussed in this context.

The value chain is becoming increasingly significant and in this chapter its implications for costs and for adding value to the customer offer are discussed within the framework of the cost structures of strategy implementation. Within this topic we shall consider the opportunities for added value offered by strategic alliances and partnerships.

Product and customer profitability conclude the chapter; in this discussion we will introduce activity and attribute based costing as methods in the analysis.

5.1 Risk and cost structure of the business

The transition between strategy formulation and implementation is not clearly defined. This is not surprising because, as the process of strategic decision making becomes operational, some issues remain to be resolved. One of these issues is the cost structure of the business. There are a number of aspects to be considered.

First there is *business risk*. We need to identify the implications of the risks for the business of the venture about to be undertaken. A new and innovatory product would be surrounded by a large number of unknowns and as such would present management with problems when attempting to reach a reliable volume forecast. Hence we could say that while the project had been thoroughly researched and evidence found to suggest it will be profitable and worthwhile, it would not be viewed (from the risk perspective) as being as safe as an established product. Furthermore, we should ask the questions: what will be the overall impact upon the business? Will it change the relationships with suppliers and, more importantly, with customers? A comparison of risk and other major issues (such as competitor activities and strengths) would identify the full extent of the business risk confronting the business.

Second is the issue of *financial risk*. While this is a concern from an investment perspective it must be considered by operational marketing managers. Managers can choose from a range of alternative production methods and these will vary from the manufacture and distribution of the product internally to minimizing both the manufacturing and distribution activities by largely subcontracting out. The issue is the extent to which the business incurs fixed costs compared with variable costs. We shall return to this topic later in this chapter.

These decisions – on production, finance and control – have one common factor – they can influence the cost structure of that part of the business undertaking the project. For example, something for the firm to consider is the type of manufacturing process it uses to produce the product. A highly automated plant will have a high level of fixed costs relative to variable costs (for the reader wishing to refresh their memory, these were defined at the beginning of Part II), as will a facility which manufactures a very large proportion of the 'finished' product. Its costs will include plant and specialist labour which are typically regarded as a fixed cost.

This situation, suggested by Hayes and Wheelwright (1979), is illustrated in Figure 5.1. As manufacturing processes and products become increasingly complex, it is to be expected that the fixed cost content of the facilities required will increase. We can see the relationship between fixed and variable costs in Figure 5.2. In Figure 5.2(a) we have a manufacturing facility with an assembly operation in which very little capital equipment is utilized; components are purchased from outside suppliers (variable costs because they are procured as required) and the fixed costs of the business are the assembly line activity. By contrast, a company preferring to maintain a comprehensive manufacturing process will have the cost structure closer to that depicted in Figure 5.2(b), in which fixed costs are considerably higher and variable costs correspondingly lower.

Figure 5.2 suggests that the risk perceptions of the two organizations differ.

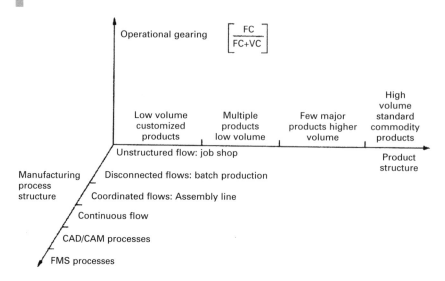

Figure 5.1   Operational gearing increases as product structure and/or manufacturing process structure becomes increasingly complex

In Figure 5.2(a) the operational gearing is typical for manufacturers of products for which specialist components are dominant inputs. Automobile manufacturing is one example and domestic appliances another. For both products extensive external sourcing exists. There are two possible reasons for this situation. One is the view that the organization has concerning its core business. A motor vehicle manufacturer may see its business as being 'the manufacture and distribution of transportation vehicles' rather than 'the development and production of motor vehicle electronics' or braking (or other) systems. The other reason concerns risk; by using external sourcing, it is possible for the firm to diversify its risk – in other words, to share the overall risk burden with its suppliers.

There is one other aspect of this topic: the impact of operational gearing on margins. Figure 5.3 uses the concept of break-even analysis to demonstrate how decisions on the fixed/variable cost structure influence the size of the margins generated. It illustrates the notion of break-even volumes and of feasible production levels.

The revenue 'curve' in Figures 5.3(a) and 5.3(b) is the same. It assumes a constant price across the volume range. Clearly what does differ is the relationship between fixed and variable costs. In Figure 5.3(a) (low fixed/high variable costs) the margin (distance between the revenue and total cost curves) is less than that for Figure 5.3(b) (high fixed/low variable costs), showing that the margins generated are higher for high fixed cost business configurations. This

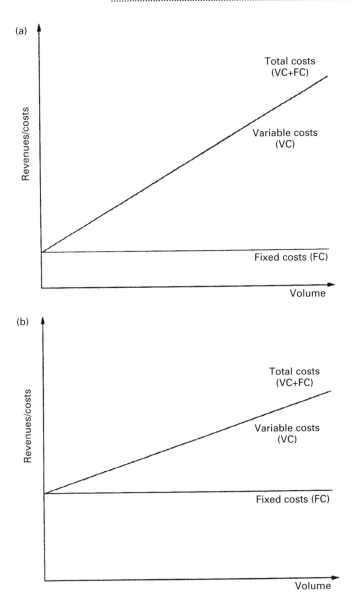

Figure 5.2   The relationship between fixed and variable costs

is because the margins generated by external suppliers are available to the manufacturer. It also follows that should there be fluctuations in volume (through changes in market demand) and volumes reduce to below break-even point then the losses experienced by the differently geared businesses will also differ. Underpinning this is the view of business risk that the organization may

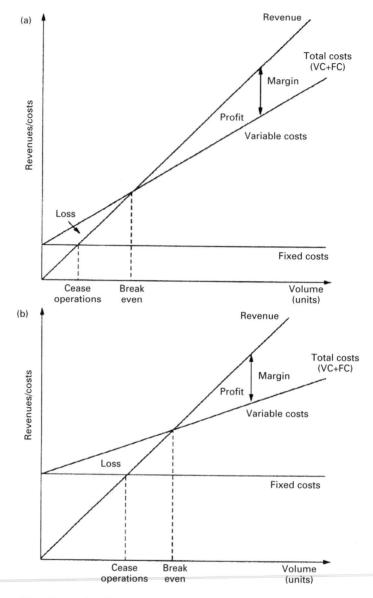

Figure 5.3　Operational gearing and the implications of margins

have. If it is uncertain of the marketplace it may prefer to operate with a low fixed cost facility, diversifying some of the risk and having to absorb lower losses but remaining flexible.

Figure 5.3 also illustrates the situation which may occur if volume decreases beyond the break-even level (or perhaps fails to even reach break even). The company may choose to continue manufacturing operations so long as this makes a contribution to its fixed costs. This occurs when *revenue equals or is greater than fixed costs* (at a particular volume); the precise location of which point is a function of the pricing/cost structures and it can be shown that the higher the price (and therefore the margin objective) the lower both the ceasing of operations and break-even volumes will be.

This point is amplified in Figure 5.4 which shows the effects of high and low fixed cost alternatives, together with changes in price levels. In Figure 5.4(a) (low fixed costs/high variable costs) the effect of a price decrease is to increase the *breakeven* and *cease production* volume levels; at the same time it has lowered the profit margin (it assumes no change in variable costs, such as advertising and promotion). What is also important to note is that the volume flexibility (the volume difference between cease production and break even) increases as the price decreases.

From a competitive response point of view it is essential that we understand these relationships. What is particularly important is the typical situation in which competition increases in the strategic business area as the mature phase of the market is reached, with possible price reductions and increases in promotional expenditure. To make an effective operational decision it is necessary to be aware of the revenue/cost relationships. Figure 5.5 illustrates these. Revenue increases and price remain unaltered through both the emerging market and high growth phase. However, towards the end of the high growth phase competition can be expected. Typically prices will be lowered and promotional activity increased.

A number of outcomes are possible. If marketing misread the marketplace and responds by initiating price reductions and an aggressive promotional campaign (TC3), which only results in revenue generation TR1, then V1 is the limit of the company's market share. By contrast if it is successful and the volume realized becomes V6, revenue increases to TR3 and market share is increased as the range of profitability increases (TR3 = TC3). However, more optimal profit margins will be at the volume levels at which the distance between the relevant TR and TC curves are at a maximum. Total profit is, of course, the area between the two intersection points of the total revenue and total cost curves. This introduces the fact that two break-even levels exist and the organization is profitable provided its volume throughput is managed between them.

It follows that intermediate outcomes are possible. Alternative revenue outcomes are shown as TR1, TR2 and TR3 and the organization's competitive response (i.e., its increases in promotional expenditure and on incentives) are shown as VC1, VC2 and VC3 (which become TC1, TC2 and TC3 when added to the existing variable costs). The volume options indicated (V1 through V7) identify the total range of volume flexibility the organization should

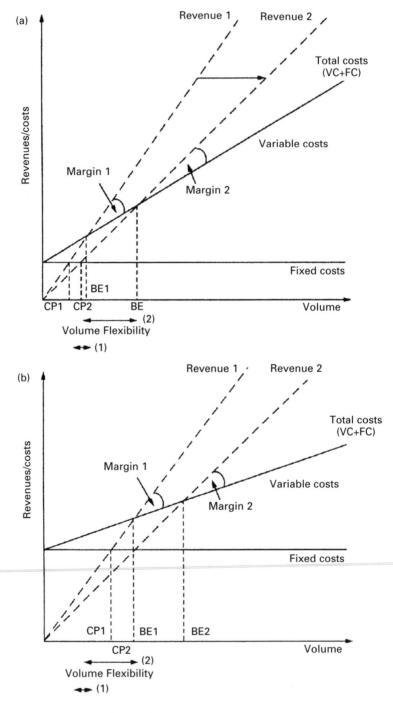

Figure 5.4 Impact of price alternatives

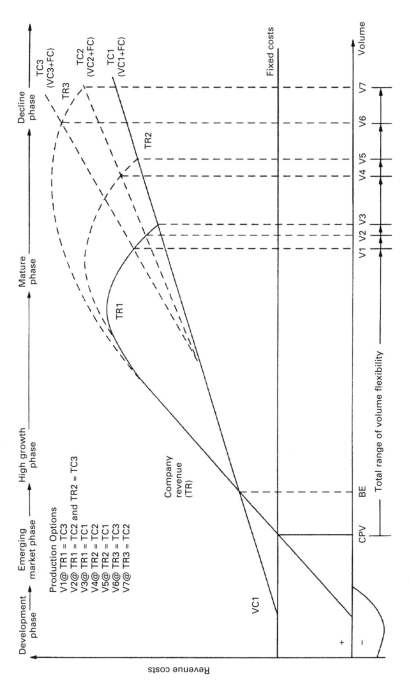

Figure 5.5 Adjusting both price and promotional costs to meet competition

consider. Clearly spending much of its time at the lower (unprofitable) end is not attractive but it should consider this possibility in detail. Together with Walters and Korkafingas (1997), we have recently developed an approach for measuring the probability of profitability outcomes using expected values for this purpose.

The objective of operational marketing should be to extend the *mature phase of the market*, provided that it can be achieved profitably and without imposing excessive opportunity costs on the organization. We should, therefore, consider the implications of economies of scale on the operational activities of the firm and the fact that they are likely to extend the profitable volume range of the organization. In Figure 5.5 we considered the cost function to be a straight line. However, we should recall, Figure 4.4 (p. 101) suggested that the cost relationship is curved. Figure 5.6(a) reflects this for the variable costs and also illustrates the effects that economies of scale are likely to have. In Figure 5.6(b) we include a realistic assumption concerning price and volume, that is, that price is likely to be reduced due to competitive pressures. If sales can be increased and a scale effect exists then the company remains profitable and the mature phase of the market is extended.

Scale and operational gearing are shown together in Figure 5.7 which suggests that a larger, and possibly more automated, plant manufacturing a large proportion of the end product increases both revenue and profitability. Clearly an accurate forecast of market demand is necessary prior to making decisions concerning plant size.

One last relationship to be considered is one typical of capacity expansion issues as depicted in Figure 5.8. Here revenue and costs are shown to vary over volume, with scale effects shown as a constant slope. The fixed costs show an increase (the step function), probably due to the firm receiving an optimistic forecast of market opportunity (which often occurs) and responding by increasing capacity. Two revenue forecasts are illustrated – the original TR1 and the new forecast TR2. The cost curves suggest that capacity (at TC1) would not have been increased and, therefore, the company limits its market capacity to the revenue forecasts. However, if the revenue forecasts are reliable and prove to be correct, and the market continues to expand (albeit at decreased rates), then the additional capacity decision was correct. As the scale effects become effective (TC2 and TC3), some additional costs are incurred (TC3) as a more aggressive promotional stance is taken. This hypothetical situation suggests this response has increased market volume for the company and profitability by a considerable amount. The volume over which the organization is profitable is shown by BE1–BE2 and BE1–BE3. Should the revenue forecasts have underestimated the actual outcome then TR3 with BE1–BE3 will occur. This has attraction as it increases the margin percentage of the profit generated as the fixed costs are amortized over the increased revenues.

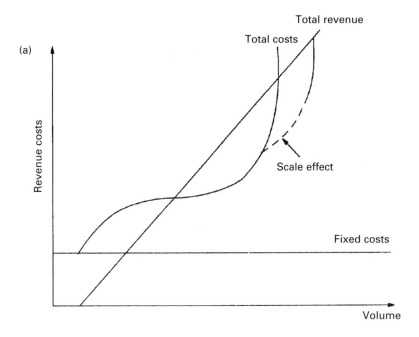

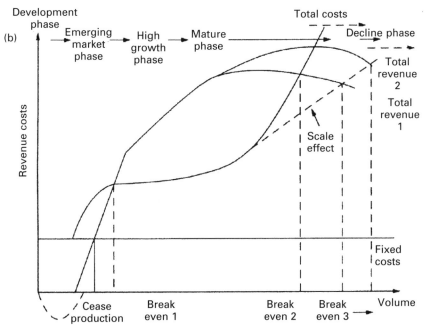

Figure 5.6 Implications of economies of scale

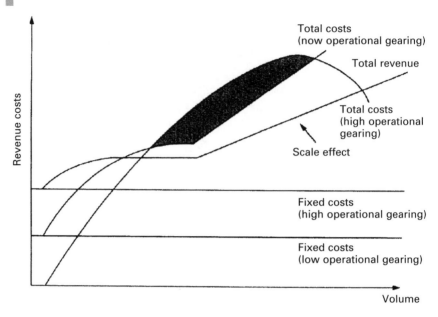

Figure 5.7 Operational gearing and economies of scale

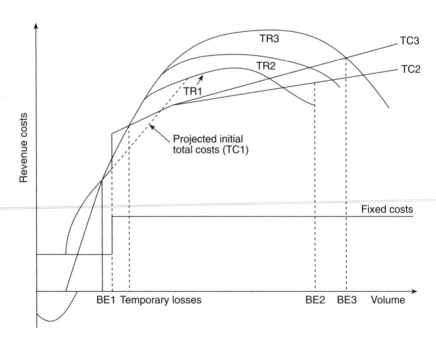

Figure 5.8 Extending capacity to increase revenue and profitability

5.2 The experience effect

During the Second World War research into aircraft production identified the fact that labour costs per aircraft produced declined as more aircraft were produced. Subsequent research (notably that by the Boston Consulting Group) and other academic researchers led to the observation that other input costs declined with this 'learning effect'. These cost decreases have a mathematical relationship with volume increases. The aircraft study found that doubling the production resulted in a total cost reduction of 20 per cent – therefore, the costs of producing the 200th aircraft could be expected to be 20 per cent less than the cost of producing the 100th aircraft. A similar effect, due to cumulative experience, was found in other production operations. Given a set of technology, there was found to be a constant experience curve effect across a significant range of output.

Three reasons have been proposed for the experience effect. The first is labour efficiency: as individuals repeat an activity they become more effective and they identify methods that they can implement to improve the process. Secondly, the process itself is improved due to modifications to plant and equipment. And, thirdly, the end product is improved due to marketing research and R&D responses to findings about customer expectations and end-user perceptions. Figure 5.9 reproduces the familiar experience curve presentation, which on logarithmic scales becomes a straight line. Note the logarithmic scales of both axes.

The experience effect has had an influence on marketing strategy. If the percentage increase in volume and percentage decrease in costs effect can be relied upon to be maintained across the range of potential market volume

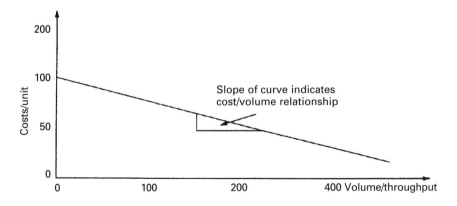

Figure 5.9 Experience effect (log scale)

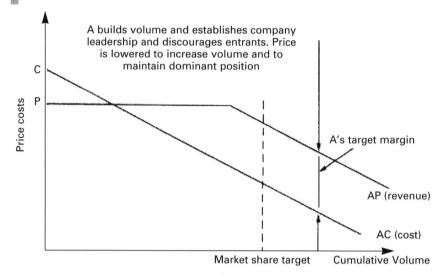

Figure 5.10   Using the experience effect to make price, volume and market share decisions

then a market-share/product-cost relationship can be projected. It follows that this useful (if not vital) piece of information permits the market-share/product-cost relationship to be extended to include pricing decisions. Provided the information is reliable, management can confidently set price *below* cost to encourage rapid sales growth. At a predetermined market share volume, price may then be set *above* cost to reflect the desired target margin. This effect is shown as Figure 5.10.

We have assumed that manufacturing technology remains constant (other than process/plant improvements). If we relax this assumption to consider the product (not the process) then it is possible to visualize a situation in which a company may introduce a product which is subsequently imitated by a competitor. Given the opportunity to evaluate the available product, as well as user perceptions, and also given the benefit of time, a competitor may introduce a similar product (in terms of benefits and performance) which has similar technology to the original. The situation which might evolve is depicted in Figure 5.11. Company B, by adopting a later entry strategy, can obtain an increase in the experience effect benefit (shown by the steeper cumulative experience curve, often based on the experience of the innovator). If company A had had a planned target volume, market share or margin objective, then unless some modifications can be made to the technology of A's manufacturing process, some revisions to A's marketing objectives and plans would be required. Often new entrants design products to take advantage of experience

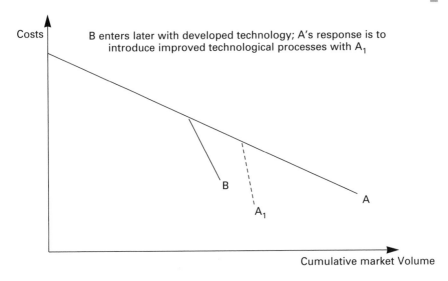

Figure 5.11   Impact of technological improvement

effects that have accrued to their competitors but which can be improved upon.

The experience effect and economies of scale differ. Cost benefits from the experience effect accrue over the cumulative output of the organization. Being more operational than strategic – in that changes may be made in response to market situations that have not been predicted – the cost benefits are not immediate. However, economies of scale offer a low cost/high volume situation immediately. Given the forecast for market demand, the strategic cost profile, estimates of both the business and financial risks involved, the capacity of the manufacturing facility can be decided and (once operational) will produce a unit cost at a predetermined level. Thus, they differ in that the experience curve cost decrease is based upon units produced over time but economies of scale costs decline because of the design of the production facility.

A second difference concerns the way in which costs decline. Economies of scale unit costs decline as a result of the amortization of fixed costs over an increasing number of units; by contrast, the experience effect will result in a continuous (constant) decrease in cost. It should be noted that managerial control is required if the benefits of both are to be maintained over time, particularly if price competitiveness is a critical success factor in the market sector.

While the concepts are based on different premises we can consider their joint effect. Figure 5.12 illustrates how, given a plant designed for economies

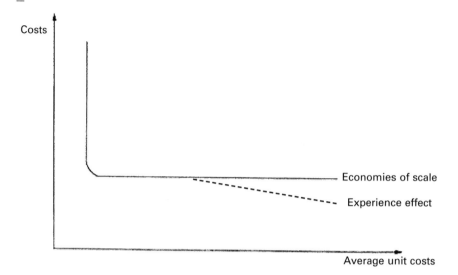

Figure 5.12   Average unit costs: scale effects and experience

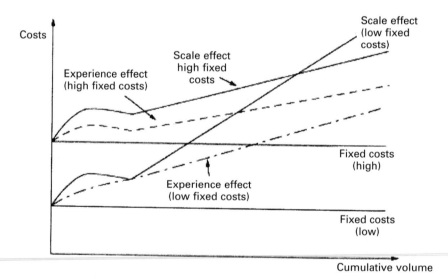

Figure 5.13   Total cost profile: effects of scale and experience

of scale benefits, over time (i.e., with cumulative throughput) we can expect average costs to decrease for the reasons discussed above. Figure 5.13 considers the behaviour of total costs. Here we see the influence of operational gearing. We assume that high fixed costs relate to a facility in which there are fewer opportunities to obtain cost reductions from cumulative throughput effects than for a low fixed cost alternative (this would particularly be the case in a high labour content process). Hence the cost reductions are smaller over the cumulative volume than those likely to be available from a low fixed cost facility with more flexibility in process management and therefore a greater opportunity to decrease costs of output over time and volume.

The benefits of a better understanding of cost and revenue relationships should now be apparent. The characteristics of market demand clearly have a considerable influence on decisions about required resources specifically in regard to technology and its volume capacity. A market demand profile also determines the 'capabilities' required to meet customer expectations for product characteristics and performance as well as the 'delivery' aspects of the offer.

5.3 The role of value

Value and price

Often the characteristics of the market can be used to determine the *value* required by customers and therefore the attributes the product-service should deliver. Value is used to differentiate a product from those of competitors, and *a value-based strategy* offers the customer more value at a *life cycle price* than the competition. Industrial purchasing usually considers *price* to include pre-purchase activities, product evaluation, negotiation, quality checking, installation, maintenance and, eventually, disposal and replacement. Therefore a value-based strategy is one in which each of these customer activities is considered along with its cost to the customer, with a view to including it within the overall productservice package. Part of the analysis includes a *pricetoperformance ratio*, which compares productservice alternatives in terms of their relative price and relative delivered utility. The productservice offering more utility is said to have the higher price-to-performance ratio. Analysis of price-to-performance ratios has benefits for both the business and its customers. For the business, the process identifies opportunity selectively to create added value and therefore competitive advantage. It also reveals ways in which the product-service may be positioned in the market and how it may be promoted to purchasers. For the customer the analysis may reveal additional capital or operating costs that were either ignored or considered as overhead items.

Figure 5.14 gives an example of life cycle pricing. It illustrates how two offers (priced similarly) may differ in the proposition made to the prospective customer. In this example we have identified some of the typical purchasing activities and considerations confronting the industrial buyer. Company A

**Customer related purchasing
activities and considerations**

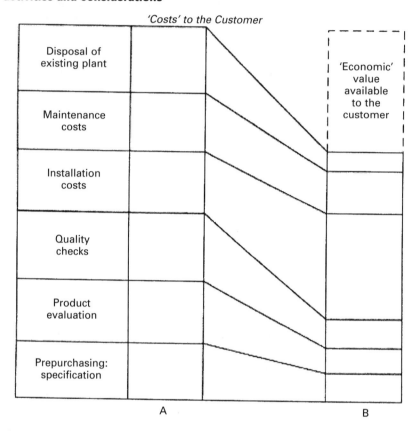

Figure 5.14 Life cycle pricing

has undertaken very little (if any) research into the sensitivities of these costs while company B has researched the customer segment very thoroughly and has 'packaged' the product-service offer such that the costs are lowered overall. And it has specifically reduced the costs of those activities which appear to the customer to be relatively high. The result is that the perceived value added for the customer is much higher in the offer made by Company B.

Value added arises from the activities of the business which add utility to the product or provide information to the buyer. Value added can be considered to be the additional benefits or utility delivered to the customer and for which the customer is prepared to pay over and above the 'going price in market'. If the benefits are unique to one particular product then the customer will be prepared to pay a premium if they can be seen to add value in turn to the customer's business. This might come through additional end uses, lower maintenance costs, higher quality, lower supervision costs, and so on. The list can be quite extensive. The purpose of life cycle costing/pricing is to identify what this premium may be priced at.

5.4   Clusters, value nets and value chains

Chapter 1 discussed the changes occurring with regard to the decline of vertical integration in favour of the flexibility and reduction in capital intensity that virtual organizations offer. The concepts of *clusters, value nets* and *value chains* have become important business structures.

Clusters

Value creation through clusters has been well documented in the applied economics literature. Porter (1990) defined clusters as 'a geographically proximate group of interconnected companies and associated institutions in a particular field linked by commonalities and complementarities'. Porter identified the components as: end-product or service companies; suppliers of specialist inputs; financial institutions; firms in related industries; firms in downstream industries; producers of complementary products; specialized infrastructure providers; governmental and other organizations providing dedicated education and information inputs and trade associations.

Porter explored a number of examples using a basic model comprising four interrelated components to explain international successes: (i) *Factor conditions* (i.e, basic factors of production that are necessary to compete successfully and to create competitive advantage); (ii) *firm strategy, structure and rivalry* (the goals, strategies and organization structures that when managed creatively result in international competitive advantage); (iii) *related and supporting industries* (the presence of national supplier or related industries that are internationally competitive); and (iv) *Demand conditions* (the quality and quantity of home demand has an impact on economies of scale and upon innovation both important influences on competitive advantage). While these remain important the developments in information communications technology has reduced their impact. The decreasing costs of *interconnectivity* have increased their importance. The use of EDI and web-based communications has reduced both the time as well as costs of transactions management thereby making it possible to expand supply and manufacturing bases across international boundaries. Porter revisited clusters (1998) and offered the following definition:

broader than industries, capture important linkages, complementarities, and slipovers of technology, skills, information, marketing and customer

needs that cut across firms and industries . . . Such connections are fundamental to competition, to productivity, and especially to the direction and
pace of new business formation and innovation.

In a broader context it can be argued that clusters comprise an effective combination of knowledge, technology, relationship and process management, that
together, in a particular combination, provide an 'organization' with the means
of developing competitive advantage. The important issue is that success is
driven by entrepreneurial vision, a vision that identifies not only the opportunities but the unique (or exclusive) alternatives for combining 'cluster capabilities', assets and resources that achieve both customer and corporate satisfaction.

Value nets

Parolini (1999) argues that the changes in the business environment require
a new or different approach to strategic analysis, suggesting that models
developed in the 1970s and 1980s are limited in a fundamentally different
economic paradigm. Parolini (as does Dunning 1997) comments on the
changes in 'strategic boundaries', suggesting that the 'new business model' is
characterized by an emphasis on specialization *and* a capacity to identify and
participate in alliance networks. For Parolini a shift in emphasis has occurred
(at least amongst the successful organizations) in which the focus has shifted
from the inward-enterprise-focussed perspective to an outward customer
focus that considers how additional value (relative to that offered by competitors) can be delivered to customers via *value-creating systems.*

Value-creating systems were identified by Normann and Ramirez (1993)
who argued that successful companies focus their strategic analysis and decisions on the value-creating system (VCS) – the suppliers, business partners
and customers – and how they can work together to *co-produce* value.

Bovet and Martha (2000) use the term *value nets* in an argument suggesting them to be: 'a business design that uses advanced supply chain concepts
to achieve both superior customer satisfaction and company profitability'.
And 'a value net begins with customers, allows them to self-design products,
and builds to satisfy actual demand'. The customer (business unit) is central
to the decision process surrounded by the company (or business unit) which
in turn is surrounded by a constellation of providers that perform some or all
of the sourcing, assembly and delivery activities.

Sawhney and Parikh (2001) ask questions concerning value trends in the
network age. They contend that value in a networked world behaves very
differently than it does in the traditional, bounded world. They suggest the
elements of infrastructure that were once distributed among different
machines, organizational units and companies will be brought together.

Shared infrastructure (*value in common infrastructure*) will include not only basic information storage and dissemination but common functions such as order management, and 'even manufacturing and customer service'.

They also suggest *value in modularity* as a trend. Here their concern is with the entire range of 'Devices, software, organizational capabilities and business processes'. These will be 'restructured as well-defined, self-contained modules' and 'value will lie in creating modules that can be plugged into as many different value chains as possible'. Examples of modularization can found in automobile production. And they conclude: 'value in orchestration' will become 'the most valuable business skill'. Modularization will require an organizational ability and the authors suggest: 'Much of the competition in the business world will centre on gaining and maintaining the orchestration role for a value chain or an industry'.

A fundamental difference between the 'value-creation system' model and Porter's value chain model is that the VCS is considered to be a set of value-creating activities (rather than companies), and these activities are defined from the final customers point of view. It is argued that:

> Taking the VCS as the focal point of strategic analysis is of utmost importance for those companies who want to avoid being trapped in outdated perspectives as to how to compete in their particular industry, and which understand that there is little sense in enjoying a strong competitive position and having a high bargaining power in relation to their direct customers, if they (and their customers) form part of a losing system. (Parolini 1999)

This assumes that all organizations are primarily customer-focused. Value net analysts assume that if customer satisfaction is maximized then so too is shareholder value – or perhaps (as the arguments of many suggest) shareholder interests are ignored!! This approach clearly has problems. Understanding customer expectations is essential, but the argument that by meeting them precisely you will guarantee shareholder satisfaction does not follow. Many practitioners would argue that corporate expectations are the overriding consideration and that provided these are met the parameters of shareholder value are satisfied. This may imply that often customer value expectations are optimized within constraints set by corporate value drivers and that marketing objectives such as market share revised, but, they argue the business will remain viable.

The value chain

The value chain approach offers a model that includes both customer and corporate expectations. It offers a means to undertake strategic and operational analysis of an opportunity at a macro (process) level and at a micro (activity) level. As with the value net approach it starts with an assumption that there are no constraints on *how* the customers' value expectations may be met. But then adds the constraint that unless the innovator/visionary organization together with its partner organizations meet specific financial objectives the VCS (the value chain system) cannot survive. Furthermore, it is argued that free cash flow is the primary requirement for success. *This view is based on the simple premise (discussed earlier) that profit – in all its variants – is opinion: cash flow is fact!*

The value chain: integrated demand and supply chains

Supply chain management supporters have argued that that the supply chain has attempted to meet all the changes identified within the new economy. *Supply chain management* has focussed on moving products and services *downstream* towards the customer. Typically the supply chain is coordinated by manufacturing companies or dominant resellers who use in-house manufacturing and distribution facilities to achieve market-based objectives such as market share volumes and customer penetration. *Demand chain management* changes the emphasis towards 'customization', *responding* to product and service opportunities offered by specific customers or customer groups sharing particular characteristics. The preference is to outsource rather than own the functions and processes that facilitate and deliver value. Focus is on asset leverage and communication through distributed assets and outsourcing. *There is a large incentive to integrate supply and demand chains* – it provides new opportunities for creating (or adding extra) market value. Working both together results in more specific and manageable value propositions and increases the returns to the value-chain participants. There is an interdependent relationship between supply and demand: companies need to understand customer demand before they can manage it, create future demand and, of course, meet the level of desired customer satisfaction. Demand defines the supply-chain target, while supply-side capabilities support, shape and sustain demand.

Implications for marketing and financial management operations

The value-creation system, by definition, is a virtual approach. It suggests that corporate boundaries can be (and typically are) extended by partnership and alliance arrangements. Figure 5.15 shows this approach. Figure 5.15 is a typical example of the structure of virtual organizations within the Australian wine industry. Within the *existing structure* the organization operates with its core processes and coordinates these very closely and at the same time keeping in

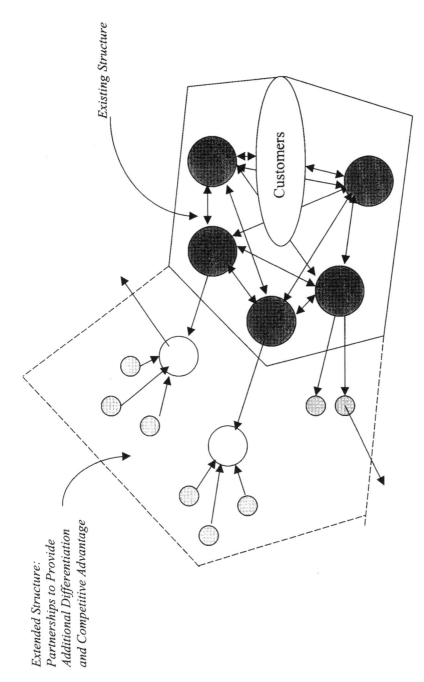

Existing Structure

Extended Structure:
Partnerships to Provide
Additional Differentiation
and Competitive Advantage

Customers

Figure 5.15   The value net enables the organization to extend beyond its traditional boundaries

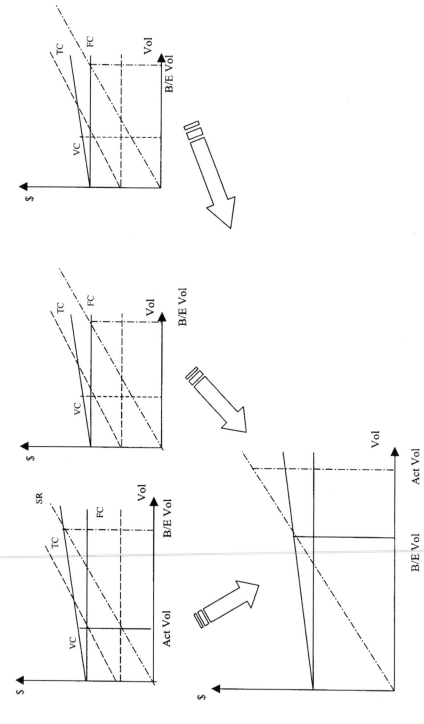

Figure 5.16 Reducing the burden of fixed costs (and financial risk) by using outsourced supply for low volume product/services

very close contact with its customer base. Non-core processes such as grape growing and processing, bottling and distribution etc. are outsourced to partner organizations – *the extended structure*. As the diagram suggests, these may be a range of processes each of which may well have a structure of partnerships, and some may be linked with other networks. The principle of the approach is described by Figure 5.16. As the diagram suggests there are often processes that are capital-intensive for which individual investment is not feasible as the break-even volume levels are unlikely to be achieved. It follows that by supporting process specialists, and achieving large aggregate volumes economies can be shared. In some industries agreement is reached where by the initial investment is shared by each of the users and it is not unknown for an ongoing fixed charge to be made to support the specialist's costs.

Much the same arrangement and understanding is reached in those industries where customers expect a form of customization (or differentiation). Small specialist organizations exist to add value in the form of product features or service characteristics. This is elaborated in Figure 5.17. Here the example given is one of additional differentiation that is outwith the capability of a main supplier. Perhaps the volume requirements are insufficient for an economical operation, or perhaps the process(es) are patented, either way the process will be outsourced. Management's task is twofold: to ensure that the process is managed in the context of quality fit and customer expectations, and to manage the overall process flow (coordination) to meet corporate, partner and customer objectives.

Procurement has become a process that many organizations outsource. The rapid expansion of information communications technology (ICT) capability accompanied by what appear to be a constant reduction in costs has led to the growth of large Internet-based buying consortia or exchanges. Again sharing the fixed and operating costs can have huge economies. The auto-industry's COVISNET, a Ford/GM initiative, was launched with suggestions that by using the buying exchange cost savings in the region of $1,000.00 per vehicle were envisaged!

Value systems

Value systems identify the links between the value chains of the companies or organizations engaged in the industry. Their purpose is to identify overlapping activities (or applications of activities) within participants in the supply chain, and to evaluate the potential for interorganizational trade-off arrangements. Value systems can therefore be used to evaluate a range of distribution/delivery alternatives against channel performance requirements and resource utilization.

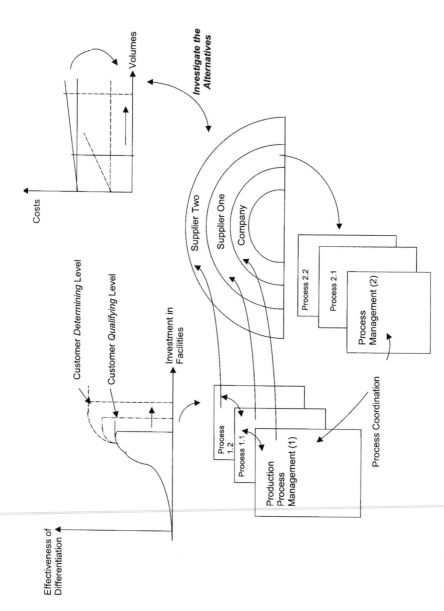

Figure 5.17 Managing processes across a range of suppliers to achieve a realistic volume/cost profile

Certainly as far as a particular organization is concerned it should be possible to establish cost profiles for its internal value chains, and provided managers can obtain the cooperation of suppliers and distributors (and ensure the confidential treatment of their information), it is often possible to construct profiles of their value chains. From this information a cost-effective and therefore optimal delivery system can be identified in which tasks are not repeated unnecessarily, but are undertaken at the most relevant point within the supply chain. The purpose of value added and value chain analysis is simple: it is to ensure that customers' productservice expectations are delivered using optimal resources. As such it implies that the marketing strategy is implemented at a level of profitability throughout the supply chain which is acceptable to *all members*. To be effective the analysis requires an understanding of cost structures throughout the value system and their implications at (and for) all levels of the delivery system. In addition the operational manager must be able to recognize and understand the implications of economies-of-scale and experience-effect cost profiles.

Recent developments within business organization design and behavioural relationships suggest that alliances and partnership arrangements are being established using the principles of the value chain and the value added chain. It is here that Hosking's views have application. Given the approach in which management assumes there are no fixed costs (regardless of the time spans involved), all costs are considered to be variable. It follows that operational choices become wider because management is no longer required to work within, and be constrained by, a fixed cost structure or an investment in infrastructure that it finds essential to continue operating. Thus if it can be established that the current operational strategy is becoming inefficient, and that to continue may result in costs increasing at a greater rate than revenues, then clearly changes should be made to ensure a more effective use of resources. The notion of 'unchangeable fixed costs' can prove to be a severe constraint requiring creative management solutions which change the nature (and often the 'ownership') of the fixed costs. The result of reconsidering fixed costs might not only simply restore the organization to profit but could well result in an enhanced level of profitability. The growth of many organizations through the use of franchising is an example. By selling the assets of a business to existing employee managers, who become 'owner operators', and agreeing to contractual arrangements for product supplies, the franchisor (as the business has now become) retains revenues, profits and cash flow, and at the same time restructures the fixed costs of the original business. Typically sales increase as the owner operators become more entrepreneurial.

5.5   Product and production decisions

Measuring product profitability: the importance of contribution

Cost categories have already been discussed at some length. It will be recalled that an important distinction was made between fixed and variable costs. The distinction between fixed and variable costs we have referred to is important when management is considering extending (or rationalizing) a product range. To make the decision process more effective we can consider *direct* and *indirect* fixed costs of producing a product. Direct costs may be attributable to the product, territory or perhaps customer. These should be allocated on some non-arbitrary basis (i.e., not the traditional 'machine hours' basis) and by doing so we obtain a much clearer view of the 'value' of the product to the business. This contribution analysis requires a number of information inputs:

sales

less variable costs of goods sold (raw materials, components, labour, etc.)

equals gross profit/margin (%)

less other variable costs (distribution and logistics)

equals contribution margin fixed

less direct fixed costs (allocatable fixed costs, R&D, selling, specific promotion and advertising, depreciation)

equals total contribution

less indirect fixed costs (non-allocatable fixed costs, corporate advertising and PR, general and administrative overhead)

equals operating profit

An example will demonstrate the usefulness of contribution analysis. Wombat Holding has four product groups, the costs of which are shown as follows:

	Total ($000)	A	B	C	D
Sales	11,600	2,100	6,000	3,000	500
Variable costs of goods sold	4,050	1,000	2,000	950	100
Gross profit/margin	7,550	1,100	4,000	2,050	400
Other variable costs	550	100	300	150	0
Contribution margin	7,000	1,000	3,700	1,900	400
Direct fixed costs:					
R&D	1,250	50	900	300	0
Selling and promotion	1,000	0	750	250	0
Production	1,700	250	850	575	25
Depreciation	750	100	500	150	0
	4,700	400	3,000	1,275	25
Total contribution	2,300	600	700	625	375
Indirect fixed costs:	750				
Corporate communications	1,500				
General and administrative overhead					
Total	2,250				
Operating profit	50				

If we now consider the contribution margins we are able to identify the responses of products if their sales were expanded (contribution margin being exposed by (price–variable cost)/price):

	A	B	C	D
Unit sales	28,000	40,000	20,000	50,000
Average price paid	75.00	150.00	150.00	$10.00
Variable cost per unit	39.27	57.50	55.00	$2.00
Contribution per unit (Average price – variable cost)	35.72	92.50	95.00	$8.00
Contribution margin	47.5%	61.5%	63.5%	80%

We see that products A and C are responsible for a large joint contribution – very nearly as large as that from B. The reason for this is the amount of the direct fixed costs that 'B' attracts. The analysis also indicates the additional contribution each product group would add if sales were expanded.

The profitability structure of products also enables us to identify cost–volume–profit relationships and the implications for product range decisions.

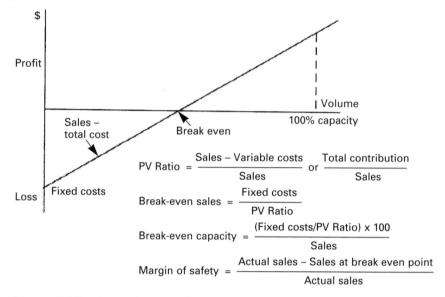

Figure 5.18   Cost–volume–profit

The cost–volume–profit model

The concept of break-even analysis was introduced earlier in this chapter and we return to it to consider how it may help with product decisions.

Break-even models can be reconfigured to show their cost–volume–profit (C–V–P) relationship as shown in Figure 5.18. Here we consider a simple application of a one-product firm. The vertical axis shows profit and loss while the horizontal axis indicates volume – this may be restricted to maximum or desired capacity. The C–V–P graph plots the profit earned at various levels of output with break even occurring at the point where profit equals zero. An important feature is the *profit/volume (P/V) ratio*, which is calculated by:

$$\frac{\text{Sales} - \text{Variable costs}}{\text{Sales}}$$

This is a measure of the contribution made to overhead (fixed costs) and profit.

There are a number of applications for C–V–P analysis. Figure 5.19 illustrates one use. By calculating first the revenue and profit performance expectations at various capacity levels, and then estimating the probabilities of achieving the sales forecast, we can, by using the probability values, derive an overall expected profit and capacity utilization level for the organization. This

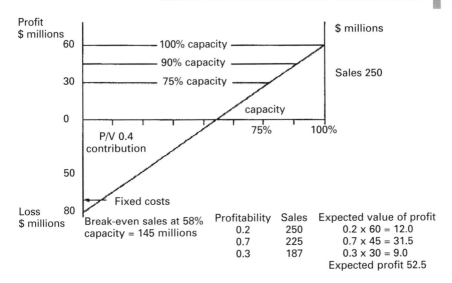

Figure 5.19   Determining an expected value profit figure

exercise should be repeated for different price levels (which would of course influence the probability factors) and a decision made concerning an optimum C–V–P influenced by market share requirements, capacity utilization and profit margin requirements. See Table 5.1 for revenues and costs.

The analysis can be extended to consider the impact of adding additional shifts which will increase the effective plant capacity. In Figure 5.20 we show an 'increase' in capacity of 25 per cent. If the same contribution can be maintained (P/V = 0.4), then profit of $75 million can be generated. However, Figure 5.19 also suggests that a price decrease of 10 per cent in order to achieve the sales forecast will result in a lower contribution (P/V = 0.3), a higher break-even volume and considerably lower profit. Note that the dollar value of the variable costs remains the same, hence the margin realized is appreciably lower. Sales at existing prices are valued at $312.5 million; with a 10 per cent price reduction the value is $281.3 million. Clearly the decision

Table 5.1   Cost–volume profit: variable capacity volumes

	($millions)		
Sales	250	312.5	281.3
Variable costs	150	187.5	187.5
Contribution	100	125	93.8
Fixed costs	80	80	80
P/V ratio	0.4	0.4	0.3

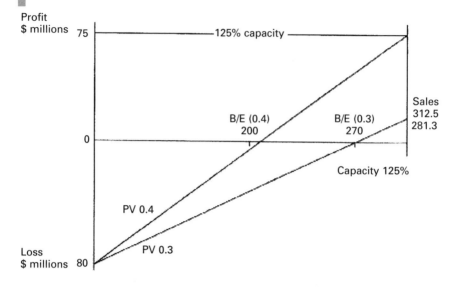

Figure 5.20   Effect of increasing capacity

to add the extra shifts is questionable and much would depend on whether controllable variable costs could be reduced to an 'experience effect'. As the volume increase is relatively small (i.e., not doubled) it is unlikely that this would occur.

We can also consider the effects of plant replacement. Here the choice may be to increase plant capacity but also increase fixed costs. Table 5.2 details revenues and costs. As the calculation demonstrates, the break-even sales value is higher ($250 million compared with $200 million) but so too is the full capacity profit. However, if it is possible to obtain the additional product volume by outsourcing (and therefore without incurring additional fixed costs) the profitability would be greater.

Table 5.2   Cost–volume profit: plant replacement

	($millions)		
Sales	250	335	+33⅓%
Variable costs	150	200	+33⅓%
Contribution	100	135	
Fixed costs	80	100	
Profit	20	35	
P/V ratio	0.4	0.4	
Break-even sales	200	250	

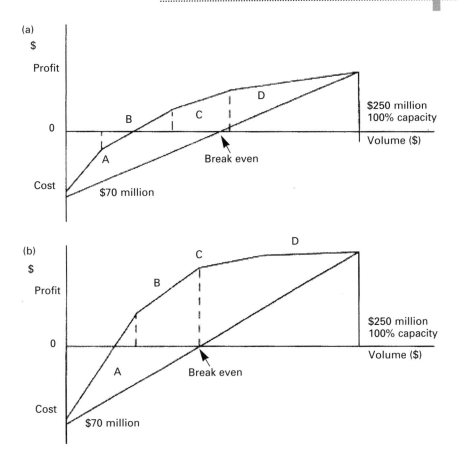

Figure 5.21 Product mix decisions

The simple C–V–P model can be extended to include more than one product and to consider product mix alternatives. Figure 5.21 illustrates a product mix of four products, each with a different P/V ratio. In Figure 5.21(a) we have the standard product sales/profit performance. However, if sales of A and B could be improved, then within the same capacity constraints the C–V–P profile will be improved (see Table 5.3 for details). Three changes have been made by restructuring the product profit mix. One is an increase in the weighted average P/V ratio (an increase of 16 per cent); the second is the earlier realization of the break-even volume and the third is a substantial increase in overall profitability of 37.5 per cent. We have made some assumptions here. Firstly, we have assumed that there have been no pricing effects and that the changes in volume participation have resulted in the same total revenue; and, secondly, we have assumed no changes to have occurred to

Table 5.3　Cost–volume profit: product mix decisions

(a)　Initial product profit mix

Product	$millions	%	P/V	Weighted average/P/V ratio
A	25.0	10	0.7	0.07
B	50.0	20	0.5	0.10
C	62.5	25	0.4	0.10
D	112.5	45	0.3	0.135
	250.0	100	–	0.405

(b)　Restructured product profit mix

Product	$millions	%	P/V	Weighted average/P/V ratio
A	75.0	25	0.7	0.175
B	62.5	25	0.5	0.125
C	62.5	20	0.4	0.08
D	50.0	30	0.3	0.09
	250.0	100		0.477

fixed or variable costs. It is likely that some pricing changes would occur, but the point of this example is simply to illustrate that a review of the product volume participation (and changes that may be made (assuming they are realistic and feasible in market terms)) will result in changes of the kind suggested in Figure 5.21. Again changes in which fixed costs are maintained, or reduced, will result in improved P/V ratios and, therefore, profitability.

Value analysis

One other aspect of product management is worth a mention. *Value analysis* is a cost reduction activity based upon the identification of physical dimensions that can be redesigned, standardized (in terms of physical dimensions or end-use application) or cheapened by using lower cost materials or production methods. The Pareto effect is quite often observed in manufacturing economics as it does in sales patterns; that is, that 20 per cent of the components will comprise some 80 per cent of the total costs. Value analysis is approached by considering five basic questions:

(i)　Can non-standard parts be redesigned so that they become standard parts? If so what will be the impact on product performance as well as on cost?

(ii)   Can a non-standard part be replaced by a standard part?

(iii) Can two or more parts be replaced by one part?

(iv)   Can component materials be substituted by lower cost materials (e.g., advanced plastics for metals) or materials that have lower cost production methods?

(v)   Can the organization work with suppliers to manufacture components at lower costs by improving production methods or by increasing volumes?

The benefit of value analysis or value engineering (an alternative name) can be extended by examining economies of scale and experience effects and applying both concepts to manufacturing problems of cost control. The objective of value analysis is to maintain full value to the customer while reducing the cost of providing the value. Figure 5.22 illustrates value analysis.

Product range management

Product range management is not dissimilar to value analysis in that often a review of end-user applications of products reveals that some products may have multiple applications. It follows that these should be investigated and, where at all possible, customers should be made aware of the opportunities. There are a number of mutual benefits for both customer and producer. An obvious one comes from the volume effect of buying more standard items and therefore lowering overall costs. Inventory holding cost benefits arise because fewer stock keeping units (SKUs) need to be maintained, and fewer SKUs implies less storage capacity requirements.

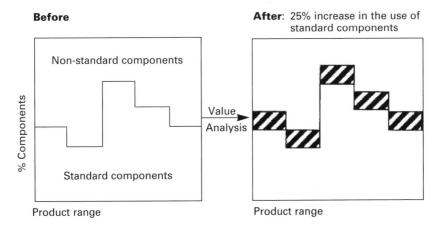

Figure 5.22   Value analysis increases profitability

Another aspect of product range management is range rationalization of slow-moving products. Often a wide range of products is necessary in order that credibility as a supplier is created and maintained. This is not unusual in retailing, nor is it unusual in f.m.c.g. manufacturing where the objective is to dominate the retailers' display areas and selling space. Therefore in some circumstances the costs of maintaining unprofitable parts of the product range are acceptable and may be considered in part, at least, as promotional costs.

As with value analysis of components so too we may find that – products in the market decline phase – can be substituted by other products. In Figure 5.23 we illustrate a common situation in which a product range might be rationalized. In this situation two items, products 6 and 7, might be considered for elimination and products 3, 4 and 5 considered as substitute or alternative components. Thus while some costs will be eliminated, it must be remembered that the fixed costs attached to the overall product range will remain and must now be recovered from sales by fewer products. Typically the volume increases (particularly the increases of items 3, 4 and 5) will compensate and the cover will be generated. However, this should not be taken as an obvious outcome and the situation of fixed cost recovery must be investigated prior to taking any range rationalization decisions. Again alternatives may exist and the fixed cost element of these slow-moving products transferred to an external supplier. This would enable their continuing presence in the range.

Direct product profitability (DPP) and customer account profitability (CAP)

Direct product profitability is a calculation method used by a number of companies in order to separate profit contribution from the sale of a product or product range. Essentially, the analysis attempts to allocate costs involved in moving the product from the point of manufacture to the point of sale. Two approaches have been taken to resolve the problem but from different perspectives. The manufacturers' perspective has been to identify total costs from point of manufacture, through finished goods storage and the physical distribution channel into retailing distribution systems and eventually onto the store's selling fixtures. In many ways this has more to do with customer profitability since these costs are typically incurred during customer transactions, but the reality is that if costs can be identified and perhaps reduced then the resulting productivity can be shared with intermediary customers and used as a component of competitive advantage (see Figure 5.24).

The retailers' approach is directed towards minimizing costs and is a

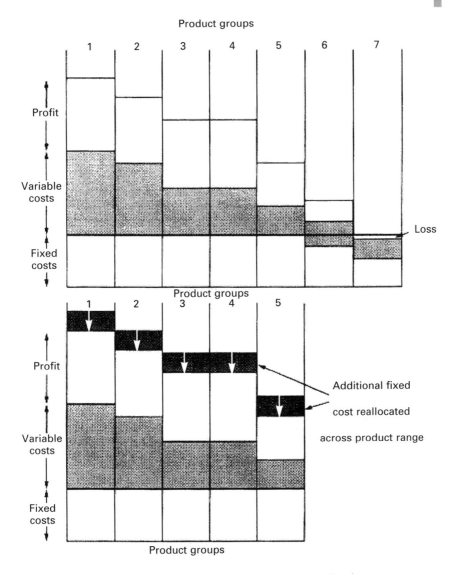

Figure 5.23 Impact of product range rationalization on fixed costs

component in the space allocation exercise. Thus, while retailers' interests are clearly concerned with cost minimization, they are also concerned to ensure that the financial return on space allocated to the product is maximized. It follows that if the rate of sale of a product related to the space utilized is attractive, the retailer may accept higher costs (lower DPP) because the cash value of the sale of the product (as opposed to the *percentage* of costs) makes a contribution larger than that of competitive products.

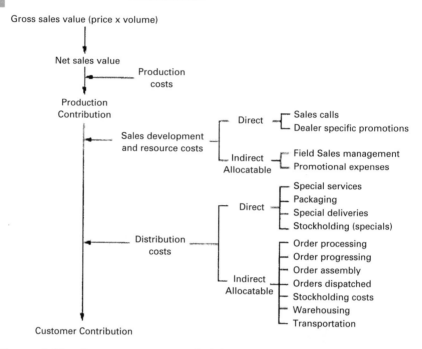

Gross sales value (price x volume)

Net sales value ——— Production costs

Production Contribution

Sales development and resource costs
- Direct
  - Sales calls
  - Dealer specific promotions
- Indirect Allocatable
  - Field Sales management
  - Promotional expenses

Distribution costs
- Direct
  - Special services
  - Packaging
  - Special deliveries
  - Stockholding (specials)
- Indirect Allocatable
  - Order processing
  - Order progressing
  - Order assembly
  - Orders dispatched
  - Stockholding costs
  - Warehousing
  - Transportation

Customer Contribution

Figure 5.24　Customer account profitability model

Typically, this situation occurs for brand leader products and often in complementary/support sales situations.

The decision to stock a brand/product by the retailer (and the ultimate profitability for the supplier) is influenced by two factors: the 'real' gross margin and the 'delivery' costs. Retail gross margins may be enhanced by the addition of discounts and allowances based upon order size. For example, it is not unusual for mainline grocery brand margins to be more than doubled in the following way:

	Purchase Price (%)
Basic gross margin	10.0
Cooperative advertising allowance	5.0
Merchandising allowance	2.0
Quantity (volume) discount	2.5
Cash discount: prompt payment	2.5
Forward buying saving	2.5
'Real' gross margin	24.5

Such incentives are clearly directed towards large retail customers. However, some of the allowances may be illegal in some countries. For example, in the

United States anti-trust law is very specific in this context and requires that all customers be made the same offer notwithstanding the fact that only a few could take advantage of it.

Direct product profitability is usually derived by identifying *direct product costs*, such as warehousing, transportation, storage and head office (overhead costs). A typical example shows the delivered margin may approach 50 per cent of the gross margin:

	Purchase price (%)
Base gross margin	19
less direct costs of:	
Warehousing	2
Transportation	1
Storage	5
Head office (overhead)	2
	10
Actual (delivered) margin	9

Clearly DPP is an important consideration for both suppliers and distributors. Christopher (1992) presented comparison data for a range of superstore products, some of which were quite revealing for both supplier and retailer:

	Gross margin (%)	DPP (%)	Average DDP/ square metre (%)
Paper products	19	7.2	0.47
Frozen vegetables	34	23.1	2.60
Cigarettes	12	13.2	6.56
Dentifrice	31	18.6	1.42
Facial tissues	15	–	(0.01)

The wide range of margins is most noticeable, as is the range of costs and the impact on profit/space. Some products – facial tissues being one – are clearly sold at an accounting loss in order that customers' choice and range expectations are met.

There are a number of ways in which the DPP of both product ranges and individual products can be improved. Pack design is one favoured by many manufacturers: often pack design is a sales incentive feature rather than a design for cube economy. Adjustments to pack size in order to avoid pallet overhang eliminates damaged product costs.

Clothing retailers have eliminated a considerable cost penalty involved in pressing clothes (at the point of sale) prior to display by delivering products ready for immediate display. Additional equipment is required and a loss of transport cube occurs; however, the trade-off proves to be economically viable.

Range rationalization often resolves many of the problems identified by DPP analysis. Boots (a UK chemist/pharmacy/retail chain) deleted the whole of its petfood and related products range following evidence from a DPP study. Woolworth (a UK variety chain subsidiary of Kingfisher PLC) has made extensive use of DPP to trim its merchandise assortment. The technique was particularly helpful in weeding out unprofitable products in its garden centre range.

However, there are a number of aspects to this rationalization task. Managers need to identify those elements of customer service and order handling expected by the customer; their relative importance; the cost of providing such services; any trade-off opportunities there might be between and among the service characteristics and the channel members involved in effecting 'delivery'; and the customers' relative perceptions of competitive offers. Even before such detailed analysis is undertaken, other more fundamental factors must be examined. These include the volume of business conducted with customers and whether there are indications that the customer base may be segmented in such a way that facilities exist for developing both service offers and methods by which they may be costed. A structured approach should be taken, commencing with an examination of a particular combination of customers – perhaps on a regional basis or by size, or, more likely, by channel of distribution. The segments or groups of customers should then be classified according to service needs, size or location (i.e., by variables other than those used for the initial classification), characteristics which are shared by the group but differ between categories. Within the categories individual customer accounts should be reviewed.

As a guide there are a number of principles which underlie the process and which it would be helpful to bear in mind during the analysis:

- *The individual customer order is the ultimate profit centre.* In other words, all costs incurred by the organization in supplying its goods/services are related ultimately to the customer's orders received. In an ideal world each order would be profitable or, at a minimum, the total trade with each customer would be profitable.
- Within an existing product/market structure, profitability is largely determined by *what happens after the product is manufactured* – that is, the efficiency with which the product is passed along to the next stage of the supply chain.

- Costs incurred after manufacture can be directly related to the servicing of an individual order.
- Although the average cost of servicing a customer is easily calculated, *it is how such costs vary by customer, order size, order type, and so forth, that is significant.* It is important to be aware of the customers who are at the extremes of the cost range.
- When considering costs and profits, managers must realize that most cost elements have both fixed and variable components, and that the profit per transaction is influenced not only by customer-orientated costs but also by sales discounts, allowances, returned goods policies, and other revenue-influencing factors which produce gross margin per order.
- Profit is influenced by both costs and revenue-producing policies.
- Customer profitability analysis requires a cost accounting system that attributes all costs forward to the revenue source, rather than back to factories, products, or their organizational units.

5.6 Summary

This chapter has considered a range of issues that are important to operational marketing decisions.

The first topic introduced concerned operational gearing – the cost structure of the production activity of the business. Here fixed and variable costs are important issues and are influenced by business and financial risk and control requirements of management. Break-even analysis was introduced to explore a number of related topics.

The experience effect (a learning effect) was introduced to discuss how knowledge of cost behaviour can influence pricing decisions and market-share objectives. We revisited economies of scale to discuss basic differences and their joint effect.

Value was introduced because delivering added value to customers has direct links to cost. The value added chain and the value chain were introduced and used to suggest how costs might be explored during the process of maximizing customer satisfaction and the implications for profitability. Within value chain analysis the role of cost pools and cost drivers is important because they enable the potential for trade-off to be identified across value chain activities, and when used in conjunction with activity based costing can be used for allocating overhead costs.

Break-even analysis was reintroduced to explore the cost–volume–profit model which was used to evaluate production and product performance decisions. This discussion led to value analysis, product range management and the examination of direct product profitability.

Finally, we considered customer account profitability (CAP) decisions and issues and outlined a CAP model.

REFERENCES

Bovet, D. and J. Martha (2000) *Value Nets: Breaking the Supply Chain to Unlock Hidden Profits*, Wiley, New York.

Christopher, M. (1992) *Logistics and Supply Chain Management*, Pitman, London.

Dunning, J. (1997) 'Governments and the Macro-Organization of Economic Activity: A Historical and Spatial Perspective' in J. Dunning (ed.) *Governments, Globalisation and International Business*, Oxford University Press.

Gattorna, J. and D. Walters (1996) *Supply Chain Management*, Macmillan, London.

Hayes, R. H. and Wheelwright, S. L. (1979) 'Matching Manufacturing Process and Product Life Cycles', *Harvard Business Review*, Jan./Feb.

Hosking, G. (1993) 'Strategic Management of Costs', *Planning Review*, Sept./Oct.

Normann, R. and R Ramirez (1993) *Designing Interactive Strategy: From Value Chain to Value Constellation*, Wiley, New York.

Parolini, C. (1999) *The Value Net*, Wiley, Chichester.

Porter, M. (1990) *The Competitive Advantage of Nations*, The Free Press, New York.

Porter, M. (1998) 'On Competition', *Harvard Business Review*, December.

Sawhney, M. and D. Parikh (2001) 'Where Value Lives in a Networked World', *Harvard Business Review*, January.

Walters, D. and C. Korkafingas (1997) 'Strategic Marketing Decisions and Cost Structure Implications', *Department of Economics Working Papers*, Macquarie University, February.

PART

III Financial Structure and Performance Characteristics

Part II dealt with cost structures and cost behaviour within the context of strategic and operational marketing decisions. The relationships that exist between marketing decisions and financial management now need to be explored in detail.

In Part III we introduce the reader to financial structure decisions that are important in a marketing context and which interrelate with marketing. An understanding of these relationships will result in satisfactory decisions and competitive advantage for the organization. We consider a number of topics including: managing working capital and the working capital cycle, managing the fixed asset base, cash flow management, financial structure, and investment decisions.

Shareholder value analysis: a key to overall performance

Shareholder value analysis is proposed by a number of authors as a fundamental factor in the performance measurement of a business. Aaker (1995) suggested shareholder value analysis 'is based on generating a discounted present value of the cash flow associated with a strategy ... However, it focuses attention on financial measures rather than other indicators of strategic performance.' Aaker continued by suggesting additional, non-performance measures, including: customer satisfaction, product/service quality, brand/company perceptions, relative cost, new product development activity, and management/employee capability and performance. Aaker's suggestion that these marketing considerations: 'Often provide better

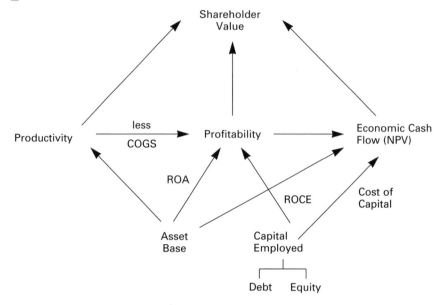

Figure III.1 Financial structure and shareholder value drivers

measures of long-term business health'. We suggest there is a link between the financial and marketing criteria. Rather than considering them as separate groups of criteria, they are mutually interdependent and performance is enhanced by viewing them as such.

Shareholder value then, is a combination of a number of factors and the model proposed in Chapter 1 (Figure 1.1) is re-presented as Figure III.1 to show the relationship between the shareholder value drivers and the organization's financial structure that influences the performance achieved. In Part III we discuss each of these in detail, but before doing so we look at each one briefly to demonstrate its influence on overall performance and to show why a working knowledge of each is useful.

The funds flow cycle

The essential element of finance for any business is cash. All firms use cash. Cash is used to pay employees and suppliers, and to meet operating expenses. Materials, components and labour are converted into products and services which are sold to customers. Typically, products and services are sold to customers on a credit basis (i.e., customers receive goods and services on the understanding that within an agreed time span they will pay the amount owing). In accounting terms the customers become debtors.

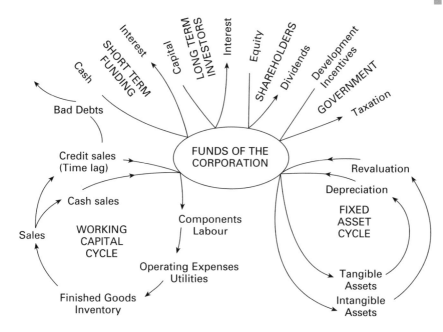

Figure III.2   Funds flow cycle: the importance of cash to the business

Eventually debtors pay the outstanding amounts in cash and this completes the *working capital cycle*. This is shown as a component of the funds flow cycle in Figure III.2. In much the same way, we purchase materials and services (other than labour) from suppliers on a credit basis (and as such are debtors to our suppliers) and eventually pay them in cash. We also purchase capital equipment or fixed assets and cash is used for this purpose, too. As we use the assets a charge is made against the profit generated for the use of the assets (depreciation). It is a non-cash expense and enables the organization to 'write-off' the cost of the capital equipment over its estimated useful life. Clearly if invoiced sales are greater than the cost of sales (including depreciation) the organization makes a profit. The important point being made here is that profit is based on invoices not cash: accounting profit is based upon sales less expenses not on cash balances. The profit reported in the profit and loss account is invoiced sales less the invoiced cost of sales plus depreciation. When fixed assets (plant and equipment) are purchased we deplete cash balances and when they are sold the cash balances are increased. However, the purchase of assets has no effect on profit until we charge depreciation. Inventories purchased for cash decrease cash balances but have no effect on profit until stock items are sold and invoiced. Depreciation reduces the profit and loss account but has no effect on cash balances. (Note: it is included in cash flow statements because, having reduced profit by the amount of depreciation charged, it must be added back, as profit is an element of cash flow.)

Cash generated from successful trading is not the only source of funds available to the organization. Financial institutions and the public lend funds, but they expect interest payments in return. Interest is accepted as a cost of doing business by government and as such it is charged against profits before tax is calculated. It should be noted that the government can and does provide funds in the form of grants and loans. After the payment of interest and tax what remains (if it is positive) is available for payment to shareholders as dividends. However, in an expanding business it is usual not to pass on all of the 'profit' to the shareholders but to use a proportion of it as funds for the growth of the business. We call this retained earnings and it is allocated to financial reserves. It is unrealistic to assume that 'reserves' actually contain cash amounts. The reported amount simply identifies the fact that over the years the company has traded successfully and that the dividends paid to the shareholders were less than the reported earnings. One last point: if the shareholders increase their investment in the business or if additional loans are taken, the effect is to increase the cash within the business but not the level of profit.

Shareholder value extends beyond cash flow and profitability. As we suggested in Chapter 1 and in subsequent chapters, shareholders' interests include growth, productivity and the economic cash flow generated by the business. Growth is a common factor to each of these characteristics and it should be understood that the growth rate should be such that the organization does not grow at an excessive rate, a rate that eventually results in the organization overcommitting itself to one or more of the stakeholders. There are numerous cases of businesses expanding without considering all of the factors involved in such a decision. For example, a common problem occurs when sales are expanded and customer credit is extended without establishing a credit policy. Typically, collection periods extend well beyond the industry average, resulting in a cash shortage which is often resolved by resorting to an increase in overdraft facilities. If these are allowed to become too large, concern is expressed by the bank and often repayment is demanded at a time when the company is unable to repay.

Shareholders' interests also include the productivity of the asset base – under-utilized assets usually suggest that much of the fixed cost burden of the company is not being recovered.

We shall consider these and other related issues, and discuss performance measures for shareholder value management in Chapter 6.

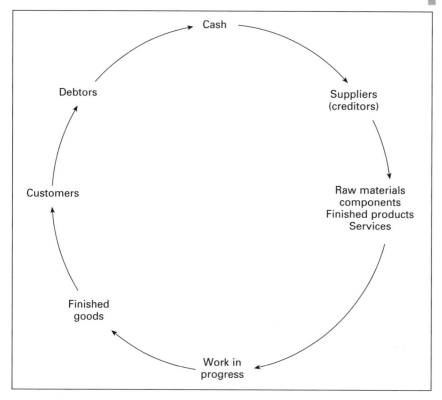

Figure III.3   Working capital cycle

The working capital cycle

Working capital is considered to be inventory, debtors and cash, which are the firm's current assets. Net current working capital (net current assets) is defined as current assets less current liabilities. Current liabilities include creditors, short-term loans and payments due within one year (such as dividends and taxation). Figure III.3 shows a detailed working capital cycle: cash is used to purchase raw materials, components or (in the case of distribution) finished products. After some form of 'value adding process' the end-product is sold to customers and they, as debtors, pay the firm in cash.

Some differences occur between manufacturers' and distributors' working capital cycles. Typically manufacturers add 'form utility value' to the inputs purchased whereas wholesalers and retailers (distributors' companies) purchase finished goods for resale and add 'place utility' as value. These differences have an impact on the rate at which cash moves through the working capital cycle. Materials and equipment purchased as components for capital equipment will clearly take longer to be processed and sold (and therefore be converted to cash) than products purchased for resale by a multiple food retailer. This raises the interesting concept of negative working capital, which is used to describe the situation that occurs when a distributor sells products purchased for resale before the supplier is paid. For example, consider a food retailer selling dairy products as part of an overall product range: supplies will be taken three or four times per week and sold at that rate, but the supplier will invoice the retailer on a monthly basis and, with payment terms of 30 or even 40 days, the retailer has extended use of its suppliers' working capital. Hence the term negative working capital. We shall return to this topic and a number of other working capital management issues in Chapter 7.

Managing fixed assets

Fixed assets are long-term resources of the business. They are purchased to provide (manufacture) goods or services over the period of their life span, rather than for resale. Fixed assets have differing characteristics. Some have finite lives. These may be prescribed by their physical characteristics or they may be determined legally. For example, plant and equipment usually has a planned life cycle over which it is used to manufacture products for sale to customers. In such cases there is a cost for using the fixed assets, and this is charged against profits generated over a period of operations as depreciation.

By contrast, some fixed assets do not 'wear out' and may appreciate in value. During the mid- to late 1980s land and property increased in value and many companies revalued their holdings of such assets, thereby increasing the value of the business.

For both forms of asset the life span may be determined by a lease or licence (as is the case for a patented product or process), which permits the use of the asset for an agreed period of time at an agreed level of payment.

Fixed assets are usually classified as tangible or intangible, or as investments. Tangible assets – land, buildings, plant and equipment – have already been discussed. *Intangible assets* include goodwill, brands, patents, copyrights and trademarks that are exclusive to the business. It is becoming common practice to capitalize the costs of obtaining these exclusive assets and other expenses hitherto seen as revenue expenses. For example, R&D and advertising etc. are considered intangible fixed asset expenditures materializing as brands. Investments, considered as fixed assets, include investments in subsidiary companies, investments in associated businesses and trade investments. Income from investments is separately identified in the company's profit and loss account. Chapter 8 discusses the management of fixed assets.

Managing cash flow and funds flows

There are two aspects to this topic – although they are interrelated. We have discussed an aspect of cash flow earlier in this section. Cash flow through the business is essential if the business is to function smoothly and over a long period of time. Companies forecast the amounts and timing of cash receipts and disbursements for a number of reasons. By forecasting the cash flows in and out of a business the financial viability of a project may be assessed prior to making specific commitments. Forecasting also identifies possible periods of time during a project life span when cash may be needed from external sources and therefore time is made available to arrange its supply at economical 'prices' – interest rates. Cash flow forecasts also identify periods when excess cash is available (to the levels required) and this may then be placed into short-term investments.

Funds flow analysis takes a macro view of changes in the funds, flowing in and out of the business. A funds flow statement shows an organization's new sources and uses of funds for its recent trading period. Various format and title differences exist and regularly undergo revision. Essentially funds flow analysis shows changes in funds allocated to current and fixed assets, funds from shareholders and external sources of funds and also includes profit and depreciation for the period. This analysis is usually referred to as the 'sources and applications of funds report'.

One other aspect of cash flow is the economic cash flow generated by the business from its portfolio of product services or activities. Economic cash flows are discounted at a specified interest rate which reflects the structure of the firm's financing and a view of the risk imposed by the industry sector in which it operates. We shall return to these topics.

Financial structure

Financing a business involves top management in determining the financial structure. These decisions have implications for the level of financial risk the 'executive' considers the organization should accept. The level of financial risk is directly proportional to the financial gearing of the firm.

Financial risk and gearing are concerned with the proportions of debt and equity in the organization's capital structure. Debt is funding loaned at an agreed interest rate by institutions and individuals whose involvement with the company is simply to receive agreed interest payments, at agreed times, and the repatriation of the amount when the term of the loan expires. These creditors have no influence in the company's governance or its strategic direction.

Equity funds are the funds raised from selling ordinary shares in the business. Ordinary shareholders are paid dividends (the amount being a board-level decision) and these together with share price appreciation are the immediate returns to the shareholder.

It follows then that gearing implies borrowing to finance the business rather than using only equity capital. A major consideration is the fact that debt funding involves the organization in an ongoing commitment to meet interest payments on a regular basis regardless of the level of success (or maybe lack of success) of the project for which the funds were borrowed. Clearly if the return generated by assets funded by debt exceeds the cost of borrowing the 'profit' benefits the shareholders.

There is a view of gearing that suggests there is an optimal range of capital structure (equity/debt combinations) over which the cost of capital (the interest rate required by investors) will vary only by very small amounts and that the market value of the firm, calculated by multiplying shares on issue by their current market price, may be increased by increasing the gearing of the company. Figure III.4 shows these effects.

We shall return to this topic in Chapter 10. It is clear at this point that marketing decisions calling for large amounts of funding could have serious implications for the organization. A project involving the business in new productmarkets, or perhaps new demand technology life cycles, will have a larger level of business risk than market penetration. The impact on financial risk may also be significant if external funding is required to finance the project.

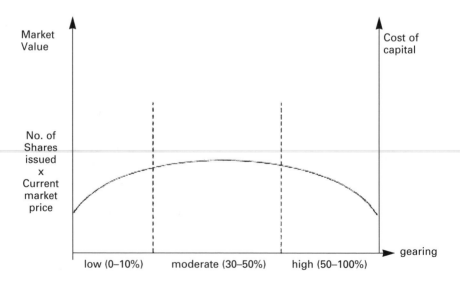

Figure III.4   Gearing, market value and cost of capital

Investment decisions: managing economic cash flow

One of the criteria used to measure the extent by which the value of the business has changed is economic cash flow. Managing economic cash flow comprises identifying, defining and evaluating long-term investment opportunities. The characteristics of these opportunities may vary. They may be expansion projects involving the business in new product-markets and adding to its production capability and capacity. Alternatively it may consist of investment aimed at reducing existing production costs without necessarily adding to the production capacity of the business. All investments, regardless of their size, have the same basic objective. Cash is sacrificed now with the expectation of increased cash returns at some time in the future.

There are a number of methods used to evaluate investment decisions and these will be considered in Chapter 11. Our particular interests are focused on the future value of cash flows which will be generated by investment projects commenced at the current time. The method favoured is to consider the 'time value' of money and adjust its future value to a current value, or its 'present value'.

The method used is essentially simple. The cash flows (both revenues and costs) associated with a project are forecast for the period of its life cycle. Clearly, the cash generated in year ten of a project will not have the same value as that generated in year one, simply because we could reinvest the cash generated in the first year and earn interest (at some prescribed rate) which would result in a larger value as the amount earns interest over the ten-year period.

Management requires an estimate of likely returns on projects, particularly when it has limited resources. Economic cash flows measure the present value of projects by applying a discount rate to the cash flow streams of project proposals in order to evaluate alternatives and to select those most suitable to its objectives and its resources. The method of evaluating cash flows over time is more complex and will be explored in more detail in Chapter 11. At this juncture we seek to establish what economic cash flows are. How they are measured will be dealt with in Chapter 11.

Performance measurement

We have discussed a number of financial management issues in this section. Figure III.5 suggests a series of ratios from which the overall assessment of performance may be appraised. Figure III.5 uses the assumption that shareholder value is influenced by overall performance across a

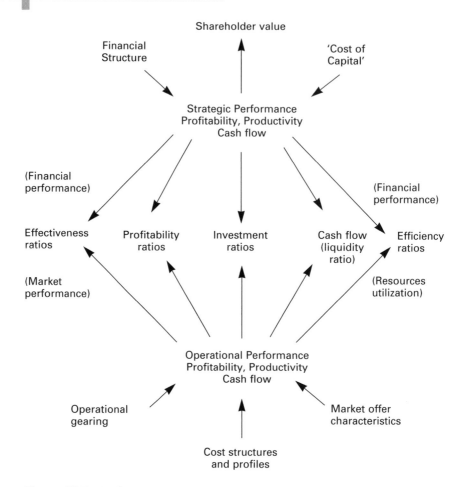

Figure III.5 Performance ratios

number of indicators, which measure profitability, productivity and cash flow. The measures proposed consider both strategic and operational performance.

Strategic performance is influenced by the company financial structure and its cost of capital. At an operational level there are a number of factors which will influence performance. These are operational gearing, economies of scale and experience effects, product mix decisions, end-user applications identified and met, and the market (and/or) segment penetration levels. These are the product-market scope characteristics and the result of the resource allocation decisions introduced in Chapter 3.

Performance measurement is comprised of a range of topics. Essentially, we are considering the effectiveness and efficiency of management decisions.

Earlier, it will be recalled, we defined effectiveness as a proactive activity in which strategic resource allocation decisions are taken with a view to achieving an optimized performance of the business. Efficiency involves ensuring the operational/implementation activities are performed to plan (i.e., to budget and within the time allotted). Performance measures comprise a range of topics.

Effectiveness is measured for both financial and marketing performance. Financial measures will include returns earned on total capital employed (ROCE) and shareholders' equity (ROE). It may also include measures such as sales and profit per sales area and employee (for distributors) or perhaps for product group for manufacturers. Marketing effectiveness may be measured by market share obtained, customer perception responses, sales from new products, sales penetration by channel/distributor type or by territory or customer type. Profitability performance is usually measured by the relevant margins. The importance of these may vary by type of business. Retailing favours gross margins and operating margins together with net margin, while manufacturing companies use a comprehensive cost of sales measure which varies (but includes cost items of relevance to the business) and will include the measure of operating and net margins.

Efficiency measures the utilization of corporate resources and these are represented by fixed assets and working capital items. Again the measures used may vary by the type of activities in which the firm is involved. For example, distribution businesses focus on stock turn because this measures the efficiency of both retail operations and distribution activities and to a degree the performance of the buying function. Manufacturing companies may be more concerned with capacity utilization because often the marketing strategy is based upon achieving sales from a specified throughput volume (and therefore level of cost) which enables promotional activities to be funded, competitive prices to be set and adequate profit margins generated.

Investment performance usually reflects value generated by the business. Measures may be the conventional *earnings per share (EPS)* or by *price earnings ratio (PER)*, both of which are reported in the financial press on a daily basis. Other ratios include the markettobook ratio (shares issued multiplied by current share price divided by the value of the company's assets). A positive value indicates that the market values the shares of the firm at a greater value than its assets and consequently the business is seen as adding value for the shareholders. The *market value added (MVA)* measure does much the same. It is calculated by adding the market value of the company's shares to existing debt and subtracting the capital invested in the business. Again a positive value will indicate a value generating business. *Economic value added (EVA)* subtracts the cost of capital from the after-tax operating profit for the period (cost of capital being calculated by multiplying capital employed by a relevant weighted cost of capital usually adjusted for industry sector risk). A positive value indicates value has been added during the period. EVA is more oriented towards the current period or recent past while MVA is arguably more future oriented as the share price, theoretically, reflects investors' views of future prospects for the firm. 'Returns spreads' are measures of the return generated (either from total capital employed or an equity) once the cost of the capital or equity has been subtracted. The argument made, once again, is that if the return spread is positive the company's activities have been adding value not destroying value in the business.

Cash flow is measured for long- and short-term periods. Measures used may need to be comprehensive. Over the conventional trading period the sources and applications of funds data together with current and quick ratios (applied to current assets and liabilities) are helpful. However, with shareholder value in mind a more significant measure may be the economic cash flow because this will consider the influence of an appropriate discount factor to adjust the cash flows to present value amounts. Each of these topics will be discussed in detail in Chapter 6. A summary of performance measures is given in Figure III.6.

The implications of marketing decisions will be discussed in detail in the following chapters.

Customer satisfaction

It should be recognized that while the role of shareholder value management is a primary driver for corporate management, this cannot be achieved without identifying and addressing customer value drivers.

Chapter 2 discussed 'value' in both the corporate and customer context and here the point is being made that unless a satisfactory level of value is delivered to the customer, long-term durable shareholder value cannot be expected. Many organizations embraced shareholder value management during the 1990s only to find, to their cost, that it distracted management's focus from delivering customer value expectations. To ignore messages from the marketplace can have a drastic impact on medium- and long-term shareholder returns. The typical reaction of most businesses to a decline in share price has been to announce plans to reduce operating costs, usually by making staff redundant and by closing branch activities. This results in a reduction in service to customers and often in limiting their choice of products and services. Customers respond by moving to competitive offers; revenues and profits decline further.

Customer satisfaction and shareholder value are inextricably linked and failure to realize this simple commercial fact, and to act upon it, inevitably leads to problems. When reading the remaining chapters the reader is advised to keep customer satisfaction in mind!

PERFORMANCE MEASURES

Shareholder Value Driver	Financial Performance Ratio
Profitability	*Profitability* Gross and operating margins EBIT ROA ROE ROCE *Investment* EPS DPS Retentions Earnings and dividend yield PER Market capitalization Market/book, MVA, EVA Returns spreads
Productivity	*Activity (Resource utilization)* ROS Sales/employee Assets/employee Fixed asset turnover Working capital turnover Stock turn Creditor turnover Debtor turnover
Cash flow	*Liquidity* Current ratio Quick ratio Operational cash flow Strategic cash flow Economic cash flow/Free cash flow

PERFORMANCE FACILITATORS

Financial Characteristics	Market Offer Characteristics
Financial gearing Operational gearing Cost structures and profiles	Differentiation (and) Value added benefits

Figure III.6   Performance characteristics and their influences

The marketing/finance decision complex

Before dealing with the marketing/finance interface, issues of working capital management, managing fixed assets, cash flow management and the implications of capital structure, we must bring these topics together and establish the importance of considering the interrelationships and identify some of the major implications of these relationships.

The overall process of creating more value out of the business is shown in Figure III.7 where a multi-dimension matrix illustrates the numerous questions to be asked and answered. In essence, the problem is simple, in practice it is

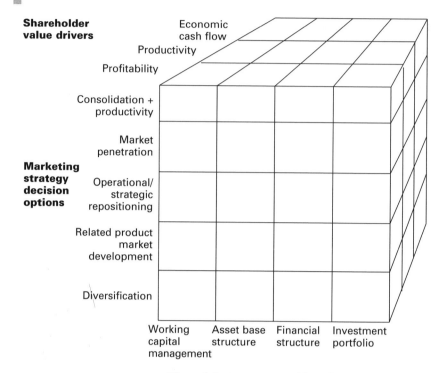

Figure III.7   Overall marketing/finance decision complex

difficult. We need to reach decisions that will create an acceptable level of shareholder wealth or value, but in doing so they should also optimize marketing and financial performance. Clearly not to do so may result in problems for either the short or long term. Figure III.7 suggests that marketing strategy options should first be evaluated in terms of their efficacy in producing results that actually do increase shareholder value in the business, but then considered within the context of their impact on existing financial strategies. This is not to suggest that either one is subservient to the other but rather there may be good reasons, at specific times, to accept that constraints may prevail. A realistic view is that constraints are likely to be resource based and consequently a financial issue.

To put some structure into the decision-making process Figure III.8 proposes a simple model which has *shareholder value objectives* as its central feature. The decision process is an interactive process which considers the impact of both marketing and financial decisions (and constraints) on the value drivers.

Clearly, we cannot identify all of the issues likely to emerge during this process but the following exhibits identify some that may occur.

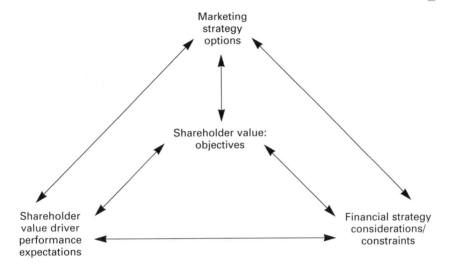

Figure III.8   Marketing/finance decision process

Exhibit III.1 proposes likely responses in shareholder value drivers to marketing strategy decisions. The responses are broad and suggest likely inter-reactions and should be seen as examples.

Similarly, Exhibit III.2 identifies the responses in shareholder value drivers that may occur with financial strategy considerations/constraints. Again it is emphasized that these are examples of possible outcomes and should not be considered as anything other than that.

Finally, Exhibit III.3 considers the resultant marketing/finance interface responses. And again, as for the other two exhibits the responses are suggested not predicted responses.

Effective strategy decisions (and their implementation) are only likely if a process is followed in which the overall implications of decisions are considered. It would be unwise to consider only the impact of marketing decisions on financial structure and strategy because the solution may not be optimal for the business. Similarly, to consider the impact of either marketing or finance decisions (in isolation) on the overall performance of the business may ignore some obvious problems. The remainder of this section will be devoted to a detailed discussion of the interrelationships between marketing and finance and finance and marketing within the areas discussed in this introduction using the approach suggested by the model outlined in Figure III.8.

REFERENCE

Aaker, D. (1995) *Strategic Market Management*, Wiley, New York.

EXHIBIT III.1

Marketing strategy options and the response of the shareholder value drivers

SHAREHOLDER VALUE DRIVERS

Marketing Strategy Decision Options	Profitability	Productivity	Economic Cash Flow
Consolidation and productivity	Product range and customer rationalization will identify poor performance. Cross-component value analysis will improve buying margins. Price adjustments based upon demand response and 'monopoly' advantages may also be used to enhance profitability.	Product range and customer rationalization will also have a positive effect on both fixed asset and working capital utilization. Some expenditure on capital equipment may increase overall productivity, e.g., IT systems for EDI and/or EPOS systems.	Rationalization activities will also improve operations and strategic cash flows and, therefore, present value of aggregate cash flows.
Market penetration	Operating and net margins can be improved by increasing volume throughout (market share) provided fixed cost increases are contained.	Utilization of primary assets (fixed and current) should be increased. Care should be taken to ensure that capacities are not exceeded; this may result in cost penalties.	The increased volume throughout should provide an opportunity to increase operational cash flows due to sales increases.
Operational repositioning	Close monitoring of the changes in customer expectations (and the modification of the market offer) should result in increased customer satisfaction. This reduces the need for price incentives.	Increased customer satisfaction should be used to increase customer transactions and, as a consequence, the productivity of the asset base.	Increased customer satisfaction (and transaction size) should result in increases in positive cash flows and, consequently, increase the NPV of overall cash flow.
Related product-market development	Development costs can be expected to be lower than those for 'new' product-market development. Provided the rate of growth of sales exceeds that of the growth of fixed costs, profit margins will be enhanced. The returns on intangible assets such as R&D and brand values will also be improved.	Utilization of primary assets (fixed and current) should be increased. But as with the market penetration option care should be taken to ensure that capacities are not exceeded; this may result in cost penalties. The productivity of the intangible assets will also be improved.	Increased activity in related product-markets should improve cash flow profiles provided that receivables and payables are closely controlled.
Strategic repositioning	This option offers an opportunity to identify segments in which the company can make maximum advantage of its distinctive competence and competitive advantage characteristics and thus maintain or enhance its margin performance.	More relevant (and specific) targeting should improve the productivity performance of fixed and current assets.	A shift towards relevant customer targets should result in improved revenues and NPV profiles.
Diversification	Overall corporate profitability can be increased by pursing product-market opportunities that have **higher** growth rates than those existing in core product-market activities.	The productivity of the intangible assets should be increased by pursuing 'new' product-market activities.	Successful diversification strategy should increase the overall NPV of the company's cash flows and should be used to lower overall risk.

EXHIBIT III.2

Financial strategy considerations/constraints and their implications for the shareholder value drivers

SHAREHOLDER VALUE DRIVERS

Financial Strategy Considerations/ Constraints	Profitability	Productivity	Economic Cash Flow
Working capital management	Changes in the levels of stock (raw materials, work-in-progress and finished goods) have significant impact on profitability. Similarly, changes in the terms made with customers and suppliers may also have important implications for short term borrowing and, therefore, interest payments. Product-market activities with long lead times and slow stock turns also must cause managers to consider the impact of stock obsolescence and 'write offs' on margins.	The rate of stock turn and the turnover rates of receivables and payables may, if both are significantly large components of working capital, have an impact on asset base productivity. It is a topic to be considered seriously when considering expansion of the product-market scope of the business.	Three elements of working capital influence cash flow. Changes in stock run will influence cash turn balances assuming supplier payment terms remain unchanged. A change in customer credit policy will have a similar effect, as will a change in supplier payment terms.
Asset base structure	The return on resources allocated (ROA) is of major importance to the business. Typically ROA is a major performance measure both internally and externally. It is influenced by the nature of the asset base size and structure which in turn is a function of product and market characteristics.	Asset base productivity is closely linked with profitability through the basic strategic profit model. Issues such as operational gearing are linked with the profit expectation of the business and its vulnerability to market fluctuations. Risk and flexibility are major considerations.	The nature of the production process and consequently the asset base structure will affect the resultant cash flows produced. Other factors to be considered are the product-market life cycle, capital intensity, technology life cycle of assets and use. All have a role in the size and timing of cash flows.
Financial structure	A concern of management should be to ensure that it maximizes shareholders' returns. Hence the decisions taken should ensure that whatever changes to structure are implemented, risk and return are in balance.	Productivity is linked with profitability. The optimal financial structure (risk and return) will influence asset base productivity. For example, very favourable interest rates or perhaps a buoyant stock market will influence a decision to purchase assets rather than lease them.	Present value calculations are influenced by the financial structure chosen for specific projects. The interest rate required to borrow funds (external or internal to the company) will have a major impact on the 'value' of the cash flow.
Investment portfolio profile	Clearly an investment should only be undertaken if it is itself a profitable venture and if it increases the overall profitability of the business. For example, it is possible that a new market offer may be very successful and because it is too close to the core activity of the business 'cannibalizes' its revenues and returns. As a consequence aggregate corporate performance is recorded.	Aggregate corporate productivity is important. It has been demonstrated that by increasing the net asset turnover of a business there can be a real improvement in profitability. Again it is important to understand both the incremental and aggregate performances.	An important feature of the portfolio concept is that it produces cash flows that may be used to 'fund' and 'support' new and recent projects. Techniques such as the value return on investment (VRO) can be used together with a 'Q' ratio to explore both individual project and aggregate performance.

EXHIBIT III.3

Marketing strategy options and the implications for financial strategy decisions

Marketing Strategy Options	FINANCIAL STRATEGY DECISIONS			
	Working Capital Management	Asset Base Structure	Financial Structure	Investment Portfolio Profile
Consolidation and productivity	Decreases in stock levels and accounts receivable.	Increased utilization of fixed assets. Disposal of fixed assets. An increase in 'productivity' assets such as MIS etc.	Decreases in short term loans, i.e., overdrafts. Expansion funds lowest risk options.	Focus on 'core products and services' to maximize profitability and cash flow.
Market penetration	An increase in both stock levels and accounts receivable. However, these should match the increased level in sales response. In overall terms the working capital/sales ratio should decrease.	If successful, improvement of the utilization of manufacturing and logistics fixed assets. Care is required to ensure that volume increases are not excessive, such that unprofitable resource allocation occurs.	No major impact. There may be an increase in short term debt to fund inventories and customer credit. Ideally this should be met from the increased cash flow.	Neither the product-market portfolio nor the fixed assets should be increased. Hence the return on capital employed should be increased.
Operational repositioning	Possible increases in both stock levels and receivables if customer expectations move towards more cutlet types (consumer goods) and for product variety and variety. Distributor response may be for longer payment terms and additional discounts.	Production and logistics facilities may need to be reviewed. If product variety and availability is to be increased and service maintained storage and perhaps transport facilities will probably need to be expanded. Service companies may be helpful in this regard.	Any permanent increase in capacity requirements will necessitate a review of funding and financial structures. Size and time spans are important issues.	Essentially the core product and service offer remain the same. However, it is often necessary to review the impact of change on portfolio performance.
Related product-market development	Working capital requirements should increase with the increase in product range (stocks) and customers (receivables).	The purpose of this strategy option is to maximize the utilization of both tangible and intangible fixed assets. Subsequent expansion of the asset base should occur only if an adequate ROA can be realized.	Expansion of the asset base will require additional funds. Any decisions taken should consider the options available. Risk is not likely to be a major issue thus the type of funding used should not be influenced by a high level of risk.	This strategy is one which should increase the overall performance characteristics of the existing core product activity. It will not diversify the business but will expand the portfolio.

Strategic repositioning	A shift in the product mix (range expansion) or product performance accompanied (possibly) by an increase in customers (new segments) will be accompanied by increased working capital requirements. Management issues should be investigated.	It is very unlikely that this option can be achieved without some capital expenditure. Some industries find that strategic repositioning occurs rapidly and frequently thus requiring a constant updating of plant and considerable R&D expenditures.	The extent of which change occurs will have an influence on the methods used for financing the business. Typically the 'hi tech' business uses retained earnings rather than continu-ously seeking external funding. Market/segment changes may require only an adjustment of short term borrowings.	In essence this option should be pursued either to protect the core product-service base in the long term or to extend it. Both should be seen as a means by which the performance of the 'core product investment port-folio' is enhanced.
Diversification	The very essence of this option 'new products/new markets' implies changes to working capital requirements. These will require considerable research because they do impact on customer service and delivery expectations.	The asset base requirements for this option may be acquired as the result of a business acquisi-tion or assembled during organic growth. The latter offers the opportunity for currency and relevant scale. Often the acquired asset base requires modifications for scale and tech-nology.	How the diversification is under-taken will have a large influence on the resultant structure. Acquisition of going concerns may be financed in a number of ways (e.g. cash, equity expan-sion, debt, equity swaps etc.). The organized growth approach will likely have fewer options. Perceptions of risk are impor-tant.	The purpose of this option is to expand the product-market portfolio. This may be within the existing 'scope' or may extend the business. Either way the performance of the reshaped investment portfolio should be planned so as to increase the return to the share-holders.

Measuring the Value Created for Shareholders – a Marketing Strategy Perspective

Our stated purpose is to link the marketing and financial implications of marketing strategy and its implementation. In order to be effective both marketing and finance require some common base. This chapter provides it. We begin by reviewing the alternatives for measuring shareholder value and derive a series of models or approaches which both measure shareholder value and identify the market characteristics and performance criteria required if shareholder value is to be maximized.

We shall revisit the topic to suggest that stakeholder issues may influence some of the decisions that can be made (i.e., the marketing strategy and the financial management and structure alternatives), and that these may result in optimizing rather than maximizing shareholder values.

6.1   Measuring value at a corporate level

Value-based management (managing for shareholder value; see Chapter 1) is 'a process of strategic management aimed at building lasting economic value for a corporation's shareholders as well as the rest of its key stakeholders: employees, customers, suppliers, bondholders and communities' (Reimann, 1989). Reimann argued that the hostile acquisitions of the late 1980s forced senior managers to be concerned about the value assigned by capital markets to their businesses. Reimann suggested that shareholder value and stakeholder value are identical. We would suggest that they differ. The increasing number of strategic alliances and partnerships suggest that as firms focus increasingly on their core business and increase outsourcing, the interests of other stakeholders may dominate the decision process in an attempt to optimize the aggregate interests of all stakeholders – and in these we would emphasize the customer.

Reimann saw the process of creating shareholder value as involving four basic independent components:

(i)   *Financial valuation*, which links internal valuation with external valuation by the stock market.
(ii) *Portfolio planning*, which links corporate- and business-level strategy analysis and valuation (this topic will be discussed in Chapter 12).
(iii) *Competitive analysis*, which links business-level valuation to competitive situations and strategies (discussed in Chapter 2).
(iv) *Value creation*, the vital step of implementing the concept of value based strategic management.

The rationale for the shareholder value approach was succinctly explained by Rappaport (1986):

> Business strategies should be judged by the economic returns they generate for shareholders, as measured by dividends plus the increase in the company's share price. As management considers alternative strategies those expected to develop the greatest sustainable competitive advantage will be those that will also create the greatest value for shareholders.

He suggested that the shareholder value approach estimates the economic value of an investment by discounting forecast cash flows by the cost of capital. These cash flows serve as the foundation for shareholder returns from dividends and share price appreciation. The broader interests of the stakeholder constituency are also included, but the emphasis is placed upon maximizing the residual claim of the stakeholder.

The argument includes the notion of the firm as a 'going concern'. If it does not satisfy the financial expectations of its stakeholders, and specifically those of the shareholders, its viability ceases. It follows that:

> a going concern must strive to enhance its cashgenerating ability. The ability of a company to distribute cash to its various constituencies depends upon its ability to generate cash from the operation of its businesses, and on its ability to obtain any additional funds needed from external sources. (Rappaport 1986)

Therefore a company's ability to borrow today is based on projections of how much cash will be generated in the future. Borrowing power and the market value of the firm's shares both depend on a company's cash-generating ability. This proposition extends to equity financing: the higher the share price for a given level of required funds, the less dilution will be borne by existing

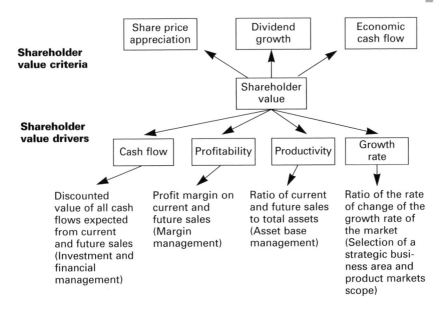

Figure 6.1   Shareholder value: management issues

shareholders. Rappaport quoted Treynor (1981) in emphasizing the importance of maintaining and increasing share price: 'Any management – no matter how powerful and independent – that flouts the financial objectives of maximising share value, does so at its own peril'.

The components of value

It was suggested in Chapter 1 that the shareholder has three primary measures of value: the increase in the share price; a dividend payment which increases steadily and reflects the growth of other investments within the portfolio; and a strong cash flow generation. These are noted in Figure 6.1 together with the four suggested *value drivers* which influence these objectives. If the concept of value is to become accepted by operational marketing managers then it must be understood; furthermore if operational management is to be responsible for implementing value-based strategies it follows that they should be perfectly clear about the concept and how their activities relate to it. Figure 6.1 begins this process by identifying shareholder value drivers in terms that are understood by managers responsible for operational functions and relating them to the managerial tasks of margin management, asset base management and investment and financial management.

Reimann (1989) evaluated various methods used to measure shareholder value on a historical basis. His comments are useful. Reimann considered earnings per share (EPS) as being a rather limited measurement of wealth. He pointed to the lack of evidence of any consistent relationship between EPS growth and share prices. The problems, he suggested, relate to the limited information content of the EPS calculation. It does not reflect capital requirements required to achieve a specific growth in earnings and Reimann suggested its largest failing is its ability to consider the simple fact that shareholders will only obtain value if the returns generated exceed their (the shareholders') cost of capital. Furthermore, changes in EPS also fail to reflect the real possibility of changes in the cost of capital and the discount rate used by investors to capitalize increased earnings. Inflation and, more importantly, risk are omitted from the EPS calculation.

The limitations of EPS as an indicator of corporate performance have meant an increasing use is now made of return on investment (ROI) spread or return on equity (ROE) spread. These compare the return on capital invested to a cost of capital determined in one of three ways. A weighted cost of capital reflects the relative amounts, and therefore costs, of the mix of equity and debt capital. If the ROE spread is used then it is the cost of equity that is used. An alternative is to establish a cost of capital determined from the capital asset pricing model, which will be featured in Chapter 11. Provided a 'positive' spread results then value is created for shareholders. Clearly a negative result destroys value. A number of companies use the equity spread approach. Its logic is quite simple: investment in positive spread businesses is advisable; business units with negative spreads should either be 'turned round' or divested. Reimann pointed to empirical evidence that both ROI and ROE spread methods give better predictions of stock market performance than does EPS. However, these measures also leave much to be desired. In any event they have limitations. The ROI and ROE measures are derived from *internal* accounting data but are compared with *external* capital costs. ROI calculations are subject to length of project life, capitalization policy, depreciation method and the timing of cash flows (Solomon, 1966). Reimann also made a significant comment relating to the calculation of both ROI and ROE. A rapid growth business is likely to have a low ROI because of the need to maintain investment, while established businesses, with significantly depreciated plant, tend to show high ROI values.

To extend the effectiveness of the spread approaches as indicators of value creation, some consultants have suggested comparing the current market value of the company with its 'book value', thus providing a comparative measure of the business's increased value. This market value/book value (MV/BV) adds another dimension to the value created/value destroyed perspective, particularly if used in conjunction with the ROE spread. As Figure 6.2 suggests, business units which cannot achieve positive returns and at the same time are not seen favourably by the stock market (i.e., the market value

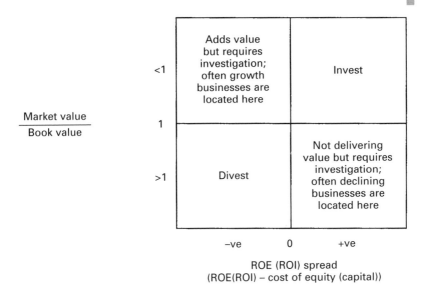

Figure 6.2 Combining market valuation and the returns spread for the evaluation problem

of the company is less than the book value of the means of production) are candidates for divestment.

The addition of market value/book value, nevertheless, fails to add much to the ROI and ROE spread approach, for are two reasons. First, the market value may be influenced by other exogenous factors. By exogenous we do not refer to accepted business environment features but to such things as computer-based share selling – issues and events that do not normally influence competitiveness. Secondly MV/BV is, for almost all businesses, an aggregate indicator which cannot easily be linked with specific strategic business units or profit centres in any direct way. Thus, it is very difficult for managers responsible for specific aspects of the business to respond to changes in any constructive way.

Alternatives to the MV/BV option have appeared. *Economic value added* (EVA) is a measure proposed by consultants Stern Stewart and Co., New York. EVA is calculated by deducting from after-tax operating profit the total cost of capital. The notion of capital is a comprehensive calculation including fixed assets, working capital and *could include intangibles,* such as capitalized expenses to maintain brands, R&D and management development expenditure, if these are significant. A positive EVA indicates that management is creating value for the shareholder, while negative values suggest value is being destroyed (Tully, 1993).

By contrast, the *market value added* (MVA) method considers a combination of debt and the market value of the shares less the capital invested in the company. Once again, a positive value indicates that value has been created while negative values indicate how much value the company has destroyed. Stern Stewart and Co. has suggested that EVA measures a company's success over the past year while MVA is forward-looking, indicating the market's assessment of a company's prospects. Again we are considering aggregate data which is influenced by external factors in addition to the overall performance of the firm. As aggregate measures and as *relative performance indicators* they have much to offer. However, we return to the central problem: how can the manager responsible for developing and/or implementing growth objectives identify and select from alternatives? In other words, how does the manager make decisions which will maximize shareholder value given data which are aggregate and largely speculative?

A number of authors have turned to discounted cash flow (DCF) methods as a means of calculating 'value' (see Rappaport 1983; Wenner and Le Ber 1989). DCF methods, too, have both advantages and disadvantages. The primary advantage is that from a planning viewpoint the company's activities can be seen as a series of projects (product groups) for which revenues and costs can be separated. When competing for scarce resources a more detailed analysis can be undertaken. For example, the sales of a well-established brand will influence the sales of a product line extension or a new product, and judgement concerning likely revenue forecasts may be reached with considerable accuracy. The impact on costs of a value analysis exercise resulting in standardizing components across a number of products within a product range can also be evaluated. The implications for costs of decisions to expand economies of scale or of scope can be included in this analysis.

Looking at the disadvantages, however, the long time horizons over which many projects extend make forecasting difficult and accuracy questionable. Time also introduces risk. The residual value of investments may be difficult to determine and, furthermore, terminal values for alternative (competing) projects may differ. These difficulties are not insignificant, nor are they insurmountable provided symmetry is applied.

Two approaches are considered here, both based upon DCF techniques. The incremental value contribution – Rappaport's *value return on investment (VROI)* – is a useful approach particularly for evaluating strategic alternatives. Rappaport's approach is a measure of the value created per discounted dollar of investment. Thus, it offers management the means by which it is possible to identify *which* alternative offers the largest benefit.

DCF techniques are applied to the existing strategy of the business and the returns likely to result, and are expressed by capitalizing the past year's cash flow (likely to be a very close equivalent of the after-tax operating profit of the business for the year). The post-strategy value is arrived at by using a DCF technique but being careful to consider planning horizons and a risk-adjusted discount rate (such as that derived by the capital asset pricing model). One further element is required: the present value of projected investments, which comprises the present value of the stream of incremental investments in fixed and working capital required by the strategy:

$$\text{VROI} = \frac{\text{Post-strategy value} - \text{Pre-strategy value}}{\substack{\text{Present value of projected investments} \\ \text{(incremental investment undertake} \\ \text{strategy under evaluation)}}}$$

Clearly VROI must be greater than zero if it is to create value for the shareholder. Given a number of competing projects those with the largest VROI values would warrant further investigation; this would require managerial experience and introduces a qualitative aspect to the exercise. The alternatives evaluated could consider the structural alternatives available from partnerships and alliances.

VROI is not without its own problems. For example, a loss situation would give an unrealistic value. Start-up businesses with little or no history make estimating cash flows difficult and low (or even zero) investment will also result in high values.

Another approach is based upon *Tobin's Q ratio*, a ratio of the market value of a company's physical assets to the cost of their replacement:

$$Q = \frac{\text{Stock market valuation of company's productive capability}}{\text{Replacement cost of assets}}$$

A Q value greater than 1 suggests the stock market values a company's assets more than they would actually cost to replace and therefore value is being created. In effect Tobin's Q ratio is very similar to the MV/BV approach of Maracon Consultants. There are a number of applications of the Q concept – one, used by HOLT Planning Associates, uses DCF techniques:

$$Q = \frac{\text{Future value of expected receipts (discounted to consider risk)}}{\text{Original purchase price of assets adjusted for inflation effects}}$$

The development of Q has eliminated much of the distortion imposed by stock prices and 'spread' approaches. Thus we can consider inflation, the economic life of assets, accounting procedural requirements, variable

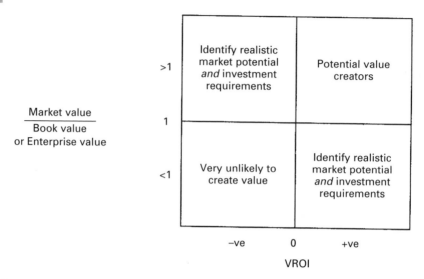

Figure 6.3 Using market valuation and the returns spread for the evaluation of shareholder value creation

depreciation, inventory valuation, capitalization policy, timing of cash flows and the implications of financial operational gearing.

While the Q ratio is more useful than the MV/BV returns spread approach for strategy evaluation it does also have problems. One is similar to that observed with the VROI approach. A project (product group) or alternative business model with steady positive cash flow but 'old' assets will indicate a low Q value because of a 'catch-up' premium which, when applied to 'update' the asset value, will decrease the value of the ROI (but we can compensate for this). Another similar problem to VROI is that if a business uses Q to evaluate the alternatives of divestment or reinvestment, a large investment requirement may result in a very large denominator and, therefore, a very low value for Q.

Reimann (1989) proposed combining Q and VROI ratios (see Figure 6.3). He suggested that business units in the upper right-hand cell would be potential value creators, while those in the diagonally opposite cell are almost certainly destroying value. The other two situations would clearly require some further investigation before a decision to abandon the product/activity is taken. This may be a marketing, financial or operational issue.

As with all of the other approaches, there is still a problem. Reimann suggested that with the combined Q and VROI we can match the stock market evaluation of the business and the effects of inflation on its assets with the more forward-looking VROI ratio which considers likely alternative strategies.

It is interesting to probe this interrelationship further. Reimann suggested: 'The numerator of . . . the Q ratio is the present value of a business determined by using . . . DCF Techniques. The present value represents the equivalent of the market value of a particular business unit.' At the same time 'VROI measures the incremental shareholder value increase per incremental dollar of (incremental) investment', and 'thus, the VROI ratio is a measure of a given business strategy's potential for adding to shareholder value relative to the capital investment required.' This suggestion assumes the shareholder had knowledge of the alternatives to be evaluated and subsequently selected – an assumption which would appear unlikely unless we accept that management acts as an agent for the shareholders. A more realistic approach would be to use a measure which reflects the market's view of the company's future, based upon its current performance and influenced by the market's evaluation of external factors. For this purpose perhaps the market value/book value approach measure or the market value added approach could be used. We shall return to this later in this chapter.

Rappaport (1986) used Porter's competitive analysis and strategy valuation to assess value creation alternatives. He used Porter's industry structure model to evaluate industry attractiveness together with value chain analysis to identify competitive advantage. The competitive position of the business within the industry is determined by evaluation of the segment structure of the industry and the company's position within the segment. Concurrently, value drivers are used to identify (and evaluate) tactics which will support both a differentiation strategy and a cost leadership strategy. The Rappaport approach is helpful in that it attempts to link the strategic considerations of shareholder value with management decision options. However, it does not link the implementation decisions to the value objectives directly nor does it provide a performance framework with which to evaluate (or assess) the efficacy of the alternative (selected) options.

6.2   Issues in marketing strategy

Early attempts by marketing strategy academics and practitioners to interface marketing and financial performance were through concepts such as the product life cycle (PLC). This considered cash outflows and cash inflows, initial investment requirements and life cycle profitability within the context of product life cycle characteristics and events over time. While there are as many arguments against the PLC as there are supporting it (see Chapter 3), the fact remains that it or its equivalent offer is a useful concept with which to explore such notions as risk, product portfolios and cash flows.

The Boston Consulting Group captured the interest and attention of

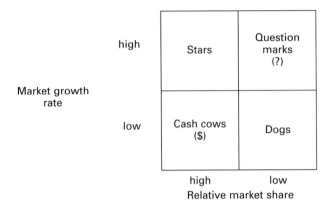

Figure 6.4   BCG growth/share matrix

academics and practitioners alike when it introduced its growth/share matrix. This now well-known approach assumed ongoing growth to be 'a given' and around this assumption proceeded to produce an elegant and convincing model for product-market portfolio analysis. The usefulness of the growth/share model was that it focussed management's attention on using the product-market or strategic business unit (SBU) portfolio to produce cash resources. The underlying assumption of the model was that volume increases bring about lower costs but to achieve growth, cash is necessary. As growth slows and the product moves towards maturity in its life cycle, cash surpluses are usually generated which are then used to support product-markets, SBU's etcetera still in the growth stages of their life cycles; these mature phase products then are the cash cows (see Figure 6.4). As the growth assumptions of the 1970s and early 1980s gave way to recession, growth became decline and the growth/share model had difficulties in providing explanations.

There have been numerous explanations for why the growth/share model did not deliver in a number of situations. One is that the assumption that growth would continue was short-lived: the result was that economies of scale and experience effects were not achieved, and the high margin, high cash expectations of 'cash cow' candidates did not materialize. Another common problem was that cash cows were not easily found and when they were, often as not, managements' expectations far exceeded the ability of the cash cow to deliver. As a result they rapidly became 'dogs'. Possibly the largest problem was (and remains) behavioural in that managers expected the model to *make* decisions rather than offer means by which past performance and potential alternatives might be evaluated. We shall return to this topic later in this chapter.

The Boston Consulting Group offered a second model, the growth/gain

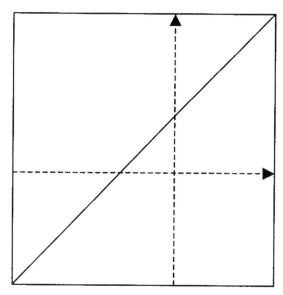

Business growth rate %

Figure 6.5   BCG growth/gain matrix

matrix. This illustrated the extent to which each product or SBU is matching the growth of the market. Figure 6.5 features the growth rate of the product or SBU on the horizontal axis and the growth rate of the market on the vertical axis. Thus products (SBUs) with growth rates matching that of the market appear on the diagonal, while those losing share are above the diagonal and those increasing share are below it. The model incorporates an interesting feature: that of the company's sustainable growth rate (see Figure 6.6). The importance of establishing the maximum sustainable growth rate becomes clear when Figure 6.6 is examined closely. At msgr 1, the company is unable to do other than fund the peripheral 'question mark' product/SBU, but at msgr 2, it could launch the question mark/star opportunity, which may then take it onto msgr 3. Thus this model introduces the importance of growth, and the necessity of attempting to manage the business such that both cash and growth can be achieved. This is an important addition because it offers the link between shareholder interests and managerial decision making, which will be dealt with in Chapter 12.

We should also review one other marketing model: the business assessment matrix. This matrix has appeared in a number of formats. Essentially, its purpose is as an analytical tool which facilitates marketing opportunity analysis and as an aid to exploring corporate competitive capability. The model was pioneered by General Electric with McKinsey and is widely known.

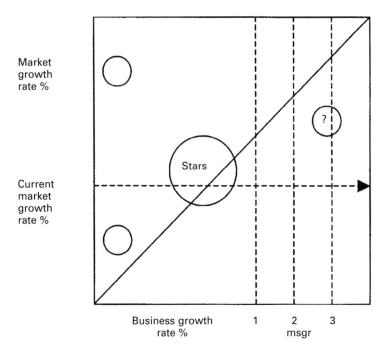

Figure 6.6   BCG growth/gain matrix illustrating the influence of the maximum sustainable growth rate (msgr) on decision making

The two dimensions used (see Figure 6.7) represent the significant elements of the internal and external environment of the firm with a facility for giving emphasis to those elements which have specific importance. Shell Chemicals developed a similar portfolio model called the directional policy matrix using as its two dimensions competitive capabilities (corresponding with GE's business strengths) and prospects for sector profitability (GE's industry attractiveness).

The criteria used for both dimensions are market and company based and need to be reviewed if they are to be more specific to shareholder value. For example, attractiveness criteria include market size and growth, pricing, structure and environmental issues. Competitive positioning criteria relate to marketing effectiveness – such things as market share, product range characteristics, pricing competitiveness, capacity and capability issues, and promotional activities. For their purpose they might be effective however, to measure their impact on creating shareholder value a range of more direct criteria is required.

For both the GE and Shell approaches a weighting and rating framework was suggested to enable emphasis to be placed on specific attributes. This is

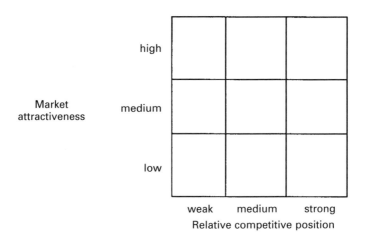

Figure 6.7 Directional policy matrix

particularly important when a company needs to pursue a strategy which will increase its profitability, cash flow or asset base utilization.

6.3 Developing a marketing approach to creating shareholder value

As we said at the beginning of the chapter, to be successful at creating or increasing shareholder value the marketing manager should understand the implications of marketing strategy decisions for the drivers of shareholder value. These were identified as profitability, productivity, economic cash flow (the present value of future cash flows discounted at a rate which reflects business and financial risk) and growth. Figure 6.8 relates marketing strategy options to the objective of creating shareholder value through these value drivers. It can be seen from the model that the basis of the process is to develop a series of strategies which themselves are based upon an optimal but successful combination of margin, asset base and investment and financial management.

The value driver components identify in broad terms the options that marketing managers may consider, while the marketing strategy options are examples of possible decisions that may be made. Space prevents a detailed examination of the options but they include conventional strategy items together with some additional but related topics.

However, if we are to see a constructive contribution from marketing implemented effectively the process by which this is achieved requires some analysis. The process comprises three stages.

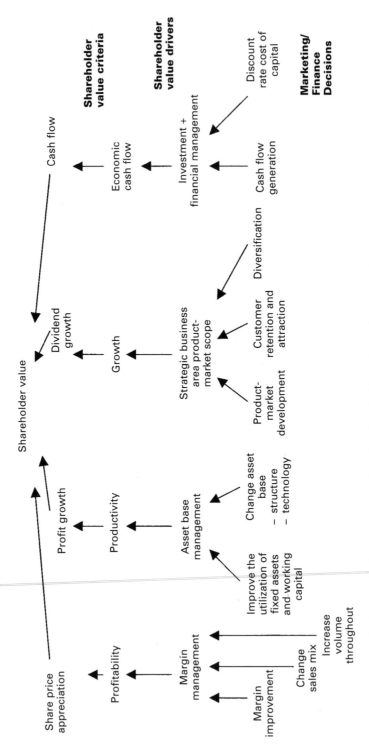

Figure 6.8 Developing marketing strategy options for shareholder value enhancement

Market opportunity analysis

Proactive marketing requires ongoing research to identify opportunities which demonstrate 'fit' with the firm's capabilities and capacities. In Figures 6.9(a), (b) and (c) a range of 'ideal market attributes' is identified for each of the shareholder value drivers. Again growth rate is assumed to be at an acceptable level for each of the value drivers. The two market attractiveness characteristics of market growth and market returns clearly relate to the value drivers. Market growth and market returns imply effective margin and asset base decisions together with equally effective resource allocation (investment) decisions. In applying the model the value drivers and the attributes should be evaluated to ascertain their relative effectiveness in achieving the shareholder value objectives. Clearly during the life cycle of the firm the value drivers will have differing levels of importance and impact on the attractiveness of market opportunities. A clear statement of shareholder value objectives is important in this respect because it will direct the market opportunity analysis towards a combination of criteria most likely to achieve shareholder satisfaction.

Competitive position criteria (Figure 6.9(c)) are not necessarily fixed. An analysis of the relevance of these items may well identify things that will either enhance or inhibit the firm's ability to add value for the shareholder, whatever opportunity is pursued. It follows that the purpose of this activity is to match the company's capabilities relative to the capabilities of major competitors active or with potential interest in the market. Competitive

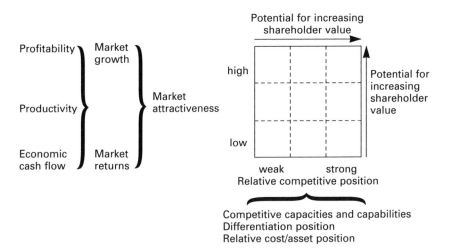

Figure 6.9(a) Market opportunity analysis

Market Attractiveness	
Market growth and market returns	
Shareholder value drivers	Ideal market attributes
Profitability (Margin management)	• High margin • Minimal direct competition • Large numbers of profitable customers • Optimal numbers of profitable suppliers • High barriers of entry • Low barriers to exit • Short 'introduction and growth' stages in product-market development process • Segmentation/positioning opportunity • Minimal government intervention • Low price sensitivity • Value chain integration
Productivity (Asset management)	• Economies of scale, scope, integration and differentiation • Low cyclical influences • Ability to use branding and brand leverage • Opportunities for value engineering/analysis • Experience effect • Increase utilization of existing assets
Economic cash flow (Investment and financial management)	• Large market • Strong steady growth • Potential for developing large market share • Large/frequent customer transactions • High-level repeat purchasing • Long 'maturity' stage in product-market development process • Short 'decline' stage in product-market development process • Optimal capital structure: financial and operational gearing requirements • Optimal cost of capital

Figure 6.9(b) Market attractiveness criteria

position analysis should be conducted with a view to evaluating the impact of market involvement on shareholder value. Some interesting opportunities might be found whereby value could be enhanced simply by extending the current activities of the firm. For example, productivity might be increased because, by entering a market, the firm's capacity could be further expanded thereby increasing both scale and scope economies. By contrast, an opportunity requiring the company to establish an entirely new brand positioning might result in diluting profitability and therefore shareholder value.

Relative Competitive Position

Differentiation and relative cost/asset position

Shareholder value drives	Ideal company attributes	
Profitability (Margin management)	• Dominant in current markets/segments • Exclusive and transferable brands • Augmentation ability • Innovative • Flexible operating systems • Integrated value chain processes • High added-value optimal costs	
Productivity (Asset management)	• Capacity/scale operations • Capacity/scope operations • Capability: design, manufacturing and marketing • Operational technology currency • Investment capacity and capability	} Review structural alternatives
Economic Cash Flow (Investment and financial management)	• Large stable current markets • Large market/segment shares • Optimal number of suppliers • Optimal number of profitable customers • Balanced product portfolio • Optimal gearing • Optimal cost of capital • Optimal capital structure: finance and operational gearing requirements • Diversified risk	} Review structural alternatives

Figure 6.9(c)   Competitive capacities and capabilities

Shareholder value/strategic marketing: opportunity evaluation

A model which may be used to evaluate strategy options is represented in Figure 6.10. In Figure 6.10(a) it is proposed to use *market value added* and a *forecast VROI* (value return on investment) as the dimensions for evaluation. The purpose of this exercise is to identify the strategy options which have the highest potential market value added and forecast VROI scores. The ideal

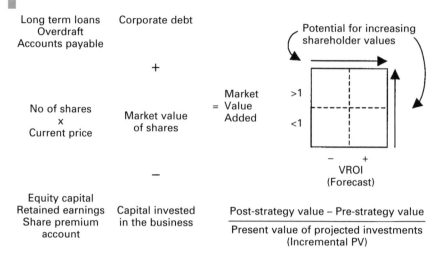

Figure 6.10(a)   Shareholder value/strategic marketing: options evaluation

location is the top right-hand quadrant where clearly maximum shareholder value is achieved. Market value added (MVA) is preferred for this exercise because, as will be recalled from earlier in the chapter, MVA is future orientated. It is possible to set specific objectives for the MVA components and thus an aggregate MVA value. In deriving the MVA objective value, a number of qualitative issues should be addressed. For example, the gearing ratio can be adjusted or left at its current value, and a range of projected share prices can be evaluated, as can changes to retentions/dividends policy. This suggests that risk may be introduced to MVA. Business risk will have an impact on the share price and financial risk will be reflected by gearing options.

The marketing strategy options identified in Figure 6.10(b) are linked to the shareholder value drivers. Some of the relationships are readily understood, but others may be less direct in their influence. An obvious link exists between differentiation (to decrease price sensitivity) and the margin improvement; similarly an expanded product range offers an opportunity for customers to complete more of their purchase with the one supplier.

Cross-component opportunities exist where component rationalization will reduce inventory holding requirements (and increase buying margins) provided that the number of common components can be increased. Lower inventory levels imply less cash tied up in raw materials and in work-in-progress stockholding and thus will improve cash flow.

The VROI process discussed earlier in the chapter is essentially a DCF (discounted cash flow) appraisal of alternative strategies, and as such the objective is to identify options which offer the largest VROI values. Again

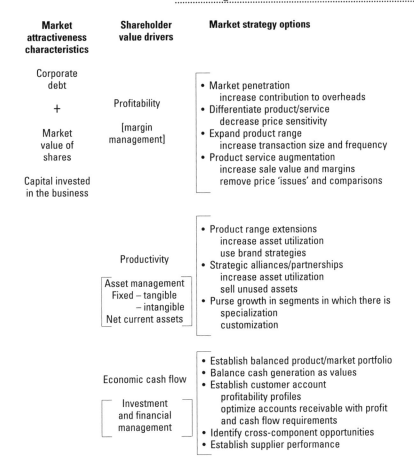

Market attractiveness characteristics	Shareholder value drivers	Market strategy options

Corporate debt
 	
 +
 	
 Market value of shares
 	
 Capital invested in the business
	Profitability
	
	 [margin management]
		• Market penetration
		    increase contribution to overheads
		 • Differentiate product/service
		    decrease price sensitivity
		 • Expand product range
		    increase transaction size and frequency
		 • Product service augmentation
		    increase sale value and margins
		    remove price 'issues' and comparisons

	Productivity
	
	 Asset management
	 Fixed – tangible
	 – intangible
	 Net current assets
		• Product range extensions
		    increase asset utilization
		    use brand strategies
		 • Strategic alliances/partnerships
		    increase asset utilization
		    sell unused assets
		 • Purse growth in segments in which there is
		    specialization
		    customization

	Economic cash flow
	
	 Investment and financial management
		• Establish balanced product/market portfolio
		 • Balance cash generation as values
		 • Establish customer account
		    profitability profiles
		    optimize accounts receivable with profit
		    and cash flow requirements
		 • Identify cross-component opportunities
		 • Establish supplier performance

Figure 6.10(b)   Market value added components

some qualitative analysis will be required to ensure that the existing business is not adversely affected by the proposed new ventures.

Shareholder value/strategic marketing: performance evaluation

The management of the implementation process should be monitored. Figure 6.11 proposes a model for this purpose using economic value added together with a Q ratio version. EVA is a performance-achieved-related measure, while the Q ratio can be modified to reflect the present value of strategies accepted and implemented at an earlier date. This will require an update of the cash flow forecasts of expected receipts and the value of the assets involved. Clearly, there may be differences due to changes that might have occurred since implementation was initiated: for example, competition may be

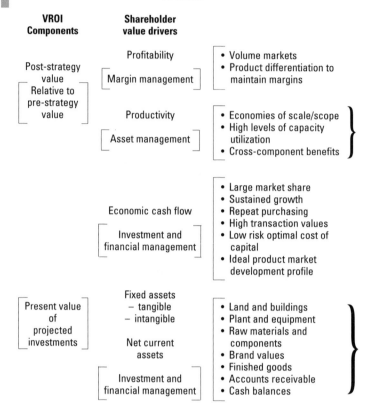

Figure 6.10(c)   VROI components

stronger than was anticipated, or raw material costs may have changed (perhaps increased due to shortages). The numerator may be influenced by changes in forecast demand levels due, perhaps, to the emergence of new technology and changes in value added available and or price levels.

Again the purpose of the exercise is to 'place' the strategies within the matrix cells and look for shifts. A strategy that appeared attractive at the option evaluation stage with a high MVA and VROI profile may over time, and because of unforeseen changes, not deliver the promised performance. While MVA and EVA differ they do share the common component of corporate debt and this is a useful link between forecast performance and actual results, because during the evaluation process it permits management to review alternative financial structures. Furthermore when the shareholder value drivers are compared, the assumptions made concerning profitability, productivity and economic cash flow generation may be reviewed and their impact on actual performance investigated.

The marketing achievement factors are described in Figure 6.11(a).

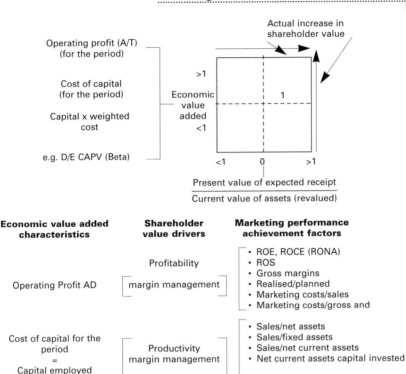

Figure 6.11(a) EVA components

These are the typical performance criteria acceptable to most businesses; some are related to financial performance. The required performance levels should be set once the strategic options have been programmed with a view to their reflecting their contribution to shareholder value creation objectives.

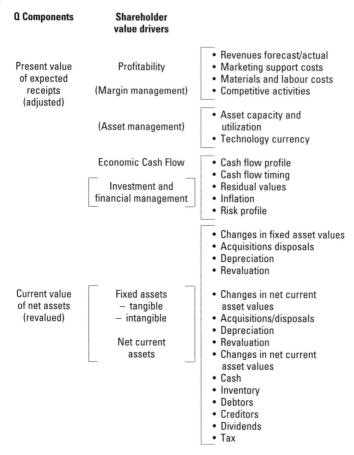

Figure 6.11(b)   Q components

6.4 Summary

This chapter has made a link between marketing strategy and operational implementation and the financial structure and performance issues which clearly will result. The approach has used corporate performance measurements currently used by companies and financial markets as criteria for the measurement of value added to the organization.

Many of the financial topics require further explanation in the following chapters. In these we shall look at working capital and asset base management, cash flow management, financial structure decisions, investment appraisal and portfolio management – again with an emphasis on the marketing/finance interface implications.

REFERENCES

Higgins, R. C. (1977) 'How much growth can a firm afford?', *Financial Management*, Fall.

Porter, M. (1980) *Competitive Strategy*, Free Press, New York.

Rappaport, A. (1983) 'Corporate performance standards and shareholder value', *The Journal of Business Strategy*, Spring.

Rappaport, A. (1986) *Creating Shareholder Value: A New Standard for Business Performance*, Free Press, New York.

Reimann, M. (1989), *Managing for Value: a Guide to Valuebased Strategic Management*, Blackwell (in association with the Planning Forum), Oxford.

Solomon, E. (1966) 'Return on investment: the relation of book yield to true yield', in *Research in Accounting Measurement*, edited by Robert K. Jaedicke, Yuji Uiri, and Oswald Nelson, American Accounting Association, New York.

Treynor, A. (1981) 'The financial objectives in the widely held corporation', *Financial Analysts Journal*, March/April.

Tully, S. (1993) 'The real key to creating wealth', *Fortune*, 20 September.

Wenner, D. L. and Le Ber, R. W. (1989) 'Managing for shareholder value – from top to bottom', *Harvard Business Review*, November/December.

7 Working Capital Management

Working capital management is a short-term operational financial activity for any organization. Working capital comprises *current assets*, that is, cash inventory and accounts receivable, and *current liabilities* – liabilities which are to be met within one year and which include accounts payable, bank overdraft and possibly taxation and dividends once declared. *Working capital* is usually defined as the excess of current assets over current liabilities:

Working capital/
Component factors
=
Inventory + accounts receivable + cash +
short-term (less than one year) investments
less
Accounts payable + overdraft + tax
payable + dividends declared

Because of the short-term nature of working capital and the dynamic nature of its components, working capital management consumes much of a financial manager's time and is likely to be an area where much of the marketing/finance interface activity occurs.

7.1 Working capital objectives

An overall issue for financial management to decide upon is the optimal structure of its assets – in other words, the balance of the company investment between fixed and current assets. Fixed assets are considered to be the means of generating revenue with working capital acting as a facilitating ingredient. For example, inventory is held to provide customer service (product availability) and accounts receivable provide a credit service to customers. Equally the organization, in its role as a customer of its own suppliers, requires similar services, credit being a major item. None of these items is 'free goods'; all have a cost. Credit services are extended by organizations to encourage customer loyalty and are funded by the supplier, which regards this as an investment.

It follows that working capital management has a number of objectives. It should determine:

- The balance of investment between fixed and current assets – the optimal financial structure which will deliver shareholder value; and
- the means and methods used to finance current assets.

If we increase sales then inventories of raw materials and components (work in progress) will also increase. To promote sales the level (or investment) in finished product (finished goods) is likely to increase, as will customer credit amounts. Hence an expansion of the business requires investment in working capital. Often, to offset the impact of the additional working capital outlay (inventories and accounts receivable), managers are encouraged to use the maximum amount of suppliers' working capital (credit) that is consonant with maintaining workable supplier–customer relationships. Working capital management is a balancing process: cash, receivables and inventory levels are maintained at levels that optimize the return to the business (i.e., shareholder value) by maximizing the net present value of the cash flows generated, which will only occur if they are sufficient to service customer expectations.

7.2 Managing working capital

The components of working capital are illustrated in Figure 7.1. In managing working capital to ensure that the optimal level of working capital is maintained a number of questions should be asked by managers:

- What levels of investment are required by each working capital component?
- How should financing be structured? Should the organization use both long- and short-term funding?
- What alternatives exist and what are the time issues to be considered (e.g., suppliers' lead times and delivery reliabilities, the production cycle)?
- What are the implications of customer service (product availability) on the *levels* of inventory to be held?
- What is the likely impact of increasing credit, product choice and inventory availability on customer loyalty?
- What are the opportunities for lowering the level of investment by using suppliers' funds and by operating credit incentives for customers?

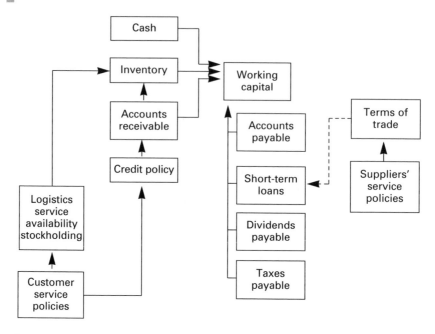

Figure 7.1   Managing working capital

To explore these issues and to examine the marketing/finance interface we need to look at details of the overall working capital management process.

The operating cycle

A company's operating cycle is the time taken between the procurement of raw materials, their conversion into products and the receipt of cash from the sale of the products. Figure 7.2 illustrates the process, its components and includes time periods, which when totalled give the overall length of the operating cycle in days.

There are seven stages in the cycle during which inventory or credit (taken or given) consume time and working capital.

Stage one is the time period between receiving materials or components and paying suppliers. It represents a working capital investment *by suppliers* in the organization which reduces the overall time and investment of the company's operating cycle. Stage two is the level of inventory of raw materials required to ensure the effective supply of inputs into the production process, expressed as 'days' stockholding'. At stage three, inventory is held as work in progress – the production time period may be hours, days, months or possibly years (such as with forestry products); clearly much depends upon

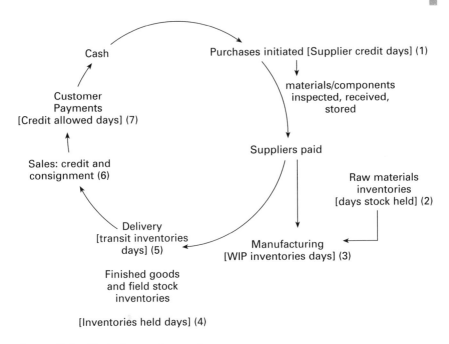

Figure 7.2 Typical operating cycle

industry practice. In recent years just-in-time methodology has been applied to both stages two and three and considerable reductions in inventory holding have been achieved by many organizations.

Stage four requires inventory to be held to ensure prompt response to customer orders and is also expressed in time. Stage five, delivery, has varying importance for companies and is a function of the number of storage facilities in use and the distance between the company's locations and its customers. There are examples of products being manufactured some considerable distance from customer plant locations and transported by slow moving mode. Clearly if long distances and large bulky items of equipment are involved transit times may be considerable and both the time and value of the product should be considered as elements of operating cycle cost. Many products are 'sold' on consignment (stage six), payment is due as and when the products are sold to the consignee's customers; again we have an element of cost in the operating cycle which must be borne by the supplier organization. Finally, at stage seven, having made a sale (or credit sale), the vendor will offer a period of time during which the purchaser can pay for purchases made. Once cash payment is received the operating cycle is completed.

While the length of the operating cycle is largely dependent upon customer responses there are a number of factors which influence it which are under the control of the supplier:

(i)   Efficiency of order receipt and preparation. A large number of information technology (IT)-based systems are available, for example electronic data interchange (EDI) communications driven by electronic point of sale (EPOS) systems, linking replenishment and in some instances manufacturing operations to reduce lead times.

(ii)   Manufacturing activities, which can influence lead times. Not only has the technology of manufacturing improved but quality control activities and policies determining the sales/manufacturing activities have significant influence over the length of the operating cycle.

(iii) Sales activities and methods. For example, not too long ago f.m.c.g. perishable products were sold to some types of customers on a 'van sales' basis; products were immediately available to customers and cash available for the supplier.

(iv)   Credit policy and management of customers' accounts. By offering discounts for prompt payment, outstanding accounts can be minimized.

(v)   Distribution channel options. These are often considered in this context. The discounts given to distributors can be seen in part as an alternative to direct sales. By selling to a distributor organization both the number of accounts and the overall time for which accounts receivable remain outstanding are reduced.

Funding working capital requirements

Figure 7.3 suggests there is a permanence among some elements of an organization's current assets and consequently these become funded by long-term financing. These same businesses may be engaged in seasonal trade activities which require them to increase levels of inventory, accounts receivable and cash balances periodically. Retailing businesses and their suppliers experience this temporary requirement prior to the Christmas season (it is a fact for many that their profitability is dependent upon being successful during these short periods of time). Typically, this has its own cycle: inventories are steadily increased, financed by bank overdraft or possibly by extending trade credit ahead of the selling period; products are sold and the 'investment' becomes accounts receivable and then cash; finally, the overdraft is reduced and the temporary current assets are liquidated. The nature of the business is such that this element of the working capital becomes a permanent requirement.

Figure 7.3 also illustrates two other important aspects of financial management of which the marketing manager should be aware. The first is the

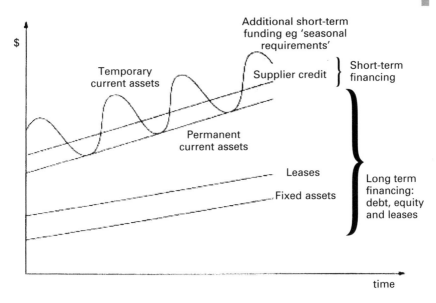

Figure 7.3 Structuring the finance of fixed and current assets

matching principle: permanent current assets (and fixed assets for that matter) should *not* be financed by short-term borrowing – the business would be vulnerable if such finance was withdrawn. The second point concerns growth: as a business expands, its financial structure should reflect this and the need to rearrange financing to fund the additional permanent current asset requirements becomes important.

7.3 Managing current assets

Marketing managers should be aware of the characteristics of current assets and the implications of marketing decisions on the levels of investment. Specifically they should understand the business of inventory, accounts receivable and cash management.

Inventory management

Inventories comprise raw materials, work in progress and finished goods. While the proportions of each vary considerably in the overall investment in inventories (e.g., typically retailers have only finished goods but manufacturers' inventories contain a mix of all three categories) the reasons for holding inventory are the same for all businesses:

- To meet customer expectations of a planned order response.
- To provide continuity in the production process thereby ensuring high levels of fixed asset utilization.
- To secure sources of supply.
- To ensure consistency of input quality.
- To obtain economies of scale in purchasing inputs and thereby optimize gross margins.

The nature of the business determines the emphasis on inventory structure. Manufacturing businesses will have large stocks of raw materials and work in progress. Depending upon the process, so the levels of work in progress may vary. The example of whisky maturing over long periods is common knowledge and is clearly an example of a product for which the time spent maturing must be considered as a cost. However, other products require time to mature, and some are not high-value products. For example, cheese is one often overlooked example. This low-value product can be formulated and processed in a matter of hours; to reach its maturity value may take 12 months. The costs involved in storing the product may be the largest cost component – clearly an issue that marketing management should consider when reviewing product planning.

Before considering other cost implications of inventory management we should identify intra-organizational issues and how inter-organizational solutions may be found. Large divisionalized companies often supply each other with inputs (raw materials, components, and so forth). These are costs.

A number of activities have markets for which it is difficult to forecast sales because of the variability of end-user demand. The consumer may be influenced by a number of things, such as competitive product offers, unpredictable weather, short-term changes in disposable income, or the availability of credit at acceptable levels. For many manufacturing companies these variables are too hard to ensure for at acceptable inventory management costs. Furthermore many companies have product ranges that are very specialized (and often seasonal) which again would present problems. Companies operating in derived demand situations are dependent upon a hierarchy of influences: the economy, seasonal influences, competitive activities, etc. These will impose a requirement to hold additional inventories. These problems can result in very large changes in production capacity utilization. These situations are illustrated in Figure 7.4. Figure 7.4(a) represents the situation in which a manufacturer sells direct to customers in a dynamic and unpredictable market (many garment manufacturers could be represented in this way, particularly those of high fashion products). Due to the lack of an intermediary to service orders from stockholding the manufacturer typically encounters problems in meeting delivery expectations and invariably has

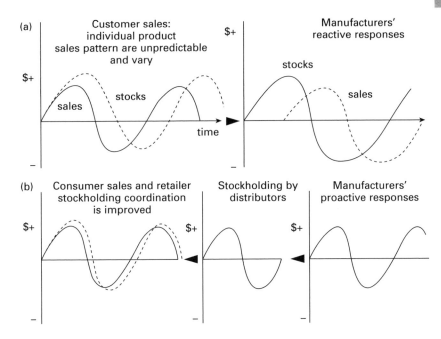

Figure 7.4 Role of distributors in improving production capacity utilization

capacity utilization problems as demand may vary between 150 per cent and 50 per cent of available capacity. One solution is shown as Figure 7.4(b): the introduction of an intermediary to act as a 'buffer' between customer and manufacturer. By maintaining adequate inventory levels, intermediaries are better able to service changes in levels of demand than are manufacturers. The benefit to a manufacturer is a manageable production risk; the cost is the margin expected by a distributor.

Another aspect of inventory management that has particular implications for cost management concerns product availability or service-level achievement. Most marketing managers are aware of customer response to high (and poor) levels of availability. Often high levels of availability are used to create market advantage, the rationale being that if a product is 'always in stock' it creates customer loyalty and therefore builds the business volumes. It may also take advantage of competitor vulnerabilities in this regard.

Availability (or service level) is measured by the percentage of orders filled upon receipt. This may be represented as orders per time cycle for replenishment, that is, it may be measured over the replenishment cycle of the vendor, or it may be a measure of 'instant response', that is, orders filled from stock (which is more the accepted measurement). Other measures that may be encountered are items per order or items per product group.

An important factor is that the level of availability offered meets customer expectations, is realizable financially and is competitive. Clearly if availability proves to be either too expensive to offer or, due to physical constraints (such as distribution capacity), or cannot be guaranteed with any reliability, a minimum level which is deliverable should be determined and some other competitive characteristic used to develop a market advantage.

Just-in-time (JIT) inventory management has changed the interpretation of availability. Hitherto we saw inventory availability as a stockholding security measure which ensured response to customer orders at a competitive (planned) level. However, the purpose of the JIT philosophy is to ensure that minimum levels of inventory are maintained at essential points of the supply chain in an attempt to lower the inventory holding costs of all members of the supply chain. JIT also lowers other costs. By restricting production volumes, storage costs are lowered as are wastage costs. The volume produced is that required at the next stage of production at a specified time rather than a production volume level influenced by economies of scale or experience effects.

In Figure 7.5 the cost, revenue and therefore profitability implications of availability are illustrated. In Figure 7.5(a) the cost profiles are shown as availability is increased. The cost of holding inventories increases as availability increases. An important feature of the cost profile is the exponential nature of the cost of providing availability: the cost of availability increases rapidly at the higher levels of availability. The quantitative implications of the choice of availability level is shown in Figure 7.5(b). At high levels, between 95 and 97 per cent inventory holding, costs can be as high as ± 15 per cent of inventory holding costs. By comparison at 75 to 77 per cent, the costs are some ± 5 per cent. Clearly, marketing management should be made aware of these cost implications during the planning stages of strategy implementation. Often the argument for high levels of availability is based upon the decreasing cost of lost sales, which (as can be seen in Figure 7.5(a)) for marketing management can be an important concern, particularly for products with little or no differentiation.

A major concern should be the basic characteristics of the product offer. As we can see from Figure 7.5(c) two quite different response patterns are typical. Sales response 2 may be expected for products where consumption is both predictable and regular. By contrast, other product categories, usually non-essential luxury products, often demonstrate an increasing response (sales response 1). There are a number of factors which will determine the level of availability offered. One important issue is the notional 'contribution' made by the inventory availability offer (which can be seen as the value of the sales response *less* the total cost of providing availability – shown in Figure 7.5(c) as the sum of the cost of holding inventory and the cost of lost sales).

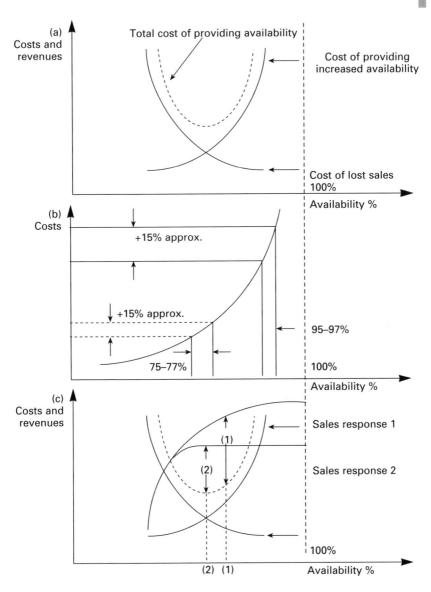

Figure 7.5   Cost and revenue implications of availability

This is not to suggest that this is the only issue. In the introduction and growth phases of a product-market the decision to trade off the costs of availability for market share may be justified if the market is seen as being competitive. Many companies resolve this decision by using a 'Pareto' analysis of product sales and customer offtake. Figure 7.6(a) demonstrates the well-known 'Pareto 80/20 relationship', seen to exist in many productmarket situations,

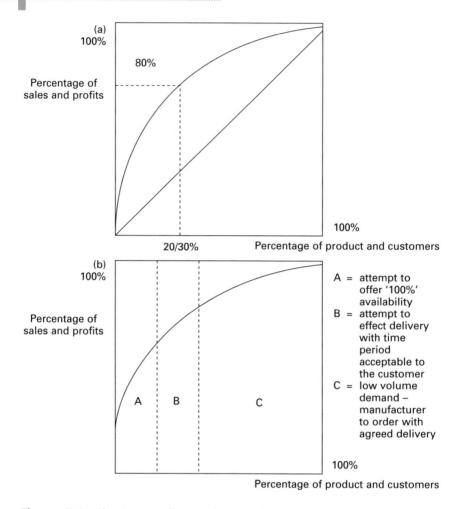

Figure 7.6 The Pareto effect and its implications for product service and customer account management

particularly volume markets for which a variety response to provide customer choice is seen as important. The usual approach is to consider the performance profiles of products (or customers) on the basis of the rates of sale of products across the range and to plan availability objectives on the need to provide service for those products which are selling in volume and for which competitive alternatives are available. Products are categorized as A, B, or C, and availability objectives set for each group: Group A products may be set at the highest availability, say 97 to 98 per cent, with B at 85 per cent and C at 75 per cent. What is important is that the levels are determined such that they are planned to a competitive, market-based response and that the cost of providing the service level is acceptable to the company. For many companies the Pareto principle extends into manufacturing. The question often asked, particularly if capacity is operating at a maximum, is why allocate capacity resources to low-volume products? Often the answer results in outsourcing of low-volume products the presence of which is essential for customer choice and market credibility.

A useful approach to overall inventory management is to consider the competitive requirements of inventory allocation, identifying the emphasis required to give market advantage. For example, consider the three major decision areas of product range management, distribution outlet coverage and availability. These are key issues throughout the life of a product and each is a major revenue and cost entity. It follows that if the inventory requirements of each phase of the product-market development process can be established, the impact on working capital requirements may be estimated and specific funding issues identified. In Figure 7.7 these three issues are compared throughout the projected life of a hypothetical product. Initially the product range is wide in order to attract target customers. As the product becomes increasingly successful adjacent market segments will be approached and this may require range expansion to meet additionally identified needs. During the mature phase the emphasis is placed on range rationalization to maintain profitability and productivity in the no-growth mature phase. During the decline phase further rationalization is likely with the possibility that outsourcing of manufacturing may be considered.

Similarly, distribution outlet coverage requires planning if effective profitability and productivity and cash flow is to result. During the emerging and high-growth phases extensive coverage is sought – the objective being to obtain exposure in outlets used by the target customer group, and in which that group expects to purchase the product type. This results in excessive costs and, if maintained, the impact on profitability and productivity is likely to be very damaging. Consequently, outlet coverage should be reviewed as the mature phase is entered. Not only does it follow that the coverage is likely to be renewed and restricted to effective outlets, but alternative structures may be introduced to 'service' low-volume territories and market sectors. As the decline phase approaches franchising possibilities may be an attractive option.

The policy for availability usually follows the pattern whereby high levels of inventory are maintained in both transaction and physical distribution channels in the emerging phase and are likely to be maintained during the high growth phase. A Pareto approach is introduced during the mature phase and extended into the decline phase, with the possibility of using selected distribution intermediaries to maintain cost-effective availability.

It follows that inventory management is important for both market advantage and customer service. It also has financial management implications:

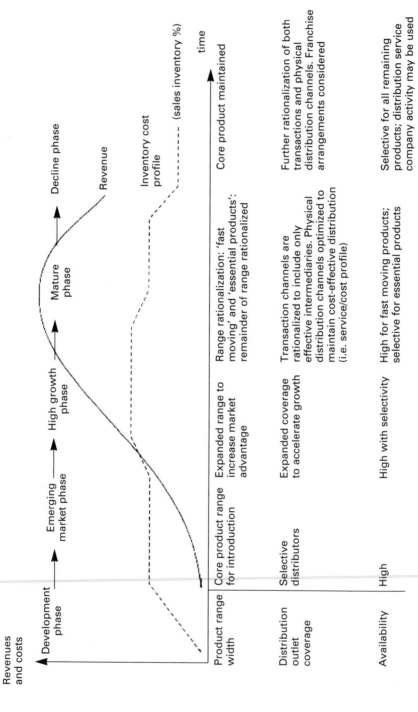

Figure 7.7 Establishing inventory requirements and costs during product life phases

holding inventory requires an investment in working capital *and* in the facilities required physically for storage and delivery activities.

Accounts receivable management

The use of credit as an element of customer service and the effect of this on
sales revenues are important features of supplier–customer relationships. The
primary concerns are how much credit should be allowed and for how long.
The answers to these questions decide the level of investment the organization should make in accounts receivable. Brayshaw (1992) suggested that
both amounts and collection time periods can vary by industry type. He
compared aggregate credit policies of UK and US companies. UK companies
have a considerable proportion of funds invested in debtors, some 20 to 25
per cent collection takes an average of 60 days in the United Kingdom and 40
days approximately in the United States. He suggested that the differences
may be due to cultural issues and not necessarily indicative of managerial
effectiveness.

It follows that customer credit can be an expensive option within the
market offer. In order to manage the cost-effectiveness of a credit policy some
initial decisions should be made:

(i)   Based upon the researched relationship between revenue generated and
      credit offered, a decision should be taken on the length of time
      customers are given to pay bills, and whether incentives (discounts)
      would be effective in accelerating payment. An additional considera-
      tion is the credit terms expected by the market.
(ii) The business should decide to which of its customers it will offer credit
      facilities and the terms of the offer (i.e., the amount of credit and the
      time period for payment). It should also consider the complete range of
      alternatives that are available (i.e., whether debt factoring is a possibil-
      ity) as a means of expanding the business.
(iii) Having established a credit policy, together with credit limits and
      payment expectations for each customer, a system of monitoring *and*
      collection should be decided on and implemented.

The effective management of accounts receivable is essential if the organization's liquidity (productivity of current assets) and profitability are to be
maintained. Credit sales involve both business and financial risk. Business
risk occurs because often there is an element of opportunity cost in the use of
resources (not only those allocated to credit). The production process, selling
and distribution activities consume resources. If the full profit margin is not
realized, this will result in a less than optimal profitability (and productivity)

return to the resources allocated. Financial risk occurs because typically working capital is funded on overdraft facilities for which interest is payable. It follows that if customers abuse the credit facility the cost becomes excessive; if customers do not meet their commitments then a financial loss will occur.

Risk can be minimized by attempting to determine the likely level of risk on a customer-by-customer basis. A number of sources of information exist and these include:

- Trade references obtained from other companies with whom a new customer has dealt.
- Bank references detailing (within the limits of confidence) the financial standing of a customer. These typically are of a standard (and guarded) form.
- Credit reporting agencies; a number exist offering general (published lists) and specific (detailed report) services. IT facilitates both accuracy and speed of this source of information.
- Published accounts; company annual reports are an indication of corporate liquidity. In addition to this there exist central records of charges made against assets when payment defaults occur.

Credit limits for customers are essentially the decision of marketing/finance management, as are the timing and methods to be used for collection. However, there are a number of issues for marketing management. For almost all companies, credit is an essential way of conducting business, clearly a credit facility is necessary. But given that there may be a significant investment made in accounts receivable it is important that the efficiency of accounts receivable as a promotional method, and credit policy in general, be evaluated.

The credit expectations of customers in new markets (or market segments) should be researched as part of the usual marketing research activity conducted prior to making an entry decision. Failure to do so may result in some surprising additional costs. For example, consider the case of Chichester Leisure Pty Ltd. In its existing markets, Chichester Leisure has found that on average 20 per cent of accounts are outstanding beyond the 30 days offered to customers. They are collected within a total of 60 days. In a new market currently under consideration they have identified this to be 33 per cent of revenues and that typically payment is extended to 90 days. The current market is valued at $20 million, credit costs are calculated as:

$16 million at 15% for 30 days: $200,000
$4 million at 15% for 60 days: $100,000
$300,000

$$\frac{\text{Credit cost}}{\text{Sales}} = \frac{\$300,000}{\$20\ 000\ 000} = 1.5\%$$

The proposed market is valued at $7.5 million; credit costs are calculated as:

$2.5 million at 15% for 30 days: $31,250
$5 million at 15% for 90 days: $187,500

$300,000

$$\frac{\text{Credit cost}}{\text{Sales}} = \frac{\$218,750}{\$7,500,000} = 2.9\%$$

The use of credit throughout a product's existence has similar considerations to those discussed earlier for inventory decisions. Figure 7.8 suggests how the use of trade and customer credit facilities may vary throughout the projected life of the product. The extent of the use of credit during the emerging market phase will depend upon the type of new product that is introduced. A competitive response to existing product offers will require less credit incentive than a new, innovative product requiring high levels of inventory by distributors if maximum market penetration is to be obtained at an early date. Options include consignment sales (SOR, sale or return) or VMI facilities to distributors and possibly credit offers to selected end users (the innovators and early adopters). Similar options are available and may be used to expand the rate of sales (and market share) during the high growth phase. Again product characteristics and marketing objectives are important considerations. During the mature phase of the product's life there should be less need of credit incentives other than for occasional promotional purposes. By the time the decline phase is reached the role of credit (together with other marketing policies) should be to manage the volume/market share to ensure that profitability and productivity objectives are maintained.

Cash management

Cash is an essential component of working capital and has three primary roles. The first is for routine *transactions*, such as the payment of suppliers, of staff and for occupancy costs and utilities. Because it is not possible to synchronize payments received with those demanded, a level of cash must be planned (throughout the trading period) to meet these requirements. A second role for cash is to allow the company the means to meet unforeseen contingencies which may result due to product failures (costs of replacement and compensation) and even legal costs (e.g., Dow Corning and cosmetic surgery implant products). Other contingencies include more routine considerations such as

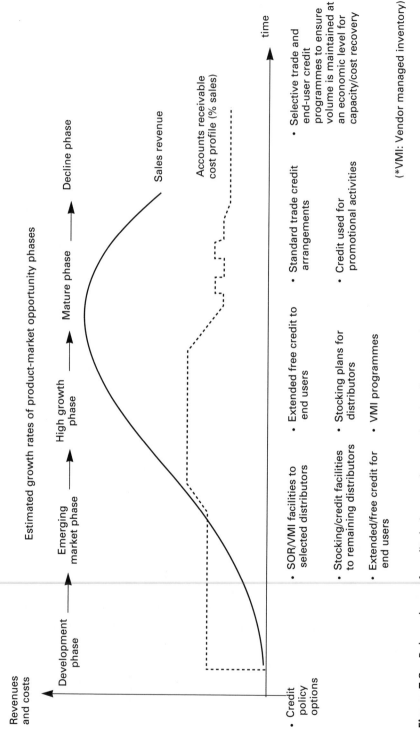

Figure 7.8 Role and use of credit during product-market development phases

budget errors. These are identified as *precautionary* measures. A third motive concerns *speculative* uses of cash, often involving supply inputs and payment offers from suppliers. Often suppliers may offer additional purchasing discounts if they (the suppliers) seek to increase their own cash balances (or decrease short-term loans such as overdrafts). They may also increase the settlement discounts offered to customers. Having cash available enables a company to take advantage of these opportunities.

An important point to be understood is that while having too little cash is a problem for the financial manager (who may have to borrow at expensive rates of short-term interest), so too excess cash is an inefficient use of cash resources, which should be invested in other assets to expand profitability and productivity (a growth issue) and, therefore, shareholder value. Under the heading of cash, a business can include 'near-cash' assets. These include securities and deposits which can be converted to cash at short notice but which are earning interest.

It follows that if management can synchronize cash receipts and payments, the need to borrow at high short-term interest rates can be avoided. The cash budget is used to identify periods of cash shortages and surpluses, thereby signifying future periods when cash sources should be approached for borrowing facilities and when excess cash balances should be made available for other uses in the business or for investment.

The routine situations can be planned relatively easily. It is important for marketing management to be aware of the characteristics of the short-term cash flow profile and avoid excessive short-term changes to marketing programmes. Not only will those be disruptive from an operations point of view but the cost of short-term funds that may be required to finance promotions or increased levels of inventories and accounts receivable is high and usually results in diluted profit margins. Marketing managers should attempt to work with financial management to minimize the need for short-term financing where it is feasible in marketing terms.

7.4 Managing current liabilities

Here our concern is with the management of suppliers' accounts and short-term financing of the business. Attention to the management of current liabilities will result in an overall optimization of working capital.

Accounts payable (trade credit)

The complement of accounts receivable is accounts payable and conversely for most transaction channels trade credit is an important source of short-term funds. It represents the time taken for the purchasing organization to pay a supplier; provided the period taken to pay does not extend beyond an agreed time the vendor will be satisfied. However, problems do occur if the nonpayment extends beyond the agreed period: the vendor incurs costs (either interest charges or opportunity costs from the loss of use of the funds) and the trading relationship becomes strained.

Terms of trade vary by industry sector and there are a number of characteristics which influence the accepted norm for each sector. Brayshaw (1992) suggested these to be:

- Product features; fast-moving consumer goods typically have shorter credit period terms than slow-moving items.
- Vendor's liquidity position; sellers experiencing cash shortages may have difficulty in offering extended credit. However, if their competitors are offering better terms they will need to seek alternative sources for funding credit.
- Buyers' liquidity position; the converse situation also obtains; a buyer with short-term liquidity problems will seek suppliers with extended trade credit terms. Payment is usually 'encouraged' by offering discounts for prompt payment and in some situations interest is charged on outstanding amounts.

These characteristics notwithstanding, trade credit remains the most important source of short-term funds. Its wide use occurs because:

- No interest is made by the vendor (the fact that suppliers publish interest charges for outstanding accounts does not mean they are imposed).
- A good credit record enables businesses to obtain supplies relatively easily, its suppliers being confident of payment within the accepted trade terms.
- Trade credit funding is correlated to turnover; as the business grows so too does this type of funding.

While supplier companies attempt to closely monitor their accounts receivable and offer discount incentives for payment ahead of the agreed time, a large number of purchasing companies very intentionally extend the time period. This is not unusual in situations where the vendor is considerably smaller than the purchasing company, a situation not uncommon in consumer goods industries where the growth of multiple retailers has resulted in very large distributor companies. For these companies with multimillion turnover figures the benefits to be obtained by extending the credit taken from suppliers by 25 per cent (e.g., seven days beyond an agreed 30 days) can provide very large amounts of interest free cash or negative working capital.

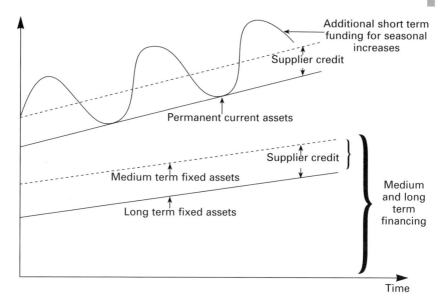

Figure 7.9   Using negative working capital for business development

Very large companies have been able to expand their activities, using suppliers' working capital to fund their new outlets. Figure 7.9 illustrates how this situation can occur and how it is managed by the distribution company. It will be recalled from Figure 7.3 (structuring the finance of fixed and current assets) that we have three groups of assets: temporary current assets, permanent current assets and fixed assets. Temporary current assets are often funded by the supplier; the products are usually very fast turnover items and sold before payment becomes due. Permanent current assets may be funded this way with payment cycles and stock turn being synchronized; slower moving items may be supported by overdraft facilities.

A favoured method for achieving this is to work with marketing/merchandise management to develop product ranges which, while responding to customer expectations, also meet stock turnover objectives. By using the Pareto characteristics of the product range the product offer can be adjusted to provide variety *and* purchasing depth (i.e., perhaps instead of providing a choice of five items in a specific category this is reduced to three). While sales may show marginal decline the buying discounts on the remainder increase, their stock turns are increased and, if payment to the suppliers is extended, large amounts of interest-free cash is made available for business development. It should be said that as consumer choice, quality and in-store ambience become important characteristics, the payback time periods become extended, making such financial policies more difficult to implement.

There are thus some important issues in trade credit for marketing management. The first is to understand the role of trade credit in the customers' business and the use of credit to gain market advantage by devising a policy which is effective. However, this also requires an understanding of the impact of trade credit on the managers' own business. For example, if there is a strict understanding between supplier and customers on outstanding credit (with almost 100 per cent compliance on a 30-day payment cycle) it would be unwise to relax trade credit terms. If the practice is industry-wide then the outstanding receivables may soon be considered permanent current assets of the customer and become a source of medium-/long-term finance. The essential issue for marketing is to understand the financial management policy concerning the use of trade credit within the company and its impact on profitability, productivity and growth (business development).

Bank overdraft

Bank overdrafts are repayable on call. That is, the bank overdraft agreement may be ended or reduced by the bank at very short notice and while this rarely occurs it should be borne in mind, particularly when considering additional marketing expenditures. Any request for an increase in an overdraft facility would be reviewed by the bank from a risk point of view and a major criterion is the 'matching principle' of short-term funding for short-term projects.

When overdraft limits and interest rates are negotiated between the company and its bank typically four factors are important:

(i) The length of time the company has been a customer with the bank, and the level and type of business conducted by the company with the bank.

(ii) The current and recent financial performance of the company which reflects its financial strength and the financial risk profile of its senior management.

(iii) A review of its business development plan with an emphasis on the risk involved, that is, if the business is developing new product-markets its business risk (and that confronting the bank) is likely to be higher than if it is expanding its current position through market penetration.

(iv) The size and nature of security offered by the organization. This may be a claim on property or equipment, as in the case of large companies, or for small businesses guarantees from principals within the business.

Overdrafts are considered an essential component of short-term finance, second only to those of trade credit. They can also represent a large source of funds and should, therefore, be used carefully. While overdrafts are seen as an important element of working capital financing, unlike trade credit they have an interest charge, and this cost can have an important impact on project margins and should be included in market appraisals.

Other short-term finance

There are a number of less frequently used forms of short-term finance. *Debt factoring* involves raising funds on the security of the company's outstanding receivables (customer accounts) so that cash is received earlier than it otherwise would be if the debts were recovered in the normal cycle of events. The services offered vary; they are also expensive and should therefore be seen as less attractive financially than overdraft facilities.

Invoice discounting is a particular form of financing using this principle. The discounting companies are usually very selective and are unlikely to accept high-risk invoice debts. Typically premiums are required and again the cost of this form of borrowing can be very high.

Deferred tax payments are also a form of short-term funds. These are possible because of the lag between profits being earned and the payment of taxes due on them. However, tax authorities worldwide are introducing regulations which are closing down this facility. Many authorities have introduced taxation prepayment systems, whereby prepayment of tax based upon previous trading is required and tax withholding payments paid on a monthly basis to the revenue authorities.

In much the same way *dividends declared but not paid* are a form of short-term funds. However, these are *very* short term as half yearly payments of dividends may be expected by shareholders.

7.5   Working capital performance measurement

The recession of the late 1980s and early 1990s was important in many ways. Mention has already been made of the changes made to management structures and philosophies, particularly in the focus on the core business and the outsourcing of non-core activities, products and product services.

However, the role of working capital and its management has also been considered widely. Tully (1994) gave examples of large US companies which undertook vigorous reviews of working capital structure and management following the recession. He discussed the concepts of zero working capital and negative working capital and the activities of large companies seeking to reduce their working capital requirements. The interesting issue presented by Tully is the size and type of business involved, including large manufacturing companies such as General Electric, Whirlpool, Quaker Oats and Campbell Soup.

The argument for reducing working capital used by these (and other companies) was expressed by Tully:

> Reducing working capital yields two powerful benefits. First every dollar freed from inventories or receivables rings up a one-time $1 contribution to cash flow. Second, the quest for zero working capital permanently raises earnings. Like all capital, working capital costs money, so reducing it yields savings. In addition, cutting working capital forces companies to produce and deliver faster than the competition, enabling them to win new business and charge premium prices for filling rush orders. As inventories evaporate warehouses disappear. Companies no longer need forklift drivers to shuttle supplies around the factory or schedulers to plan production months in advance.

And

> The most important discipline that zero working capital necessitates is speed. Many companies today produce long-term forecasts of orders. They then manufacture their product weeks or months in advance, creating big inventories; eventually they fill orders from the bulging stocks.

Clearly these companies are undertaking more than a review of working capital components. Rather they are undertaking a comprehensive review of the entire operations process; this includes procurement, manufacturing operations, inventory policies and customer order communications and handling. The impact is significant as the examples given by Tully suggest:

> Over 12 months that ended last May [1994], Campbell Soup pared working capital by $80 million. It used the cash to develop new products and buy companies in Britain, Australia and other countries. But Campbell also expects to harvest an extra $50 million in profits over the next few years by lowering overtime, storage costs, and other expenses . . .

> In 1988 American Standard wallowed in over $725 million . . . 25 cents per dollar of sales . . . [in 1994] . . . working capital [was reduced] to $525 million about 14% of sales. He has used the $200 million . . . to pay down debt and make capital investments. Lowered costs have raised annual operating earnings by $100 million, or 33%, since 1990.

These and other examples of savings have not been achieved by reducing customer service or damaging supplier–distributor relationships. Quaker Oats moved away from a situation where it shipped large stocks to customers, which then sold the product over long periods of weeks, even months. Costs rose and margins declined as Quaker Oats carried huge inventories and met overtime payments. The trade loading was expensive due to the extra discounts demanded by customers as recompense for their carrying large inventories. A change in operations philosophy and methods resulted in production methods which operate to replenish shelves with promotions programmed to meet financial as well as marketing objectives. Since 1990 Quaker Oats has reduced working capital from 13 per cent of sales to 7.3 per cent, there by freeing US$200 million in cash. Changes in operations methods have increased the number of hours spent resetting equipment but while this has increased costs by some US$20,000 per year the reduction in inventories has exceeded US$500,000 per year!

Clearly if customer service can be maintained (and perhaps enhanced) then efforts to decrease working capital produce considerable benefits.

Product management is an important activity (see Figure 7.10). The phases of a product-market development cycle are shown together with the working capital components (and uses of cash). The diagram also illustrates the implications for working capital should the decision be taken to extend the mature phase of the cycle. During the emerging market phase, total costs may increase if variable costs such as inventory building, credit allowed and promotional expenditure (use of working capital: cash) are increased to accelerate or reinforce the product-market launch.

7.6 'New economy' opportunities

The business models that have been influenced by the 'new economy' have a number of common features. It will be recalled that in Chapter 2 it was proposed that free cash flow has become a primary performance measure. This point was emphasized with Figure 2.2. An important element in the model for this discussion concerns *Cash flow from Assets*. This comprises operating cash flow +/– short-term working capital requirements +/– capital structure (restructuring) costs. The recent business models introduce the notion that some aspects of working capital management may be more efficiently managed by partner organizations. Three items can be considered.

An obvious candidate is inventory. Supply chain management discipline suggests that inventory should be minimized within the supply chain meeting specified 'availability' objectives and avoiding excess amounts resulting in a number of cost reductions. For example inventory-holding costs comprising the levels of inventory held in specific locations should be planned to ensure that customer service expectations are met but excess inventory is avoided

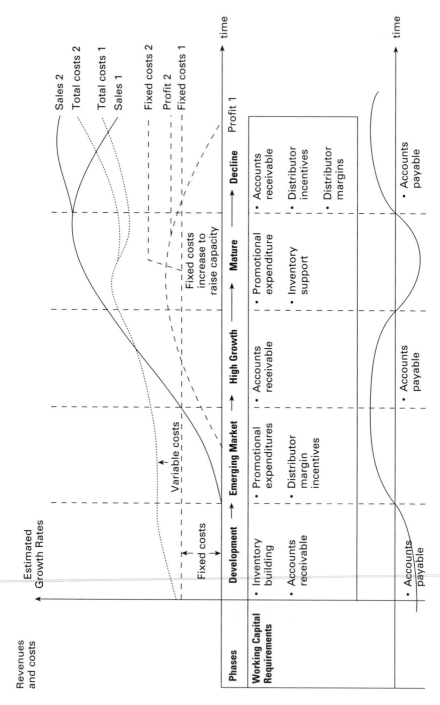

Figure 7.10 Working capital requirements during the product-market development phase

and with it the costs of additional storage and 'obsolescence'. The build-to-order (BTO) approach adopted by Dell Computers extends this by introducing 'postponement' into the model. Products are assembled to meet specific customer (paid-for) orders. This further reduces costs because not only are the inventory components maintained at relevant levels but the labour costs that would have been included if the products had been made available on a 'speculative' basis would be included.

Customer credit is another element of working capital that may be reduced by the 'new economy' models. Effective relationship management policies should be based upon an evaluation of the roles and tasks required within a distribution channel. Thus a credit policy that encourages distributors to manage their specific tasks more efficiently is likely to have a positive impact on credit (accounts receivable). The adoption of Internet web-based ordering models has also had a positive effect on this aspect of working capital management. Web-based transactions that require prepayment arrangements have reduced accounts receivable considerably.

The Internet has also introduced 'buying exchanges', such as COVISNET (automobile industry) and ELEMICA (pharmaceutical industry). These not only reduce the accounts payable (and therefore the accounts receivable) within an industry and consequently working capital requirements but also offer cost reduction benefits (see Figure 7.11).

Performance measurement criteria

We have already discussed the use of financial ratios for performance measurement (see Part II). Some ratios are of particular interest when we are considering the efficiency of the organization's use of resources:

Activity ratios:
  current asset turnover
  stock turnover (sales, value, purchases value)
  debtor turnover
  average collection period of receivables
  average payment period of suppliers

Liquidity ratios:
  current ratio
  liquid ratio

Working capital ratios:
  current assets/fixed assets
  working capial turnover

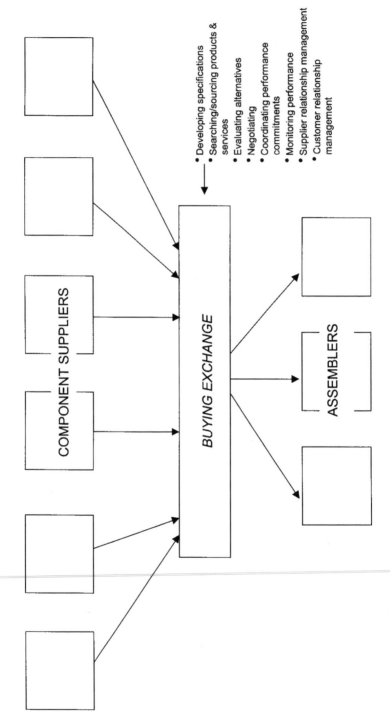

COMPONENT SUPPLIERS

BUYING EXCHANGE

• Developing specifications
• Searching/sourcing products & services
• Evaluating alternatives
• Negotiating
• Coordinating performance commitments
• Monitoring performance
• Supplier relationship management
• Customer relationship management

ASSEMBLERS

Figure 7.11 Buying exchanges reduce interaction and transaction costs

Marketing-based ratios, which consider the relationships between market performance and working capital components:

$$\frac{\text{Working capital (\%)}}{\text{Sales}} \text{ and } \frac{\text{Working capital (\%)}}{\text{Market share}}$$

Working capital turnover:

$$\frac{\text{Sales}}{\text{Working capital}}$$

On a specific product range basis we might consider ratios which indicate the efficiencies of specific applications of working capital components. For example:

$$\frac{\text{Sales: product (range)}}{\text{Product (range) stocks}} \text{ (Measures turnover and trend)}$$

$$\frac{\text{Sales: product (range)}}{\text{Product (range) credit allowed}} \text{ (Measures debt, turnover and trend)}$$

$$\frac{\text{Debtors (product range)}}{\text{Sales}} \times 365 = \text{(days credit allowed)}$$

Similarly for specific customers we could measure:

$$\frac{\text{Sales per customer}}{\text{Customer credit}} \text{ (measures credit, turnover and trend)}$$

$$\frac{\text{Customer credit}}{\text{Customer credit purchases}} \times 365 \text{ (days credit allowed)}$$

Financial management would be interested in these ratios but would also be concerned with creditor based ratios:

$$\frac{\text{Credit purchases (by locatable product group)}}{\text{Creditors (by group(s) of suppliers)}}$$

$$\frac{\text{Creditor(s)}}{\text{Credit purchases (by supplier)}} \times 365 = \text{(days credit taken by supplier)}$$

Richman (1995) discussed working capital management from the viewpoint of productivity improvement. He quoted George Stalk (Boston Consulting Group): 'working capital productivity is not a driver of improvement like a focus on time or cost. It is a measure of the divisionwide or company-wide improvement that the drivers create.' Increasing working capital productivity results in savings on capital, which is important because manufacturers can tie up as much as 30 per cent of their total capital in working capital support. There is also a substantial saving in labour cost through eliminating materials handling steps and streamlining order processing and the payments collection process.

Because working capital can be manipulated by extending supplier credit many companies omit it from the productivity calculation; some even *add* payables to the working capital total to ensure that management cannot do so! Working capital productivity improvement minimizes the capital tied up in a range of support operations. The implications for marketing are that any decisions (such as increasing product choice and availability and customer credit) should be evaluated for cost effectiveness prior to their implementation.

7.7 Summary

We have considered the components of working capital and their influence on marketing decisions (and the influence of marketing decisions on working capital components).

Working capital is an essential element of the operational marketing activities of the business and of the manufacturing functions which support marketing. As Tully (1994) quoted from a Boston Consulting Group consultant, 'working capital is the grease that keeps the manufacturing motor running'.

REFERENCES

Brayshaw, R. E. (1992) *The Concise Guide to Company Finance and its Management*, Chapman & Hall, London.

Dobbins, R. and Witt, S. F. (1988) *Practical Financial Management*, Basil Blackwell, Oxford.

Richman, T. (1995) *Briefings from the Editors*, Harvard Business Review, May/June.

Tully, S. (1994) 'Raiding and company's hidden cash', Fortune, 22 August.

Wilson, C. and Keers, B. (1987) *Introduction to Financial Management*, Prentice Hall, Australia.

Managing the Fixed Asset Base

Fixed assets are the organization's means of production. The acquisition of fixed assets is concerned with adding value to the product offer and ultimately to the organization itself. This differs from the acquisition of current assets where the concern is with their value as part of the product sold to the customer. It is this difference which concerns the marketing/finance interface. Marketing management concern with customer satisfaction differs from that of financial management to minimize the purchasing and ownership of assets which do not increase in value. Typically fixed assets (currently this includes property) lose value as assets and the financial manager's concern is, therefore, to ensure that the value added through ownership and/or use of fixed assets exceeds the cost of ownership.

This chapter is concerned with managing fixed assets such that both customer added value and the overall value of the business is increased. It will identify the types of assets businesses usually deal with and will consider issues of performance in the context of profitability and productivity. Ownership and use of fixed assets are two quite different things and these will also be discussed in this chapter.

8.1 Components of the asset base

Figure 8.1 depicts a typical asset base. We have included working capital, or net current assets, in it to complete the aggregate situation but clearly will not make reference to working capital in any detail because this was covered in the previous chapter.

In the introduction we suggested that the decision to procure the use of fixed assets is driven by their value in a production process. For a manufacturing

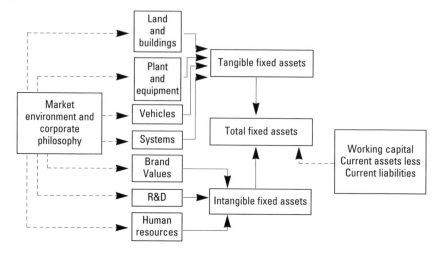

Figure 8.1   Managing and fixed asset base

organization such a decision will cover the property, plant and equipment and other infrastructure required to convert raw materials and components into saleable products. A distribution company will view its fixed assets differently: much of the utility will already exist and its use of fixed assets are primarily to add time and place utility to the form utility which exists. However, the difference is not quite as clear-cut as this might suggest. Manufacturing organizations also have location decisions to deal with; an important issue in manufacturing decisions is whether the production facility should be located adjacent to raw materials sources or closer to its markets.

A number of factors influence this decision, and these often involve marketing/finance interface issues. An obvious one is customer satisfaction and these typically concern product characteristics such as product shelf life; handling characteristics – volume, cube and weight; and customer expectations for service and availability.

Shelf life is a feature shared by consumer and industrial products. We are well aware of 'sell-by' dates for food products and these products' requirements for rapid but economical delivery systems. Often the fixed asset decision is a composite solution whereby a large manufacturing facility is located close to the largest proportion of its market, thus reducing transportation time and the costs involved in servicing the majority of its customers. Market size is important if managerial economies and economies of scale are to be obtained from the operations process. To ensure that customer delivery and availability expectations are met a distribution infrastructure is put in place comprising warehousing and transportation facilities (together with inventories, a working capital concern).

Handling characteristics of a number of products are such that specialist transportation facilities are required. Very large manufacturing equipment and components and the movement of construction equipment from one site location to another (a service product example) are typical examples of this. The fixed asset issues here include manufacturing facilities and the 'delivery' element of the product. (The issue of whether the company should own a fixed asset, such as a specialist transportation vehicle, or purchase the use of the asset as a service we will consider later.)

Customer expectations have a large influence on fixed asset decisions. There are a number of product-markets for which customer expectations of immediate (or very short lead time) availability are important – for example, pharmaceuticals. Many prescription drugs are very expensive and also have short shelf lives. Consequently there is a reluctance by pharmacists to hold stocks of these drugs, preferring to rely on high levels of availability and very rapid delivery from suppliers.

There are also aspects of customer psychology which influence fixed asset decisions. The economies of scale available in manufacturing and distribution led to considerable consolidation in the 1980s. In order to manage production and distribution fixed costs manufacturers built larger but fewer manufacturing and distribution facilities. However, many found anxiety among their customers, who were concerned that because the physical (or geographical) distance between them and the supplier had increased, the level of service they would receive would, as a consequence, decrease. Much of the subsequent investment in systems for customer order processing and management was motivated by the need to consolidate supplier–customer relationships *as well as* to benefit from improved control and lower costs.

Our discussion so far has concentrated on tangible fixed assets. Figure 8.1 suggests that intangible fixed assets are also important, and increasingly we see organizational concern for intangible fixed assets as sources of value to the business. Thus we have begun to see brands, research and development, and a number of aspects of human resources (e.g., management development and employee training) being considered as capital expenditure items.

Brand values are significant in both consumer and industrial product-markets, and this significance extends across manufacturing and distribution. Brand values increase not only as organizations invest in customer communications (i.e., advertising and promotional expenditure), but also because of investment in product differentiation and service characteristics: in other words, investment in the product-market scope characteristics of marketing operational strategies. Figure 8.2 reminds us of the decisions required at the strategy and operational levels (see Chapter 3).

Product mix decisions involve investment decisions in the market offer characteristics (i.e., variety, quality, product features, etc.); delivery decisions

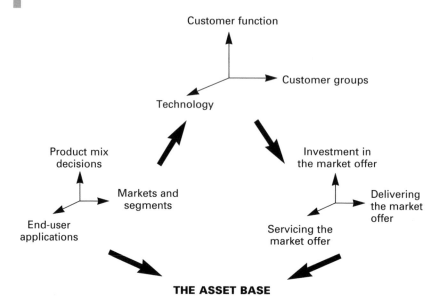

THE ASSET BASE

Figure 8.2   Marketing/finance interface: implications for asset base decisions
Based upon Abell, D. (1980) *Defining the Business: The Starting Point of Strategic Planning*, Prentice Hall, New York.

are concerned with investment in technology, product-market distribution facilities and customer communications; while servicing the market offer can involve product-service reformulation to meet customer expectations, which may change either by product type, market location or perhaps over time. Each of these resource allocation decisions contributes towards the brand value perceptions of existing and potential customers.

Another intangible fixed asset we identified was research and development (R&D). Research and development in technological products is critical in ensuring success. Without considerable investment in product and applications development many companies would surrender their differentiation and competitive advantage to their competitors. An obvious example is the computer sector where R&D activities form an important element of the competitive base of the market leaders. It follows that R&D expenditure is a significant investment and an important feature of the total assets for such organizations.

For a number of organizations the skill and expertise which accrues within its management and employees can also be considered to be an intangible fixed asset. Consequently any expenditures on staff development should be considered as an investment in the asset value of the business. There are many examples of companies which focus on their ability to offer high levels of advice and service based upon the expertise of well-trained and long-serving employees. Often it is the problem-diagnosing and -solving skills of staff that are the basis of the productservice offer. For example, consultancy businesses and technology applications areas in data communications companies fall into this category. In such cases the staff themselves and the expenditures allocated to their development are an asset and as such are of value to the organization.

8.2 Asset performance criteria and influences

There are some basic quantitative performance requirements, each of which has an influence on the performance of the asset base. These are shown in Figure 8.3.

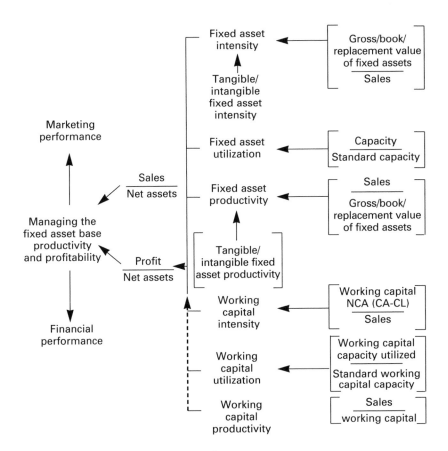

Figure 8.3 Influences on asset performance

Fixed asset intensity (or fixed capital intensity) is a measure of the value of fixed assets expressed as a percentage of sales; a 50 per cent ratio implies that one dollar of sales requires 50 cents of investment in assets. The actual value used (i.e., gross or book over replacement value) will depend upon the use being made of the ratio. For example, gross value would be used at a strategy evaluation stage of planning, while book value would be used as an ongoing performance measure. Replacement value would be used for incremental expansion of the asset base or perhaps in a situation where the impact of inflation should be considered. There is often the need during strategy option evaluation to consider tangible and/or intangible asset intensity. To take an actual example, a f.m.c.g. manufacturer was confronted with two alternatives: one was to use a plant extension for increasing sales of its nationally branded range of products in a highly competitive market; the other was to accept the offer of a major multiple retailer to manufacture an own-branded version. The retailer offered a guaranteed volume schedule for a three-year period (to be reviewed after that time). The decision was complicated. Not only was plant asset intensity an issue but so also were intangible assets such as brand values. On the one hand these would not require promotional investment expenditures, but on the other they could decline in the long run (through the impact of the retailers' own-label product version). Maintaining the investment would maintain the brand equity value and continuity, thereby ensuring impact as and when new products were introduced.

Fixed asset utilization is typically measured as the average percentage of standard capacity utilized during a specified period (usually a budget year). Fixed capacity utilization concerns the investment in both tangible and intangible assets. Standard capacity is the sales value of the maximum output a business can sustain with facilities (tangibles and intangibles) normally in operation and under normal constraints. Both tangible and intangible asset values should be considered during planning and implementation of strategies, and during evaluation. While there may be some difficulties in the initial valuation of intangible asset entities, once established they offer an additional joint marketing/financial performance measure.

Some amplification may help at this point. Given an investment over time to establish a strong brand, a business not showing interest in the effectiveness of the investment decision (i.e., the utilization of the brand as an asset) is unlikely to know whether or not to continue the investment or to consider alternative uses for the other assets such as developing alternative brands and moving into new product markets.

Fixed asset productivity may be considered either as an aggregate measure or broken down into component items. Clearly, in a computational sense it is the reciprocal of the intensity measure; however, it is a useful component of the return on investment/assets performance measure when combined with a margin performance measure (see Chapter 1 and the discussion of the strategic profit model). A view of the performance of components is useful when evaluating ongoing activities and when making reinvestment decisions.

Working capital intensity, utilization and productivity: If the business could forecast its activities with perfect accuracy, it would have sufficient cash and inventory to meet its sales and sourcing requirements and have exactly the level of debtors to meet an optimal customer credit policy. Working capital performance is largely influenced by industry sector, for example, retailing companies have lower levels of working capital (because of the absence of raw materials, work in progress and negative working capital influence of supplier stocks and credit); hence the working capital intensity differs.

As we mentioned earlier in the chapter, we are concerned here with the overall performance of the organization and therefore *working capital* (or net current assets) should be included in a measure of asset performance. There is also the potential for trade-off situations to be evaluated. These may include situations in which a product is sold in kit form requiring the customer to contribute to its value by assembling the components and completing the product. In these situations the supplier reduces costs (i.e., the labour content of manufacture, the storage space requirements, transportation costs, etc.). The cost reductions are shared with the customer. IKEA is one company that has developed this approach, with considerable success.

In Chapter 5 we introduced the concept of operational gearing. It will be recalled that operational gearing identifies the relationship between fixed and variable costs. High fixed cost activities typically operate with a much higher investment in plant and equipment, that is, high fixed asset intensity, with relatively higher margins than an organization which prefers a lower combination of fixed assets and fixed costs. The investment issues here concern marketing factors as well as financial management preferences.

Typically, the high fixed cost company manufactures a much higher proportion of the final product. The benefits are often cost-effective quality control improvements, component availability and, possibly, improved flexibility of the use of labour. The disadvantages are those described earlier in Chapter 4 and concern the implications for profitability and productivity if demand should fall. The low fixed cost/high variable cost company model reverses the situation. It is, however, vulnerable to supplier-based problems, such as industrial disputes, supplier: capacity problems, and so on. Marketing factors which could influence this trade-off situation include: customer preferences (and their importance for differentiation and competitive advantage), market size, growth rate and stability, supply and sourcing, and overall risk.

Customer preferences for product variety, quality and price competitiveness obviously influence the asset intensity decision. Preferences for choice should imply flexible manufacturing systems with short-run production scheduling. This may result in decisions for an assembly-based activity in which the standard components are manufactured internally and external suppliers used for components specific to individual products within the range.

Quality control is usually more difficult to manage if a large proportion of components are outsourced from a number of different suppliers. From a control viewpoint, therefore, the high fixedcost situation (with its high risk profile, see Chapter 5) may be preferable. Price competitiveness usually has at least one other component in the equation such as style, quality or reliability. It follows that the manufacturing decision is not decided by opting for the lowest cost structure facility but the one which offers an optimal solution.

Competitive advantage results from an effective response to customer preferences. It follows that competitive advantage is linked closely to the asset intensity decision through the specific characteristics of productservice differentiation identified as important for customers.

Market size, growth rate and stability have a significant influence on the choice of manufacturing facility and therefore its fixed cost/variable cost structure. A large market demonstrating a steady rate of growth, with little or no seasonal variation, is likely to result in a more highly operationally geared facility than a market with the opposite features. The former offers an ideal situation in which production scheduling is relatively simple and the overall stability offers an opportunity to maximize margins by manufacturing a large proportion of the product within the organization.

As we noted in relation to customer preferences and quality control, supply and sourcing issues are important. However, innovatory products often cannot be manufactured externally (e.g., fasteners, some instrumentation gauges, etc.). Similarly existing products typically have supply markets established, which offer quality and reliability together with high levels of technical/design services. In this situation there have to be very strong (often not financially influenced) reasons for preferring to manufacture internally. Access to specific materials or components may be difficult due to supply monopolies, distance or other factors; these, together with poor quality, reliability or price levels, may influence a decision in favour of internal sourcing.

The asset intensity decision therefore may require some detailed analysis and the choice between high levels of fixed assets and correspondingly lower working capital commitments (or vice versa) be identified and evaluated. A longitudinal approach will be particularly useful. Using judgements of the marketing factors, managers can begin to reach conclusions concerning the levels of business and financial risk unresolved in a strategy and, together with financial management, agree on an asset base structure which would optimize profitability, productivity and cash flow. Figure 8.4 illustrates how asset structure decisions (fixed assets/working capital alternatives) may vary throughout the product development phases.

During the emerging-market and high-growth phases the objective is to provide an asset base which supports the product. However, being aware of business and financial risk, management would prefer not to invest unnecessarily in fixed assets and would seek options to trade off fixed asset commitment at this stage with net current assets; for example, many of the components might be outsourced where to do so has no major impact on customer expectations. As the product becomes established so the business would become more willing to undertake investment. During the mature phase the firm faces the options of expansion, contraction or maintaining its size. This decision will be influenced to a large extent by market share and activities of competitors. Clearly if the intention is to withdraw from a market there will be an incentive to reduce fixed asset investment (or not to maintain existing fixed assets) and outsource as much of the productservice as is consistent with maintaining the market offer.

The influence of marketing decisions

The decision on the precise form of asset base with which to respond to market opportunities has a number of influences. Figure 8.4 suggested that a risk/opportunity view of the market would result in a balance of fixed and net current assets over the life span of a product. However, as we suggested earlier there are a number of issues that affect the decision.

Figure 8.5 offers a more formalized view of these influences. The task of financial management is to manage the net asset base so as to ensure that its structure and performance make it possible for the business to pursue and realize its objectives. Therefore, if the business is to be capable of making and implementing strategic marketing decisions which result in gaining competitive advantage, customer satisfaction and increase the value of the business, the optimal balance of fixed and net current assets should be aimed for. However, what may appear to be ideal in terms of asset structure and cost of capital may be inappropriate in so far as the characteristics of the marketplace go. A high-volume/low-cost/low-flexibility operations structure with a high fixed asset intensity, for example, may be ideal for the company, but if its market opportunity is characterized by numerous segments (each having very different product-service expectations, and with perhaps considerable turnover of customers and competitors) it follows that flexibility is essential

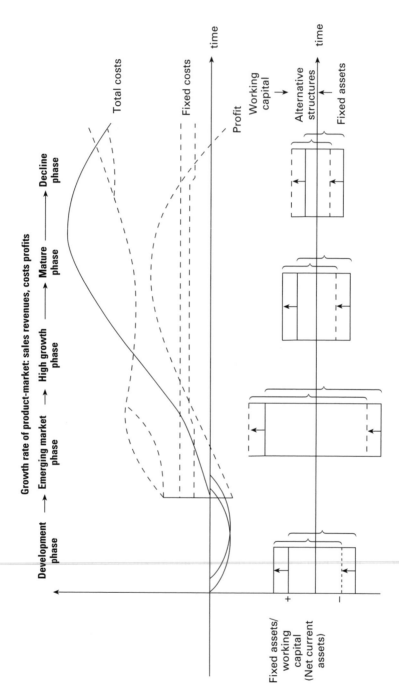

Figure 8.4 Asset base structure and product development phases

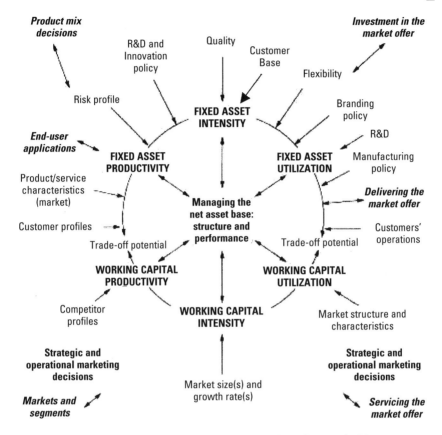

Figure 8.5 Influence of strategic and operational marketing decisions on asset base structure and management

and that a rigid system would be very restricting. Figure 8.5 suggests that the asset base decision should be one which explores the market opportunities and trade-off potential available and is influenced by the dimensions of the strategic business area and the implementation functions.

Internal factors Among the internal considerations and influences are some we have discussed previously; nevertheless, each has an influence on asset base decisions.

Innovation policy determines *R&D policy*, which is an essential feature of competitive advantage for technology-based companies, and may have significance as an intangible asset. *Quality* may require investment in sophisticated plant (tangible assets); furthermore, if quality is a major competitive issue the investment (and replacement/refurbishment) of plant may feature prominently. *Flexibility* in both manufacturing and distribution operations may have high levels of costs; associated with fixed asset costs are high costs for training (human resources). Thus, the investment in *manufacturing and operations facilities* may have a number of facets. One is the response to customer expectations within time constraints (availability and reliability), another concerns order size handling capabilities and the implications for product and customer account profitability; and yet another concerns customer expectations for variety. *Branding decisions* have been discussed earlier in this chapter and all that need be added at this point is an acknowledgment of the impact of brand equity and brand values as intangible assets. For f.m.c.g. companies, product development decisions may be motivated by brand continuity concerns and distribution presence in major retail outlets. For these reasons it is important to consider branding policy and value decisions as asset and investment decisions as well as marketing decisions.

Sourcing and supply factors can have a major impact on asset base decisions. At one end of the spectrum there is the question of the lengths to which the company should go to ensure availability and quality of raw materials (which may result in complete or partial ownership of supply chain elements) prior to manufacturing or may involve a high-cost procurement activity (human resources, intangible assets) to source on an international scale.

External factors Among the important external influences are *customers' operating structures* and policies. Recent years have seen considerable changes in operating philosophies and methods. We have discussed JIT and quick response (a logistics/distribution service discipline offering rapid inventory replenishment) techniques and clearly these and subsequent developments should be considered at the marketing strategy development stage. Marketing management should ascertain the volume of business it is likely to obtain from each customer or customer group and determine the costs of servicing them. A major determinant of these costs will be the service response that the customers' own operating methods require. It follows that they can have a major impact on the asset base investment.

Market structures and characteristics are important in so far as they may determine the way business is conducted and, perhaps, competition (the competitive differentiation) within segments and sectors. It is likely that the basic market characteristics of concentration and/or fragmentation will influence the conduct of business. A few powerful customer companies (such as those dominating f.m.c.g. retailing) can and do have a strong influence on suppliers to their service requirements. A large number of customers within a market offers more scope for competitive differentiation and, consequently, more options for asset base structures. The same argument applies to markets that have supplier concentration. Here market leadership usually implies some level of control over competitive characteristics in the marketplace: again, we are likely to have a situation which will influence the tangible and intangible asset base characteristics required for effective response and market leadership. Clearly, *competitor profiles* and *customer profiles* should be researched and evaluated prior to making firm decisions concerning asset structures.

Equally important to the asset base decision is the *market size* and *growth rate* of market opportunities. As we saw earlier, in Chapters 4 and 5, market size and potential growth rates can have significant implications for scale decisions and the scope for price competitiveness offered by experience effects. Market size and growth rate are important, but should be considered together with the *product-service characteristics* of the marketplace. As we found earlier both economies-of-scale and experience-effect cost profiles are often influenced much more by the characteristics of the product. A customer preference for variety and quality in ranges can restrict the cost benefits offered by experience effect based manufacturing systems.

Market expenditures are important in that not only do they determine the levels of advertising and promotional expenditure, and therefore the investment in barriers to entry, but they also determine the levels of investment in intangible assets and influence branding decisions.

A thorough evaluation of the implications of both internal and external factors from both marketing and financial points of view helps to formulate more precise approaches to *business* and *financial risk*. It is important to approach this analysis from 'both sides' by asking what are the financial implications for the asset base structure if the organization implements a particular marketing strategy what are the implications for marketing decisions if there are specific constraints imposed by financial management on levels of investment in fixed assets and working capital. Such an approach er.compasses managements' exploration of all alternative asset formats.

8.3   Asset base performance: characteristics and relationships

There are a number of important characteristics and relationships of the asset base that should be understood by marketing management. Figure 8.6 identifies those of significance to marketing management when strategy and implementation decisions are under consideration.

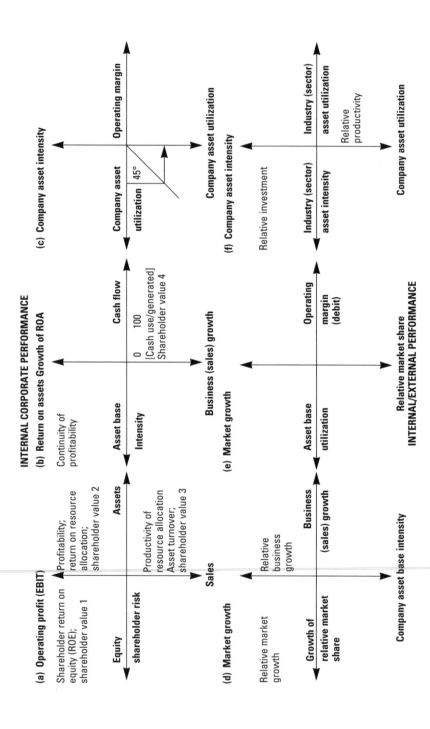

Figure 8.6 Planning asset base performance: criteria for planning and control

Figure 8.5 identified a range of factors influencing the asset base decision. The issue for management is to identify the most cost-effective combination of assets – that is, both fixed assets and working capital – with which to implement the strategy that has been decided upon. Alternative strategies require different asset combinations and, consequently, are accompanied by different levels of risk. Effective management seeks to maximize returns with a minimum level of risk.

With this in mind Figure 8.6 identifies the internal and external performance characteristics which should be of concern to both marketing and financial management and which should be used individually and together.

The internal (corporate) performance characteristics and relationships offer planning and control measures. The *profit/equity* relationship provides a primary indicator of required shareholder value and its current value. *Equity/sales* indicates any change that may occur (or is planned over time) and therefore is a view of shareholder risk. For example, if over time the level of equity in the company increases at a rate greater than the increase of sales then the shareholders may consider their investment riskier than it was at a lower level of sales volume. Clearly there are also other issues. The phase a product-service currently is at will be important (at the emerging market phase the actual sales volume will be small) and if the equity base was expanded to fund the venture and the corporate view may be held that the risk is high. By contrast, during the mature phase, when sales volume is higher, the risk/sales perspective changes. Profitability is another shareholder value issue that should be established as a planning objective and measured regularly. *Profit/assets* indicates the intended and the actual efficiency of resource allocation, and measures the return on assets managed (ROAM) at specified levels of business activity. If we consider the various marketing strategy alternatives, introduced in Chapter 2, it is possible to set ROAM performance criteria for consolidation and productivity, market penetration, operational repositioning, etcetera. For example, we might consider the ROAM on a product range, or the ROAM achieved by a territory, in terms of ideal and minimum levels: persistent performance at the minimum level would require a review of the activity and attempts made to improve profits generated (sales increases or cost decreases) or to reduce the resources (a rationalization of fixed assets) – either production or distribution facilities, or, possibly, net current assets (inventory levels or credit allowed). There is a relationship between risk and ROAM but at this point it is sufficient to simply say we would expect to see a positive correlation between them. (More detail will be given in the discussion on portfolio management in Chapter 12.)

Productivity is measured by considering the *sales/asset* ratio. As with the return on equity (ROE) and profitability (ROAM) ratios it is a primary shareholder value indicator, and likewise we would expect to see a range of values for it across the activities of the company. The range of sales/assets ratios throughout the product development process were suggested in Figure 8.4 which showed the fixed asset/working capital levels throughout the product development phases. We might expect low asset productivity in the emerging-growth phases followed by a much higher value during the mature phase. During the decline phase management would be focusing on productivity options: for example, if a preference for maintaining a full product range during the decline phase is validated by customer and competitor research, the asset productivity performance could be enhanced by outsourcing all but fast-moving products. This option releases fixed assets (plant and equipment, etc.) for alternative uses and provided a JIT distribution method is introduced with the suppliers of the remaining product range items, the increases in inventory levels may be contained resulting in an overall much improved asset productivity ratio.

Changes in ongoing performance can be planned and then monitored. In Figure 8.6, an internal (corporate) performance ratio set, we have a range of indicators that may be established to measure planned and actual change in major performance areas. Asset base intensity is a particularly important concern for both marketing and financial managers. The relationship between investment (asset) intensity is shown by ROA/asset base intensity (we can monitor change over time by considering incremental changes in both items). Clearly, as asset intensity increases there should be an increase in the growth of return on assets if *profitability continuity* is to be maintained. The PIMS (profit impact of marketing strategy) programme identified this as a major concern for both marketing and financial management. Whatever the increase in asset value was (or is) meant to achieve (i.e., asset replacement, product added value etc.) as the asset base intensity increases so the profitability continuity decreases, unless specific profit targets are established ensuring that the overall value of the ratio is maintained. Robinson (1986) suggested this to be a major, significant issue.

> The finding is totally unexpected. Conventional wisdom expects that a positive correlation should exist between modernity and progressiveness and profitability. It is expected that modern technology, elaborate machinery, extensive automation and capital intensity should result in higher productivity and improved margins. The rationale for increased capital spending is frequently that costs should be driven down, prices maintained and margins improved, thus improving profitability and amortizing the increased capital costs. This does not occur.

Robinson used the evidence from PIMS which showed that as investment intensity rises, gross margins rather than increasing are squeezed. The reasons for this are that as the investment base expands there is a need to maintain (or preferably increase) the capacity utilization of the expanded asset base if margins are also to be maintained. This suggests that using price reductions as a means by which volumes are maintained can be damaging to margin performance. The competitive process in an investment-intensive industry can degenerate into volume contests with suicidal price competition, advertising and sales promotional activities; the result is a failure to meet the profit expectations of the shareholders. It follows that other measures are required if decision making is to be effective.

One such measure is the *sales growth (business growth)/asset base intensity* ratio (Figure 8.6(b)) at differing levels for both variables. Clearly, the ideal situation is for the growth of the business (sales) to exceed that of the asset base required to support it. Situations requiring close monitoring of this are those such as market penetration and related product-market development: for both of these strategic options, if they are to be effective, it follows that asset base intensity should remain at the same value. If this does not occur, and an increase in asset base intensity accompanies the growth in the business (sales), then growth will have been achieved at a lower margin. Cash generation and use is an important criterion. It is preferable that the growth of the business occurs using company self-generated cash. Success in this regard will limit the extent to which the use of external funds is made (this topic will be considered in more detail in Chapter 10). However, as can be seen in Figure 8.6(b), it should be viewed in the context of both *business (sales) growth/cash flow* and compared with the *return on asset growth/cash flow performance*. It is, as suggested, an important component in the shareholders' assessment of value generated by the business.

This issue concerning *asset intensity/asset base utilization* raised by Robinson (1986) and discussed a little earlier is addressed in Figure 8.6(c). Ideally any expansion of the business activity incorporating improved operating technology and/or the expansion of the asset base should be accompanied by an increase in asset utilization. There are some interesting marketing/finance interface issues to be considered here. It does not necessarily follow that an increase in intensity implies an increase in capacity. A consolidation and productivity strategy may result in an increase in asset base intensity due to the purchase and introduction of more efficient production methods and equipment. Robinson's argument suggests any decision on new means of production should be preceded by market and company internal research to establish whether the overall result will be favourable: in other words, will intensity and utilization be matched, and what will be the impact on operating margin? Figure 8.6(c) illustrates how the company can consider both issues before and after making the decision to expand.

The performance of any business should be compared with that of similar competitor organizations and with trends in the marketplace. Figure 8.6(d) compares the growth of the business with that of the market. *Business (sales) growth/market growth* provides an organization with an indication of its competitive position; if the company's business growth rate exceeds that of the market it is in a strong position and should consider continuing investment. Clearly a growth rate lower than that of the market should cause concern and changes made after reviewing other indicators. One useful indicator in this regard is the ratio relationship which compares market growth to relative market share. This measure is particularly useful if markets can be segmented. The comparison of the company's relative market-share growth with that of the market gives a trend review of growth performance; and the growth of *relative market share/company asset intensity* indicates the effectiveness of investment and the potential advantage to be gained from continued investment. At an aggregate level the *business (sales) growth/company asset base* intensity relationship provides a macro view of past and current investment efficacy and an input into the decision to continue investment.

In Figure 8.6(e) market growth and relative market share are compared with asset base utilization and operating margin (utilization and operating margin were compared in Figure 8.6(c)). Here the emphasis is on efficiency. *Asset base utilization/market growth* is an indication of the impact on changes in market-level activities on the utilization of assets within the company, and *asset base utilization/relative market share* provides an indication of relative changes in both utilization and market share. This may disclose some surprising things. For example, an increase in relative market share not accompanied by a change in utilization may suggest a declining market and therefore raise questions concerning both marketing strategy and investment in the market. A decrease in relative market share together with a decrease in asset base utilization raises serious concerns about the competitive characteristics of the product-service offer. By examining *operating margin/relative market share* we can evaluate the effectiveness of marketing strategy implementation decisions: a growth of relative market share should be accompanied by a comparable growth in operating margin as the effect of amortizing fixed costs over increased volume is seen. A similar view should be taken of the *business (sales) growth/operating margin* ratio. However, an additional issue to emerge is the trend indication, and of particular interest is the comparison of *rates* of change. An operating margin which increases at a greater rate than that of the business is an indication of increased efficiency and suggests further expansion is a worthwhile consideration.

The final set of performance comparison data compares relative investment and relative productivity for the organization and its competitors within the industry sector (see Figure 8.6(f)). Relative investment is indicated by *company asset intensity/industry (sector) asset intensity*; this is a useful measure of asset intensity from a number of points of view. First, if it is monitored over time it indicates the need for capacity changes or perhaps plant renewal. Secondly, if used in conjunction with market growth and growth of relative market share, it may indicate changes in competitive intentions and capabilities. Relative productivity is indicated by *company asset utilization/industry sector asset utilization*; the industry performance may need to be estimated but typically managerial experience can be used to make reasonably accurate assessments of competitor activities. In some countries these data are available on subscription and are compiled by a confidential third party. The measure is a very useful indication of marketing activities (or potential activities): underutilized capacity, if it is widespread, may result in price competition in an attempt to increase volume and therefore utilization factors. Clearly, other features enter the equation; for example, the size of the plant product characteristics, market share and the importance of the product (Pareto effect) for competitors are but a few. In addition the asset base structure is a particularly important issue: an organization with low operational gearing usually has greater flexibility over changes in volumes and capacity utilization than a company preferring to control a large amount of the supply chain activity.

8.4   Asset base management

There are a number of key management variables that influence the performance of the asset base. In this section of the chapter we are considering assets in the broad context of fixed and net current assets or working capital. The PIMS programme identified a number of significant issues, which we will review now because they have implications for the marketing/finance interface.

Marketing expenditure and investment intensity

It has been found that heavy marketing expenditure does not reduce the pressure exerted on profitability by high levels of investment (net asset) investment intensity. Evidence from PIMS research has suggested that high levels of marketing expenditure decrease profitability across the database and that this effect is most marked when high levels of marketing spend and high levels of investment intensity occur simultaneously. This is not a surprising revelation. In the emerging-market phase and during the high-growth phase it is to be expected that both expenditures will be high, thereby depressing profitability. However, this problem is one which can be accepted if, eventually, the net present value of the income stream generated by the activity is strongly positive. Further, it suggests to management that a review of marketing expenditure and investment intensity relationships in the product development stages should be conducted and considered within the context of the economic cash flow measure. It is possible (if not desirable) that plant renewal and product relaunch expenditures may occur at frequent intervals and such persistent dilutions of profitability may ultimately prove to be unacceptable. The intense competition and rapidly changing technology confronting competitors in the computer industry may be because of these problems: investment in R&D and plant is high and the marketing expenditure/sales ratio not inconsiderable.

Investment intensity and productivity

For the PIMS study, productivity was measured by value added per employee; value added is the contribution of the business to the product, measured by selling price less the cost of raw materials and components. The PIMS results suggested that value added does not increase over a wide range of investment-intensity. A significant favourable effect occurs only for highly investment intensive businesses. Typically the results imply that employees working with low levels of investment intensity produce more than those with larger investments; the reason for this appears to be that intensive price competition in investment-intensive industries reduces the market value of the product and hence the value added.

There is an issue to be resolved concerning the number of employees within an organization. However, administrative activities may not contribute towards value added to the same extent as the work of production employees, and if significant differences exist they should be considered. From the marketing/finance consideration this relationship may be particularly significant in the mature and decline phases of product-market development as competition becomes intense and price reductions dilute the value added of the productservice and therefore productivity. In an attempt to maintain margins a number of alternatives might be considered. Product rationalization may reduce costs (and thereby maintain margins and value added), but it may also result in a decline in customer perceptions of value (in a differentiation context) and this, in turn, results in a loss of sales. An alternative may be to expand end-user applications: there is an opportunity to hold price levels and increase sales if this is feasible. One other option is to investigate other market segments: while the promotion costs may be higher the benefits may be lower competitive activity and higher realized margins.

The relationship between fixed and working capital

Any type of capital intensity has an impact on profitability. The PIMS experience suggested the impact is most pronounced at high levels of both fixed and working capital. If high levels of fixed capital are inevitable because of the level of technological sophistication, the solution may be for management to maintain very tight controls on working capital. The operations management techniques of just-in-time manufacturing and quick response distribution are typical solutions. A comprehensive review of the structure of the supply chain may result in a reduction of both fixed and working capital *throughout* the supply chain system if each member cooperates.

Investment intensity and product breadth and depth

A product range which offers wider end-user application and choice appears to be beneficial in investment-intensive industries. The reasons for this are because the business does not only depend upon one or two products and because of the seasonal and cyclical flexibility offered by a diversified product range. It also follows that utilization and operating margins share this independence.

8.5 Financing fixed assets

Chapter 7 considered the issue of funding working capital requirements. This chapter concludes by discussing alternative means by which the fixed asset base might be funded. We have established that the objective of the firm is to maximize its current market value – that is, to maximize shareholder wealth. Shareholder wealth, or value, is created by making successful investment decisions resulting in positive net cash flows, profitability (an optimal return on shareholder equity) and productivity (an optimal use of resources). An important element in the process of maximizing shareholder value is the *financing decision*, which concerns the capital structure of the firm – that is, the balance of debt and equity in the firm, or its *gearing*.

There are two forms of gearing and both are usually used in most organizations. Operational gearing was discussed in Chapter 5. It will be recalled that *operational gearing* is determined by the extent to which operative fixed costs are used in a firm's fixed cost structure. By contrast, *financial gearing* can be described as the extent to which funds with a fixed cost (interest) are used to finance the company's operations. Whereas operational gearing bears a relationship with the assets in the balance sheet, financial gearing is influenced by how the assets are financed. Financial management, by varying the mix of its finance sourcing, will vary its commitment to pay interest. Clearly the higher the level of interest-bearing debt the higher the impact on profit and the lower the resultant value returned to the shareholders.

The benefits to the company (and therefore the shareholder) of using debt in the funding mix is that the interest payment is tax deductible and therefore reduces the taxable profit. Consider three companies:

($000)	Company A		Company B		Company C	
Equity shares of $1	100,000		80,000		50,000	
Debt (interest 15%)	–		20,000		50,000	
Capital employed	100,000		100,000		100,000	
	A		B		C	
Profits	10,000	2,000	10,000	20,000	10,000	20,000
Interest	–	–	3,000	3,000	7,500	7,500
	10,000	20,000	7,000	17,000	2,500	12,500
Taxation (40%)	4,000	8,000	2,800	6,800	1,000	5,000
	6,000	12,000	4,200	10,200	1,500	7,500
Earnings per share	6c	12c	5.2c	12.75c	3c	15c

For company A there is no effect from tax as earnings increase; the earnings per share (EPS) are 6 cents then 12 cents as profit is doubled. Company B, with 20 per cent gearing, shows EPS increases by a factor of 2.4 for the same increase in profit; while for company C the increase is by a factor of 5. It follows that financial gearing can increase the value delivered to the shareholders provided profits are being generated.

However, interest commitments do not vary with the propensity (profitability) of the business and we can deduce from the example that the benefits from financial gearing are high if revenues and profits are high, but can give serious problems if the revenues and profits decline. This is an illustration of the *financial risk* confronting the company that was discussed in Chapter 5.

Sources of funding for fixed assets

There are essentially two sources of funds for the long-term financing of fixed assets: equity funds and debt. Before considering the practical issues of debt, some other sources should be identified. The example of the impact of debt on the return to the shareholder illustrates the importance of the funding decision, particularly if we add *business risk* to the equation.

Equity funds Companies are usually incorporated with an authorized share capital stated in the authorization document. The amount of authorized capital represents the maximum number of shares which can be offered to individuals and organizations. There are three main types of shares: ordinary, preference and deferred. While a detailed discussion is not essential for our purposes the distinguishing features should be identified.

Ordinary shares have a designated 'par value', which usually indicates the amount payable by the shareholder to obtain ownership. Ownership is accompanied by voting rights (such as appointment of directors etc.) and entitlement to a share of profits earned in the form of dividends. It is interesting to note that quite often successful companies' shares are purchased in large quantities by insurance companies and pension funds (known as institutional shareholders), which can, through their large shareholding, influence the decisions that are taken. Ordinary shareholders carry the main risk of the company and receive returns as decided by the board of directors.

Debt funds   Debt funding is used by companies wishing to maintain control of the business. Equity funds require the company to relinquish a proportional amount of control to the new shareholders. Debt funding has no such requirement. Debt funds have an agreed term and interest rate which are legally enforceable but have no voting rights attached. Debt funding may be secured against a specific asset or be unsecured. As the earlier example illustrated, interest payable on debt is tax deductible and therefore offers the facility to increase shareholder wealth (or delivered value) by using financial gearing: the combination of debt with equity.

Off-balance sheet funding   The alternatives to equity and debt funding are leasing, hire purchase agreements, and the short-term funds such as overdrafts and trade credit discussed in Chapter 7. These forms of funding are collectively known as off-balance sheet funding. Here we shall consider aspects of leasing.

Technically, a lease is a contract between the owner of an asset (the lessor) and the user (the lessee) whereby the lessor agrees to allow the lessee to use the asset for an agreed period; the lessee agrees to pay rental and comply with other conditions of the lease.

There are a number of benefits to be obtained from leasing. Clearly, a major benefit is that no major capital outlay is required to obtain the services of the asset, thus, capital may be used elsewhere in the business. Usually the view of management is that if its task is to maximize shareholders' return it will do so by using its capital in the high return core activities of the business. Another important benefit obtained by leasing is that the risk of obsolescence is avoided; in fact, it is more likely shared because the leasing company will determine leasing rates such that they are compensated for excessive effects of obsolescence. Maintenance costs may be included in the lease payments, to the benefit of the lessor who can typically take advantage of economies of scale to pass on lower costs and therefore leasing rates than can the lessee. It should be added that by purchasing maintenance as part of the lease additional capital expenditure is avoided. Lease rentals are usually allowable deductions for tax purposes at a rate comparable to the depreciation and interest which would be allowed if the asset had been purchased.

Two broad types of leases are available. An *operating lease* offers the lessee the right to use an asset over an agreed period of time, usually less than the economic life of the asset. Rental payments cover maintenance and servicing requirements. The lessee often has the option to cancel the agreement without penalty before the expiry of the lease. Rental payments typically amount to less than the value of the asset.

By contrast, a *financial lease* may be closely related to an asset purchase. The characteristics of these leases include a lease term which matches that of the life of the asset. The lessee is responsible for maintenance and servicing of the asset. Cancellation of the lease will result in substantial penalties. Rental payments will usually amount to a total greater than the cost of the asset.

The three most common leasing options on either of the above are direct leases, sale and lease back and leveraged leases. *Direct leases* are when the assets leased are items not previously owned. *Sale and lease back arrangements* are when the owner of an asset sells it to a finance company and then leases the asset back from the buyer. Sale and lease back arrangements are common methods of financing shopping centres and industrial and commercial facilities. The benefit to the original owner is the ability to continue in business in the original facilities, and use the cash released from the sale to finance other areas of the business. *Leveraged leases* are used for financing extremely expensive assets, whereby the leasing is undertaken by a principal lessor together with a consortium of lenders. From the lessee's point of view the leveraged lease does not differ from any other financial lease.

Make or buy: the lease or purchase decision   The direct finance lease is, essentially, another means of financing the acquisition of an asset. Wilson and Keers (1987) suggested that the method of financing an asset is a separate decision from that of deciding whether or not to invest in the asset. Evaluation of a lease proposition disregards operating cash inflows and outflows, as these will have been considered during the evaluation of the role of the asset as investment.

Wilson and Keers suggested three steps in the evaluation of a financial lease:

(i)   Ascertaining the net annual cash flows resulting from leasing rather than purchasing.

(ii)   Discounting the net annual cash flows to their present value at the after-tax cost of borrowing, which would be required if the asset was purchased rather than leased.

(iii)   Comparing the present value of net cash flows with the purchase price of the asset. *If the present value exceeds the purchase price, the asset should be purchased; if not, it should be leased.*

A number of reasons make leasing attractive. The first concerns taxation. The effects of taxation vary from one tax authority to another, thus, in a general text we can only suggest that the taxation situation for the lessee and the lessor be explored to derive the most mutually advantageous arrangements. A second reason, which is generally applicable, concerns the availability of finance, particularly for small companies without the necessary creditability and balance sheet base. Thirdly, fixed lease payments may end up being less costly if interest rates rise, particularly if the lease payments are fixed for the period of the lease. Clearly, interest rates move downwards as well as upwards and it follows that in a period of fluctuating interest rates some advice on interest rate futures may be necessary prior to making a decision. A fourth reason making leasing superficially attractive is its use as off-balance sheet financing. This suggests a misunderstanding of leasing. Leasing payments involve similar contractual arrangements and commitments as those for borrowing. They also reduce net cash flows in a similar way to interest payments and repayment of capital. As Dobbins and Witt (1988) suggested: 'For practical purposes both leasing and borrowing increase the amount of leverage on a $1 for $1 basis and hence both add financial risk to business risk.'

8.6   'New economy' opportunities and threats: a return of the enterprise value model

The *enterprise value model* was introduced in Chapter 4. It will be recalled that the model has a simple structure:

$$
\begin{array}{l}
\text{Enterprise} \\
\text{value} \\
= \\
\text{Market} \\
\text{value}
\end{array}
= f
\begin{bmatrix}
\text{NPV of} \\
\text{returns on} \\
\text{Fixed and} \\
\text{working} \\
\text{capital}
\end{bmatrix}
+
\begin{bmatrix}
\text{NPV of} \\
\text{returns on} \\
\text{Growth} \\
\text{opportunities}
\end{bmatrix}
+
\begin{bmatrix}
\text{NPV of} \\
\text{returns on} \\
\text{Latent} \\
\text{value}
\end{bmatrix}
$$

based upon generating . . .

$$
\begin{bmatrix}
\text{Tangible} \\
\text{value}
\end{bmatrix}
+
\begin{bmatrix}
\text{Premium} \\
\text{value}
\end{bmatrix}
+
\begin{bmatrix}
\text{Latent} \\
\text{value}
\end{bmatrix}
$$

from . . .

$$
\begin{bmatrix}
\text{Tangible} \\
\text{assets}
\end{bmatrix}
+
\begin{bmatrix}
\text{Intangible} \\
\text{assets}
\end{bmatrix}
+
\begin{bmatrix}
\text{Efficiency} \\
\text{improvements}
\end{bmatrix}
$$

. . . where *market value* is derived by multiplying share price by the number of shares outstanding and subtracting long-term debt but could be replaced by aggregate economic cash flow.

The approach taken by this model offers a number of options hitherto unavailable with traditional models. The vertical integration structures of recent years constrained expansion into new product-markets. To pursue many opportunities typically required organic growth or by merger and acquisition. The assets that were required were unavailable unless they were 'acquired' through either strategy alternatives. The 'new economy', with its preference for virtual structures rather than vertically integrated structures, offers a facility to 'leverage' partner's assets. This becomes more significant when the options that are identified and explored suggest that to expand the assets within an industry sector will result in excess capacity and lead to unwanted and unnecessary price competition.

The enterprise value model encourages management first to identify the growth options and the assets required to make a competitive entry and then to evaluate the alternatives. Typically this evaluation is based upon a DCF (discounted cash flow) appraisal of alternative asset base structures and ownership structures. In Figure 8.7 typical growth options confronting an organization are identified. Using the enterprise value model we are able to determine the ideal asset base with which to pursue the options and the most *cost-effective* method of doing so. The model also offers an effective means by which performance can be planned *and* monitored. This is shown as Figure 8.8.

Implications for marketing decisions

Marketing management should understand the financial managers' approach to asset base management and ownership. Financial management would prefer to own only assets likely to increase in value – these would be seen as investment opportunities. Typically assets are used to produce income and in this respect are seen as an expense item. Consequently the financial managers' approach will evaluate the contribution of an asset to producing shareholder value and as such will recommend purchasing or leasing depending upon the most favourable contribution likely.

To enable an optimal decision to be reached the marketing contribution should identify the market characteristics likely to influence the evaluation of optimal asset base structure and the infrastructure required to maximize shareholder value. It follows that marketing managements' assessment of key issues should make the decision both easier and more effective. Information that both marketing and finance will find useful for the asset procurement decision is suggested in Table 8.1. The purpose of this information is to be able

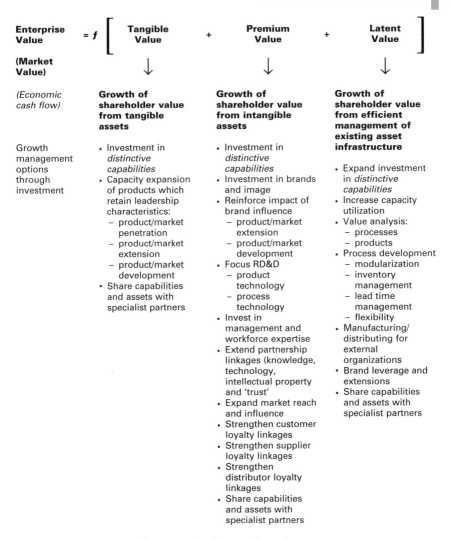

$$\text{Enterprise Value} = f \left[\text{Tangible Value} + \text{Premium Value} + \text{Latent Value} \right]$$

(Market Value)	↓	↓	↓
(Economic cash flow)	**Growth of shareholder value from tangible assets**	**Growth of shareholder value from intangible assets**	**Growth of shareholder value from efficient management of existing asset infrastructure**

Growth management options through investment	• Investment in *distinctive capabilities*
	• Capacity expansion of products which retain leadership characteristics:
	  – product/market penetration
	  – product/market extension
	  – product/market development
	• Share capabilities and assets with specialist partners
		• Investment in *distinctive capabilities*
		• Investment in brands and image
		• Reinforce impact of brand influence
		  – product/market extension
		  – product/market development
		• Focus RD&D
		  – product technology
		  – process technology
		• Invest in management and workforce expertise
		• Extend partnership linkages (knowledge, technology, intellectual property and 'trust')
		• Expand market reach and influence
		• Strengthen customer loyalty linkages
		• Strengthen supplier loyalty linkages
		• Strengthen distributor loyalty linkages
		• Share capabilities and assets with specialist partners
			• Expand investment in *distinctive capabilities*
			• Increase capacity utilization
			• Value analysis:
			  – processes
			  – products
			• Process development
			  – modularization
			  – inventory management
			  – lead time management
			  – flexibility
			• Manufacturing/ distributing for external organizations
			• Brand leverage and extensions
			• Share capabilities and assets with specialist partners

Figure 8.7 Managing the growth of enterprise value

to take a composite view of the market opportunity and the accompanying business risk, together with the implications of the market characteristics and asset decisions relating to financial risk.

8.7 Summary

This chapter has considered the marketing/finance interface issues of asset base management. It is important that marketing managers are aware of the

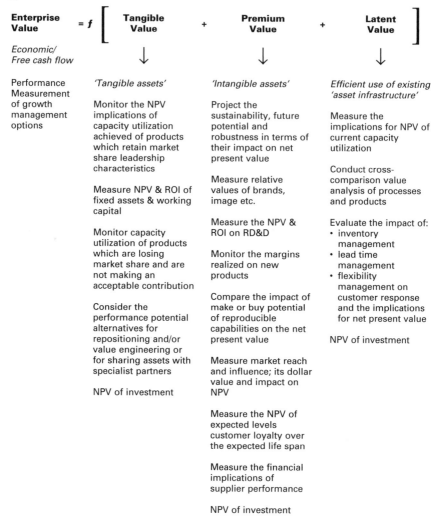

Figure 8.8　Evaluating the options and measuring performance

impact of their proposals when capacity decisions are being taken, and we identified a number of customer-based marketing decisions that may have significant impacts on the structure of the business and the business's response to customer expectations.

We considered some specific asset base elements such as fixed asset intensity, utilization, productivity and working capital issues. Examples were used to explore the marketing and financial management implications of decisions which are taken concerning the asset base components. Decisions concerning

Table 8.1   Market characteristics for asset base planning

Market characteristics	Asset base considerations
Product-market development profile:	
• Expected market volume	Capacity, location, technology (intensity)
• Expected growth rate	Economies of scale
• Expected market share	Current/future capacity size extent of vertical integration
• Anticipated segmentation	Flexibility: volume and product range characteristics
	Experience effect potential
• Planned operating margins	Operational gearing (fixed cost profile) and capacity utilization
• Competitive structure and competitive profile	Impact on utilization and margins
• Capital replacement program	Future intensity/utilization profile desirable
• Industry investment	Relative investment, productivity and impact of competition on future utilization

the combination of fixed assets and working capital were explored using the product development process discussed in Chapter 7.

A review of the influence of strategic and operational marketing decisions on asset base structure and management used the earlier models developed in Chapters 2 and 3 and identified (through examples) issues requiring both marketing and financial decisions. The comprehensive approach taken was illustrated in Figure 8.5.

To make effective decisions concerning the size and characteristics of the asset base we suggested a number of important relationships. The significance of the approach taken is that it relates the activities of the business, and its resources, to performance achievements and to external factors that affect the company's positioning and the eventual value it delivers. These inter-relationships were represented in Figure 8.6.

Finally, the chapter considered the alternative financial structures by which the asset base could be supported and funded. Here, the emphasis was on types of funding (the issues of costs will be discussed in Chapter 10).

REFERENCES

Channon, D. F. (1982) *The Stratpac Directory*, Manchester Business School, Manchester.

Dobbins, R. and Witt, S. F. (1988) *Practical Financial Management*, Basil Blackwell, Oxford.

PIMS (1981) *The PIMS Programme*, Cambridge, Mass., Strategic Planning Institute.

Robinson, G. (1986) *Strategic Management Techniques*, Butterworths, Durban, SA.

Wilson, C. and Keers, B. (1987) *Introduction to Financial Management*, Prentice Hall, Melbourne.

Managing Cash Flows **9**

Cash flow management is a vital function for any organization and the typical view of marketing as being a cash user and finance the cash generator requires some clarification. The importance of cash in the business was introduced in the introduction to Part III of this book and was developed in Chapter 7 (Working Capital Management). As we noted there, cash is important for three primary reasons: to conduct transactions; for precautionary or contingency reasons; and for speculative uses. The coordination of marketing activities to identify cash uses and requirements during the operating plan period of the organization was discussed.

We also discussed the difference between profit flow and cash flow: profit flow being an opinion while cash flow is a fact. Many organizations make notional profits while their cash balances decline. The management of cash flow in the short and long term is an important issue for the marketing/finance interface. It is as important to the survival and the value maximization of the firm as the management of its assets or liabilities.

A number of questions should be asked by both management and shareholders concerning cash flow situations. Among the most common are:

- Why are profits decreasing (increasing) and our working capital increasing (decreasing)?
- The company used external funding for new plant when there is a large cash reserve – why?
- Where are the proceeds from the divestment of a subsidiary?
- Why are profits increasing but dividend remaining unchanged?
- What cash will the planned product development programme require (and eventually provide) in the short and long term?

Table 9.1 Comparison between traditional accounting reports and sources and uses of funds

Traditional reports	
Balance Sheets	*Sources and Uses of Funds*
Provide details of assets and liabilities in the company at a specific date	Explain the changes that have occurred in both assets and liabilities over the period covered by the report
Provide information on types of finance used by the business	Provide additional information on financial flexibility, liquidity and investment decisions
Income Statements	
Show how proprietorship has been affected by the profit (or loss) for a specified time period	Explain all other changes affecting proprietorship over the period of time
Provide the profit (or loss) from operations over a period	Indicate cash flow from operations over a period

This chapter considers these and similar questions. We shall review contributions from the literature and consider the cash flow issues confronting marketing decisions at both the strategic and operational levels.

9.1 Cash flow: a financial management perspective

Accounting reports do not readily answer the questions posed above, but looking for changes in the balance sheet items over the year of the report can help. Most companies provide a funds flow or sources and applications (uses of funds) statement with the income statement and balance sheet they publish, which begins to answer these questions and others as well. Presentation of data may differ due to the different reporting formats available. However, the information given is essentially the same.

Wilson and Keers (1987) offered a useful comparison between traditional reports and statements of sources and uses of funds statements, and this is set out in Table 9.1.

Note that in the comparison, funds are used to refer to cash and cash equivalents. An increase in trade credit, for example, is a source of funds. Sources of funds and applications of funds include:

Sources	Uses
• Funds from operations (profit and non-cash expenses such as depreciation)	• Losses from operations
• Increases in supplier credit	• Decreases in supplier credit
• Reductions in stock	• Increases in stock
• Reductions in debtors	• Increases in debtors
• Sales of fixed assets	• Purchases of fixed assets
• Decreases in lease payments	• Increases in lease payments
• Increases in loans/debentures	• Redemptions of loans/debentures
• Increases in share capital	• Decreases in share capital
• Repayments of tax (refunds and tax concessions)	• Payments of tax
• Dividends received	• Dividends paid
• Increases in overdraft	• Decreases in overdraft
• Reductions of cash balances	• Increases in cash balances

Changes in fund movements can be both short term and long term, influencing the operating cycle and the long-term financial structure of the firm.

Sources and uses of funds can be identified from balance sheet changes. An analysis of these changes and changes in marketing and financial performance in the short and long term can be revealing when conducted on competitors. It is a useful exercise to do at the strategy planning stage and we shall return to this application. Meanwhile an example from Kookaburra Pty Ltd in Table 9.2 illustrates the concept.

Revenues for 1994 and 1995 were $30 million and $35 million respectively, with operating income of $1.5 million and $2 million. Kookaburra would appear to be a growth business. While its net margins are not particularly high (12.5 per cent and 10 per cent after expanding the asset base) there appears to be growth and profit potential. However, before firm conclusions could be made we would need to undertake a more detailed analysis of the business, and certainly for expansion decisions.

9.2 Cash flow: a marketing perspective

Here we must look again at two concepts previously mentioned: the product process and the experience curve. Both have market share as a common denominator.

Robinson (1986) suggested that if the experience curve is to influence the competitive positioning of the business it can only do so if market share is pursued as a principal objective in the long run. A dominant market share

Table 9.2 Kookaburra Pty Ltd balance sheets and sources and uses of funds

Kookaburra Pty Ltd Balance Sheets

Fixed assets		
Property, plant, equipment	12,000	16,000
Less accumulated depreciation	4000	5000
	8000	11,000
Current assets		
Cash	3000	3000
Accounts receivable	5000	7000
Inventory	4000	6000
	12,000	16,000
Less		
Current liabilities		
Accounts payable	3000	3000
Overdraft	2000	2000
Others	1000	2000
	6000	7000
Net current assets	6000	9000
Net assets	14,000	20,000
Shareholders' funds		
Ordinary share capital	5000	7000
Retained earnings	4000	5000
	9000	12,000
Long term liabilities		
Debentures	5000	8000
Capital employed	12,000	20,000

Sources and Applications of Funds 30 June 1995

Sources of funds	($000)
Decrease in net current assets	0
Sale of fixed assets	0
Issue of long term liabilities	3000
Sell equity (ordinary shares)	2000
Operations: income (before dividend)	2000
Depreciation	1000
Total sources of funds	8000
Uses of funds	
Increase in net current assets	3000
Purchase of fixed assets	4000
Redemption of long term liabilities	0
Decrease share capital	0
Operations: losses	0
Dividends	1000
Total uses of funds	8000

should provide the organization with a considerable cost advantage over competitors:

> Lower costs imply that the company should have higher margins than competitors and, as a result, much higher profitability and cash flows. It becomes convenient to use market share as a surrogate variable for experience in an industry, since market share is highly correlated with experience . . . High market share then means high experience and low costs, implying high margins and profitability. High market share means improved cash flows. Low market share points to the unavailability of cash and profits.

The market dynamics of the product development phase influence the cash flow determining ability of a product. The rate of growth of a product-market is important and is likely to be a major influence on the ease and cost with which market share is obtained. In markets with low growth, market share increases can only be obtained by activities which reduce the market share of competitors. By contrast in high-growth markets, volume increases are relatively easy to obtain as the market expands. There is very little competitive rivalry; organizations are intent on expanding their primary market share rather than targeting competitors in order that they might make secondary market share gains. The exception is likely to be seen in capital-intensive industries, where (as we saw in the previous chapter) it is essential that capital utilization be maintained if planned margins are to be realized. Robinson argued that the organization might expand market share by increasing capacity incrementally and ahead of competitors. Certainly in an industry sector where product availability and frequent, reliable, delivery are critical success factors this can be important. He suggested that competitors may be unaware of the loss of market share as capacity continues to be fully utilized; they may not be concerned if the high utilization of assets is sustained. In any event the fact that high rates of growth require strong cash flows to fund increases in fixed assets and working capital is indisputable.

The Boston Consulting Group (1970) offered an approach by which products, product groups or strategic business units could be assigned strategic roles within an organization. Roles were assigned on the basis of market growth rate and company competitive position, as reflected by relative market share.

The Boston Consulting Group (BCG) growth/share matrix has been well documented and it is not necessary to repeat its characteristics here. What is necessary in the context of this discussion is to focus on the cash flow relevance of the model. The market growth rate scale (the ordinate) reflects the relationship between growth rate and cash requirements. At high rates of

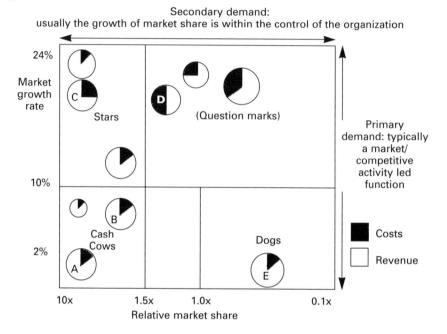

Figure 9.1   Growth/share matrix

growth the product requirements for cash resources are high, while in the mature phase the competitive emphasis decreases and with this there is relief in the demand for cash. BCG decided upon an arbitrary 10 per cent as a figure to differentiate growth categories. Clearly this may differ by industry. Indeed, the impact of the recession of the late 1980s and early 1990s was such that growth rates anywhere near 10 per cent were exceptional.

The abscissa in the BCG model indicates relative market share and a relative measure of 1.5 was selected by BCG as this was thought to reflect the order of market share (relative to the nearest competitor) which would ensure a sufficiently dominant position. A low-growth industry may well put this level at 10.

Combined, the axes provide the well-known matrix presentation in which 'products' are positioned and whose area reflects sales or capital intensity. Figure 9.1 identifies a hypothetical range of products in this way. As well as indicating the proportional weights of the sales generated, the circles indicate the utilization of the assets. For product A, a dominant product in the mature phase, capacity is almost fully utilized, whereas product B, still an important product, indicates proportionately more under-utilization, which should be of some concern for the company. Product C is still in its growth phase and for this product (and others in this quadrant) it is not unexpected that capacity is available for expansion. Much the same argument may be made for D, and the others in that quadrant, where they represent products in the emerging phase. Product E, however, is in the decline phase, and ideally management concern should be to attempt to maintain high utilization rates during the withdrawal of the product. Clearly no further investment should be contemplated.

A general rule concerning the matrix is that 'products' to the left of the 1.5× market share datum are expected to have high profitability, productivity and sustainable cash flows. Those to the right are expected to have lower profits and less, possibly negative, cash flow. 'Products' below the market growth cut-off rate (here shown as 10 per cent) are expected to require relatively little investment in order to maintain market share, while those above the cut-off rate are very likely to require cash if growth is to be maintained.

The BCG model suggests a structured and orderly approach to strategy decisions. In reality it is not: 'businesses cover a smooth spectrum across the matrix. There is no sudden formula . . . which transmits a star into a cash cow as its growth declines from 11% to 9%. Changes occur gradually and the transition points are merely guidelines to assist in strategic thinking' (Robinson 1986). Robinson's comments identify a major 'problem' with the matrix or, to be more accurate, with the expectations of managers attempting to use it to produce strategy decisions. The matrix indicates which products are not where they should be; furthermore the business environment has a major influence on 'product' performance. Management makes strategic decisions; models such as the BCG matrix are simply support systems.

Given that the matrix is a decision support system, how should it be used? The location of 'products' within the matrix is indicative of the current strategic position and cash flow status of the portfolio (Abell and Hammond 1979). The ongoing success of the portfolio depends upon the *existence* of businesses that generate cash and provide acceptable profits, and businesses that use the cash generated to fund future market dominance and continue the cash generation activity. Returning to Figure 9.1, it is suggested that market growth (primary demand) is a market-led activity, whereas marketshare growth/ market dominance (secondary demand) usually depends upon the strategic innovation of the individual business.

Given that the matrix offers an input into planning future cash flow and growth, the following criteria were suggested by Hedley (1976) and are illustrated in Figure 9.2:

(i)   The first objective should be to maintain the position of cash cover and to guard against a temptation to invest excessively.

(ii) A second objective should be to use cash generated by the cash covers to maintain and consolidate the position of star products which have unique differentiation characteristics.

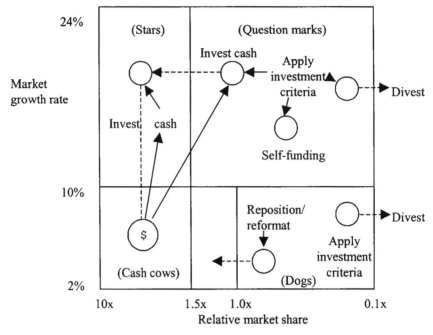

Figure 9.2 A value-based strategy to generate profitability, productivity and cash flow using the BCG growth/share matrix

(iii)   Question mark products should be evaluated and a number selected for investment. Those selected should demonstrate features that suggest positive customer response will occur and from this a strong competitive position. On the assumption that cash is a scarce resource, the assessment of question mark products should be such that only those with clear potential should be investment candidates. Those not meeting the criteria may succeed if their cost structures can be modified in order to improve their margins (perhaps by value engineering and by reviewing corporate expectations for overhead recovery).

(iv)   The 'dog' products are usually a statistical inevitability. It is important that they are recognized as such and dealt with constructively. It may be possible to maintain cash flow and profitability through operational repositioning and/or some creative segmentation. One other possibility is to revise performance expectations: it may be possible for the 'dog' product to continue to generate cash if it is subjected to rationalization or value engineering (or some similar activity), which results in a less ambitious role but one which contributes to overall corporate objectives for profitability, productivity and cash flow generation.

The BCG growth/share matrix offers a structured approach to managing the financial aspects of marketing planning that is essentially qualitative. Given quantified parameters for market growth and relative market share, as well as a structure and behaviour of costs, it also gives an anticipated revenue, profit and cash flow performance that is quantifiable, but with some difficulty. Furthermore, it lacks specificity in that it is not always clear which aspects of performance arise from strategic planning and operational implementation and which are the result of unforeseen responses from the marketplace. In the following section we suggest an approach that overcomes these problems by identifying the influences on cash flow and by using the notions of operational and strategic cash flows.

9.3 A marketing/finance cash flow management model

Figure 9.3 represents the cash flow management model. The idea of considering cash flow at operational and strategic levels is not new. Schlosser (1992)

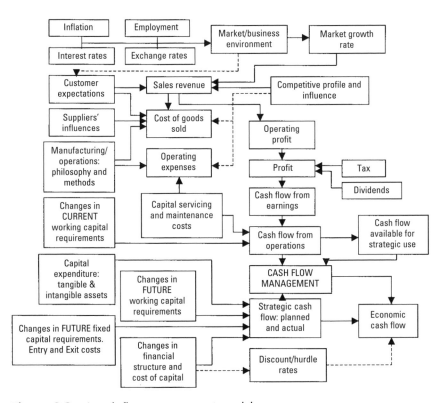

Figure 9.3 A cash flow management model

suggested that operational cash flow be calculated by adding depreciation to the after-tax profit and adjusting this by changes in working capital requirements, that is:

$$
\begin{array}{l}
\text{Profit after tax} \\
+ \text{ Depreciation} \\
= \textbf{Cash flow from earnings} \\
\pm \text{ Working capital requirements} \\
= \textbf{Cash flow from operations}
\end{array}
$$

Both measures are essential to marketing/financial planning but we need to consider long-term cash requirements for strategic marketing considerations. In the long term we are concerned with additional fixed assets and possibly with the alternative financial structures required to fund the reconfigured asset base. The free cash flow model can be expressed as:

Operating Cash Flow = Revenues Less Discounts less Wages and Salaries less Materials, components and services Less Capital servicing and maintenance costs less Overhead expenses.

Cash flow from Assets = *Operating Cash Flow* +/– Short-term Working Capital Requirements +/– Capital structure (restructuring costs.

Strategic Cash Flow = *Cash flow from Assets* +/– Fixed Assets (Tangible & Intangible) +/– Long-term Working Capital Requirements +/– 'Entry and Exit' Costs.

Free Cash Flow = *Strategic Cash Flow* +/– Changes in Equity & Debt funding.

It follows from the model that fundamental changes to the business can be explored in terms of changes to cash flow, and this may be extended to consider *economic cash flows* (which will be discussed in detail in Chapter 11). The purpose of considering economic cash flows here is to evaluate strategic options on an equal basis, that is, their current (present) values.

The model described in Figure 9.3 acknowledges the influence of the *market/business environment* (seen at the top of the model). Schlosser illustrated the importance of including a comprehensive review of the competitive environment with an example taken from the industrial gas industry in Europe. There the major competitors used their retail customers to generate negative working capital by encouraging cash payments. Purchasers of gas in cylinders were asked to pay advance rentals for the cylinders. Large users were asked for a cash contribution towards the construction of in-plant gas production facilities. Users with volume requirements not large enough to justify inplant installations were invited to reserve a share of the capacity of a shared plant; this required an initial cash payment which was recovered through low price benefits subsequently. In an extremely price-competitive market, with profit margins squeezed and profit contribution to operating cash flow consequently less than it might be, these measures increased cash flow at an operational level.

We can now see a link with the discussion in the previous section. It will be recalled that the BCG matrix focussed on relative market share and market growth in exploiting benefits from the experience effects on costs as volume increases. Lower costs contribute to cash flow through the enhanced margins. However, it will also be remembered that in price-sensitive markets aggressive price cutting and high promotional expenditures require large amounts of cash. It follows from Schlosser's example that marketing creativity is necessary to develop alternative cash generation strategies.

Operational strategies may also be reviewed in a similar manner. Customer service strategies governing inventory policy have a significant impact on operational cash flow. A customer service policy which focuses on product availability anywhere, usually requires a stockholding commitment from which orders are dispatched immediately. An alternative is to use just-in-time methods (or purchasing), which complete the ordering process. The implications for cash flow are quite clear. The stock-building (speculating) approach uses a sales forecast to construct a production/procurement schedule, which is used to buy/build inventory items to meet demand: often this involves paying suppliers (including labour) ahead of receiving payment from customers. Justintime (or quick response) systems require low working capital needs (often negative working capital) which may be enhanced by requesting partial payment. There is also a halfway situation in which products are held as subassemblies and are completed upon receipt of order.

All three options have advantages and disadvantages. Speculative inventory holding does permit the use of economies of scale and experience effects together with scheduling to maximize utilization. Clearly it works best if the demand forecast is accurate, but often this cannot be relied upon and surplus inventory is held to meet contingencies when forecasting errors occur. For some products stock excesses create obsolescence and markdowns.

The just-in-time approach has a number of benefits. The 'certainty' of demand reduces stockholding costs; waste is minimized; the system usually has greater flexibility and a wider variety of products may be offered. However, success does not come without prior involvement in IT-based systems; also while the reliability of IT systems is much improved a system failure can be expensive.

Other features of the market/business environment are also important and can have a variable influence. The macroeconomic factors have been seen to influence both customer and corporate attitudes. For example, periods of high *inflation* have resulted in increased stockholding in anticipation of continued price increases and therefore cost of goods sold; this may result in reduced cash flow as stocks are built up. Levels of *employment* affect consumer confidence. High unemployment can be expected to lower consumer confidence, resulting in a decrease in the rate of sale of non-essential consumer goods. *Interest rates* have an influence on both industrial and consumer borrowing. If rates are low both producers and consumers are willing to increase their levels of borrowing: industry for expansion, consumers to purchase holidays, durables and other nonessentials. As interest rates increase corporate finance, managers begin to seek out alternative methods of financing their (reduced) expansion or asset maintenance programs opting for leasing or other alternatives. *Exchange rates* have a similar impact upon stockholding: as rates change and imports become increasingly expensive inventory levels may be increased in an attempt to offset cost increases. We now consider the impact of customer expectations.

It follows that *customer expectations* have a large influence on sales revenue and cost of goods sold. Expectations of quality, availability and choice impact on costs, and as we have seen, alternative philosophies and operating methods exist whereby service may be maintained and costs optimized. *Competitive influences* have a large impact on sales revenue. Large competitors with a dominant presence can influence competitive methods, most of which have an impact on operating cash flows. The dominant competitor typically selects an organizational strength on which to compete (i.e., its competitive advantage) and while this may create problems for other competitors it also offers opportunities for them to target customers with particular value preferences and create a strong loyalty.

Suppliers can *influence* cash flow. Attempts to increase sales with a customer may result in a number of benefits to cash flow. For example, extended credit terms, stock financing, distribution services (e.g., stockholding, frequent/responsive delivery schedules) are but a few influences on cash flow. *Manufacturing/operations philosophy* was discussed above in relation to just-in-time methods, however, to these comments we should add the application of information technology. As mentioned in Chapter 7 the introduction of electronic point of sale (EPOS) systems has had a dramatic effect on inventory levels and in-transit inventories and the investment (and therefore cash committed) to inventory holding has been considerably reduced.

Moving further down the left-hand side of the model, *changes in working capital requirements* have much in common with operations management methods: the application of technology over time in manufacturing and distribution has tended to reduce the level of current working capital requirements. However, when considered in terms of business expansion, where often there is an incremental increase in working capital (e.g., finished goods inventory in a stock-based order/sales system), this may be excessive when expanding into new territories. Both the availability of cash flow and the cost (actual cost or opportunity cost) should be considered when future working capital requirements are reviewed. Often some synergy is obtainable. For the stock-based order/sales system, in which typically safety stocks are carried, the stochastic economies of scale are such that the required increase in stock levels necessary to provide availability service cover are proportionately less for the same level of cover.

A major cash flow issue concerns *capital expenditure* and the ways by which it is financed. Capital expenditure usually implies changes to the *financial structure* of the business unless, of course, the existing business makes sufficient *cash flow available for strategic use*. Changes in financial structure will be discussed in the next chapter and economic cash flow with investment appraisal methods in Chapter 11.

The model in Figure 9.3 offers management a facility for planning and reviewing cash flow situations that may occur as a result of strategic and operational changes. In effect it is a *cash flow management* model with which management is able to respond to the questions posed at the beginning of the chapter:

Question: Why are profits decreasing and our working capital increasing?
Response: A review of the model may indicate market/business environment changes or perhaps supplier-based reasons.
Q: Why use external funding when there are large cash reserves?
R: The company's use of external funding can be evaluated and the optimal structure (external funding versus the use of reserves) be thoroughly considered with changes in dividends policy and customer and supplier options all considered prior to a decision being made.
Q: Where are the subsidiary divestment proceeds?
R: When large divestments are made decisions to use funds may be made *after* a review of the overall cash flow management situation of the firm. A strategic view may result in a review of the options initially identified. The model permits their subsequent monitoring.
Q: Why are profits increasing but dividends remaining unchanged?
R: Or is the current retentions policy more or less effective in producing cash for investment than the use of external funding?
Q: What cash will planned product development programmes require and produce?
R: The requirements of product development programmes can be projected. This gives the BCG matrix a dynamic perspective *and* identifies current and future sources of cash flow.

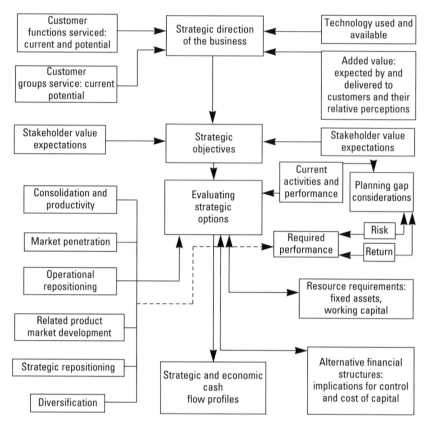

Figure 9.4   Determining strategic and economic cash flow

Strategic perspectives

By now the importance of forecasting cash flows has been established. Figure 9.4 suggests an approach to this important activity. It commences with deciding upon the *strategic direction* and then considers the company's *strategic objectives*. Given these, management can then identify and *evaluate the strategic options* that are available if the objectives are to be achieved. The options considered are based on those described in Chapters 1 and 2. The analysis requires a comparison of the *required performance* with *current activities and performance*. This will identify *resource requirements* and the *alternative financial structures*. Given a *strategic direction* (see Chapter 2) it follows that profitability, productivity and cash flow characteristics will have been identified and by and large incorporated into the marketing/finance decision-making complex. These are likely to be similar for competitors in similar industry sectors with similar business scope characteristics. The efficient companies will be those which service customer functions, dominate selected customer groups (segments), use leading-edge technology, and maximize the added value delivered to their customers. If this is the case it is not unreasonable to assume that the range of margins earned, the asset base productivity and the cash flow generated will show small variations around a mean outcome.

Any changes to the scope of the business may result in changes in these three areas. For example, a shift in the scope (additional functions, segments or added value) may be towards more cashintensive activities; the example (given by Schlosser 1992) of the industrial gas companies is a good illustration of this. Clearly, the investment increases in gas production facilities would have required funding from corporate resources (either from retained earnings or additional equity and/or long-term debt); however, to provide the cash the customers were offered a range of benefits (e.g., availability, price, personal services), which from a cost–benefit view offered mutual added value. These moves may be considered in strategic terms as market penetration, operational (or strategic) repositioning, or perhaps related product-market development. In the case of any of these options the marketing strategy/financial strategy changes are much more 'incremental' in nature.

However, diversification will usually require a review of the scope of the business because the change in direction may have quite serious implications on the financial infrastructure. Such was the situation confronting a specialist-food/delicatessen processor which was approached by a large food multiple retailer for supply. The processor's existing customer base was satisfied with the product range, distribution service and sales representation offered. They paid their accounts well within the 30-day term offered, with many paying early to benefit from the prepayment discount.

The multiple retailer soon began to dominate the specialist manufacturer. Product exclusives were demanded, with own-brand versions of fast-moving items; packaging was to be redesigned and distribution frequencies increased. A major problem for the processor was the cash flow that arose with the large company: it expected and usually was given 45 days (which often stretched to 60 days) for payment of accounts. Initially, this represented a manageable proportion of the total accounts receivable and caused no major problems; but as the business undertaken with the multiple retailer expanded, the accounts receivable problem increased and resulted in a restructuring of the smaller company's working capital requirements.

Other issues that have implications for strategic cash flow concern shareholder and stakeholder value expectations. A change in *shareholder expectations* (usually for an increase in dividends and/or share price appreciation) will require a review of *objectives* and have implications for the performance of the business (i.e., its profitability, productivity and cash flow). This in turn requires a review of *strategy options* in which *current activities and performance* are compared with *required performance*, which will identify *planning gap considerations* together with the accompanying *risk* and *return* issues. These in turn raise questions concerning the *resources required* and how they might be funded.

Changes in *stakeholder value expectations* will initiate a similar sequence of events. Stakeholder expectations may vary from requests for increased pay and/or reduced working hours and other benefits to mandatory issues such as pollution controls in manufacturing operations. For example, within the European Union (EU) there are beginning to emerge mandates concerning the recyclable content of products. This has obvious implications for both marketing and financial management. Marketing issues concern not only costs and their impact on pricing flexibility but also on positioning. Within many of the EU's constituent countries consumer attitudes towards the central EU drive on conservation and pollution vary. It follows that if a producer wants to attract a market segment which may contain a number of potential customers with more than average positive attitudes, the product-service offer should reflect their values and meet the most stringent requirements. Thus the issue assumes quite large dimensions, which may result in changes to the business and have far-reaching financial as well as marketing implications. These may well require plant renewal or modifications which will change resource requirements and raise funding considerations.

Implementation/operational perspectives

Effective strategy implementation occurs when performance objectives are met within the constraints of the fixed assets and working capital budgets. Figure 9.5 identifies the steps by which this occurs. The process is initiated by *implementing the strategy* which has been developed (the previous four steps) and proceeds with decisions on *product-market scope* and *resource allocation* required by the strategy selected.

Given that the basic objectives are to meet profitability, productivity and cash flow, the three key (performance-based) activities noted in Figure 9.5 are *determining the operational budget*, and *increasing* the *operating profit* and the resultant *cash flow from operations*. The task of the marketing group is to optimize profitability, productivity and cash flow if the primary objective of maximizing shareholder value is to be achieved by effective management of product-market scope and resource allocation decisions.

Product-market scope and resource allocation decisions reflect the strategic direction already decided on. For example, a consolidation and productivity strategy suggests a number of implementation activities. A product range rationalization programme will release working capital by reducing stock-holding and improve fixed asset productivity, releasing under-utilized plant,

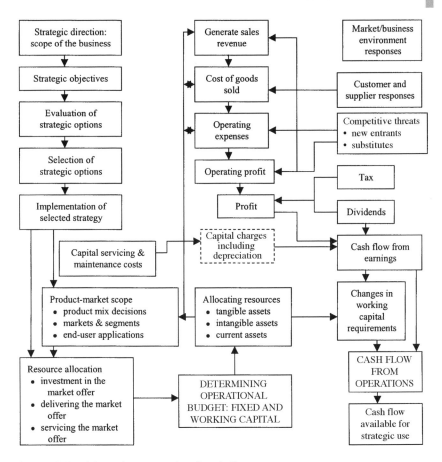

Figure 9.5 Managing operational cash flow

equipment and distribution facilities for use in the manufacture and distribution of the more profitable products within the range. However, care should be exercised to ensure that vital end-user applications are not reduced as a result of the rationalization. An investment in the market offer may occur if IT systems are introduced to improve the efficiency of the current offer with a faster, more accurate order management system.

Market penetration may be achieved by increasing either the product range or by increasing market share by an aggressive promotional campaign: both activities would require use of working capital – cash to increase stockholding and to increase the intensity of advertising. Some increases in the fixed asset utilization would therefore occur and management should ensure that either this capacity exists internally or that the capacity can be 'bought in' at an acceptable cost. A market penetration strategy may be based upon expanding the uses of the product by existing customers. The f.m.c.g. household cleanser manufacturers provide examples of this in their promotion of kitchen cleansers as equally effective bathroom cleansers.

Operational repositioning usually requires both fixed and working capital budget allocation. The earlier example of the response of mineral water manufacturers to meet a shift in consumer preferences for 'light lunches' is matched by the response of retailers (that is, food retailers and department stores) which allocate sales area and chilled storage space together with staff to provide an easily accessed fast food/rapid service offer to customers.

Strategic repositioning requires a larger commitment of resources and may involve product reformulation, product augmentation or the introduction of delivery alternatives. There have been a number of examples where this has occurred. The introduction of catalogues by department stores and clothing durables specialists is a response to the changes occurring in consumer purchasing preferences and habits. Car maintenance and valet services have become mobile, enabling these services to be delivered to the customer rather than offered from specific locations the customer is required to visit. And financial services (banking, insurance, savings and investment products) are now available to telephone customers. In each of these examples there were productmarket scope and resource allocation decisions to be made; these in turn required fixed and working capital decisions.

As the strategy options are expanded so too are the demands on resources. Related product-market development requires a budget for product development and/or modification and may alternatively require an investment in distributor development and sales development activities as and when new geographical markets are considered.

Diversification strategies may well stretch across a number of operational/implementation activity periods. The in-company development of new product/new market activities may require a serial approach which requires an investment in fixed tangible and intangible assets (such as R&D, operations technology and capacity, handling service facilities and staff development). Eventually working capital investment is required in the form of cash for distributor development, promotions and, of course, for inventory support.

The task confronting operational marketing and financial managers is to manage the operational budget effectively. Clearly, they have involvement in the strategy development process by identifying feasible options (and identifying those options which would be difficult to pursue due to lack of customer expectations (market research) or competitive responses (competitors with much larger market share) or supplier response (a lack of capacity in the existing supplier markets)). The result is an agreed strategy expressed in broad terms and for which the marketing and financial details are subsequently developed.

It follows that a major component of the activity comprises evaluating the cost effectiveness of the product-market scope and resource allocation decisions such that the profitability, productivity and cash flow objectives are achieved.

9.4   Current and future cash flow

We have referred to the importance of cash flow in order to meet transactions for contingency purposes and for speculative uses. To this end a review of the cash flow currently available and that which will result from proposed strategies is necessary. A review of the cash flow uses and generation of the product-market development process will help. It will identify how the firm may be able to control these later phases of the productmarket development process and generate above-average profits, productivity and cash flow. However there are costs. To continue to commit resources to an existing strategic business area usually implies they cannot be used elsewhere; it follows that opportunities to develop strong competitive advantage in new strategic business areas may be lost. The cash flow implications of rejuvenation are indicated in Figure 9.6: additional fixed capital requirements and working capital are included and the cash flow attributable to the disposal of the fixed assets may be reduced.

9.5   Summary

This chapter has considered the financial and marketing approaches to cash flow. Financial measures are typically expressed in the standard annual reporting format as sources and applications of funds. The marketing approach has been more qualitative and has been based upon concepts espoused by the Boston Consulting Group using market share and the experience effect as the foundation of their arguments.

The chapter developed the approach of Schlosser (1992), who considered cash flow to have two aspects: cash flow from earnings and from operations. We have extended these to include strategic considerations, the thesis being that from a planning view it is essential to be able to project operating and strategic cash flow profiles. By doing so, strategic as well as operational cash requirements may be forecast. Models to consider the sources and applications of operational and strategic cash flows were developed.

The hypothetical cash flow profile of the strategic business area was discussed in the context of marketing and financial decisions.

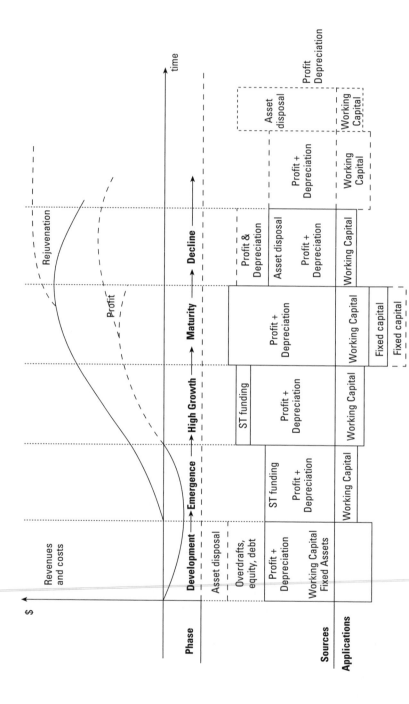

Figure 9.6   Cash flow planning for the product-market development process

REFERENCES

Abell, D. F. and Hammond, J. S. (1979) *Strategic Marketing Planning*, Prentice Hall, Englewood Cliffs, NJ.

Boston Consulting Group (1970) *Experience Curves as a Planning Tool*, Boston Consulting Group, Inc., Boston.

Hedley, B. (1976) 'A fundamental approach to strategy development', *Long Range Planning*, December: 2–11.

Robinson, G. (1986) *Strategic Management Techniques*, Butterworths, Durban, SA.

Schlosser, M. (1992) *Corporate Finance*, 2nd edn, Prentice Hall, London.

Wilson, C. and Keers, B. (1987) *Introduction to Financial Management*, Prentice Hall, Melbourne.

10 Capital Structure Decisions

In the introduction to Part III financial structure, financial risk and financial gearing were introduced. The concept of financial gearing was introduced as a measure of the proportions of equity and debt in the organization's overall capital structure. Financial risk relates to the levels of debt only within the overall capital structure.

In Chapter 8 we reintroduced financial gearing together with operational gearing (the extent to which operating fixed costs are used in the firm's cost structure). Financial gearing has an influence on the nature of the activities the company undertakes. While a detailed knowledge of the theory of capital structure decisions is unnecessary for the reader (and is beyond the scope of this text), an understanding of the issues and implications for marketing/finance interface situations will prove to be useful.

10.1 Financial gearing: some characteristics

Gearing reflects the extent to which the firm is financed by borrowing. Investors see equity investments as riskier than debt and therefore expect a higher rate of return on equity investments. Gearing, or leverage (its North American label), may be defined as the use of low-cost debt. However, as we have already indicated, gearing has a problem in that it adds financial risk to the existing *business risk*. Shareholders are averse to risk and consequently expect higher returns for accepting an above-average level of risk.

Financial managers are responsible for capital structure decisions and try to maintain a balance of debt and equity that optimizes the overall cost of financing the organization's capital requirements (i.e., dividend payments and interest charges on the debt). Capital structure theory argues that if taxation and costs of financial failure are ignored then it is unlikely that an optimal financial structure can exist. Interest is tax deductible (as a cost of doing business) and should the firm fail and be forced into liquidation, the costs associated with the ensuing financial distress are considerable and, of course, are the responsibility of the shareholders.

It follows that there is a trade-off between the tax benefit of borrowing and the costs of financial distress; the firm should use debt to maximize the benefit of tax relief on interest payments but not borrow to the extent that it risks incurring the costs of financial failure.

The cost of borrowing has an important impact on the business's marketing strategy. Gearing attempts to lower the overall cost of borrowing. There is likely to be a range of rates of return across the spectrum of strategies that may be pursued by the firm because customer and competitor responses will vary, supply markets and resource availability will not be uniform (shortages may increase input prices, etc.) and operating costs will differ. The task of marketing management is to identify opportunities which offer high rates of return and low risk. Given a weighted average cost of capital it follows that it is to the firm's advantage to pursue high return strategy options with, preferably, low risk. To do so is to maximize the shareholders' value of the business.

There are a number of theories concerning the impact of debt on the value of the firm. Dobbins and Witt (1988) suggested that as the market value of the firm is based upon the cash flows generated from operational and investment (strategic) activities (less expenditures) discounted at its cost of capital, it follows that marketing decisions have an important influence on both the revenue generation and the cost of capital.

The argument that interests us here is the traditional one that suggests shareholders have increasing expectations of returns as the level of borrowing increases. Figure 10.1 illustrates that point. The influence of increased levels of debt (i.e., as the debt/equity ratio increases) is to lower the cost of capital up to a point; but beyond this investors consider levels of risk to be increasingly unacceptable; from this point their expectations of higher returns increases (i.e., rate of return on *their* investment in the firm) as the debt/equity ratio increases.

These arguments were summarized by Brayshaw (1992). While there are clear benefits to the firm from the deduction of tax due to debt interest, this obtains only as long as there are taxable profits. A point can be reached where the increase in risk and potential failure make the tax benefits increasingly less attractive. Furthermore, as an increasing level of debt is added to the capital structure so the company may find that its lenders impose conditions upon courses of action it wishes to pursue. In addition, there is the fact that the flexibility that an unused debt capacity offers is increasingly reduced as the debt/equity ratio is increased.

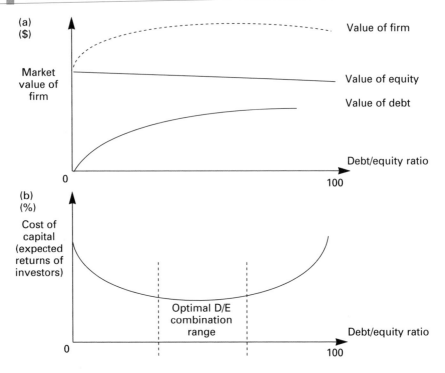

Figure 10.1 Combination of debt and equity that minimizes the cost of capital

The nature of the business often influences the level of gearing of individual companies. Those with tangible and marketable assets may be able to operate with higher levels of gearing than those with intangible assets. However, some caution should be exercised here. For example, while property is a tangible asset it may be very specialist and therefore not necessarily marketable; superstore building owners fall into this category. If one owner has not been able to earn acceptable levels of profits in a particular location it follows that the trading environment will be difficult for subsequent owners. However, because of a lower level of gearing, the levels of profit and cash flow generated may be adequate for one company but not for one whose debt funding represents a significantly higher level of its capital employed.

Consider, in a declining market, two supercentre companies of equal size, that is, with the same amount of capital employed – $1 million. However, Company A has a $100,000 debt compared with a $500,000 debt held by Company B:

	Company A Low geared ($1000)	Company B High geared ($1000)
Equity	900	500
Debt (financed at 15% interest)	100	500
Capital employed	1,000	1,000

Consider three years' trading:

	Year 1		Year 2		Year 3	
	A	B	A	B	A	B
EBIT	300	300	200	200	75	75
Interest (at 15%)	15	75	15	75	15	75
Profit (B/T)	285	225	185	125	60	0
Tax (at 35%)	100	80	65	45	20	0
Profit (A/T)	185	145	120	80	40	0
Return	21%	29%	13%	16%	4%	0
on equity (ROE)	(A 38%↓)		(B 45%↓)			

As the ROE decreases it does so at an increasing rate. The percentage decreases in ROE between year 1 and year 2 are, for A, 38 per cent, but for B the ROE percentage decline is 45 per cent. In year 3 the decline continues and the 50 per cent debt/equity ratio of B requires all of the EBIT to service the debt. Clearly debt favours the shareholders if high levels of profit can be maintained. Failure to do so results in poor returns: hence high levels of gearing increase financial risk. Add to this business risk and the overall expectations of shareholders will be higher, to compensate for the total risk. Returning to the hypothetical situation, the lower geared business is in a position to accept the lower margins from the low sales for a longer period of time, during which it may be possible to make sufficient changes which will restore the sales and profitability of the superstore location. Without the flexibility of a superior gearing position such options are not available.

10.2 The cost of capital

The cost of capital for any organization has both quantitative and qualitative considerations. Qualitative costs relate to the extent, involvement and nature of control that equity investors expect. Clearly, it is difficult to ascribe value to these. The quantitative costs are not difficult to derive arithmetically but, as we shall see, some assumptions concerning the current levels of returns, business risk and tax-shielding benefits are necessary.

Qualitative costs of capital

If company management chooses to expand the company's equity base, it has a number of options available; some of these were identified in Chapter 8. Here we are concerned with the costs of these options. The qualitative costs are important to both marketing and finance managers. A major qualitative factor for consideration when expanding the financial structure and size of the business is the impact on decision making and control.

The equity-owning shareholders enjoy voting rights and theoretically can influence the major decisions made by their company. Increasingly shares are held by large institutions (referred to in Chapter 8) and these institutional shareholders can (and do) exert influence over the strategic direction of the business. Institutional shareholders are charged with the stewardship of the funds of their investors and are therefore concerned to ensure that the companies in which these funds are invested are secure (taking the necessary steps to minimize financial and business risk) and not likely to make decisions that would seriously change their risk profile. To this end they may, albeit discreetly, comment upon the strategic plans of companies in which they have large investment interests.

If the equity base is expanded it follows that this influence may increase. For large public companies this has become an accepted way of business. However, there remain a few companies with privately owned equity, and other companies (particularly in high-technology industries) whose rate of expansion can only be maintained if external funding is obtained: it is these companies which may experience difficulties in obtaining funds without constraints.

It has been suggested (Berle and Means 1932; Holl 1977) that ownership of many businesses is separated from control by the management structure. This argument is based upon the extent to which many shareholders are not qualified to comment constructively on company decisions, and that furthermore they have little interest beyond dividends and the growth of the share price. Nevertheless, the fact remains that to expand the financial base of the firm by issuing equity does invite some dilution of management control.

A *rights issue* is one means by which the control structure of the shareholding remains undisturbed. The company offers existing shareholders an opportunity to purchase additional shares *in proportion to the amount* of shares currently owned. The subscription price is set at below the market price to make the offer attractive but not so low as to damage the price of shares subsequent to the offer when trading recommences. Thus no dilution of ownership or control occurs.

There are a number of other options available to management for the issue of additional equity shareholding. *Private placing* is a means by which the expenses associated with equity issues may be avoided. Placements involve offering packages of shares to large institutional investors, usually at prices below current market value. There are both advantages and disadvantages to this. As well as minimizing costs, private placings can be arranged more quickly than other forms of issues (if empathetic investors are approached); and control and the 'direction' of investment (the risk profile) can be controlled. The major disadvantages concern existing shareholders' interests because the discounted prices may lower the market price of shares and dilute the control existing shareholders currently have.

Share options are one other alternative. An option is simply an offer to purchase shares in a company at a specified price within a specified time period. Options are typically included in recruitment packages for senior executives, offering performance incentives and, of course, some (very small) measure of control. Options may also be offered as part of a financial package when making a private debt issue. The option to purchase equity may act as encouragement to the investors of long term debt.

Debt funding does not have the implications for control that we find with equity financing. However, there are some indirect issues. Debt interest payments cannot be deferred and therefore act as a constraint on the business, possibly preventing its expansion. Debt funds must be repaid at a predetermined date; it follows that if an investment has not grown at the rates initially assumed, any fixed asset funding met by the debt is only flexible to the extent to which refinancing is possible. If the debt was to have been repaid from cash flows generated from operations some embarrassment may occur. The major 'control' exercised by debt is a limitation imposed on borrowing capacity, as debt expenses are a component of the financial structure of the business. The control issues are important in the development of marketing strategy and should influence decisions in so far as acceptable levels of business and financial risk are decided.

One final, but obvious source of funds is *retained earnings*, which avoid the capital issues (at least in the short term, although low dividends and low growth are likely to be met with shareholder discontent eventually). Using retained earnings offers a low-cost (and almost instantaneous) source of funds. Often tax incentives are offered to stimulate reinvestment by corporations, such as 'negative tax rates' on reinvested profits.

Quantitative costs of capital

Regardless of the types of funding used by a firm each has a cost. The cost of funds is measured by the returns expected by the investors as payment for the use of their funds. The cost of capital to the company depends upon the various amounts of equity debt and any other capital employed. An average cost is calculated by using the proportion each represents in the total funding of the business. This weighting is usually based upon balance sheet values. Brayshaw (1992) suggested that there are assumptions here concerning the relationship between the investors' expected rate of return and their view of the accompanying risk (of the current activities of the firm) – that is, its activities in current strategic business areas. Brayshaw argued that this risk/return combination is based upon historic values of tangible and intangible assets. This is of concern to the marketing manager. If we consider the firm's business activities to be described by its strategic direction or business scope we have implications for fixed asset values (technology) and intangible asset values (such as brands) which correspond to customer loyalty and perceptions of the business. These are likely to have different values for proposed business activities. The problem of arriving at a quantitative value has no easy solution, particularly for investors. Internally, for planning purposes, adjustments can be made to the expected rate of return (or hurdle rate) used when evaluating strategic options. We shall discuss these issues in detail in Chapter 12.

Given these problems we remain concerned with investors' expectations of return on their investment in the business, and if balance sheet values are used for evaluative purposes it is assumed that:

(i)   The risk/return profile for new activities will be similar to the average of existing projects.
(ii) Future financing methods will reflect the current level of financial gearing.
(iii) Taxation and the implications for debt funding will continue into the future.

These assumptions may not be realistic for a growth business seeking expansion through unrelated product-market development or perhaps through diversification.

Cost of equity funds

Equity shareholders receive no fixed return on their investment but are entitled to a share of the profits remaining after other expenses have been met.

Investors' expectations of returns are based upon their view of the dividend stream they will receive and the increase in value of the share price. The expected rate of return represents the cost of equity funds to the firm. We can express this value as:

$$\text{Return to Investors/Cost of equity to the firm} = \frac{\text{Future dividend payments}}{\text{Current value of shares}} + \text{Expected growth rate of future dividends}$$

An example will illustrate how this relationship works. Acme Pty Ltd has paid a 15 cent dividend per share on its ordinary shares which are currently valued at $3.30 exdividend (i.e., after the payment of the dividend). The recent performance of Acme shows that dividends and earnings have grown at 10 per cent per annum. During the accounting period the company has retained 50 per cent of its earnings. The company has enjoyed a 20 per cent return on assets. The cost of equity can be calculated by:

$$\frac{\text{Dividend paid (in cents)}\qquad \text{Retentions} \times \text{ROA (return on assets)}}{\text{Annual growth rate}}$$
$$\frac{15(1 + 0.1)}{330} + 0.1$$
$$\text{Current share price in cents} = 15 \text{ per cent}$$

Cost of debt

It is usual for interest payments and redemption dates to be fixed prior to loan offers being accepted. In this case the cost of debt is easily calculated. However, redemption values may be index linked (e.g., to the retail price index) although index linking is not particularly popular with private sector companies.

A not unusual form of debt is the fixed interest security with no repayment date. Perpetual debts are transferable and while the interest rate is fixed the value of the debt reflects current interest rates. This can be expressed as follows:

$$\text{Current value of debt} = \frac{\text{Annual interest payment}}{\text{Rate of return required by investors}}$$

or:

$$\text{Rate of return required by investors} = \frac{\text{Annual interest payment}}{\text{Current value of debt}}$$

However, it is more usual for debt to be repayable and the redemption value should therefore be included:

Time adjusted

$$\text{Current value of debt} = \frac{\text{Annual interest payment}}{\text{Rate of return required by investors}} + \frac{\text{Redemption value of debt}}{\text{Rate of return required by investors}}$$

Again an example will serve to illustrate how the cost of debt may be calculated. Acme Pty Ltd has one ten-year term debt liability. The debt interest rate is 10 per cent (paid annually) and the debt is to be repaid at its issue value of $10 million. The loan is traded in $100 bonds and currently is quoted at $89. Using the relationship described above we have:

$$\text{Quoted current \$ value } 89 = \sum_{t=1}^{10} \underbrace{\frac{10}{(1 + R)^{10}}}_{\substack{\text{Debt} \\ \text{interest rate}}} + \underbrace{\frac{100}{(1 + R)^{10}}}_{\substack{\text{Redemption value} \\ \text{(issue value)}}}$$

Which gives (using the annuity tables for calculation):

$$89 = \$10 \times 5.0188 + \$100 \times 0.2472$$

Using the appropriate discountable values at a rate of 12 per cent (the present value of the *future* cash flows) this will equal the market price of $88.70. Assuming the tax rate to be 35 per cent, the after-tax cost of capital will be:

$$12\% \ (1 - 0.35) = 7.8\%$$

The weighted average cost of capital

The weighted average cost of capital reflects the debt/equity mix in the capital employed. The actual cost can be calculated from a relationship reflecting the proportions of each type of funding and their cost:

Weighted average cost of capital

$$= \frac{\left(\begin{array}{c}\text{Market value} \\ \text{of equity}\end{array} \times \begin{array}{c}\text{Cost of} \\ \text{equity}\end{array}\right) + \left(\begin{array}{c}\text{Market value} \\ \text{of debt}\end{array} \times \begin{array}{c}\text{Cost of} \\ \text{debt}\end{array}\right)}{\text{Market value equity} + \text{Market value of debt}}$$

Using the hypothetical Acme Pty Ltd again to illustrate the calculation, we can assume the company to have 10 million shares issued (nominal value $1.50) currently with a market value of $3.30 ex-dividend (dividend paid: 15 cents) and $10 million debt with an aftertax cost of capital of 7.8 per cent. We therefore have:

$$\frac{(10 \times 3.3)\,(0.15) + (10 \times 0.89)\,(0.078)}{(10 \times 3.3 + 10)} = 13.3\%$$

10.3 Marketing/finance interface issues

Having discussed the issues of financial structure and the costs of debt and equity financing we conclude this chapter by considering the issues that have an influence on the financing decision. These are presented in the model in Figure 10.2.

The *market/business environment* (in the top middle of the model) is influenced by the same factors that affect cash flow (see the cash flow model in

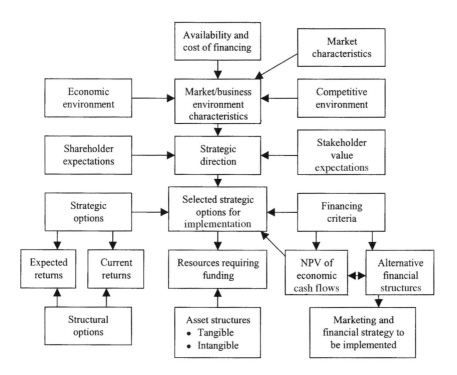

Figure 10.2 A marketing/finance approach to determining financial structure

Figure 9.3). There may be some additional issues to be considered specifically relevant to the financing decision. For example, the use of overseas sources of funds is not unusual and potential borrowing companies should be aware of the views of overseas investors concerning the domestic economy. Indeed *interest rates, exchange rates, GDP/GNP growth* and *employment* have implications for both the borrowing company and the potential source of funds. Borrowers will wish to satisfy themselves that the projected returns will be secure. Investors will wish to satisfy themselves that the economy as well as the company has a secure future.

During the process of confirming (or modifying) strategic direction two important things should be considered. *Shareholder value expectations* are central to the eventual decision because the financial structure decided upon will impact upon share price performance, dividends and cash flows. Shareholder expectations should be established prior to extensive evaluation of the alternatives because they may be such as to exclude some options. For example, a shareholder preference for a low level of risk may set limits to the use of high levels of debt financing. *Stakeholder value expectations* may be extensive; they can be expected to vary according to company size and strategic business area. (It should be remembered that stakeholders comprise employees, suppliers – including suppliers of finance – government and, of course, existing and potential customers.)

Current marketing performance is also significant, particularly positioning and market share. Positioning indicates a degree of qualitative strength (e.g., brand equity and customer loyalty) while market share gives some quantitative measures: strong market share indicates market power; it also indicates financial strengths in terms of revenues, costs and therefore margins. Both positioning and market share have significance with investors who tend to favour 'winners'.

Having determined the ideal marketing strategy, *risk* and *return* are evaluated and compared with values of existing activities (*current risks* and *returns*). Clearly, the company should not expect to be able to continue to expand (if that is what its objectives imply) with the levels of risk remaining at those of current values. What is required is an examination of viable strategic options and their risk/return combinations against those experienced by the company's current strategic business areas. The purpose should be to identify how large the differences are. If the risk/return profile is vastly different from the expectations of the shareholders and the financial stakeholders it may imply that additional financing is either difficult or expensive to obtain.

For this reason the *financial criteria* that are included in Figure 10.2 form a useful check list. Each item should be considered with respect to proposed financial structures. Clearly, the purpose of the analysis is to identify a financial structure that optimizes the return on investment of the business and this can only occur if the firm does not adopt an 'expensive' financial structure. However, it is equally important that *qualitative costs* are also optimized. Flexibility to add additional short term finance and to permit marketing decisions in both the short and long term without hindrance is part of the trade-off process.

The *marketing and financial strategy* that evolves should be a response to the market-led opportunities that may be pursued with an acceptable level of risk, and which meet the value expectations of the shareholders and other stakeholders. The balance is not easy to obtain, but the process of attempting to reach an optimal financial structure for the company will ensure that all issues have been addressed. It does not follow that they have all been totally satisfied; rather that the solution reached represents an effective allocation of financial resources.

10.4 Summary

This chapter has discussed the issues of financial structure confronting a business.

We have discussed financial gearing and the implications for risk that gearing combinations may impose. Of particular importance is the influence that gearing exerts on the cost of capital. We identified the benefits and the costs of high levels of gearing with worked examples.

The cost of capital was introduced and we suggested that both qualitative and quantitative aspects exist and that both are important. Examples of quantitative costs of capital were given. The costs of equity and debt funding were discussed and calculated. These led to the calculation of a weighted average cost of capital.

Finally we proposed a model with which to approach the financial structure decision given the requirements of the marketing strategy. Its purpose is to offer a methodical approach which considers many of the indirect influences, as well as the more obvious ones.

REFERENCES

Berle, A. A. and C. Means (1932) *The Modern Corporation and Private Property*, Macmillan, New York.

Brayshaw, R. E. (1992) *The Concise Guide to Company Finance and its Management*, Chapman & Hall, London.

Dobbins, R. and Witt, S. F. (1988) *Practical Financial Management*, Basil Blackwell, Oxford.

Holl, P. (1977) 'Control Type and the Market for Corporate Control in Large US Corporations', *Journal of Industrial Economics*, 25(4): 259–73.

11 Investment Appraisal

If the objective of the firm is to maximize the value delivered to the shareholder, management must look beyond the single criterion of profit maximization. Wealth is created by maximizing the present value of economic cash flows. Investment decisions are central to value creation because it is the investment decisions which determine the level of future cash flows generated from successful trading. It follows that both marketing and finance have important roles in the identification, appraisal and selection of market-based investment opportunities.

There are a number of methods available for evaluating investment alternatives, which vary in terms of suitability, simplicity and realism. We shall review the currently favoured methods prior to discussing the important issues confronting management during the investment appraisal and decision-making process. It is assumed that the reader is familiar with the principles and methodology of investment appraisal and therefore only a brief review of the methods will be undertaken.

11.1 Investment appraisal alternatives

The purpose of investment appraisal is to identify the costs and benefits associated with a project. For our purposes we will assume a project to be a strategy-based alternative. Thus, we consider the process as applicable to the spectrum of strategy alternatives we have referred to throughout that confront the business – diversification, related product-market growth, repositioning (strategic and operational), market penetration, consolidation and productivity and divestment. Investment appraisal techniques may be applied to individual projects or to a broader strategy which may combine a number of product-market activities.

Nondiscounting methods

Nondiscounting-based investment appraisal methods are simple to apply, easy to understand because of their simplicity and are often favoured by businesspeople. Two of the most prominent examples are the accounting rate of return and payback.

The *accounting rate of return* (ARR) uses accounting values rather than cash flows to evaluate investment alternatives. It is calculated by expressing the average accounting profit generated (after charging depreciation and tax) as a percentage of the average capital employed invested in a project. If there is likely to be a residual value from the original investment this is subtracted to arrive at the average investment.

The ARR measures a return in accounting terms over a project life span, and there is a possibility of subjective assessment for depreciation and costs. The time value of money is ignored; hence a dollar to be received in ten years' time is given the same value as a dollar received today. ARR is familiar to management and, as Brayshaw (1992) has commented, as managers' incentives are based on profits and profitability it is not surprising to find them preferring an investment appraisal method which has links with their performance incentive appraisal.

Payback appraises projects by measuring the time required to recover the original investment in a project. It uses profit after tax *plus* depreciation. Payback's users claim that it emphasizes liquidity and can make an allowance for risk. It is both simple and easy to use. However, as with ARR it ignores the time value of money as cash flows received after the recovery of the investment and this is a major deficiency. According to the payback method, risk is considered to be a function of the time taken to recover the investment, which may not be an effective measure. Payback will favour short-term projects, which may not be the most profitable, and its use may result in the selection of low profit projects simply because they have rapid payback. Long-term technology-based projects, for example, with high R&D and large capital expenditures, would not receive favourable appraisals. An argument favouring the use of payback (in conjunction with discounting-based methods) as a secondary appraisal method has some support among company managers pursuing growth strategies. Payback is attractive for distribution companies and others with low investment/high cash flow characteristics that plan their expansion around cash recycling.

Clearly, the failure of ARR and payback to incorporate the time value of money in their appraisal methods is a serious deficiency. While they are both simple and easy to use they must be seen as inefficient in comparison with discounting-based techniques, which do take into account both interest and time.

Discounting methods

Discounted cash flow (DCF) methods use the cost of borrowing and (as we said) take interest and time into consideration in the appraisal. The two most commonly used discounting methods are net present value (NPV) and internal rate of return (IRR).

DCF methods are based upon the *present value* of future cash flows. The argument is simple; a dollar to be received in ten years from now is worth less than the dollar held today. Furthermore, we can calculate future values by using compound interest given by:

> Compound value (or Terminal value)
> = Initial investment × Interest rate × Time in years as a multiplier

or:

$$CV \ (\text{or} \ TV) = S(1 + r)^3$$

where:

$$CV \ (TV) = \text{compound or terminal value}$$
$$s = \text{sum invested}$$
$$r = \text{interest rate earned}$$
$$t = \text{time period over which S is invested}$$

It follows that a dollar amount received immediately is worth more than the same amount to be received at some future time because the sum received immediately can be invested for the intervening period and earn a return. It therefore follows that an amount promised in the future has a *present value* and this can be found by *discounting* future income values to calculate their present value:

$$\text{Present value} = \frac{\text{Future amount}}{\text{Interest rate} \times \text{Time in years}}$$

or:

$$PV = \frac{F}{(1 + r)^t}$$

where:

$$PV = \text{present value}$$
$$F = \text{future amount}$$
$$r = \text{interest rate/discount rate}$$
$$t = \text{time period over which value is to be calculated}$$

The net present value (NPV) is arrived at by deducting the initial investment from the present value:

$$\text{NPV} = \sum_{t=1}^{n} \frac{F_t}{(1+r)^t} - I$$

where:

NPV = net present value

$\sum_{t}^{n}$ = the summation over years

$t = 1, 2 \ldots n$
F_t = the forecast net cash flow arising at the end of year t. This represents the difference between operational cash receipts and expenditures (including capital replenishment during the life of the project)
r = required rate of return on the discount rate
n = project life in years
I = the initial cost of the investment

The present value is arrived at by aggregating the forecast net cash flows for the planned life span of the project discounted at a rate of interest which reflects the cost of a loan of equivalent risk on the capital market.

It follows that an investment is wealth-creating if its NPV is positive. All projects offering a positive NPV (when discounted at the required rate of return for the 'project' investment) could be accepted with the aim of maximizing the value of the shareholders' equity holding in the business.

The *internal rate of return* (IRR) also uses discounting but it does so to derive a rate of interest which equates the present value of future flows with the original investment:

$$I = \sum_{t=1}^{n} \frac{F_t}{(1+i)^t}$$

where:

I = initial investment
n = project life in years
Σ = the summation over years
t = 1, 2 ... n
F_t = the forecast net cash flow arising at the end of year t, etc
i = the interest rate found by trial and error which equates the present
value of the forecast flows to the value of the required investment

As with the nondiscounting methods we can review the advantages and disadvantages of this approach. NPV indicates the increase in shareholder value which a 'project' delivers when discounted at the cost of capital or discount rate determined by the company's management. NPV does consider the time value of money and NPV values can be aggregated to give a total of the value to be delivered. NPV is often difficult for nonfinancial managers to understand and so they tend to prefer rates of return and payback periods.

IRR calculates a rate of interest which can be compared with the company's cost of capital or required discount rate. IRR does have problems handling cash flows which do not follow a conventional format. While it is preferred by managers because it expresses its findings as a rate of return, it is nevertheless more difficult to calculate manually, often requiring interpolation to reach an exact rate of return. IRR, being a rate of return, does not reflect the size or importance of an investment to a company, whereas NPV is a measure of deliverable value. In other words, IRR may indicate a very large rate of return in percentage terms, but the project may not be large nor particularly significant for the firm.

11.2 Expected rate of return, cost of capital, risk and inflation

The value of the rate of interest used for discounting the forecast cash flows is influenced by the company's cost of capital. For NPV calculations the rate is a management decision while IRR methods derive the rate achieved by the investment. Both ignore inflation and risk and it is a management task to determine the extent to which the discount rates are adjusted to reflect these. It is agreed by practitioners that generally inflation influences both costs and prices and that exhaustive attempts at calculating DCF values at different values of inflation are, in most instances, not worthwhile. However, there are situations in which the rate of inflation of costs differs from that affecting price. For example, products or components sourced from countries with significantly different levels of inflation to those prevalent in the end-use markets can, if the purchases or inputs are sufficiently large, be an exception to this 'rule'. Another example concerns the influence of capacity and competition in reseller markets. Quite often (and particularly in the case of consumer durable products) reseller capacity exceeds the current consumer demand and the resultant price competition has a deflationary effect on product prices within the sector.

Risk is a different issue. As we saw earlier, the NPV of a project is derived by adding together the forecast net cash flows over the span of the project, discounted at a rate which reflects the cost of a loan of equivalent risk on the capital market *less* the initial capital outlay. Hence an investment 'creates' value if the NPV is positive and 'destroys' value if the NPV is negative. However, to be sure about the *amount* of value created (or likely to be destroyed) we should consider the impact of risk. The *capital asset pricing model (CAPM)* can be used for this purpose.

The CAPM is based upon the assumption that investors are risk-averse and the greater the risk of a variable return on an investment, the greater will be the actual return expected by investors (see Chapter 10). It follows then that there is a trade off between market risk and expected return which must be reflected in the required rates of return from the investment alternatives.

The trade-off between risk and return may be represented graphically (see Figure 11.1). The 'trade-off' line indicates the trade-off between expected return and market risk combinations. Therefore activities at A, B and C fall on the trade-off line and the expected return compensates for their risk as the NPV equals zero. Activities F and E have strong positive NPVs and offer good opportunity to create shareholder value while G and D – particularly G, which has very high risk and low return – should not be considered.

The capital asset pricing model was developed to evaluate securities in the

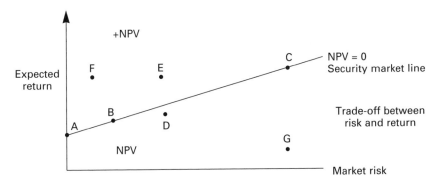

Figure 11.1 Risk/return options of alternative opportunities

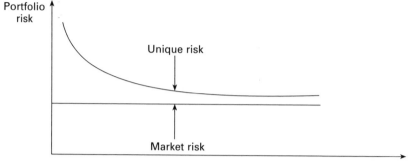

Figure 11.2 Risk/return options of investment opportunities: diversification reduces risk

Note: As the number of investments increases, so the level of unique risk declines. However, market risk remains at the same level.

investment market. It considers risk to have two components: *market risk*, which affects all securities to much the same degree, and *unique risk*, which is specific to an investment and, as suggested by Figure 11.2, may be reduced by diversifying the investments or product-market activities. The underlying principle of the CAPM is that the *expected return* on an investment comprises two components – a *riskfree return* and a *risk premium*:

$$\text{Expected return} = \text{risk-free return} + \text{risk premium}$$
$$ER = Rf + ß(Emr - Rf)$$

where:

    ER = expected return
    Rf = the current short term risk-free interet rate (government bonds etc.)
    $ß$ = coefficient which measures the market risk of the individual share/investment
Emr = expected market return for the next priod

For practical purposes, we can assume the risk-free rate, Rf, is represented by government bonds. *Emr* is the expected return from an investment in *all* shares available on the market – it is a market return.

The beta factor is determined by calculating the relationship between the returns on a specific asset (or investment) and those of the market. For our purposes we can consider it to reflect the relationship between a product-market

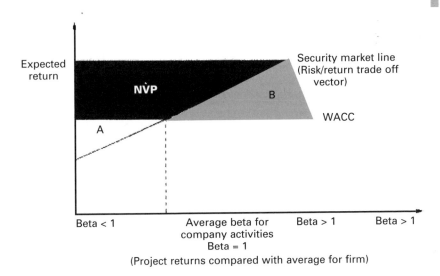

Figure 11.3   CAPM and the cost of capital

and a market segment or a strategic business area and an industry sector. The beta value for the market as a whole is equal to 1. Investments with beta values greater than 1 are sensitive to movements of the market as a whole; if the economy expands, the investment will perform well, but if the economy declines these investments will reflect that lower level of performance. Individual investments (shares) with beta values equal to 1 are expected to match the performance of the economy.

CAPM is of interest because it provides a forward-looking, 'project'-based variable interest rate evaluation model, in which the required rate of return (and therefore the rate used for discounting) can be related to risk as suggested by the beta value. The weighted average cost of capital (WACC) is, as we have seen, a cost of capital that reflects capital structure and investors' perceptions of risk based upon this current structure. Figure 11.3 suggests that this approach may result in the rejection of low risk but viable projects (the shaded area) and the acceptance of high-risk projects which fail to offer an adequate risk/return profile. The use of a beta value enables a more project/company specific measure for evaluation. The benefits are that the approach separates marketing issues from financial structure considerations.

If we use the beta concept in the context of corporate investment decisions (rather than taking the view of an investor in the stock market), the notion of the beta value as an indication of risk does not change: in effect, the beta used should reflect the overall investment market view of the industry sector which the firm is planning to enter. Thus, while the financial management literature suggests that shares with high beta values are sensitive to movements of the market (which in turn reflect the expected performance of the economy), we can say that companies active in these sectors (with high beta values) are more exposed to the vagaries of the economy than those with low beta values. If the economy is expected to perform well then the companies can be expected to generate good results. By contrast, in a recession they are expected to produce poor results. Thus, we see property, travel, leisure services, luxury durable items (high-priced automobiles) and exclusive/speciality stores with high beta values. It follows that companies, the shares of which have a beta of 1, are generally expected to perform in line with the economy. Those with low beta values are companies which may perform independently of the economy; these are likely to include food processors and distributors and utilities companies (i.e., energy and communications). Using Figure 11.4 we can illustrate how expected returns may vary depending upon the relationship existing between the company and the market as perceived by the aggregate investors.

Figure 11.4 plots various investments together with their relative expected returns based upon our earlier comments. The discount rate to be used for investment appraisal should reflect the rate indicated by the beta value, its intersection on the security market line and the corresponding expected rate of return on the vertical axis. The first step is to estimate the security market line. This is usually possible by working with a specialist financial services company, which will also identify the beta values for industry sectors within the economy. Typically, beta values do not vary significantly over time and

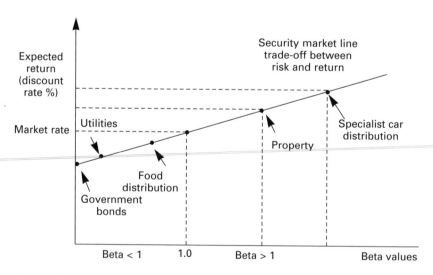

Figure 11.4 Risk/return relationship across industry sectors

are published quarterly along with betas for quoted companies. However, it has been found that the beta values of industrial sectors are more reliable than the beta values for individual companies, simply because the industry betas are based upon larger data samples. This finding has some significance for investment appraisal.

Schlosser (1992) identified the consequences of this industry-return/market-risk relationship:

> *The cost of capital/expected return used depends on the industry with which you are concerned when making strategic investment appraisals.* The beta used should reflect the industry being evaluated.

> *The cost of capital/discount rate does not depend a great deal on the company.* A strategic decision to expand within the industry sector should be appraised with the current cost of capital. A decision concerning sectors outwith the company's current activities should be investigated using the beta value and discount rate of the industry sector not that of the company.

> *Diversified companies should use the beta values and therefore the cost of capital of the industry sectors in which they are active.* This approach will give a more realistic 'answer' for appraisals and therefore make resource allocation more realistic.

An example may help here. Kirribilli Holdings Pty Ltd operates in a range of activities with assets allocated thus:

	Percentage of assets	Beta	Weighted value
Food distribution	40.0	0.8	0.32
Apparel retailing	30.0	1.25	0.375
Property	20.0	1.5	0.30
Specialist car distribution	10.0	1.7	0.17
	–	–	–
	100.0		1.165

The overall beta for Kirribilli is 1.32 and the expected rate of return (indicated by Figure 11.5) is 19 per cent.

Any further diversification should be based on the beta value for the proposed sector and, using the security market line, by identifying the required rate of return.

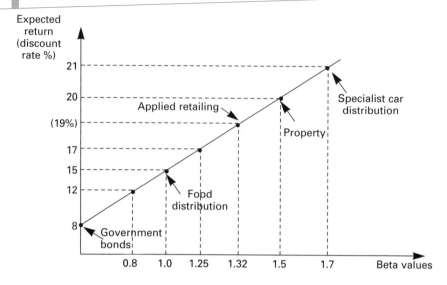

Figure 11.5 Kirribilli Holdings: risk and return of a conglomerate

Implications of debt funding

Brayshaw (1992) reminded us that published betas reflect the risk of the underlying business activity *and* the financial risk that is inherent in the capital structure of the company(ies) used in the sample. This is becuase of the existence of debt. To evaluate the economic risk in a potential project the published betas should be 'ungeared' for an analysis of capital expenditure. This may be done by using the following relationship:

$$\text{Ungeared ß} = \frac{\text{Published ß}}{\text{Tax adjusted D/E ratio}}$$

or:

$$\text{ß}\mu = \frac{\text{ß}\rho}{1 + (1 - t)\frac{D}{E}}$$

where:

   ßμ = ungeared beta
   ßρ = published beta
    t = tax rate
   D = market value of debt
   E = market value of equity

Consider the example of a company with a published beta (or the beta for its industry sector) of 1.7, a debt/equity ratio of 0.5 and a tax rate of 35 per cent. The ungeared beta is:

$$\frac{1.7}{1 + (0.65)(0.5)} = 1.28$$

If we now assume that the after-tax risk-free rate of interest is 6 per cent and the expected market return is 12 per cent then using the CAPM approach we would have an expected return of:

$$ER = Rf + \text{ß}\ (Emr - Rf)$$
$$= 6 + 1.28\ (12-6)$$
$$= 13.75\%$$

(If we had used the published beta of 1.7 the expected return would be higher at 16.25 per cent. This 2.5 per cent increase may have excluded some projects.)

We can now determine the required rate of return on projects in this *industry sector* using low, average and high risk categories. *Average risk* is 13.75 per cent; *low risk* 13.75–3.75 per cent (guide), which gives 10 per cent; and high risk 13.75 + 3.75 per cent = 17.5 per cent.

A typical situation at the marketing/finance interface is the evaluation of a proposed expansion and the financing options for it. Quite often the expansion requires more funding than is available from existing reserves and the decision concerns how funds should be arranged, as well as how much should be allocated.

The previous chapter raised a number of factors concerning the debt/equity structure of a business. It will be recalled that beyond an optimum combination of debt and equity, the investors' expectations for returns will increase as they perceive a greater level of risk accompanying the increased level of debt and interest payments.

The consequence on the cost of capital of borrowing can be shown using the security market line. In Figure 11.6 a hypothetical situation is illustrated. If the proposed company expands its current SBA (strategic business area) activities by gearing, the business will increase its beta value and therefore the rate of return expected by shareholders. If it then diversifies, the beta value may be higher due to the additional debt *and* the perceived higher risk of the new product-market or SBA activity. This may be an important consideration for both marketing and financial managers. The issue becomes one of comparing the long-term growth and the potential value for the shareholders with the risk and their expectations given that changes to the marketing and financial strategies have been made.

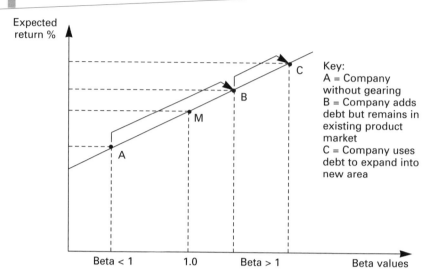

Figure 11.6 Impact of borrowing on expectations and the cost of capital

Factors influencing beta values

Beta values can change over time (albeit slowly) and reflect both the level of economic activity and key indicators of economic performance.

We have considered the influence of changes in gearing (debt/equity ratios) and the fact that individual company betas will increase as the gearing of the firm is increased. A similar influence may be expected with fixed costs: the higher the fixed costs the higher the beta value. It might be expected that a move by a company into an SBA with significantly higher fixed costs would be accompanied by an increase in the beta value. This is because fixed costs, like debt interest, have to be paid regardless of the level of sales and profits. Consequently, changes in cost structure can lead to changes in the beta value. A significant change in the mix of business activities will also have an influence on a company's beta value.

Implications of beta values for the marketing/finance interface

It is apparent that the discount factor used in investment appraisal can influence management decisions. If a very low discount rate is used it will indicate a very high NPV, resulting in the allocation of resources which may have produced more shareholder value in an alternative application. A discount rate which is too high precludes projects which may have had strategic marketing significance as well as short- to medium-term shareholder value implications.

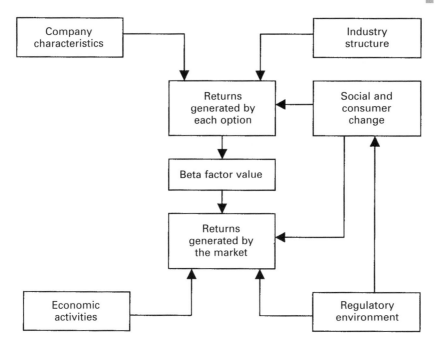

Figure 11.7   Internal and external influences on beta factor values

As we have seen, the beta value can influence the discounting factor and, as a result, the outcome of the investment appraisal findings – and, ultimately, of course, the decision whether to accept or reject. In the long term this may be seen to be a strategic marketing issue rather than one of financial management. It follows that the calculation of beta values should become a major consideration for both marketing and financial managers – who should use both internal and external information sources. Figure 11.7 summarizes the issues and influences. As can be seen, the range of factors influencing corporate and industry beta factors is extensive. *Company characteristics* include many of the topics discussed in earlier chapters; however, some additional items are introduced which should be commented on. *Sales/distribution effectiveness* is an important one – an ability to obtain market coverage at low cost may well be a critical success factor or possible competitive advantage. Share of business spread across *key accounts* is also seen as an element of competitive advantage. The critical issue here is the balance of the business: it is possible to become dependent on one or more of these key customers and, because of this, to lose control of marketing decisions and influence. Similarly a position where there is insufficient share of the business can be a disadvantage: if key account customers do not regard the company as a major supplier there is a risk of rationalization or delisting should there be pressure to sell facility capacity. *Relative advantages* identify a company's industry strengths (distinctive competence(s)) in activities that are important to developing competitive advantage; for example, innovative research and development and customer service are two characteristics that are important in most businesses. *Market characteristics* (such as overseas activities often seen as more risky than domestic markets) will influence betas.

Moving to *industry structure*, this includes a number of issues which have an impact on the investors' perceptions of stability and therefore growth. Clearly both *market size* and *growth rate trends* are important. Large industries with a history of growth are seen as relatively less risky than smaller industries with erratic growth patterns. A number of *market segments* often lowers risk because segments offer diversification, particularly where price is an important variable. The industry *activity* is also important: a commodity-based activity will have a lower risk profile than an industry dependent upon excess disposable income and fashion. *The stage of productmarket development* may be regarded as important by investors. An industry in the emerging stage (or perhaps the early stage of growth) is likely to be considered riskier than one in the mature stage. The decline stages of an industry will influence investor risk perception adversely.

The characteristics of the industry will provide an insight into funding requirements, cash generation, productivity and profitability. The *number of competitors, their size* and the *rate of entry/exit* have implications for risk. The existence of a few large competitors may mean a controlled rate of growth and the entry of new competitors. This may indicate the likely pattern of costs and therefore profitability in the industry. *Price structures* and price dynamics have implications for margin size and stability: fluctuating margins are less attractive to investors than are stable margins; *profitability trends* are likely to be viewed similarly. *Fixed capital intensity* also has implications for profitability; if it is high and industry volumes are liable to fluctuate, price competition and margin dilution are very likely. High levels of *working capital intensity* may dilute profits or may be seen as an opportunity to improve working capital productivity by implementing just-in-time practices. *Investment levels* in both tangible and intangible asset items indicate the potential growth of shareholder value items as well as an indication of the costs of entry for new competitors. The pattern of expenditures, that is, on R&D, plant refurbishment and modernization, promotional expenditures or customer service, are indicators of existing competitors' views on competitive advantage factors. *Technology* has a number of implications. The rate of change of technology in the industry provides an indication of profit levels available to shareholders; it also indicates barriers to entry; and the type of technology suggests the industry view on trends for capital (or labour) intensity. *Unionization* and its influence may be seen by investors as a threat to revenue, profit and cash flow generation if industrial relations actions are commonplace in the industry.

Turning to the *social and consumer change* box, such change has short- medium- and long-term implications. For example, *demographic trends* have long-term effects. Population trends are slow to emerge, but can be significant for companies (and their shareholders) if the business activity is dependent upon specific population characteristics, such as age groups. In developed societies in which the average age is increasing there are both opportunities (health care and retirement finance products) and threats (a decline in the productmarkets targeting families with children). Any business that is firmly committed to a specific demographic segment which is indicating change and is failing to seek diversification opportunities will likely find the share- holder/investor view of its vulnerability reflected in an increase in their expected returns. *Socioeconomic* change occurs more rapidly. Changes in taxa- tion (direct or indirect) can change the disposable income available to socioe- conomic groups quite rapidly. Similarly, changes in industry structure can bring about domestic shifts in spending power. The growth of information technology application has resulted in large reductions in the number of middle and junior managers; many have found it difficult to find alternative employment quickly, if at all, and the result has been a major reduction in the expenditure patterns of those groups.

Consumer confidence is closely linked with socioeconomic change but may be more general in its influence. The impact of the recession of the late 1980s to early 1990s had serious consequences for consumer confidence, particu- larly regarding consumer willingness to undertake lengthy periods of personal gearing, such as house purchases and automobile purchases on extended credit. The importance of consumer credit cannot be underestimated because its impact is widespread: any reluctance to purchase houses and durables is accompanied by a decline in sales in related products. The marketing manager should be well aware of these links when forecasting future activity levels and the financial manager aware of the possible impact on share- holder/investor expectations. *Activities, interests and opinions* have long been used by marketing management to segment markets. Any changes to these attitudinal and behavioural characteristics may have implications for market- ing performance and consequently for shareholder/investor expectations.

Regulation: industry and government constraints on market behaviour, seen in Figure 11.7 feeding into *social and consumer change*, come in various guises. Clearly it is changes in these constraints that interest shareholders. The impo- sition of pollution controls requiring industrial effluent to be processed prior to discharge is an increase in costs and a decrease in profit available to the shareholder. The decision by a company (either in isolation or in conjunction with others) to restrict trade with governments failing to meet minimum requirements for human rights (and other similar controversial issues) may meet the ethical views of investors but not their expectations for returns. It follows that *codes of practice*, which may protect consumer interests, are not always in the interests of maximizing shareholder value but do form a framework within which all industry members operate. Consequently we might expect shareholder expectations to be similar. Encouragement by government with offers of incentives to business for *industrial development* purposes may have a beneficial impact on beta factors. The guarantee of enhanced profitability for a specific period of time can be seen as a reduction in risk. As business becomes considerably more expansive, and global environment and conservation controls increase in their complexity, what may be acceptable in a domestic market is often unacceptable in overseas markets. Some markets have what may appear as excessive controls (e.g., Switzerland's attitude towards motor vehicles), while others have an urgent need for the product benefits and are more concerned with obtaining these at minimum currency costs. Sophisticated investors (particularly the institutional shareholders) are fully aware of the impact of overseas activities and will identify the risks associated with them. This is in addition to the risk of overseas marketing and relates to cost complications and profit repatriation controls as well as the difficulties of managing overseas product-market activities.

Such regulations as we have discussed flow on to *economic activities*. Economic activities may have either specific implications which concern certain companies or the effects may be uniform. For example, *demand characteristics* may differ by sector; consumer durables and home improvement sectors may share depressed sales with residential construction companies, while the mining and extractive industry sectors boom as their overseas customers enjoy growth situations. *Inflation* may have a differential effect. In industries with excess capacity there may be fierce price competition, but at the same time such industries may be subject to the impact of increases in inputs, such as raw materials, occupancy costs and utilities. In this situation the differential inflation will be identified as an inhibiting influence on growth and a risk factor.

Fiscal policy is a way by which government, through control of its own spending, can influence the fortunes of businesses. The most widely known influence concerns the multiplier effect whereby government expenditure (such as an expansion of transport and roads) will increase the overall expenditure on industrial and, eventually, consumer goods. The extent of the effect of the multiplier will depend upon individuals' propensity to save, their propensity to purchase imported products and the taxes imposed on their spending. A similar effect may result from reductions in taxation, but here the effect is unlikely to be large because, unlike increases in spending, tax changes leave the GDP unaltered and taxpayers may choose to save rather than spend the increase in disposable income.

Monetary policy (governments' decisions concerning interest rates and money supply) is easy to implement and very effective at influencing output and inflation. Changes in interest rates affect activity and inflation in three ways. By altering the cost of borrowing they affect the incentive to save. A fall in interest rates redistributes income from savers to borrowers, which may lead to an increase in expenditure because borrowers tend to have a higher propensity to spend. Interest rate changes may also redistribute income by changing asset prices and wealth, such as equities (and bonds) and property; this may encourage new entrants into the market. Monetary policy is effected by central banks and while most companies (and individuals) borrow for periods that are much longer than the short term rates (typically a 24-hour rate) it is the effect on longer-term borrowing that is important. This is significant for shareholder value. A period of sustained high interest rates will be seen as imposing difficulties for industry. Again some companies will experience greater difficulties than others; housing, motor vehicles and high-priced durables are particularly vulnerable. Not surprisingly beta values tend to reflect this vulnerability.

Exchange rates are particularly important to companies with either a large proportion of revenues attributable to overseas activities or to those whose inputs are dominated by overseas suppliers. A prolonged decrease in the value of a currency (relative to those of its customer markets) should result in increased sales revenues, profits and therefore shareholder value. While we may expect some reflection in the beta factor value, it is likely to be discounted by virtue of the fact that the control of exchange rates is extended to both the firm and the domestic government and changes may occur at short notice. The reverse situation, currency appreciation, presents problems for pricing in overseas markets. Volkswagen has encountered serious pricing problems when attempting to maintain market volumes overseas when the DM has appreciated against local market currencies. Because governments use exchange rates to manage inflation and output levels they are of particular importance in making an assessment of both market and company net cash flows over time.

Levels of *employment* have fallen in developed countries over the past twenty years. While not underestimating the serious social implications there are issues for investors to consider. Given that the trend will continue, and that redundancies resulting from restructuring are likely to affect relatively highly paid occupations, there are some long-term issues concerning the returns likely to be earned by companies in industries marketing discretionary purchase items. Residential property companies, motor vehicles and durables are constantly offering incentives to prospective customers, and these clearly dilute margins and have an impact on investor perceptions. It is also obvious that a company or industry sector that has a history of labour relations problems is considered to be a higher risk than one without such a history. Disruptions and pay demands clearly prejudice profit and cash flow.

We have intentionally dealt with the issues which influence investors' perceptions of risk because it is a topic which may have quite different meanings for the marketing and financial manager. The simple example (Figures 11.4 and 11.5) demonstrated the impact that beta values can have on the cost of capital: if the shareholders' expectations are not reflected in the calculation of the cost of capital the results may be punitive, particularly if the project is extensive in both the size of the investment and the time over which it will operate. A major benefit that also accrues from a beta profile review is that it may identify issues that should have been considered but were missed during the initial marketing research.

11.3   Strategy decisions and their appraisal

To conclude this chapter we should consider the use of investment appraisal methods for evaluating strategy options. Figure 11.8 uses the net present value approach for this purpose. The primary objective is to obtain quantified values of the *annual net cash flows* and to reach an accepted value for the *discount rate* (see centre of model).

The model proposes a process which first identifies the *strategic options* available to the organization and within each goes on to identify specific factors, each of which may have an influence on the cash flows generated by each strategy. For example, the *growth-related strategies* (related product-market and diversification) should be considered within the context of their impact on the sales of current product-services. If it is estimated that existing sales would be damaged this may present difficulties for recovering specific (dedicated) fixed costs and therefore threaten the overall cash flow, profitability and productivity of the business. It would also cause concern among shareholders and therefore increase their view of risk. Qualitative issues are also important. Employee morale (and attitudes) may be influenced in a positive way if the company is seen to be innovative and this may be reflected in labour relations, increased productivity, and so on.

Repositioning strategies entail a number of questions. The obvious concern here is whether the increase in revenues provides adequate return for the risk incurred in increasing fixed assets and working capital. Competitors inevitably respond in some way to repositioning moves and this unknown represents an increase in risk. Furthermore, until customer response is measured (positively) there is an element of risk.

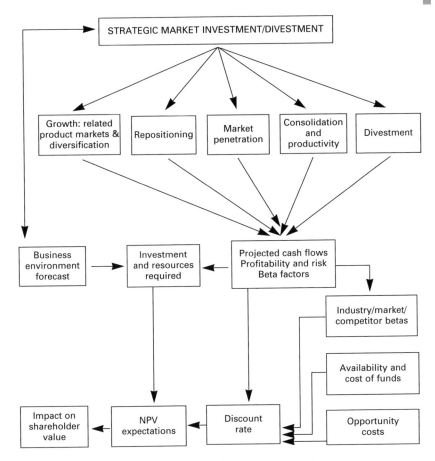

Figure 11.8 A qualitative view of the investment appraisal process

Divestment strategies should be evaluated using an NPV approach. We can quite easily evaluate the quantitative issues. These include cash flow increases from the sale of assets and the costs that are avoided by withdrawal from the market; these should be adjusted by the loss of revenues following the decision. In addition, there are the qualitative concerns, some of which can have far-reaching implications for the business. For example, employee morale may be affected by uncertainty: suppliers may be concerned about continuity, and the quality and service expected on other products and components may be affected. Possibly the most important concern is that of customer response, particularly of those for whom the product has importance: what may have been a slow-moving product consuming excessive resources for our company may well have been a critical input to a small customer.

The NPV appraisal process appears in the lower section of Figure 11.8. It suggests that ultimately any investment should be evaluated on the basis of what it will deliver for the shareholder. The qualitative aspects of the process are, as we suggested for the strategy options, equally as important as the quantitative results. Therefore the NPV analysis should seek to address the qualitative aspects of the market/volume/time relationship: in particular, managers should consider the marketshare/control and volume/cost relationships over time.

There are occasions when it is seen as essential that a firm move into a specific position relative to its competitors; these should be evaluated and the cash flow profiles identified. Customers inevitably have an impact on both the cash flow profile and the size of the NPV of a 'project'. It is useful to estimate and evaluate *customer response* in order to identify the alternative sales and perception responses that may result following different product-service format options. In essence, this is really a segmentation exercise and managers should consider issues such as the development of brand equity over time. How the marketing elements are perceived by customers initially will shape their attitudes towards repeat purchasing of the existing and subsequent products. The NPV process should also be used to consider the impact on net cash flows of maintaining *competitive advantage* over a specified time period. This will necessitate a review of downstream investment requirements to update product, service and operating facilities. Very few companies fully understand the need to do this; even fewer plan around the fact that competitive advantage is rarely (if ever) sustainable and that therefore they should plan their investment funding to meet specific objectives in this regard.

The realistic life expectancy of a strategic business area (SBA) (or project) is one of the first considerations to be made. It will have an important influence on annual net cash flows, the cost of capital (as influenced by risk through the beta factor), the cost and availability of alternative sources of funding, and the opportunity costs. It will also have a major influence on the size and type of the initial investment to be made. A number of factors therefore arise. For example, if the life expectancy of the SBA (or project) is likely to extend over a considerable period of time, an investigation into the ways in which a proportion of the fixed costs may be shared with other activities should be sought. The possibility of phasing in other activities over time should also be considered as this may improve (or help to attain planned levels of) capital utilization.

11.4 Summary

We have considered the issues that affect investment analysis in this chapter. Our starting point was a brief review of alternative methods for appraising investments, considering their various advantages and disadvantages. Much of this discussion was spent on methods using discounted cash flows and working with net present value (NPV) or the internal rate of return (IRR).

Investment decisions involve the allocation of corporate resources and there is always a level of risk which accompanies the decision. Furthermore, because investment requires the use of shareholders' funds the amount of risk they are prepared to accept is important to incorporate in the decision making process.

We used the capital asset pricing model (CAPM) to discuss ways in which risk can be included in the process with some objectivity. The concept of the beta factor (or coefficient) was introduced and discussed in some detail. This discussion was extended to consider the influence of debt funding, changes of strategic direction and overseas marketing activities on the shareholders' perceptions of risk.

The beta factor has both quantitative and qualitative aspects and we identified six areas of influence: the company; the industry within which the investment was planned (or within which the company operates); social and consumer change; the regulatory environment of industry; self-regulation and government control; and economic activities and influences.

The chapter ended with a section considering the marketing/finance interface issues of strategy decisions and how these influence the investment appraisal process. We emphasized there that investment appraisal should be undertaken with the primary purpose of investigating how best the shareholders' value interests in the business may be enhanced.

REFERENCES

Brayshaw, R. E. (1992) *The Concise Guide to Company Finance and its Management*, Chapman & Hall, London.

Schlosser, M. (1992) *Corporate Finance*, 2nd edn, Prentice Hall, London.

12 Developing and Managing a Business Portfolio

Given the primary task of delivering shareholder value, both marketing and financial management seek to maintain the growth of profitability, productivity and cash flow by building and managing a portfolio of strategic business activities and product-market activities.

Because both the business and the environment within which it operates are dynamic, the portfolio which emerges from strategic planning, requires constant monitoring and modification. The profitability, productivity and cash flow requirements may also change over time and this requires some skills to plan and control activities.

Both marketing and financial management have contributions to make. The literature from both management disciplines when combined, equips managers to balance the marketing/finance interface.

The concept of the planning gap was developed by Ansoff (1968) whose model of strategic analysis and classification of strategic options has, as we have commented earlier, formed the basis of numerous subsequent contributions to the literature on strategy. The planning gap results when management estimates the performance required if growth objectives are to be achieved.

More recently, as we have also noted, there has been a clear move by companies to focus upon the 'core business'. Their view has been that it is the core business that should generate shareholder value and that resources should be directed towards developing the profit (and cash) generation capabilities of the core business assets. Support functions and activities of these companies have often been divested. In so doing we have seen them focus on consolidation and productivity, product-market development and repositioning (strategic and operational) strategies. High risk diversification activities have been (and continue to be) avoided.

12.1   Marketing considerations

Development work by the Boston Consulting Group (BCG) between 1970 and 1975 offered a very useful point of departure from Ansoff's planning gap. The BCG growth/share matrix, introduced in Chapter 6 and reviewed in detail in Chapter 9, is probably the group's best-known contribution. The thesis of the growth/share matrix is that a well-managed portfolio of products (or businesses) will provide the cash required for developing other products (businesses) and thus will avoid the need to resort to external sources of funds. The growth/share matrix, together with the product-market cycle, provides a useful introduction to a discussion on planning and controlling product-market/strategic business area portfolios. Although it may be argued that the BCG approach is now dated, it remains a powerful analytical tool, particularly when both cash and profit generation are essential to the success of the business.

The BCG portfolio approach suggests to management that it should review the cash-generation capabilities (and requirements) of products (or individual businesses) and manage the 'mix' of products, thereby identifying the characteristics of the products and using them in such a way that the overall portfolio contributes a planned cash flow contribution. There are a number of issues to be considered in relation to this point. The first is volume. It is obvious that as sales volumes increase so too should revenues. However, revenue does not mean cash and the Boston Consulting Group's work on cost behaviour (the experience effect) resulted in the suggestion that as market share increases many of the costs of production and distribution decrease at a constant (and predictable) rate (see Chapter 9). As volume increases, market share should also increase and average costs decrease. The result is that large market share implies low costs *and* relatively large cash generation. From this the emphasis on growth rate and market share in the growth/share matrix follows logically.

There are some conditions, however. It is assumed that a large degree of standardization exists in both the production and distribution processes: if this is absent it presents problems, particularly for the production process, because low-cost volume processing becomes difficult and cost reductions are not readily available.

There is also an implied assumption concerning product/business management activities. The cash generators are likely to be *low* risk and have 'ideal' life cycle profiles. These two aspects are connected. Kotler (1994) suggested the ideal strategic business area (SBA) cycle to have:

- Low risk.
- Low R&D market development costs.

- Rapid introduction and growth readily accepted by distributors and consumers.
- A prolonged maturity period during which both customer acceptance and technology exhibit stability.
- A sufficiently long period of decline for both customer acceptance and technology to change and for the product/business to be withdrawn gradually, ensuring that remaining cash and profit residuals are maximized and a minimum disruption to customer satisfaction occurs.

Ideally products with such cycles (see Figure 12.1) should form the basis of the product range, and typically these cycles are the characteristics of core product groups. They can, and do, change over time but these changes can be easily accommodated by monitoring consumer expectations (and perceptions) through tracking studies and similar research methods.

If core products form the basis of the offer, then the customer groups looking for product differentiation and other variations may not be attracted to the offer unless their requirements can be incorporated into the range. Clearly, such demand attributes are likely to change more rapidly and have a much higher risk profile. Although the precise timing of fashion (and fad) life cycles is difficult to forecast, their shapes follow predictable patterns.

The product offer typically comprises a 'range' which is planned to appeal to a target customer group and which should appeal to both their basic and varying needs. Hence we expect an assortment to be planned around core ranges and items supported by products which reflect the changes acceptable

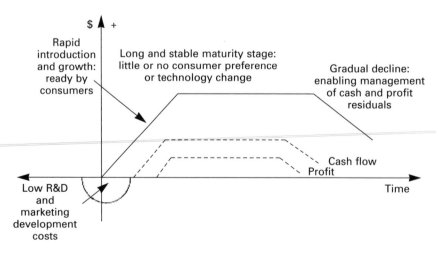

Figure 12.1 An 'ideal' product life cycle

to the target customer group. Performance at any particular time, for example, will comprise contributions for each assortment category.

Returning to the earlier discussion on portfolio issues, it follows that there is a strong relationship between life cycles and the BCG growth/share matrix. Products in their growth stage of the conventional product life cycle are classified as *stars* in the BCG terminology; products in the mature stage are *cash cows*; those in decline are *dogs*. *Question mark* products are usually in, or about to enter, the introduction stage of the life cycle.

Many markets are very large and very clearly segmented (for example, most clothing markets). It follows that specialist companies will be interested primarily in their close competitors, which are targeting similar customer groups. It often happens that performance variations across segments are quite marked and concern with overall trends may be quite misleading. Figure 12.2 shows the way in which the 'pathways' of SBAs, SBUs (strategic business units) and product groups may be plotted. It is suggested that cash cows are derived from categories for which demand becomes well established and for which the business builds a strong reputation: these products may, over time, become core products. The impact of this view on the growth/share matrix is shown in Figure 12.3 as the market develops distinct segments.

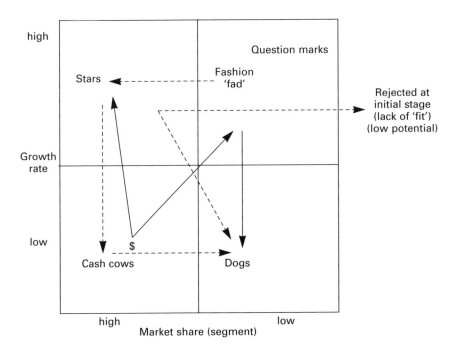

Figure 12.2 Product mix: cash generation characteristics and portfolio patterns

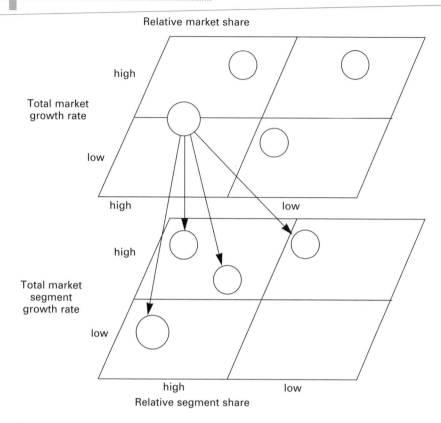

Relative market share

Figure 12.3 The importance of considering market segment characteristics

Performance characteristics may also be examined using another BCG tool: the growth/gain matrix. This was introduced in Chapter 6 but will be reviewed here. The growth/gain matrix has not received the same exposure as that afforded the growth/share matrix. Whereas the weaknesses of the growth/share model were exposed by external factors, such as the impact of recession and other economic problems which constrain growth, the growth/gain matrix offers a useful planning aid which, when extended, is applicable to all environmental influences (see Figure 12.4). The growth/gain matrix indicates two additional useful aspects. The first is the comparison between business growth rate and market growth rate (or product group growth rate). The second concerns the maximum sustainable growth rate, the rate of growth the business is able to maintain within specified growth/risk parameters. Though as managers we may have what we consider to be an assortment currently producing satisfactory levels of both profit and cash flow, it is possible that in 'market' or 'market segment' terms it does not share the same rate of growth. (Rates of growth may be compared by the position

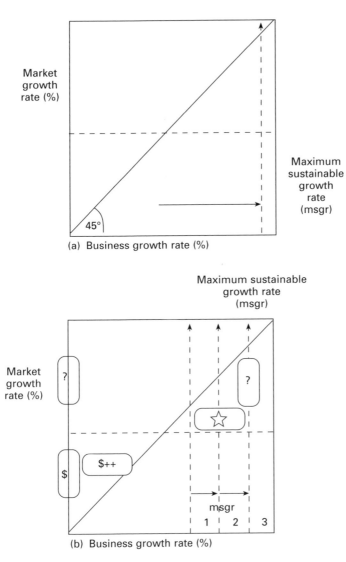

Figure 12.4 Growth/gain matrix showing the influence of the maximum sustainable growth rate on decision making

of a product or business relative to the 45° diagonal in Figure 12.4(a): any product/business growing at the same rate as the market will be *on* the diagonal; if the growth rate is less than that of the market, the product will be positioned above the diagonal; and if it is greater, then it will appear in a position below the line.)

The *maximum sustainable growth rate* is of particular interest for productivity and profitability planning and control. The determinants of corporate growth are:

- The rate of return of the business.
- The use of debt.
- The dividend/retentions policy pursued.
- The recourse to external equity funds.

Dividend payout and capital requirements determine the availability of funds generated by the return on the assets employed in the business. It is essential that management understands the implications of product-market management activities on the *availability* of funds.

The rate of return

The *rate of return* a business generates is usually a reflection of the going rate for the industry. It is influenced by size, the competitiveness of the industry and the environment. Robinson (1986) argued that it is difficult to exceed the 'industry norm' by very much, because if the firm generates too high a margin (for a sustained period) it will attract competitive entry; lose market share; forego turnover (a function of elasticity); and will grow more slowly than the market average. From this we can conclude that long-term excessive returns are unlikely. The extent to which the improvement in the resultant rate of return will prompt competitive entry depends very much on factors such as industry structure, barriers to entry and overall market/segment growth rate.

The use of debt

This can increase the return on shareholders' equity (the realistic measurement of management's success). As we saw in Chapter 10 the use of high levels of debt permits the firm to gear up (use leverage on) the returns on investment into a higher return on equity. The advantages and disadvantages of debt in the financial structure were also discussed in Chapter 10.

Dividend policy and retained earnings

This influences growth rate simply because there exists a trade-off between current and future dividends. Future growth may be funded by reducing the dividends paid to shareholders and using retained earnings to finance expansion. The benefit to the shareholder becomes longer term as current dividends are foregone in return for a growth in both future dividend and share price.

Clearly, current high levels of dividend *and* growth can only be maintained if the rate of return on investment is high or if debit is used.

External equity funding

The use of external equity funding is not necessarily an easy solution to obtaining additional funds. Two major problems are of concern:

- The additional equity may have the effect of diluting control and may also generate conflicts of interest between established and new equity holders – particularly large institutional shareholders.
- The cost of servicing new equity can be very high when equity financing is substituted for debt, particularly with a high dividend payout policy.

Let us return to the growth/gain matrix and the notion that growth activities may be funded from a well structured and managed product/business portfolio. This was demonstrated by Zakon (1971), who derived a relationship to express the factors influencing the maximum sustainable rate of growth of a firm by using internal sources and the use of debt:

Profit = f(return on investment, gearing and interest rate)

$$P = \frac{r\,(D + E) - iD}{E}$$

where:

$$P = \text{profit}$$
$$r = \text{return on investment}$$
$$D = \text{debt}$$
$$E = \text{equity}$$
$$i = \text{interest rate}$$

Collecting the terms and dividing by equity (E):

$$g = \frac{D}{E}\,(r - i)\,p + rp$$

Dividend payments reduce the rate of growth. The effect of dividend payments can be modelled by multiplying by the proportion of retained earnings. This gives

$$g = \frac{D}{E}\,(r - i)\,p + rp$$

where

$$g = \text{sustainable growth rate}$$
$$D = \text{debt}$$
$$E = \text{equity}$$
$$r = \text{return on investment}$$
$$i = \text{interest rate}$$
$$p = \text{the proportion of earnings retained}$$

Returning to Figure 12.4, we can see how the maximum sustainable growth rate (msgr) can influence the shape of the product portfolio. In Figure 12.4 three possible positions of the msgr are shown. At msgr 1 there is limited growth potential within the firm's capabilities as there are no cash-generation candidates (cows). However, an expansion of the msgr to msgr 2 would improve the company's prospects significantly, because at msgr 2 it has growth star products and potential question mark products for future growth. At msgr 3 the stars are increased and further capacity for growth can be funded. Figure 12.5 provides a hypothetical example of a firm which has determined its msgr. At the selected business growth rate it can finance capacity for the expansion of its star product and its portfolio of products includes a core SBA, an obsolescent SBA and some potential (question mark) SBAs.

Zakon's (1971) relationship suggests an msgr that considers internal funding as its only option. Clearly, this constraint may be relaxed. For example, if there was a change in dividend policy whereby a larger proportion of the residual profit was retained for investment, or perhaps if debt was to be

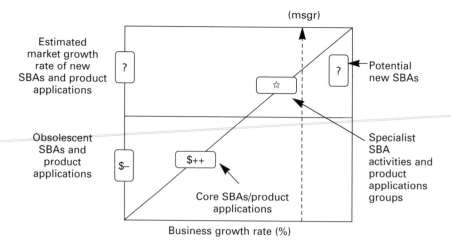

Figure 12.5   Hypothetical assortment/business profile

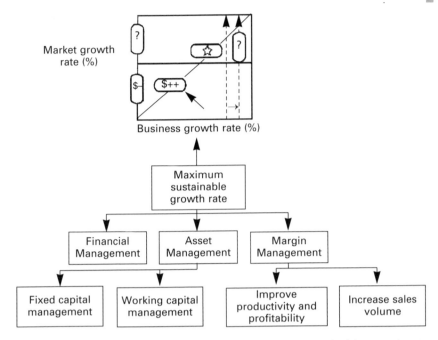

Figure 12.6 Factors influencing the size of maximum sustainable growth rate

increased or lower rates of interest funds became available, the msgr could be increased. The msgr could also be increased by increasing the return on investment through improved productivity performance.

Figure 12.6 illustrates a situation in which it is desirable to increase the msgr. To do so would effectively move question mark products into the star category by enabling investment to be directed into expansion of the business. The two components of msgr are identified as asset management and margin management. These will determine how much of the expansion may be financed from internal sources and how much will be financed from external sources together with the nature of the funding.

Both asset management and margin management were discussed in detail in Chapter 6. Figure 12.6 shows that there is a *financial management/capital structure* influence which is exercised through the nature of the funding of the assets.

Traditionally, discussions concerning business growth have considered the notion of a planning gap. The planning gap is concerned with both revenues and profits. In Figure 12.7 we use the planning gap concept to illustrate the dynamic requirements of cash flow. The diagram demonstrates the importance of thinking through the cash needs of the business as individual SBA cycles are pursued. It suggests that it is necessary to make estimates of future

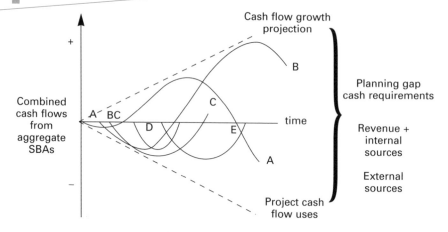

Figure 12.7 Using the planning gap for cash flow projection

cash generation and cash uses. From these estimates, cash flow shortfalls can be identified ahead of their occurring and action may be taken accordingly. This may involve a review of internal operations with a view to asset or margin management improvements to alleviate the problem, or enabling management to negotiate overdraft facilities (or alternatively to revise future planned activities). The comments made on working capital productivity (in Chapter 7) are particularly relevant.

Another contribution by BCG is helpful in this respect. *Frontier curve analysis* is a seldom used, but helpful technique, which portrays the growth rate of the business in a portfolio compared with the cash used (Moose and Zakon, 1972). Figure 12.8(a) illustrates the technique. The annual growth rate of profits is shown on the vertical axis and the cash used (as a percentage of earnings) is plotted on the horizontal axis. The company's SBAs/profit centres are plotted on the resulting matrix according to their growth and reinvestment characteristics over a selected period of time. The location of the profit centres (and these may be SBAs, SBUs or product groups) indicates the value of the profit centre to the business. For example, an SBA showing a 15 per cent growth in profits and a 100 per cent use of cash generated is using all of its resources to grow at 15 per cent. Such a situation, which was high growth and is self-financing, suggests a star. By contrast, a product group which is not increasing its annual growth rate in profits, but only using 60 per cent of its generated cash to maintain a competitive position (thereby making the remainder available for redeployment), may be described as a cash cow. The BCG authors suggested that in general:

> . . . cash cows would be expected to have profit growth rates of less than 5 per cent and cash usage rates of 70 per cent or less. Stars would be expected

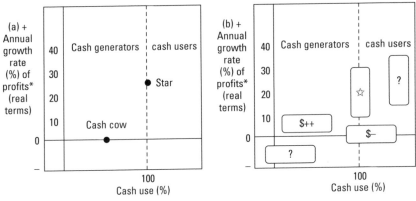

Figure 12.8   Frontier curves: growth versus use of cash

to be roughly in cash balance with growth rates in excess of 10 per cent. Wildcats (question marks) would be expected to have similar growth rates of profits to stars, but higher cash usage rates. Dogs, if properly managed, should have low growth rates and be cash generators, albeit small. (Moose and Zakon 1972)

The theoretical position of the portfolio is shown in Figure 12.8(b) and a detailed classification appears in Figure 12.9. Moose and Zakon suggested that businesses (or product groups, etc.) not conforming to these guidelines are problem areas and may represent cash traps.

Robinson (1986) contended that corporate cash needs in the form of dividends, interest and overheads are to be covered from revenues and that often the analysis overlooks this requirement. The BCG suggestion is that each business should be assessed on the percentage of net assets employed and that the given percentage of corporate dividends, interest and overhead should be deducted from profits before the percentage reinvested is calculated. Clearly, the result will be to reduce the number of cash generators and/or the amount of cash generated. Robinson also directed attention to the fact that care should be exercised concerning cash use and cash generation: proportions of both can be represented by the 'area' (or 'size') of the merchandise group/format used in the plot.

The formula quoted earlier for modelling the effect of dividend payments can be modified and restated to consider overhead and dividends:

$$g = \frac{D}{E} (r - i) \, p + (r - e)p$$

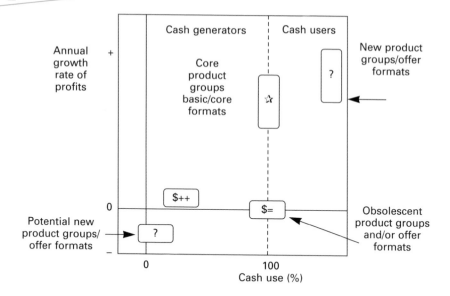

Figure 12.9 Hypothetical assortment/format profile using frontier curve analysis

Where e is an after-tax charge on assets to cover corporate overhead and dividends. Robinson suggested that for given, constant values of D, E, r, i and e, the equation reduces to:

$$g = Ap$$

Where A is a constant. If p (proportion of earnings retained) equals 1 (100 per cent cash retention) then g is equal to the msgr for the corporation and the result is a series of straight lines for various targeted rates (see Figure 12.10). Opportunities along the line are equally attractive; those below the line are less attractive; and those above the line are more attractive because of their *potential* for higher growth with the same cash use. The areas of the rectangles representing the chosen portfolio above and below the line can be compared to assess the cash flow characteristics of the desired portfolio. The straight lines in Figure 12.10 assume that the debt/equity ratio is constant. Frontier curves can be generated for different debt/equity ratios as a function of cash usage.

This discussion suggests that productivity of resources and corporate profitability are critical if growth objectives are to be met. At an operational level management activity to improve both the margin spread and the utilization of operational assets can increase the return on assets (profitability) and

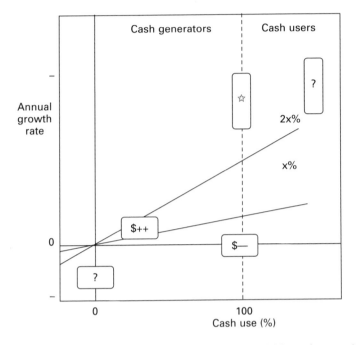

Figure 12.10 Target growth rates for the business (100% cash retention)

improve cash flow. In the long term the use of financial gearing can be supported by low-growth cash-generating businesses. High-growth businesses should be less highly leveraged. The decision as to the level of gearing can only be reached after an analysis of the cash generation/cash use situation of the portfolio. An important conclusion that may be reached is that effective planning of overall SBA performance may reduce the requirement for external funding to finance growth.

12.2 A closer consideration of financial issues

Thus far our discussion has focused on the marketing/finance interface aspects of portfolio management and risk has only been given cursory attention. Clearly, we should look more closely at the implications of risk.

The financial management literature offers a very useful concept in its approach to portfolio theory. Portfolio theory assumes that investors appraise their investments on the basis of expected return and the 'variance' of expected returns – variance being described by the standard deviation(s) of the expected returns. Figure 12.11 illustrates both expected return (the mean value) and variance plus the standard deviation of return values around the

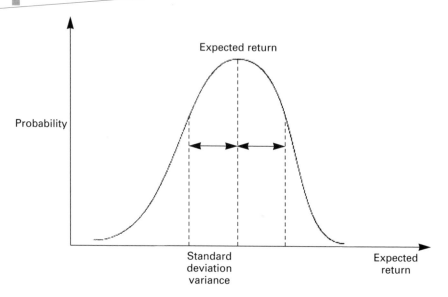

Figure 12.11   Shareholder returns: a combination of expected returns and variance (standard deviation)

mean – typically more than 34 per cent approximately. If two shares (or SBA projects) offered the same expected return the one with the lower variance would be preferred: if both have the same variance then the one with the higher expected return would be the obvious choice. Figure 12.12 suggests two risk/return profiles: A is preferable to B because the expected return of A is higher than B, but also because the variance of A is much less. In Figure 12.13 a hypothetical example is given of two 'projects' offering the same expected return but with a different variance. In this example A would be preferred to B simply because the variance implies greater risk.

Clearly, investors do not like risk and, as the previous chapter suggested, the higher the risk of a return from an investment the higher will be the return expected by investors. The trade-off between risk and return then must be identified and reflected in the rates of return offered to investors.

Investors can reduce risk by diversifying their range of investments (or their investment portfolio) as in Figure 12.14. What is happening is intuitively obvious: the wider the range of investments the less likely it is that *each* will be influenced by events occurring in *each* of the industries of the economies in which it operates. In other words, problems in the industry sector in which investment 5 operates are offset by above-average results from the industry sector in which investment 4 is operating. Diversification can eliminate the *specific risk* (or unique risk, as it is otherwise known). However,

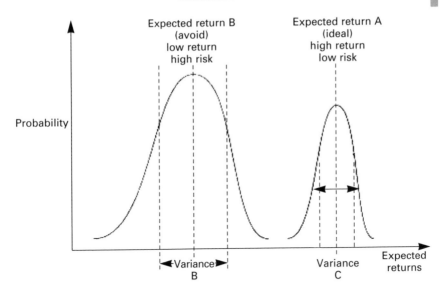

Figure 12.12 Profiles of returns

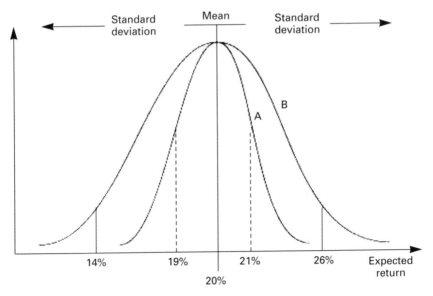

Figure 12.13 Risk can differ around the same expected return

as Figure 12.14 suggests there is a limit to risk reduction which is the *market risk* common to all investors. Brayshaw (1992) showed how this could be quantified using the expected returns, variance values (for each investment) and the covariance of the returns of the investments. *The covariance is a measure of the extent to which the returns of each investment vary with each other*

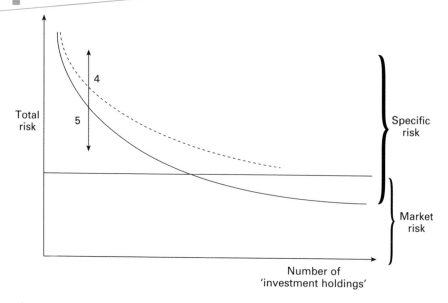

Figure 12.14 Risk is reduced by diversification

in different market conditions. The covariance is multiplied by the proportion invested in each investment and by the number of investments.

An alternative expression is given in terms of the variance of each investment and the correlation coefficient or returns between the investments. It will be recalled that the coefficient of correlation measures the relationship between changes in the values of two variables, say, expected returns: if they are perfectly correlated, that is a change in one variable is accompanied by a similar change in another, then they are positively correlated and if the changes are matched the coefficient of correlation is +1. Clearly the reverse obtains: equal and opposite changes result in the variables being perfectly negatively correlated and the coefficient of correlation is −1. This is expressed as:

$$\text{Covariance}_{AB} = \text{Coeff}_{AB} V_A \times V_B$$

where

$$
\begin{aligned}
\text{Coeff}_{AB} &= \text{coefficient of correlation between A and B} \\
V_A &= \text{variance (standard deviation) of A} \\
V_B &= \text{variance (standard deviation) of B}
\end{aligned}
$$

Diversification, therefore, attempts to obtain a low (negative) value of covariance in order that the overall standard deviation of the portfolio may be minimized.

An example will be helpful. Assume we have two investment situations, one in which the coefficient of correlation is +1 (perfect) positive correlation and the other the opposite with perfect negative correlation of –1. If the performance of the investments is as follows we can determine the overall risk profiles.

	A	B	Investment
Expected returns (ER)	15%	20%	50% (A)
Standard deviation (SD)	17%	25%	50% (B)

The expected returns would be the weighted average returns:

$$ER = (0.5 \times 0.15) + (0.5 \times 0.20)$$
$$= 0.175\ (17.5\%)$$

Using the covariance concept we have with $\text{Coeff}_{AB} + 1$

$$SD = (0.5^2 \times 0.17^2) + (0.5^2 \times 0.25^2) + 2(0.5 \times 0.5 \times (+1) \times 0.17 \times 0.25)$$
$$SD = 0.2098\ (21\%)$$

If $\text{Coeff}_{AB} = -1$ we have:

$$SD = (0.5^2 \times 0.17^2) + (0.5^2 \times 0.25^2) + 2(0.5 \times 0.5 \times (-1) \times 0.17 \times 0.25)$$
$$SD = 0.0396\ (4\%)$$

If it was desired risk could be reduced by shifting some of the investment from the relatively higher B to A. This would then give:

	A	B	Investment
Expected returns	15%	20%	80% (A)
Standard deviation	17%	25%	20% (B)

Expected return:
  ER = 0.16 (16%)
Standard deviation:
  $$SD = 0.8^2 \times 0.17^2) + (0.2^2 \times 0.25^2) + 2\ (0.8 \times 0.2 \times (+1) \times 0.17 \times 0.25)$$
  SD = 0.1859 (18.6%) with perfect positive correlation
and
  $$SD = (0.8^2 \times 0.17^2\ 4\ (0.2^2 \times 0.25^2) + 2\ (0.8 \times 0.2 \times (-1) \times 0.17 \times 0.25)$$
  SD = 0.08596 = (8.6%)

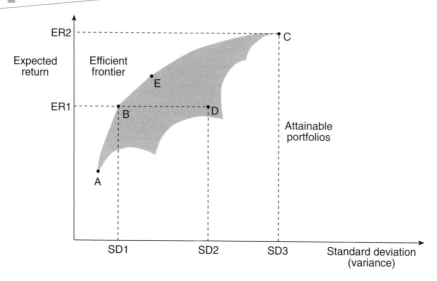

Figure 12.15 Markowitz' 'efficient frontier' capital market

It follows that provided the correlation is less than perfect a combination of investments may be developed which will offer a higher return for their risk or a lower level of risk for their given level of return. As the number of investments is increased so the overall risk can be reduced. This principle led Markowitz (1959) to propose a model for portfolio selection in which an efficient set of investments could be derived such that at each given level of risk a maximum expected return could be obtained or at a given level of expected return, the minimum risk required could be seen. Figure 12.15 illustrates the Markowitz model.

In Figure 12.15, the shaded area defines all combinations of expected return and risk that may be achieved. The *efficient frontier* identifies all of the possible combinations of return and risk considered to be efficient. For example, at an expected return ER1, B offers less risk than D (the variance of B at SD1 is less than that of D at SD2). At A both risk and return are at their respective lowest values while C represents maximum return and maximum risk.

The Markowitz model has limited practical value. Dobbins and Witt (1988) made the perceptive observation that 'to generate the efficient portfolios an enormous amount of data is required even if the number of available securities is relatively small'. They showed that for 100 securities, 100 expected returns and standard deviations need to be calculated together with 4,950 pairs of correlation coefficients!

12.3   Planning the business portfolio

There are some useful planning concepts which emerge if we combine the contributions from both discussions.

From the marketing portfolio literature we can develop some thoughts using growth rates, market share and cash flow. Financial management offers expected returns (ROE) and risk (beta values and variance measures) in the planning of product-markets.

If the primary objective of a business is to maximize shareholder value – with value expressed as a combination of profitability, productivity and cash flow – it follows that an *effective* allocation of resources resulting in an *efficient* portfolio of strategic business areas and productmarket activities is necessary.

Our discussion of the Markowitz portfolio (and the background concepts of expected return and risk measurement) returns us to the capital asset pricing model (CAPM) introduced in Chapter 11. CAPM provides a useful starting point for integrating the BCG model (growth/cash generated and used approach given by frontier curves) because it suggests a relationship between risk and return through the current risk-free interest rates (government/treasury bonds) and the beta value which measures risk on a market/sector basis. If we assume that, as the beta value indicates the perceptions of investors in the markets in which a company operates (or may operate), it is acceptable to use the beta value/risk-free interest rate relationship as a benchmark for investment appraisal purposes (see the next chapter) and for business portfolio planning.

The capital market line/security market line indicates a trade-off profile for return and risk (see Figure 12.16). This in turn suggests that in constructing a business portfolio other trade-off considerations should be made. For example, we should consider the options between returns and cash flow, and risk and cash flow. We should also consider the implications of the CAPM model for strategic direction decisions.

Earlier in this chapter we reviewed the Boston Consulting Group's *frontier curve analysis* model, which compares business profits growth and cash flow generation. We established a link between growth rate and internal funding: growth can be financed from retained earnings (at a cost to the shareholder in the short term) or by using external funds with their associated considerations. If retained earnings are used, actual returns to the shareholder are reduced but long-term returns may be enhanced.

Figure 12.17 suggests a method by which these trade-off situations may be approached. The return/risk trade-off may be resolved by using the security market line (SML) along which expected returns and risk are in equilibrium. The relationship between expected returns and cash flow may be examined

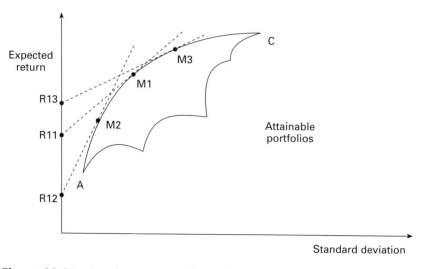

Figure 12.16   Developing the capital market line

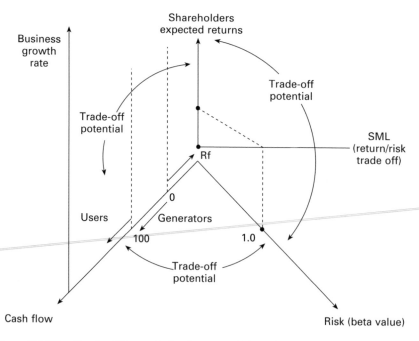

Figure 12.17   Trade-off issues in business portfolio selection and management

by first identifying the cash users and cash generators across the product-market portfolio, and then establishing the balance – that is, is more cash required than is generated or does the reverse situation hold? In the event that insufficient cash is being generated, managers must consider the trade-off possibility of reducing dividends and increasing retained earnings, these being the lowest (economic) cost of finance available to the firm. However, if this is not suitable, for whatever reason, then external financing must be required. This may be in the form of long-term funds (i.e., equity and/or debt) or it may be made available by reviewing working capital policy (i.e., accounts receivable and payable). Here there is another trade-off situation to be considered: that between increased cash flow and increased risk. If the funds for expansion are raised through long-term debt then the risk involved is that of increased financial gearing (which is likely to increase both risk and expected returns – dealt with in the final chapter of this book). Long-term debt may also have an impact on fixed costs and this too may be seen as a problem if there is excess capacity in the marketplace with high levels of capital intensity and the 'risk' of margins being diluted by price competition (see Figure 12.18).

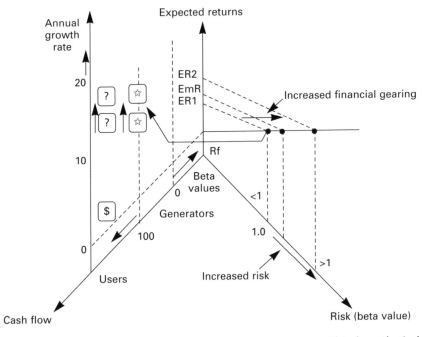

Figure 12.18 Trade-off issues in portfolio management. This hypothetical company increased its gearing to fund the growth of a star (☆) and to develop a new (SBA) (?) This has increased risk. It is anticipated that expected returns will increase (ER1–ER2).

(a) Followers: companies with no specific competitive advantage or distinctive competencies
Leaders: innovative companies; companies with strong competitive advantage and/or
distinctive competence(s) e.g. product development, manufacturing, selling and
distribution operations

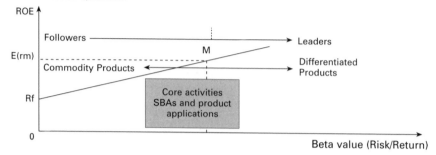

(b) A follower has expanded its R&D function and has developed new technology; to open up
the SBA its current activities are constrained to generate cash; debt and equity are issued to
fund the SBA. The follower attempts to become a leader over a 5-year period

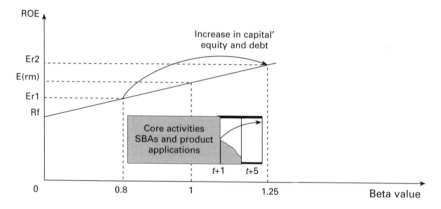

Figure 12.19 Innovation, differentiation, competitive advantage and competence(s) and the return/risk trade-off

We can assume that investors' views of risk in a particular sector may be determined by their view of an 'average' business. This average business may be expected to operate with a balanced portfolio of activities based upon distinctive competences and competitive advantages reflected by the *core activities* of the business and its track record for innovation/imitation. In other words there are 'followers' and 'leaders' and together they influence the overall sector beta value; individually, they will have beta values reflecting investors' and corporate management's view of risk. This situation is shown in Figure 12.19(a). Followers are likely to perform around the E(rm)/M datum, while leaders may operate above the datum, offering returns which reflect above-average and below-average performances. This is because a firm would not be expected to maintain a 100 per cent success record for innovation or possibly because it might be more highly geared than competitors (or paying lower dividends). It would therefore have beta values in excess of 1 with returns greater than average for much of the time. Technology-based industries and pharmaceutical businesses might be classified in this category. The issue for marketing and financial management is to identify an appropriate trade-off position. One which offers market leadership and returns, but at the same time does not jeopardize the financial structure and security of the business. Figure 12.19(b) suggests a follower's response.

12.4 Planning the business portfolio in the 'new economy'

When assessing the choices of the best way to structure the firm's business model the issue of the risk associated with pursuing each option also needs to be considered and is addressed in detail below. The traditional terminology of 'risk' has been used for these purposes, but it should be noted that the concept of '*robustness*' might be more accurate, implying that the assessment of the suitability of any structure or process option involves more than simply understanding what can go wrong.

Given the assumption that the primary objective of the organization is to generate (and maximize) free cash flow (albeit within legal, social and corporate imposed constraints) the ultimate, comparative, performance model will be the net present value (NPV) of the free cash flow generated. Using a '*new economy virtual approach*' offers an opportunity to reduce the risk of a planned product-market venture but at the same time to pursue realistic objectives by considering and evaluating the alternatives available to optimize the free cash flow objective.

Drawing on the framework outlined above, it is proposed that an appropriate performance measurement model to determine the anticipated value of performing an activity or process in a certain way is:

Expected return = NPV anticipated free cash flow × structural risk factor

The *anticipated free cash flow ('AFCF')* incorporates the three cash flow components:

Operating cash flow (op cf), *which* is the traditional direct and indirect costs associated with performing the process in question, and includes in the case of outsourced services the vendor's profit margin.

Cash flow from assets (asset cf), which takes into account the short-term working capital and capital structuring or investment costs, required to perform the process.

Strategic cash flow (strat cf) encompassing the cost of fixed assets, long-term working capital requirements and entry and exit costs associated with performing the process.

Risk premiums are dealt with in the notion of **structural risk factors** which itself constitutes a number of variables. These are best seen as operating at four levels:

Capability Risk (cap risk): is the most obvious and important measure of risk and is the actual ability to operationally perform the process in question – can you actually make the widget or deliver the service? High capability risk should be a significant discount factor to any anticipated free cash benefits.

Business Model Risk (bm risk): is a measure of the overall risk to its viability that an organization attracts (or avoids) by owning, or acquiring (or delegating the ownership and management) of a core process. It reflects either the avoidance of, or increase in, internal transaction costs and the impact on process fusion within the firm's business model generally. For example, a firm may have what seems a relatively unimportant manufacturing process such as a paint shop that can be outsourced with low capability risk, but in doing so this may disrupt the entire manufacturing flow and incur substantial hidden internal transaction costs.

Strategic Risk (strat risk): reflects the importance of the process and the degree of direct control over it needed to impact the firm's overall strategic positioning in the market – for example, outsourcing a process that is driven by unique intellectual property that is key to the firm's market positioning and competitive advantage would entail a high strategic risk.

Alliance Risk (ar risk): reflects the introduction of virtual integration. It is more than simply the viability and dependability of particular partners, which is inherent in the notion of capability risk, but reflects the strength of the alliance (or holonic network) as a whole. Alliance risk may be influenced by a number of factors. For example, an established alliance undertaking a new or expanded venture will increase the risk previously identified. A new alliance will be 'riskier' than one built from known partners. Equally, an alliance built around a new business model and one that has members from a diverse group of industries (that have yet to prove they can work together) also attracts high levels of risk.

Structural risk then is the aggregation of these risk factors and for the purposes of this model a low structural risk factor will be 1. The comparative weighting of the risk factors will obviously be driven by the particular circumstances and will be, to some degree, subjective. In this sense the purpose and usefulness of this model is as much to act as a checklist of critical factors as anything else.

As Magretta (2002) points out the business model is the 'system, how the pieces of a business fit together', while a firm's strategy is the choices made about how to deploy that model in the marketplace. And 'a successful business model represents a better way than the existing alternatives. It may offer more value to a discrete group of customers. Or it may completely replace the old way of doing things and become the standard for the next generation of entrepreneurs to beat.'

Again, the CAPM is of interest because it provides a forward-looking 'project'-based variable interest rate evaluation model, in which the required rate of return (and therefore the rate of interest used for discounting) can be related to risk as suggested by the beta value. If we use the beta concept in the context of organizational options and the risk of each alternative the notion of the beta value as an indication of risk does not change: in effect, the beta should reflect the risk involved from the adoption of any of the options identified. Clearly, the purpose of considering a partnership structure is based on the assumption that the better the 'fit' the more relevant the structure between the market opportunity becomes. Using the beta concept facilitates the process by which the structure that *optimizes* both the expected return (the NPVAFCF) and the risk of the structure is derived. This is represented as Figures 12.20 and 12.21. Figure 12.20 suggests that market

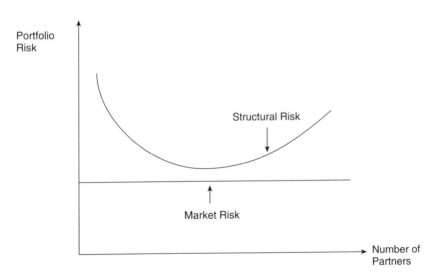

Figure 12.20 Risk/return options of investment opportunities: diversification reduces risk

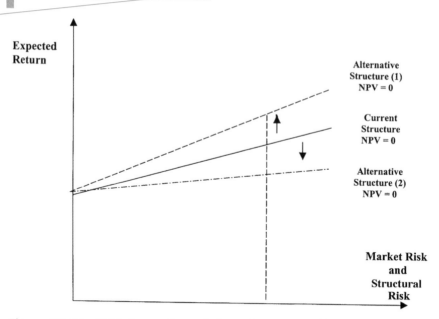

Figure 12.21   Risk/return options of alternative opportunities

risk confronts each competitor and is a constant. Structural risk can be managed by combining the relevant processes and capabilities of a group of partner companies into a structure capable of increasing the expected return of the organization. This effect is shown as Figure 12.21 in which the expected return is increased at the same level of risk. Figure 12.22 represents the procedure to be followed.

The firm's positioning within the model should therefore be aimed at an optimum that trades off risk against the generation of free cash. It should, however, be explicitly recognized that there is not necessarily a linear relationship between risk and the generation of cash. Some low-risk activities may be large cash generators – the proverbial 'cash cow' – and some high-risk processes may produce minimal returns. Some processes in the firm, what have traditionally, been termed 'overheads', will be net users of cash, but may still be critical to the firm's overall business model.

This is where a portfolio approach is of interest. When assembling the appropriate set of business structure or process options, or in other words building the firm's business model, an understanding of where value is generated or destroyed may be a useful tool, both to prioritize management efforts, and to initiate the strategic alignment of the firm's business model in the market. A portfolio approach may also foster the establishment of targets against which structural and process options are measured, not only

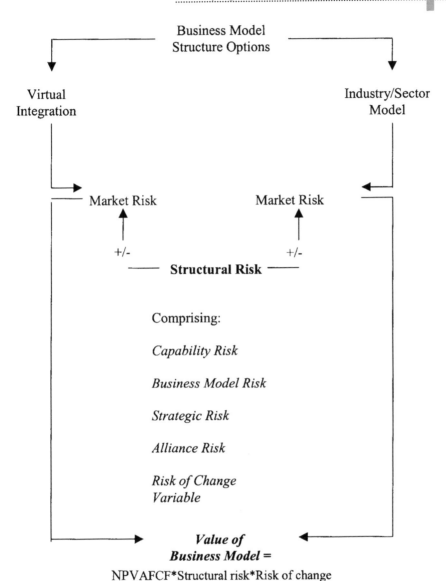

Figure 12.22 Deriving the risk profiles of alternative business models

individually but also collectively. This implies not only cash generation targets, but also structural risk targets. It may also indicate the need for strategic review of the company's direction if the sum of those process values fails to generate both adequate and reliable returns to shareholders. Figure 12.23 illustrates this approach.

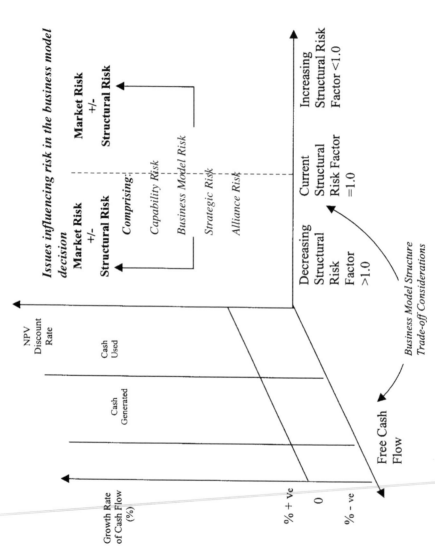

Figure 12.23 Risk and cash flow considerations in the vertical/virtual structure organization decision

12.5   Summary

This chapter has taken a detailed review of profitability, productivity and cash flow management from both a marketing and financial perspective.

The work conducted by BCG in the 1970s was reviewed and developed in some areas and in particular the financial management aspects were explored in depth.

This led to a review of the contributions of the financial management literature with an emphasis on portfolio theory. Of interest to us is the risk and return relationship that can be extended into marketing strategy decisions.

REFERENCES

Ansoff, I. G. (1968) *Corporate Strategy*, Pelican Books, London.

Boston Consulting Group (1970) *Experience Curves as a Planning Tool*, Boston Consulting Group Inc., Boston.

Brayshaw, R. (1992) *The Concise Guide to Company Finance and its Management*, Chapman & Hall, London.

Dobbins, R. and S. F. Witt (1988) *Practical Financial Management*, Basil Blackwell, Oxford.

Kotler, P. (1994) *Marketing Management: Analysis, Planning, Implementation and Control*, Prentice Hall International Inc., New Jersey.

Magretta, J. (2002) 'Why business models matter', *Harvard Business Review*, May.

Markowitz, H. M. (1959) *Portfolio Selection: Efficient Diversification of Investment*, Wiley, New York.

Moose, S. A. and Zakon, A. J. (1972) 'Frontier curve analysis: a resource allocation guide', *Journal of Business Policy*, Spring.

Robinson, G. (1986) *Strategic Management Techniques*, Butterworths, Durban.

Zakon, A. J. (1971) *Growth and Financial Strategies: a Special Commentary*, Boston Consulting Group Inc., Boston.

Note: For a detailed review of financial portfolio theory the reader is referred to both Dobbins and Witt; Brayshaw offers a management approach to the topic.

13 Performance Planning and Control

13.1 Introduction

> Knowing the cost of your operations, however, is not enough. To succeed in the increasingly competitive global market, a company has to know the costs of its entire economic chain and has to work with other members of the chain to manage costs and maximize yield. Companies are therefore beginning to shift from costing only what goes on inside their own organizations to costing the entire economic process, which even in the biggest company is just one link. (Drucker 1995)

Drucker was discussing the changes in business organization structures and the 'need to know' information portfolio of management. As ever with Drucker his views are expansive. In this particular article he was focusing on the role of costs in the economic chain as a tool for creating corporate wealth (or value). Drucker suggests that the shift from cost-led pricing to price-led costing is a powerful force driving companies toward economic-chain costing: he emphasizes that it is only in the mid- to late 1990s that companies have, in any number, switched to price-led costing, in which the price the customer is willing to pay determines *allowable costs*, beginning at the design stage and from that point exerting an essential influence on subsequent processes: 'Companies can practice price-led costing . . . only if they know and manage the *entire* cost of the economic chain.' And:

> The same ideas apply to outsourcing, alliances, and joint ventures – indeed, to any business structure that is built on partnership rather than control. And such entities, rather than the traditional model of a parent company with wholly owned subsidiaries, are increasingly becoming the models for growth, especially in the global economy.

Drucker comments that the transformation to economic chain costing is far from easy, suggesting success is built upon compatible accounting systems and a willingness to share information on an inter-organizational basis. The example of the close cooperation between Proctor & Gamble and Wal-Mart is used to demonstrate how information sharing and economic chain management can lead to a cost-effective planning *and* control system.

The role of the enterprise is to create wealth (or shareholder value); Drucker argues that this is not obvious from traditional accounting information where the emphasis is on the liquidation value of an enterprise. Wealth-creating enterprises are going concerns, and to fulfill their roles management requires information that facilitates informed decision-making.

As Magretta (2002) points out the business model is the 'system, how the pieces of a business fit together', while a firm's strategy is the choices made about how to deploy that model in the marketplace. Using the example of American Express and the invention of the traveller's cheque in the nineteenth century, Magretta states that: 'a successful business model represents a better way than the existing alternatives. It may offer more value to a discrete group of customers. Or it may completely replace the old way of doing things and become the standard for the next generation of entrepreneurs to beat.' In particular:

> all new business models are variations on the generic value chain underlying all businesses. Broadly speaking, this chain has two parts. Part one includes all the activities associated with making something: designing it, purchasing raw materials, manufacturing and so on. Part two includes all the activities associated with selling something: finding and reaching customers, transacting a sale, distributing the product or delivering the service. A new business model's plot may turn on designing a new product for an unmet need . . . Or it may turn on a process innovation, a better way of making or selling or distributing an already proven product or service.

13.2 Information for wealth creation

Drucker's executive toolkit for managing the business is the economic chain comprising:

Foundation information: the most widely used set of data are cash flow, liquidity projections and relevant ratios that indicate the efficient use of working capital and the effectiveness of investment in assets.

Productivity information: these data extend the information provided to measure the productivity of assets. Typically, we were concerned with plant and labour productivities. Increasingly the focus is upon the productivity of tangible and intangible assets that are knowledge based, but more significantly the measures are becoming inter-organizational. Data generated for performance monitoring is concerned with *total factor productivity* – regardless of who actually owns the 'assets'.

Competences/capabilities information: Drucker suggests that the Prahalad and Hamel work on 'core competences' identified the notion that 'leadership rests upon being able to do something others cannot do at all or find difficult to do even poorly'. It is essential for management to know the strength (or indeed the weakness) of capabilities. It answers the questions: do the capabilities remain relevant and if so for how long? Kay (1993) discussed capabilities as comprising architecture, reputation, innovation and strategic assets. While they all have significance, *architecture (the network of relational contracts within, or around, the firm)* is particularly interesting. He suggests:

> the value of architecture rests in the capacity of organizations which establish it to create organizational knowledge and routines, to respond flexibly to changing circumstances, and to achieve easy and open exchanges of information. Each of these is capable of creating an asset for the firm – organizational knowledge which is more valuable than the sum of individual knowledge, flexibility, and responsiveness which extends to the institution as well as to its members

This is particularly relevant to the virtual structure to which Drucker referred in 1995 and which are now becoming significant as organizational structures. Kay describes three *types of architecture*: *internal*, between the firm and its employees and among employees; *external* architecture structures exist between the firm and its suppliers and customers; *networks* comprise groups of collaborating firms. Clearly 'organizational knowledge and routines' are the basis for building inter-organizational or stakeholder performance planning and monitoring networks.

Resource allocation: this last item is more significant now than when Drucker raised it in 1995. Resource allocation is becoming an inter-organizational activity. The influence of resource decisions on wealth or value creation has not changed, but the process has. Increasingly, the decision is becoming one of allocation and coordination as the concept of distributed assets (or asset leverage) becomes more common within corporate structures. Kenevan and Xi Pei (2003) discuss the need for an equity approach to resource allocation, suggesting that rewards and comparative financial commitments should be a guiding metric in the development of alliances and partnerships.

13.3   Some basic requirements

In an environment that is constantly changing and in which competition can often come from the unexpected it is essential that organizations have systematic processes in place with which to modify performance-measuring systems and performance measures. Kennerley and Neely (2003) present evidence to show that few organizations have such responses in place that will ensure their performance measurement systems continue to reflect their environment and strategies. The authors present case study evidence to show that:

a well designed measurement system will be accompanied by an explicitly designed evolutionary cycle with clear triggers and:

- *Process* – existence of a process for reviewing, modifying and deploying measures.
- *People* – the availability of the required skills to use, reflect on, modify and deploy measures.
- *Systems* – the availability of flexible systems that enable the collection, analysis and reporting of appropriate data.
- *Culture* – the existence of a measurement culture within the organiza-tion. ensuring that the value of measurement, and importance of maintaining relevant and appropriate measures, are appreciated.

Through the case study the authors demonstrate the factors facilitating the development of measurement systems that are relevant to the changing envi-ronment in which this particular company found itself. They contend:

The data collected ... shows that the managers ... now recognize the process, people, culture and systems capabilities necessary to manage a measurement system over time. They recognize that these capabilities did not exist within the organization during the first phase of their manage-ment systems evolution, and action has been taken to ensure that the capa-bilities are in place to ensure that the evolution is effective in the future.

Perhaps it is the conclusions the authors reach that are the most significant directions for the 'visionaries' or 'integrators' responsible for developing virtual organizations: without a structured and relevant approach to perfor-mance measurement the organization may not be aware of the extent of the success of the innovative organizational structure, but nor will it be aware of the need to make changes if the performance is to be maintained.

An 'SAS White Paper' proposes a broad approach. While this is an attempt to sell software, the seven topics introduce a framework that, regardless of whether or not a particular 'brand' of software is used, has some validity.

Enterprise performance management: is a key factor comprising:
- A company (organization) wide strategy that is identified, accepted and managed by all 'partners'.
- An organization wide 'vision' is used to align processes and capabilities. Where these are not available 'in-house' they are identified and incorporated.
- This implies that functional units are aligned to meet the strategic direction of the organization.

Proactive rather than reactive structures:
- Business cycle compression creates the need for organizations to identify opportunities and threats ahead of potential competitors.
- Virtual organizations that are flexible and lean are able to respond more effectively and more quickly than vertically integrated organizations.

Abandoning the 'Silo' mindset:
- By extending corporate transactions and interactions beyond the organization's existing boundaries.
- Embrace value chain and value net concepts to their full extent.

Understand and leverage relationships:
- Worthwhile relationships are long-term, they are not managed on a transaction by transaction basis.
- Processes should be managed on a relationship basis extending across functional, organizational and even international boundaries.
- 'Value' is a stakeholder issue; value criteria should be determined and monitored for long-term success.

Automate 'Best Practices':
- Ideally processes should be 'self-learning' and 'self-tuning' and be able to capture and share best practices, performance metrics and experience. In this way knowledge is created and it follows that;
- Decision making becomes more effective.

Communicate 'Customized' information:
- Stakeholders must understand the vision, direction and structure they have agreed to be part of.

Create knowledge rather than just capturing data:
- Understand the messages from 'day-to-day' transactional data.
- Creating knowledge systems that relate to the business model is essential.

SAS suggest that there are common problem areas. For example, *financial management* typically lacks vision in creating structures and is more secure with well-established performance measures. For many organizations *customer relationship management*, while recent as a 'collective concept', has a quantity rather than quality perspective preferring to measure its success on market share rather than share of market value. Combining 'knowledge' with structured data processing analysis can result in a powerful method or tool for exploring long-term customer relationship scenarios, identifying how value propositions *might* be met by valued customers. *Supplier relationship management*, not typically practiced in most companies, is another process for which clear performance metrics are necessary. And again these should be qualitative as well as quantitative. For example, organizational spending patterns should be identified, and suppliers' performance should be 'ranked and rated' against meaningful criteria such as organizational objectives. A knowledge base should be established that enables potential areas for cost rationalization, consolidation and buying power indices to be identified and used. Such a knowledge base would also permit the exploration of procurement strategies on both intra- and inter-organizational bases. *Human resource development and management* can also benefit. Combining strategic information with workforce performance analytics will facilitate the evaluation of HR alternative strategies against qualitative and quantitative organizational expectations. Not only can the HR strategy be considered but more importantly so too can the future organization structure.

Bryan and Hulme (2003) identify the comprehensive nature of corporate performance management:

> By definition, corporate-performance management involves corporate- and not just business-level managers. Unlike operating performance, which can be driven by 'vertical' line-management processes, corporate performance requires 'horizontal' processes involving company-wide collaboration to generate and share ideas, establish accountability, and help allocate resources effectively. Scarce resources now include not only capital but also discretionary spending as well as the talent and management focus needed to find, nurture, and manage new projects that could boost future performance. Major corporate-wide initiatives, such as programs to improve the management of client relationships and to create new product-development and corporate-purchasing processes, would all be part of the effort.

And:

> A particularly important part of the portfolio mix should be initiatives to communicate with and influence the expectations of major stakeholders – customers, regulators, the media, employees, and, above all, shareholders and directors. The involvement of all parts of the company in this area is essential, since strong corporate performance means results that meet or exceed the stakeholders' expectations.

13.4   Some basic issues

Neely *et al.* (2002) comment: 'Performance measurement is a topic that is often discussed but rarely defined. Literally it is the process of quantifying past action, where measurement is the process of quantification and past action determines current performance.' The authors continue by making an essential point: 'Organizations achieve their defined objectives – that is, they perform – by satisfying their stakeholders' and their own wants and needs with greater efficiency and effectiveness than their competitors.' This is a valuable contribution. Neely *et al.* are suggesting, as does Porter (1996), that performance planning and measurement occurs at two levels; a strategic level and at an operational level. *Strategic* success requires *effective* planning and control while *operational* success is achieved with *efficient* planning and control systems. They suggest this perspective is helpful in identifying qualitative aspects of strategic decisions that are qualitative in their nature and influence such as product/service reliability – an effectiveness metric. Efficiency measures are typically related to cost performance. And, further, the authors identify the role of stakeholders, and the need to consider their roles and expectations, if both strategic and operational objectives are to be realized. They offer the basis for a working definition of a performance measurement system:

> A performance measurement system enables informed decisions to be made and actions to be taken because it quantifies the effectiveness and the efficiency of past actions throughout the 'organization' through the acquisition, collation, sorting, analysis and interpretation of appropriate data. (Neely *et al.* 2002)

In their work in this area the authors suggest five criteria that any performance measurement approach should address:

- A clear understanding of *who* the stakeholders are and *what* they require.
- For the 'organization to establish and articulate *what* it requires from its stakeholders' clearly.

- Strategies that reflect the interests of all participants.
- Processes that are in place to ensure the 'organization' can implement its strategies.
- Capabilities that facilitate the operations of the processes.

Neely *et al.* discusses performance from a traditional corporate perspective and this requires modification to meet the needs of the organization structures of the 'new economy'. Stakeholders become partners and their requirements and their contributions become as central to the success of the 'organization' as are those of the coordinator and visionary who may initiate the structure.

The notion of interrelated systems is not new. Koch (1994) refers to the role of information technology and its ability to span corporate boundaries necessitating a review of inter-organizational structures and relationships. Well before the 'IT' revolution, thought was being given to the functional aspects of distribution versus the view that considers distribution as an activity performed by a number of institutions. Intermediaries are seen as system functionaries, their designations are incidental: 'what is critical is the system design through which functions can best be performed' (Dommermuth and Andersen 1969). The impact of information systems extends beyond distribution channels (as suggested by Short and Venkatraman 1992) and now has an impact across entire operational processes. Thus their comment concerning the impact of information systems, '(they can) redefine market boundaries, alter the fundamental rules and basis of competition, redefine business scope, and provide a new set of competitive weapons', is particularly relevant. Add to this: 'Just as importantly, they change the emphasis in interorganizational relations from separation to unification' (Stern *et al.* 1996) and the contention that inter-organizational functions and processes are becoming increasingly integrated leads to a significant role for strategic operations management.

The growth of 'virtual organizations' has added emphasis to the need for a strategic perspective. Oates (1998) discusses outsourcing in the context of virtual organizations. He refers to a contribution by Moran (in a *Daily Telegraph* supplement on outsourcing, 28 May 1997) to the effect that outsourcing was no longer seen as: 'a way to reduce costs, it is now perceived as a route to improve business performance and competitive strength'. Oates also refers to a survey by Andersen Consulting, aimed at finding out what 350 executives expected their companies to look like in 2010. Comments regarding outsourcing suggest cost reduction remaining as a prime motivating force, but six other reasons were offered:

- To improve overall business performance.
- To sharpen business focus.

- For accessing external skills.
- For improving quality and efficiency of the outsourced process.
- To achieve competitive advantage, and:
- To create new revenue sources.

These benefits are often more easily realizable through virtual organization structures which 'Rather than owning assets, companies look to outsource functions to achieve a high level of flexibility in providing services. There is a shift in focus to communication and linkages between the various outsourced functions and distributed assets' (Beech 1998). It extends its interest and influence into developing and managing networks of logically related assets (the virtual organization). The owners of the processes clearly have their own objectives.

13.5 Strategic market analysis

Given a complex business environment how should an organization approach the planning and performance measurement process? Clearly the point at which to commence is one at which the characteristics of the market can be analysed, evaluated and from the analysis decisions be made to pursue opportunities that emerge.

13.6 Market opportunity analysis

Market opportunity analysis comprises market analysis, environmental analysis, customer analysis, competitor analysis and company (self)-analysis. There are a number of essential questions to be considered on different aspects when constructing a market analysis exercise.

Size, structure and growth rate(s) Questions here include what is the overall size of the market and what rate of growth is apparent now and for the planning horizon? Do segments exist? If so, how large are the segments and what are their characteristics? How significant are the differences? What are their growth rates? What is driving market development? Is it primary demand (i.e., unsatisfied consumer demands) or perhaps secondary demand? (i.e., sales effort focussed on customers who have yet to become users)?

The analysis should aim to identify demand life cycles and technology cycles for the total market and/or its major segments (see Exhibit 13.1).

EXHIBIT 13.1

The product life cycle is but one concept that has been debated by marketing theorists for some time. Its value is 'that it provides insights into a product's competitive dynamics. At the same time, the concept can prove misleading if not carefully used' (Kotler 1994).

Ansoff (1984) offered a different perspective to the product life cycle. His suggestion was to consider not the product but the 'need' that products satisfy. Thus personal written communications or word processing is a need and the 'changing level of need is the demand life cycle' (shown in Figure 13.1). Needs are satisfied by technology. Word processing technology has developed over time from a quill and vellum, through various mechanical writing applications (pens, pencils, etc.) to typewriters and computer-based software processing packages. As each 'technology' is introduced it creates its own demand technology *life cycle*.

Within any given demand technology life cycle a number of product alternatives appear. For example, mechanical writing applications have had numerous variants (refillable 'fountain pens', ballpoint pens, etc.) and word processing packages are continually updated. Each development is a product for which a *product life cycle* can be determined.

The shape of the product life cycle within its demand technology life cycle is shown in Figure 13.2.

The issue confronting the firm is which technology life cycle should it invest in. In Figure 13.3 we suggest that in a dynamic industry such as computing, the demand technology changes very rapidly. Added to this feature is the reality of continually increasing cost-effectiveness in which we

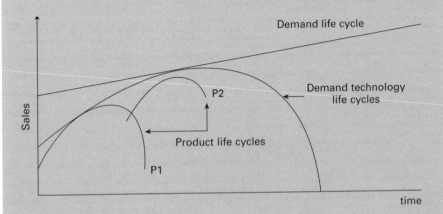

Figure 13.1

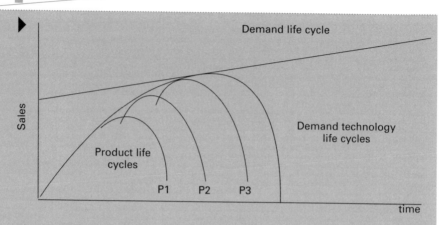

Figure 13.2

see not only an accelerating rate of technological development but also decreasing costs.

Ansoff calls a demand technology a *strategic business area* (SBA) which is 'a distinctive segment of the environment in which the firm does or may want to do business'. The decisions are not easy ones for the individual company. The issues are therefore the cost of entry, the time required to become operational (i.e., profitable) and the time period over which the strategic business area is likely to be effective. The concept of the product life cycles is interesting and has aroused quite differing views.

For a detailed discussion see Ansoff (1984). A less detailed but very clear and succinct discussion appears in Kotler (1994).

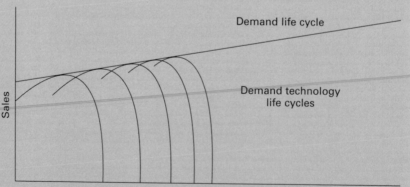

Figure 13.3

Profitability and margin profiles   For the total market (and each significant segment) the analysis should determine the profit generated, including gross, operating and net margins. It should also include a sensitivity analysis of the profitability components and identify influences such as materials and components, labour, customer service concessions (such as credit allowed) and any abnormal items.

Cost structures and behaviour   Here, we are considering fixed/variable cost structures, profit/volume relationships, industry capacity utilization and individual company utilization situations. This analysis is closely related to the review of size, structure and growth rates of the business in that these have implications for cost structures and behaviour patterns.

Competitive activity profile   Who are the competitors and how do they compete? The potential for new entrants, substitute products (and processes which may influence costs) must be identified. An estimate of the strength of intra-industry rivalry is essential. The identification and review of potential entrants should also be undertaken.

Value creation   Where in the industry value chain is value added? It is necessary to identify the competitive issues and the relative ease (or difficulty) with which value added contributes to competitive advantage and the strength of the advantage.

Distribution   The key issues to be considered here are the ease of access to customers and end-users through transactions channels and the costs of providing logistics services (i.e., product/service delivery and availability).

Market trends   The analysis here is to identify key quantitative and qualitative trends in the market. Clearly, the rate of change of volume growth is important but so too is changing customer demand for attributes such as product quality and choice, customer service and after-sales service.

Value drivers/critical success factors   What are the important characteristics, assets, skills and other resources that are necessary to compete in the market successfully enough to guarantee a level of profitability which will satisfy shareholders' value requirements?

Environmental analysis

There are five areas which comprise an analysis of the company's business environment.

Technology   Available technology and trends for the future can be critical in the decision-making process. Evidence from high tech product-markets (for example, personal computers) suggests a rapidly changing environment in which product acquisition costs decrease and application scope of the product, and effectiveness for end-users increase. Questions here should aim to identify the demand technology cycles of the industry and their rates of change. They should also identify developments which could affect industry investment patterns and competitive profiles.

Government   There are a number of initiatives of government which require close monitoring. One of increasing importance is the trend towards economic unionization as seen in the European Union and the North American Free Trade Association. These developments can change the pattern of trade and the structure of competition markedly. Another area of government interest concerns resource conservation. When the German government, for example, issued a mandate to companies concerning product design and the recycling content of products, there were clear implications for costs. Imposition of or changes to taxation, particularly such taxes as VAT (value added tax), may have major implications for consumer goods companies. One final consideration of major importance for international operators is the action (or likely action) of host governments. A discussion of the problems of operating in overseas markets is beyond the scope of this text, but it is necessary to point to the risks that exist when operating overseas and the need for a thorough evaluation of political problems that may occur.

Economics   Economic trends and government responses are important elements of the environmental analysis. Of particular interest are the trends for inflation, unemployment, interest rates, and foreign exchange rates.

Sociocultural changes   Cultural changes occur very slowly. However, the impact of satellite communications and the activities of global marketing have caused a convergence in consumer preferences in many markets, for example, motor vehicles, travel products and computers. However, business managements should be alert to subcultures which are responsible for fashion and fad product successes. These subculture markets can offer opportunities to companies with relevant products and often they become quite large if the fashion/fad gains international acceptance. However, while their rate of acceptance is often very rapid, their life spans can be short.

Demographics   The population characteristics of a particular market may offer a company an opportunity or pose a threat. Many characteristics, such as age profiles and residential and lifestyle patterns do not change rapidly. Nevertheless, a review of demographic characteristics is an important element in the analysis particularly at the strategic marketing level.

Customer analysis

The more detail we have concerning customer (and potential customer) expectations, preferences, perceptions and purchasing behaviour/product use, the more accurate will be the evaluation of the market opportunity. There are four important aspects to customer analysis requiring close attention.

Consumer profiles   A detailed analysis of the consumers comprising a product market is always required. Data should include estimated consumer numbers and consumption points (households, etc.); demographic profiles (age, sex, residential location); socioeconomic characteristics (occupation, income and disposable income); product preferences and characteristics, and product use.

Bases for segmentation   Consumer profile data provide a basis for identifying segments within the overall market. It is usual for segmentation to be analysed on the basis of customer characteristics: that is, location, type of organization, size of consumption unit, lifestyle, sex, age, occupation and income. In addition, (often alternatively) product-related approaches are used. These include type of user or usage, product benefit preferences, price sensitivity, brand/manufacturer committed customers.

Purchasing processes   It is useful to know how the product purchasing operates and whether there are differences within market segments. Thus the sequence of becoming aware of a product, seeking information, evaluating the product, deciding to purchase, choosing the purchase location, and post-purchasing evaluation may differ across market segments and between purchasing groups, and detailed knowledge of these differences can be critical in the decision to enter a market.

Product-market potential   It is not unusual for there to be 'gaps' in the range the market offers which provide opportunities for innovative new entrants. Customer dissatisfaction (customer complaints) or perhaps the fact that there are no strong brands or suppliers may be seen as evidence of these opportunities. Research should identify the potential of such 'gaps'. It should also suggest changes that are occurring or which may occur.

Competitor analysis

The three components to competitor analysis are studies of companies comprising current competition and potential entrants, and competitor evaluation.

Current competition   The number of competitors and their respective market shares, together with detail on their competitive activities, is essential information. Given this we can identify serious and not-so-serious competitors and set strategic responses to cope with their activities. An important issue to decide before entering a market is the extent of the barriers to entry existing competitors may have established.

Potential competition   Clearly other companies may be planning market entries. Often new entrants do so with substitute products and processes; it follows that it may take some creative research to identify potential competitors and their likely entry methods. Their product/process responses may emerge as by-products from their core business.

Evaluating the competition   There are a number of issues to be considered here. Most important are the major competitors' objectives and strategies; their target market segments and customers; their corporate and brands positioning; their cost structures; and their apparent competitive advantage characteristics.

Competitive response options

Once a company has analysed the market environment and customer base, it can assess the options available to it. Essentially, these are the optional segments, target markets and alternative positioning (the nature of the differentiation and competitive options available to the firm). But before any of the options are adopted, other issues should be identified and addressed. Not the least of these is the current positioning of the business. Important here is the company's distinctive competence (its core skills and expertise), its current differentiation and competitive advantage, and its core productmarkets and customers. Alternative supply chain and addedvalue chain partners (both upstream and downstream) should be identified. This identifies a broader range of alternatives available to the company for both current and future use. Competitive response options provide a basis for decisions concerning future strategic direction.

Company analysis

Given the response options that have been identified, a company self-analysis or audit will disclose the strengths and weaknesses within the performance of the company, and of its asset and financial structure. This is essential if the company's capabilities and capacities are to be determined and matched with the response options already identified. Three areas of performance are important: financial; market; and shareholder value creation.

Financial performance It is usual for financial performance to be reviewed using a structure of ratios grouped to provide a logical method of review. These were introduced in Chapter 1. There are a number of approaches to defining the ratio groups. One, suggested by Holmes and Sugden (1992), is to use three main groups:

(i) *Operating ratios*, which are solely concerned with trading performance and provide information on:

$$\frac{\text{Trading profit (\%)}}{\text{Sales}} \qquad \frac{\text{Trading profit (\%)}}{\text{Capital employed}}$$

Or margin management

$$\frac{\text{Sales (}\times\text{)}}{\text{Total assets}} \qquad \frac{\text{Stocks (\%)}}{\text{Sales}} \qquad \frac{\text{Sales (}\times\text{)}}{\text{Capital employed}}$$

$$\frac{\text{Debtors (\%)}}{\text{Sales}} \qquad \frac{\text{Creditors (\%)}}{\text{Sales}} \qquad \frac{\text{Working capital}}{\text{Sales}}$$

Or asset management

(ii) *Financial ratios*, which indicate the financial structure of the company and relate this to trading activities. Financial ratios are usually presented in two groups: gearing ratios are concerned with the structure of the capital employed, while liquidity ratios are concerned with the company's cash position.

Financial gearing

$$\frac{\text{Debt}}{\text{Equity}} \qquad \frac{\text{Debt (\%)}}{\text{Capital employed}}$$

Investment and financial management

Operational gearing

$$\frac{\text{Fixed costs (\%)}}{\text{Fixed costs + Variable costs}}$$

Indicates the sensitivity of profit performance with changes in sales revenue

Liquidity

$$\frac{\text{Current assets}}{\text{Current liabilities}} \qquad \frac{\text{Current assets} - \text{stock}}{\text{Current liabilities}}$$

Indicates the company's cash position

(iii) *Investment ratios,* which relate the shareholders' equity holding and the market value of their shares to profit, dividends and the assets of the company:

$$\frac{\text{Share price}}{\text{Earnings per share}} \qquad \frac{\text{PER of the company}}{\text{PER of the market}}$$

(Price earnings ratio, PER)   (Relative PER)

$$\frac{\text{Net dividend (cents/share) (\%)}}{(1 - \text{basic tax rate}) \times \text{ordinary share price (cents)}}$$

(Dividened yield)

$$\frac{\text{Earnings per share}}{\text{Net dividend per share}}$$

(Dividened cover)

$$\frac{\text{Ordinary shareholders' funds (OSF)}}{\text{Number of ordinary shares in issue}}$$

(Net asset value)

$$\text{Market price of ordinary share} \times \text{number of shares in issue}$$

(Market capitalization)

To the investment ratios we should add measures of shareholder value:

Cash flow
  = Profit + depreciation ± changes in fixed assets and working capital
  ± changes in shareholders funds ± changes in long-term debt

Economic cash flow (Net present value)
   = Future cash flow × discount rate (cost of capital or other relevant rate)

Economic value added (EVA)
   = Operating profit – taxes – (Capital employed x cost of capital (risk adjusted)

(Financial performance is indicated by value of EVA components. A positive value indicates that wealth or value is created for the shareholder; negative values indicate that value has been destroyed.)

Market value added (MVA)
   = Corporate debt + market value of shares – capital invested in the business
(Here financial performance is indicated by a positive value of MVA: the higher the value, the greater the value generated for the shareholder.)

Marketing performance   There are a number of items which indicate marketing performance. We can identify them as quantitative or qualitative measures. *Quantitative measures* will include:

Sales: revenues	(existing and	Expressed as trend
Sales: units	new products)	indices, percentages,
Market share	(Products)	percentges/sales and/or
Relative market share	(markets)	indices
	(territories)	

Margins generated		
Transactions	(direct/indirect)	
existing customer		
new customers		Budgeted and actual
Communications costs		
Distributor discounts		
Manufacturing costs		

Clearly other measures will be included for specialist activities. For example, retailing will look to identify sales and contribution on a per-square-metre and employee basis.

Qualitative measures will include:
Customer satisfaction monitoring   Continuous measurement of customer perceptions and responses to the company's products and services and to

those of its competitors. Customer satisfaction indices are used for this purpose.

Stakeholder performance The increasing extent to which companies are relying on outsourcing as an internal component of their activities makes the consideration of stakeholder interests an important performance issue. There are a number of stakeholder categories; the customers and the shareholders have been discussed, but two other similarly important groups are the suppliers and the employees. It is important that suppliers' businesses remain healthy, with sales volumes and margins meeting budgets and capacity utilization at economic levels. If these performance requirements are not considered it is possible that suppliers will be unable to meet price, quality and availability requirements. Consequently, the firm may be unable to meet the expectations of its customers due to supplier performance problems. Suppliers have also played an important role in the success of a great many companies through the close cooperation in product and market development activities.

Similarly, employee performance and satisfaction should be monitored. The links between employee performance and their levels of satisfaction over pay and conditions have been well documented over many years. It follows that employees are important stakeholders.

Distributor networks are also important and distributors therefore are significant stakeholders. Indeed, the importance of distributor networks in industrial, automotive and consumer durable product-markets should not be overlooked.

13.7 Strategic marketing decisions

The core business: its competitive advantage

Fundamental to the process is a view of what the *core business* comprises and the dimensions of its competitive advantage. One approach is to ask: what business are we really in? Theodore Levitt's 'Marketing Myopia' (1960) first suggested this question as a point of departure for a discussion concerning marketing strategy and planning. Since then we have heard a number of convincing arguments suggesting that companies should first define their business in generic terms on the grounds that: 'It forces an organization to look at its markets from a customer perspective . . . It widens the perspective on what currently and potentially constitutes competition, i.e., it helps define competition . . . It helps identify key factors in competitive marketing success' (Lancaster and Massingham 1993). Abell (1980) suggested that markets could be defined in terms of customer function, technology and customer groups. Day (1988) broadened this approach by adding the notion of added value to the definition. Day's approach used the value chain to identify the relative strengths (or weaknesses) on which to build differentiation. This can be achieved by either using specific, relative performance characteristics within the value chain activities of research and development, procurement, inbound and outbound logistics, production, marketing and customer service or by developing cost-led differentiation. This extends the original concept of the value chain, which was to identify the activities and the costs of producing and delivering customer satisfaction.

Day's approach can be said to give emphasis to shareholder value management and may be used to link strategy decisions and strategy implementation through the shareholder value drivers. Clearly, if a company chooses to focus on its differentiation characteristics, the growth of profitability, productivity and cash flow will follow. The task of management is to decide upon how to deploy the resources it has available to achieve its growth objectives.

Customer functions or needs will be enhanced through differentiation by providing benefits through specific product attributes. The identification of the relevant benefits (and the subsequent response by the producer in the shape of product or cost led differentiation) is typically based upon the uses for which the product is to be put by the customer. It follows that there can be a wide range of uses for a product, which will vary by customer, all of which should be identified by the supplier.

Customer groups (or segments) are identified as those who share similar needs or characteristics which are relevant in a strategic planning context. Segmentation proposes that companies focus on a specific set of needs or customer characteristics.

Technologies describe the ways in which customers' needs can be satisfied or functions performed. Clearly there are often a number of ways in which a need may be satisfied.

Scope

Scope refers to the extent of the business's involvement in a market. This may take a number of characteristics. For example, a company may decide on geographic scope by which it specifies an area within which it will operate. This decision may be based on either inbound or outbound logistics costs. Day's approach (also using the value chain) considered scope from what is best described as a supply chain perspective. He proposed that management consider scope from an activity perspective by identifying where within the supply chain in the production process, i.e., how far forward (toward the end-use/customer) or backward (towards the supplier), the business should participate.

Davidow and Malone (1992) developed this further by proposing that the value chains of suppliers, intermediaries and customers are merging increasingly. (The literature on strategic partnerships and alliances reinforces this view.) They suggested the interchange of information and the recognition by both supplier and distributor (or perhaps between distributor and end user) that 'for either to succeed, they both will have to prosper . . . mutual dependence will characterize the relationships'. It follows that an increased focus on outsourcing (and hence the development of partnerships and alliances) will be based upon mutual dependence and mutual profitability.

They suggested 'It is not difficult to imagine a further step . . . in which the supplier begins to look downstream to the distribution channel and even to the final consumers themselves. A supplier might even conduct its own market research, offer its own service guarantees, even solicit design advice from end users – anything to support its customers' success.' This *extends* the approach of relationship marketing (which looks to develop the supplier/customer relationship beyond just one transaction into a long term commercial relationship). Davidow and Malone were suggesting a value-based approach whereby a number of supplier value chains are *combined* to ensure customer satisfaction is increased.

Both Abell and Day described the concept of using a three-vector diagram, which is reproduced as Figure 13.4. The result is a market cell comprising customer functions (or customer needs), customer groups (segments) that are satisfied, and also the technology used. In Figure 13.5 a hypothetical market cell for an airline is illustrated. For the airline there are four market segments based upon the primary segments of that market. The technologies reflect those currently available. Customer functions (needs) represent an extensive range of requirements, some of which are applicable to both segments and technology. It does not follow that each segment will have sufficient demand for each of the customer needs. Clearly, the technology applications are equally applicable to each of the segments, but may have greater potential for one or two specifically.

If we agree that the value-added considerations are becoming increasingly important, they should be included in the graphical presentation. The impact of alliances and partnerships is likely to increase the value added both to the business and to the stakeholders. This effect is shown in Figure 13.6. Thus the scope of the market cell may be expanded (profitably) provided the end-user and target customers are satisfied that the value added has overall benefits.

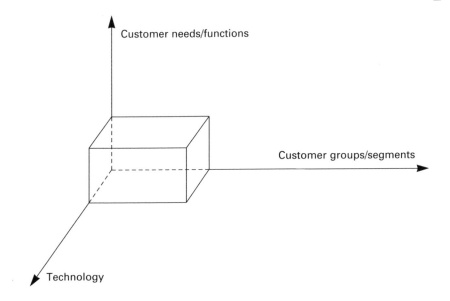

Figure 13.4 The market cell bounded by capabilities to service customer needs and segments with current technology

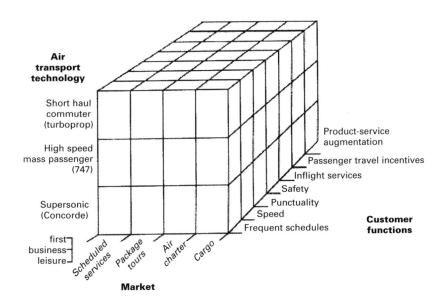

Figure 13.5 Defining the market cells of an airline

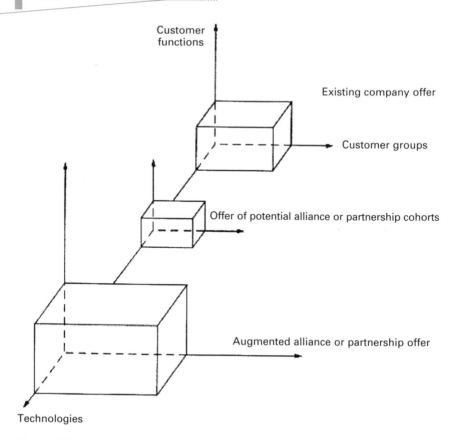

Figure 13.6 Outsourcing using alliances and partnerships to increase the value added of the customer offer

13.8 Resource requirements and availability

Before making final decisions concerning strategic direction and corporate and brand positioning the issue of resource availability and opportunity cost should be considered. It is very unusual for a firm to be in a situation in which it can fund all of the strategic options identified. Rather, the situation is likely to be one in which resources are limited and as a consequence options must be evaluated from a number of aspects.

Resources management is a critical function: if too many resources are allocated to an option, the returns generated will be low; on the other hand, an under-resourced venture may fail. The important issue is that the skills and resources should be sufficient to meet the objectives set and should be compatible with the means of achieving them (i.e., the strategies).

If we consider the requirements for shareholder value management (growth, profitability, productivity and cash flow) the resource allocation process should anticipate performance returns which will satisfy these.

13.9   Value migration: opportunities to add value and improve performance

Kay's (1993) measure of 'corporate success' is helpful in identifying where added value is generated within an industry value system. The components (it will be recalled) are

Revenues
Less (wages and salaries, materials, capital costs)
Equals
Added Value

Kay's model may be illustrated and Figure 13.7 depicts two possible outcomes, one (Figure 13.7a) shows a successful organization making a positive added value (in Kay's terms, it must be remembered that added value > operating profit because it includes a return on capital therefore it *may not* be profitable). In Figure 13.7b the organization represented has difficulties; wages and salaries and capital costs are greater than revenues. Figure 13.8 suggests the added value structure of a value chain. At the raw materials (primary production) stage materials costs are a low proportion of total input costs, but as value is added by successive processes, materials costs become significantly more important as do the capital costs of inventory financing.

13.10   Combining scope and added value opportunities

Best (2004) offers a useful view of market scope by introducing the concepts of *vertical and horizontal markets*: 'Vertical markets represent market opportunities along the vertical market's "value chain". . . . Horizontal market opportunities exist in substitute product-markets.' Best's treatment of this is to consider more the vertical integration aspects of the opportunity. However, a more comprehensive approach would consider the collaborative opportunities available through partnership and alliance structures. The objective being to maximize the opportunity to leverage assets within the overall value system (see Chapter 3).

Best's model has been adapted as Figure 13.9. The vertical markets are

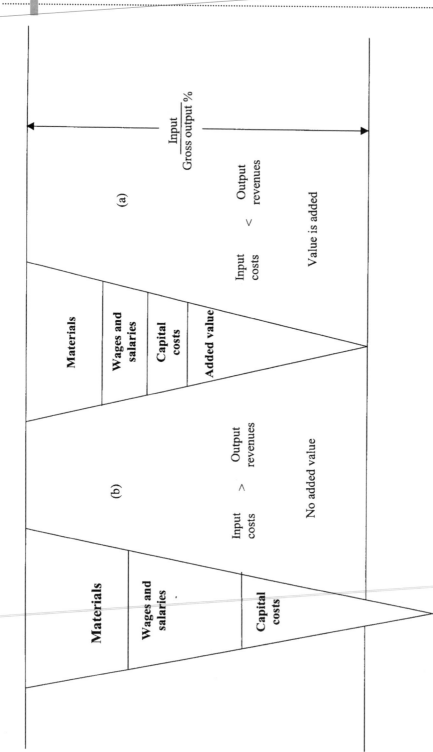

Figure 13.7 Kay's Added Value perspective

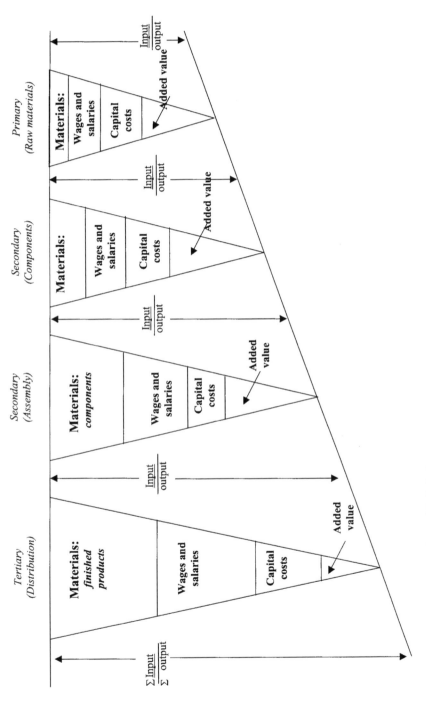

Figure 13.8 Stages in the value added chain

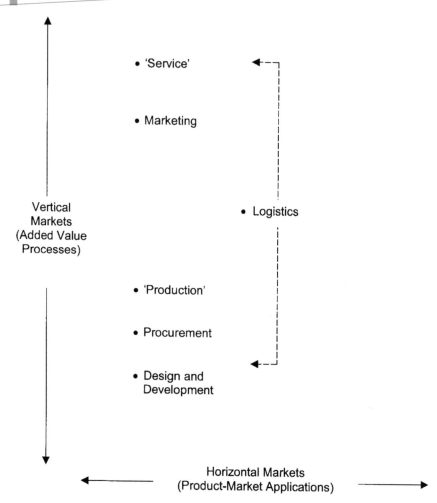

Figure 13.9 Exploring vertical and horizontal markets for competitive activities and corporate opportunities

considered as value-adding processes. The proposition is that it is not necessary to own and control the process but rather to access the process(es) (or the resources) in order to increase the effectiveness of the business model design and to increase the efficiency of its implementation. An example may help. Consider the biotech industry. The industry is R&D-based with a focus on pure research (and applied with some larger organizations). However, if an individual organization is to do it, it will need access to the other value-adding processes between the organization and the end-user. As Figure 13.10 shows, the typical approach is to partner with a pharmaceutical organization possessing the resources required for successful commercialization of the

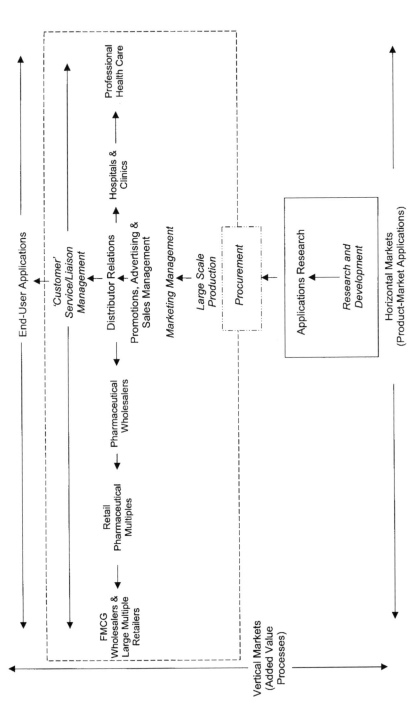

Figure 13.10 Exploring vertical and horizontal markets for competitive activities and corporate opportunities: an example from the pharmaceutical industry

product or process. The pharmaceutical and chemicals industries have pioneered web-based supply chain partnerships, similar to those in the automotive industry. 'Elemica' is a global electronic network comprising 22 of the largest international chemical corporations. By forming a negotiations/transactions hub, interactions and transactions costs are significantly reduced and asset productivity throughout the 'organization' was improved by the elimination of unnecessary inventories, automated transaction systems, reduced transportation costs (not to mention a vast improvement in 'mode' utilization) and storage costs. The potential savings for organizations within Elemica are beginning to appear. Within North America and Europe the potential savings from 'e-market' initiatives are estimated to be around $US15–20 billion!

Other industries demonstrate similar growth structures. Within the Australian wine industry there are a number of *virtual wineries* such as Cockatoo Ridge and Cheviot Hills – both are small organizations (unlike the larger wine producers and brewers) operating in selected segments of the wine market domestically and overseas.

Probably the most notable example of the application of this approach is Dell Computer. Dell 'owns' very few tangible assets, relying on partnership structures with well-known, reputable suppliers such as Sony, to supply essential components. Dell's argument is simple, and can be summarized as: 'Why invest capital in an industry, such as computer microprocessors, that has more than enough capacity – and to do so would only introduce excess capacity with accompanying management problems, thereby distracting the focus of management away from the core business?'

13.11 Performance measurement in 'new economy' organizations: the Performance Prism

Neely *et al.* (2002) have developed an approach to performance planning and measurement that addresses the expanding spectrum of stakeholders. A review of recent business trends identifies by the authors leads them to conclude: 'The point is that the only sustainable way of delivering shareholder value in the 21st century is to deliver stakeholder value and this means enhancing, maintaining and defending the company's reputation on a broad range of fronts.' Neely *et al.* suggest that the 'demands' made on organizations are in fact two-way. While the stakeholders seek to improve their 'lot' through more 'profitable' relationships (looking for closer and longer relationships, not simply increased profitability and productivity) organizations are beginning to programme and structure their expectations of stakeholders. The authors identify typical contributions expected of stakeholders:

- *Investors*: capital for growth, assume more risk and long-term support.
- *Customers*: profitable and long-term loyalty, feedback.
- *Intermediaries*: planning and forecasting, inventory management.
- *Employees*: flexibility, multi-skilling, anti-social hours, loyalty.
- *Suppliers*: increased customization, total solutions, integration.
- *Regulators*: cross-border consistency, advice, involvement, grants and aid.
- *Communities*: skilled employment pools.
- *Pressure groups*: closer cooperation, shared research.
- *Alliance partners*: co-development, co-productivity, shared information and shared costs.

Clearly the interrelationships between stakeholder and organization are becoming structured as corporate boundaries reach beyond their legal entities and become inter-organizational. Neely and his colleagues conclude that: 'Indeed the very concept of stakeholder value itself should perhaps be quantified in terms of the strength of the interrelationship.'

13.12   Value-led management

The argument developing here is that corporate structures (as well as decision-making processes) and corporate behaviour are changing dramatically and rapidly. The point may be made a little stronger: it is becoming very clear that 'value' is migrating in many industries and is being captured by an increasing number of 'participants'. For example, the automotive industry is experiencing a shift in value profile. Hitherto, value *was* maximized in the production process, current indications and expectations for the *future* are that this will migrate towards the marketing and service processes.

Three major changes are suggested. The first concerns the emphasis on performance. Currently many organizations emphasize cost-led efficiency as a primary objective. Not only is this constraining, it has been shown not to be in the shareholders' interests: cost reductions typically have a negative impact on customer service and this, in turn, has the same impact on revenues. The second change involves a switch from an internal focus in which assets and resources *must be owned* to one of cooperation and collaboration in which assets and resources are *managed*. The third shift is one in which the organization becomes *proactive* in its operations and this obtains for both customer and supply markets. *Market-responsive* organizations tend to be inflexible and typically have very slow 'time-to-market' responses. In other words they are imitators rather than innovators!!

This notion can be expanded upon. The role of the entrepreneur is to balance the allocation of resources between *transformation inputs* and *interaction inputs.* Central to the decision is not who owns the inputs but rather how they may be incorporated into the business organization and how this then is structured to ensure that customer and stakeholder expectations may be met. There are a number of important decision areas. The first concerns decisions that influence physical products; quality and production costs are important and the resource allocation decision can be influenced by production alternatives that offer an organization the opportunity to utilize the production facilities of partner organizations that have production expertise or cost advantages. The management of 'intangible assets' can add differentiation to the physical product and improve the customer appeal by a 'brand promise' that in some way increases customer perceptions of the benefits received. Innovative product and/or service design is another factor. Designs that increase, or extend, 'value-in-use' for customers also differentiate both the organization and its products. The third decision concerns where, how much, and who should invest in both tangible and intangible assets and how these should be integrated and coordinated. The 'virtual community' approach that value nets and chains propose, offers to increase an organization's abilities for focused response, flexibility of response and an ability to organize a 'timely' response.

Tapscott and Caston (1993) proposed a 'generic' model of the value chain/virtual organization. By modifying their model and using it to contrast the traditional and emerging organization the structural *and* resource inputs requirements of the new model become apparent. The significant, and perhaps fundamental, difference is its interrelationship focus. The emphasis shifts from ownership and intra-functional capabilities towards one based upon cooperation and collaboration and towards managing inputs without necessarily owning them. This in turn suggests that profitability becomes less significant. Rather the value delivered to the shareholders is oriented towards free cash flow discounted to give a net present value.

Earlier Davidow and Malone (1992) suggested:

> The complex product-markets of the twenty first century will demand the ability to deliver, quickly and globally a high variety of customised products. These products will be differentiated not only by form and function, but also by the services provided with the product, including the ability for the customer to be involved in the design of the product . . . a manufacturing company will not be an isolated facility in production, but rather a node in the complex network of suppliers, customers, engineering and other 'service' functions . . .
>
> . . . profound changes are expected for the company's distribution system and its internal organization as they evolve to become more customer driven and customer managed. On the upstream side of the firm,

supplier networks will have to be integrated with those of customers often to the point where the customer will share its equipment, designs, trade secrets and confidences with those suppliers. Obviously, suppliers will become very dependent upon their downstream customers; but by the same token customers will be equally trapped by their suppliers. In the end, unlike its contemporary predecessors, the virtual corporation will appear less a discrete enterprise and more an ever-varying cluster of common activities in the midst of a vast fabric of relationships.

The challenge posed by this business revolution argues that corporations that expect to remain competitive must achieve mastery of both information and relationships.

And later Pebler (2000) commented:

The virtual enterprise of the future will be much more dynamic and sensitive to the need for tuning operational parameters of the enterprise as a whole, including capital spending for both producers and service companies, optimizing the whole chain of value creation. The future world will be characterized by knowledge management and collaborative decision-making by way of virtual teams. Virtual enterprises will be empowered by a willingness to do business in more productive ways and by information technologies that eliminate barriers between stakeholders and radically improve work processes.

Clearly, the way in which we measure performance needs to be reviewed in light of these changes.

13.13   The Performance Prism

Neely *et al.* argue that the *balanced scorecard* focuses on financials, customers, internal processes, plus innovation and learning. In doing so it downplays the importance of many of the stakeholders. As discussed earlier, it can be modified to do so. They also consider the strengths and weaknesses of other models. The *business excellence* model takes a broader view of performance and considers a wider set of stakeholders: 'but also contains a host of dimensions that are effectively unmeasurable.' Similar comments are made concerning the *Baldrige Award* and others yet to be implemented. Neely *et al.* conclude that 'they are all partial or point solutions, offering insights into some of the dimensions of performance that should be measured and managed, but by no means all of them'. They suggest the Performance Prism rectifies this shortcoming by integrating the strengths and weaknesses of them all, thereby: 'offering a more comprehensive and comprehensible framework.' They argue:

> In order to satisfy their own work and needs, organizations have to access contributions from their stakeholders – usually capital and credit from investors, loyalty and profit from customers, ideas and skills from employees, materials and services from suppliers and so on. They also need to have defined what strategies they will pursue to ensure that value is delivered to their stakeholders. In order to implement these strategies they have to understand what processes the enterprise requires and must operate both effectively and efficiently. Processes . . . can only be executed if the organization has the right capabilities in place – the right combination of people skill-sets, best practices, leading technologies and physical infrastructure.

This is the structure provided by the Performance Prism. It provides a comprehensive framework that may be used for a communication model as well as for performance measurement (see Figure 13.11). In the Performance Prism model, strategies are applied at relevant levels of the organization. They reflect overall corporate strategic direction and the strategies at other levels that contribute to these. Supporting processes and capabilities are developed and performance measures developed for both.

13.14 Modifying the Performance Prism for the 'new economy'

The Performance Prism makes a significant contribution in an academic and pragmatic context. By identifying the role of the stakeholders in the strategic decisions of the organization a more effective as well as efficient model results. However, for many industries the predominant structure is one in which corporate structures (as well as decision-making processes) and corporate behaviour are changing. Furthermore, it is becoming very clear that 'value' is migrating in many industries. This raises two issues not met by the model; the characteristics of the value strategy to be delivered and a means by which the appropriate strategy can be developed and subsequently monitored for effectiveness. The principle set by Neely et al. is that partner (stakeholder) expectations or value drivers that are of primary importance. Futhermore, Neely et al. are discussing the more traditional business model. The needs of the virtual organization differ.

It is safe to assume that an inter-organizational approach to strategy will differ from that of a single company working with (and recognizing the needs

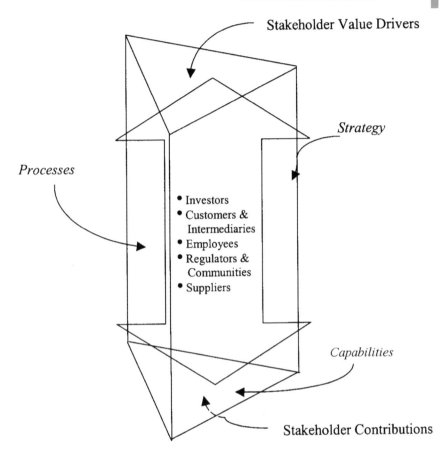

Stakeholder Value Drivers

Strategy

Processes

- Investors
- Customers &
  Intermediaries
- Employees
- Regulators &
  Communities
- Suppliers

Capabilities

Stakeholder Contributions

Figure 13.11   The Performance Prism

and contributions of) its stakeholders. And here another assumption; given the dynamic nature of value in many industries, the most likely 'common denominator' will be cash flow. Margins are changing as both value and profit migrate (see Gadiesh and Gilbert 1998) it follows that the success of the virtual organization and of its component partners is more readily measured in the overall *free cash flow generated*.

The eventual success of the business is the *free cash flow* that is generated. To calculate this we need to consider the additional funding required by the business if it is to achieve its objectives. These will be equity and/or debt combinations. This introduces not only the cost considerations, but also the perceptions of risk that the 'market' may assume and issues of corporate control. The 'value of the business' then becomes the discounted value of the free cash flow at a discount rate that is judged to be appropriate reflecting this risk. These levels of cash flow form an important feature of Figure 13.12.

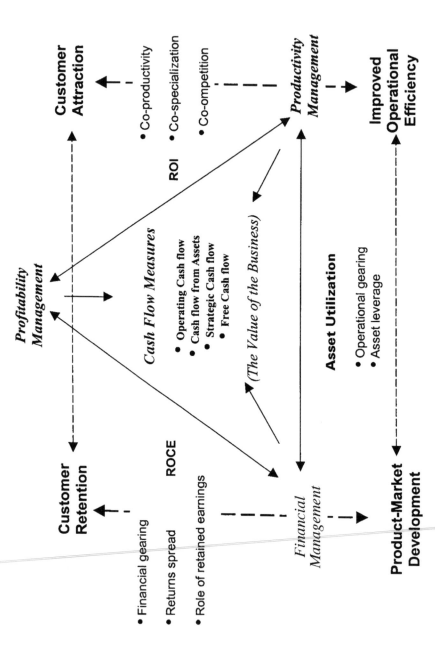

Figure 13.12 Integrating the objectives and strategies

Figure 13.12 links strategies to objectives. Given the assumption that free cash flow is the *primary objective* of the virtual organization, Figure 13.12 first identifies the components of this primary objective. The model uses the principle of the Dupont model – that there are links between profitability management, productivity management and financial management and, further, that these links can be used to explore the options available to the organization to maximize free cash flow (see Chapter 3, in particular Figures 3.4 and 3.11). The *primary strategies* that will drive the organization towards meeting its free cash flow objective are: product-market development, customer retention, customer attraction and improved operational efficiency.

13.15   Structural issues

However, it is important that the performance implications of structural alternatives are considered. Campbell's (1996) typology of virtual organizations (see Chapter 3) brings out some important differences that impact on performance outcomes i.e., internal virtual organizations, stable virtual organizations, dynamic virtual organizations and agile virtual organizations.

13.16   Processes and process management

In addition, performance planning and measurement models will be required to consider the implications of more recent views on process management. Following the attention given process re-engineering, business processes run horizontally *across* organizations, organizational boundaries and often across international boundaries. Neely *et al.* (2002) remind us that processes typically consider four separate categories these being to: *develop products and services, generate demand, fulfill demand* and *to plan and manage the enterprise*. They add: 'Processes are what make the organization work . . . They are the blue prints for what work is to be done where, when, and how it will be executed.' To make this effective for the emerging virtual structures we must add 'who' to their qualification. They add that for process management to be effective five characteristics should be measured because they quantify the measurement criteria for success: how good, how many, how quickly, how easily and how expensive:

Quality: consistency, reliability, conformance, durability, accuracy, dependability.
Quantity: volume, throughput, completeness.
Time: speed, delivery, availability, promptness, timeliness, schedule.
Ease of use: flexibility, convenience, accessibility, clarity, support.
Money: cost, price, value.

In virtual structures such an approach is essential if the strategic goal of an *effective* response is to be developed. However, for the model to be successfully applied to the virtual organization the structural options should be a major consideration.

13.17 Capabilities

Similarly for capabilities. Hamel and Prahalad (1994) have defined a core capability as: 'a bundle of skills and technologies that enables a company to provide a particular benefit to customers'. An interesting perspective that may be derived from this definition is that it is an aggregate of 'skills and technologies' and as Hamel and Prahalad contend: 'it represents the sum of learning across individual skill sets and individual organizational units'. They suggest 'it is unlikely to reside in a single individual or within a small team'. A primary reason for an organization to consider partnerships with other organizations is simply for that reason, together with the fact that the dynamics of competition, technology and consumer value expectations make investment in core competencies unattractive. This view is reinforced by the assertion that:

> In the concept of core competence there is no suggestion that a company must make everything it sells . . . although Cannon has a very clear sense of its core competencies, it buys more than 75% of components that go into its copiers. What a company should seek to control are those core competencies that make the biggest contribution to customer value.

This view also identifies both the clear need for core capabilities to be linked with customer value generation and the trend towards *virtual integration* in which the core capabilities required to complete are identified and, rather than being developed or acquired, they are leased and aggregated to create an entity which answers the question 'What can we do that other organizations could not easily do as well?' Competitive advantage is determined by capabilities, and these vary. Kay (2000) identifies two categories: *distinctive capabilities*, such as institutional sanctioned items (patents, copyrights, statutory monopolies). But these also feature 'powerful idiosyncratic characteristics . . . built by companies in competitive markets'. These are strong brands, patterns of supplier and/or customer relationships, specialist skills, knowledge and processes. *Reproducible capabilities* can be created (or purchased or leased) by any company with reasonable management skills, skills of observation and financial resources. Both process and product technology are reproducible, the automotive industry is but one example of this (see Chapter 2).

13.18   Assets

It follows that any performance model should now be capable of evaluating the alternative combinations of tangible and intangible assets and asset ownership structures that are emerging with the recent business models and structures. Boulton *et al.* (2000) contend (for fuller discussion, see Chapter 2):

> The encompassing challenge that companies face in this new environment is how to identify and leverage all sources of value, not just the assets that appear on the traditional balance sheet. These important assets including customers, brands, suppliers, employees, patents, and ideas – are at the core of creating a successful business now and in the future . . . But what assets are most important in the New Economy? How do we leverage these assets to create value for our own organizations in a changing business environment? What new strategies are required for us to create value?'

13.19   Planning and Performance: a 'new economy' total organization perspective

Given the changes in strategy and structure perspective it follows that neither the balance scorecard nor the Performance Prism offer precisely the approach needed to plan and measure performance in the virtual communities that are beginning to become a feature of many sectors. The 'interrelated approach' of Kaplan and Norton and the 'stakeholder approach' of Neely *et al.* can be combined into a performance planning and measurement mode. Figure 13.13 presents a framework for the model. It extends the Neely *et al.* model by adding structure and asset base decisions. Both are justified by the composition of the virtual organization model that works on the premise that it is *managing* assets rather than *owning* assets that has impact on performance (Normann 2001).

The model is explored in more detail in Figure 13.14, where the components are presented in detail. The overriding purpose of any business organization is for it to increase its 'value' to its owners. The ownership may be diversified. This does not detract from this primary requirement: without ongoing financial success the survival of the organization is under threat. Accordingly, the purpose of the organization is to increase the NPV of the free cash flow generated. This can only be achieved if the stakeholder expectations are met *and if* the stakeholders make the necessary contributions. These are suggested in Figure 13.8 and include capital for growth, long-term loyalty, feedback, 'solutions', together with a shared view of success and what is required to achieve success.

398

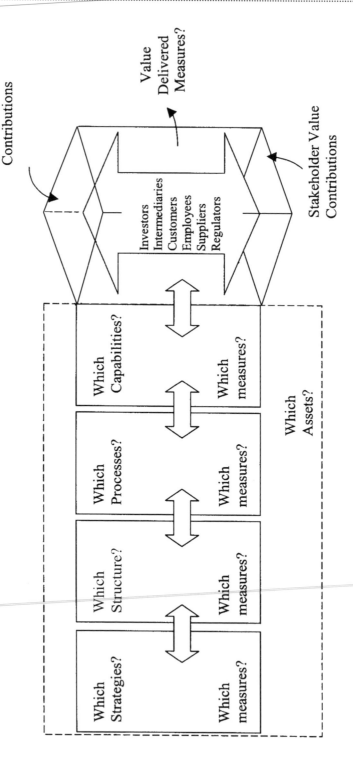

Figure 13.13 Performance management: integrated objectives, strategy, structure, processes and capabilities

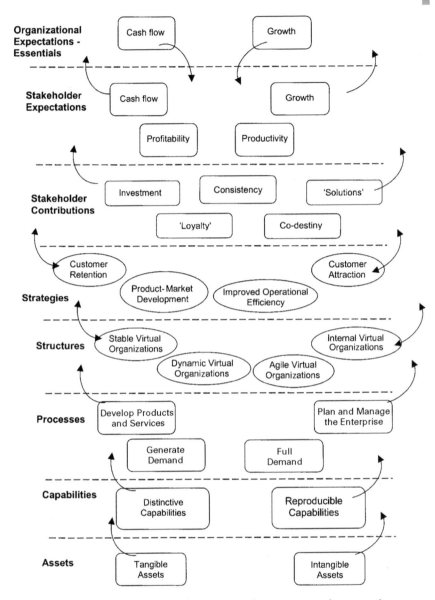

Figure 13.14   Planning and performance: a 'new economy' perspective

The selection of appropriate strategies is essential. Four basic strategies are crucial: product-market development, customer retention, customer attraction and improved operational efficiency. These strategies ensure the growth of the 'organization' by maintaining growth from the existing business but at the same time exploring and exploiting new opportunities.

The appropriate structure is also crucial in improving the likelihood of success. The concern here is not simply about performance – it is also focused on qualitative issues such as control, commitment and flexibility. Decisions on performance options should only be made when there is a clear agreement on the terms of value delivery set by the customer.

Processes are also central. Processes are 'strategy facilitators'. Unless the 'strategy–structure–process fit' is appropriate it has been found that the long-term success of the organization is very doubtful. Capabilities 'underwrite' the success of the processes in implementing strategy. There is another issue and this concerns the development of an asset base from which the capabilities can be developed. Kay (2000) argues that the development of a strong capability base is key if the momentum of competitive advantage is to be maintained. Indeed, it could be argued that neglect can lead to competitive rigidities, and these in turn eliminate any advantages that may once have been established. It follows that the asset portfolio be regularly monitored for relevance as well as performance.

Performance metrics are proposed in Figure 13.15. Empirical evidence from ongoing research suggests that the measures indicated are typical. Some are new and some are difficult to obtain. However, a number of organizations that are becoming increasingly involved in alliances and partnerships are beginning to adopt both the structure and the metrics.

13.20 Summary

Planning and control should be integrated processes, rather than being separate and sequential, because if approached in the latter manner it typically fails. This chapter has considered the planning and performance concerns of a business organization from the perspective of *all* of the stakeholders that work with or have interest in the organization's activities, not simply from the marketing and finance interfaces. The approach adopted throughout this text has been to embrace the emerging strategies and structures that are confronting business in the 'new economy'. It has taken the opportunity to review some of the recent contributions to planning and control, such as Neely et al. and Kaplan and Norton.

Performance planning and control should be seen as an opportunity to ask questions not usually asked and then to continue with other questions concerning alternative means (strategies and structures) to the ends (the objectives). The 'new economy' is now an opportunity for organizations to be different and to create the essential differences that in turn create sustainable competitive advantage.

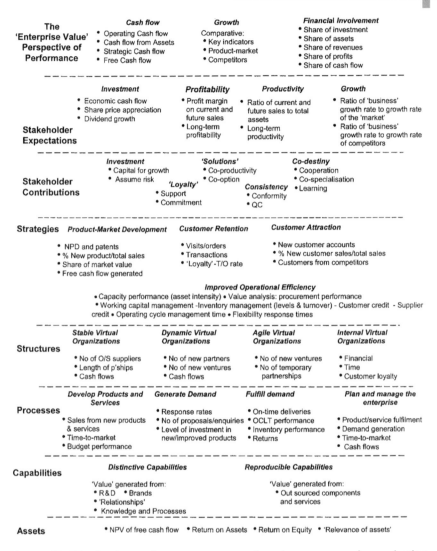

Figure 13.15 Setting performance measures for a 'new economy' organization

REFERENCES

Abell, D. F. (1980) *Defining the Business: The Starting Pions of Strategic Planning*, Prentice Hall, Englewood Cliffs, NJ.

Beech J., (1998) 'The supply-demand nexus' in Gattorna editor, *Strategic Supply Chain Alignment*.

Best, R. J. (2004) *Market-Based Management*, Prentice Hall, Englewood Cliffs, NJ.

Boulton, R. E. S., B. D. Libert and S. M. Samek (2000) 'A business model for the new economy', *The Journal of Business Strategy*, July/August.

Bryan, L. and R. Hulme (2003) 'Managing for improved corporate performance', *The McKinsey Quarterly*, Number 3.

Campbell, A. (1996) 'Creating the virtual organization and managing the distributed workforce', in Jackson P. and J. Van der Weilen (eds), *New Perspectives on Telework – From Telecommuting to the Virtual Organization*, Report on workshop held at Brunel University.

Davidow, W. H. and M. S. Malone (1992) *The Virtual Corporation*, Harper Collins, New York.

Day, G. (1988) *Market Driven Strategy*, Free Press, New York.

Dommermuth, W. P., and R. C. Andersen (1969) 'Distribution systems: firms, functions and efficiences', *MSU Business Topics*, vol. 17, no. 2 (Spring).

Drucker, P. (1995) 'The information executives truly need', *Harvard Business Review*, Jan./Feb.

Gadiesh, O. and J. L. Gilbert (1998) 'How to map your industry's profit pool', *Harvard Business Review*, May/June.

Holmes, G. and A. Sugden (1992) *Interpreting Company Reports and Accounts*. Woodhead Faulkner, London.

Kalmbach Jr, C., and C. Roussel (1999) 'Dispelling the myths of alliances', *Outlook*.

Kaplan, R. S., and D. P. Norton (1992) 'The balanced scorecard – measures that drive performance', *Harvard Business Review*, Jan./Feb.

Kaplan, R. S. and D. P. Norton (1993) 'Putting the balanced scorecard to work', *Harvard Business Review*, Sept./Oct.

Kaplan, R. S. and D. P. Norton (1996) 'Using the balanced scorecard as a strategic management system', *Harvard Business Review*, Jan./Feb.

Kaplan, R. S. and D. P.Norton (2000) 'Having Trouble with Your Strategy? Then Map It', *Harvard Business Review*, Sept./Oct.

Kay, J. (1993) *Foundations of Corporate Success*, Oxford University Press, Oxford.

Kay, J. (2000) 'Strategy and the delusion of Grand Designs', *Mastering Strategy*, Financial Times/Prentice Hall, London.

Kenevan, P. A. and Xi Pei (2003) 'China partners', *McKinsey Quarterly*, No 3.

Kennerley, M. and A. Neely (2003) 'Measuring performance in a changing business environment', *International Journal of Operations & Production Management*, vol. 23, No. 2.

Koch, C. (editor) (1994) 'The power of interorganizational systems', *Indications*, vol. 11, No. 1.

▶

Lancaster, G. and L. Massingham (1993) *Marketing Management*, MacGraw-Hill, London.

Magretta, J. (2002) 'Why business models matter', *Harvard Business Review*, May.

Neely, A. C. Adams and M. Kennerley (2002) *The Performance Prism: the Scorecard for Measuring and Managing Business Success*, FT Prentice Hall, London.

Normann, R. (2001) *Reframing Business*, Wiley, Chichester.

Oates, D. (1998) *Outsourcing and the Virtual Organization*, Century Business Books, London.

Pebler, R. P. (2000) 'The virtual oil company: capstone of integration', *Oil & Gas Journal*, March 6.

Porter, M. (1996), 'What is strategy?', *Harvard Business Review*, Nov./Dec.

SAS Institute Inc (2003)

Stern, L. W., A. I. El-Ansary and A. T. Coughlan (1996) *Marketing Channels*, Prentice Hall, Englewood Cliffs. New Jersey.

Tapscott, D. and A. Caston (1993) *Paradigm Shift*, McGraw-Hill, New York.

Index